Psyche and Society

PSYCHE and SOCIETY

Explorations in
Psychoanalytic Sociology

Robert Endleman

New York   COLUMBIA UNIVERSITY PRESS   *1981*

Library of Congress Cataloging in Publication Data

Endleman, Robert.
Psyche and society.

Bibliography: p.
Includes index.
1. Nature and nurture. 2. Psychoanalysis.
3. Social psychology. 4. Human evolution.
5. Sex differences (Psychology) 6. Homosexuality. 7. Deviant behavior.
8. Psychology, Pathological. I. Title.
[DNLM: 1. Psychoanalytic theory. 2. Social
sciences. WM 460 E56p]
BF341.E53   302   81-1646
ISBN 0-231-04992-7   AACR2

Columbia University Press
New York   Guildford, Surrey

Printed on permanent and durable acid-free paper.

To
Julie
and
Lezlie *and* Mark

CONTENTS

Preface

This book is the product of a number of lines of work I have pursued over many years. It tries to show that a psychoanalytic social science, integrating psychoanalytic theory with relevant parts of sociology and anthropology, is not only possible, but has already come into being. It seeks to demonstrate work in that genre applied to four major topics: human evolution, sex differences, homosexuality, and the relationship between deviance and psychopathology.

Some parts of this work are reworkings of earlier of my writings. Part 2 builds on, expands, and updates my 1966 paper, "Reflections on the Human Revolution." Sections of parts 1 and 5 develop themes introduced in my *Personality and Social Life* (1967). Discussion of student rebellions of the 1960s in chapter 15 derives from published and unpublished work of mine written at the time of those events, then so disturbing, now so seemingly remote. They were the context of my formulation of how would-be liberation movements develop their own "reactive and mitigating mythologies," that can be as distorting and as repressive as what they perceived the "established" or conventional world to be. Comparable mythologies appearing now in the women's liberation and the gay liberation movements of today are dealt with in chapters 10 and 14. The battles of both of these movements with psychoanalytic formulations of the psychology of women and of homosexual preference are a major concern of parts 3 and 4. Analysis of these issues needs a combination of psychoanalytic and sociological-anthropological expertise. That is what I try to bring to them.

Parts of the work, or preliminary versions of them, have been presented at various professional conferences: the colloquium of the New York University Psychoanalytic Society, that of the Adelphi University Graduate Sociology Department, the International Forum for Psychoanalysis, the New York Academy of Sciences, and the Pacific Sociological Association.

I have tried in the writing to appeal to each of three disparate audiences, psychoanalysts, social scientists, and lay readers interested in the issues involved. This is not an easy task. I have endeavored to avoid the opposite dangers of oversimplification and technical turgidity. The underlying issues that present obstacles to efforts at integration of psychoanalysis and the social sciences are themselves material that has to be confronted. That I try to do in chapter 2.

The range of relevant material in all of the applicable disciplines is of course very large. I have therefore worked very selectively, choosing those studies and lines of analysis I think most pertinent to the task at hand. Inevitably I have left out others that I am aware of as relevant, and unintentionally must have missed many more that are beyond my present ken. Specialists in particular areas will no doubt perceive lacunae at many points.

My biases within psychoanalysis and within sociology and anthropology will be evident to discerning readers. The rationale for these is articulated fairly explicitly in the first section of chapter 3, also elsewhere in part 1, in part 5, as well as at many other points in the work. Also, to psychoanalytic readers it should be clear that this work is concerned with psychoanalytic *theory*, not with psychoanalytic clinical practice.

I am indebted to numerous friends, relatives, colleagues in several fields, students, mentors, and professional and political antagonists, for the influences that have gone into this work. I am especially indebted to my patients who have given me humbling lessons in the complexities of applying psychoanalytic theory to clinical practice, and of formulating theory adequate to the ambiguities of their psychic reality.

The New York University Postdoctoral Program in Psychoanalysis and Psychotherapy has been influential in recent years in sharpening my psychoanalytic understanding and clinical skills. Its graduate organization, The Psychoanalytic Society, has been a particularly supportive network of fellow-graduates, and a microcosm of conflicting trends in contemporary psychoanalysis. Dr. Ruth-Jean Eisenbud has been an inspiration in the poetic application of psychoanalysis in clinical practice (though I suspect that she will dissent from many of the formulations I make here in this work.)

Two sociological colleagues merit special appreciation: Dennis Wrong for his painstaking critical reading of an earlier draft, and Helen M. Hacker for an equally meticulous and critical reading of earlier drafts of various parts, especially of what is now part 3 (on sex differences), from a searching feminist-sociological viewpoint obviously at odds with my own, therefore all the more valuable as critique. Neither of these, it need hardly be mentioned, is to be held responsible for what deficiencies persist in the book as it now appears. (At many points I have resisted their corrections.) Helen Hacker has long been a stimulating friendly antagonist on most of the issues dealt with in part 3. On many critical points, we have "agreed to disagree."

Conversations with George Devereux in Paris have been influential, as have been those, years earlier, with that Renaissance man of an intellectual, Benjamin Nelson, whose death is mourned by many of us in many fields.

To Adelphi University, gratitude for a sabbatical leave which facilitated the writing of the book, and for the intellectual stimulation of faculty colleagues and students.

I want to express appreciation also to all those who helped with the nuts and bolts of putting together the manuscript. To John Moore of Columbia University Press for his interest and encouragement at an early stage of the work, and persistent help on many aspects of it at later points. To the editorial staff at the Press for painstaking attention to details of the manuscript that needed work as it approached publication. For help on many details regarding bibliography and indexing, special appreciation to my daughters Lezlie Weiner and Julie Endleman.

Responsibility for the composite portrait that is here presented, warts and all, is of course my own.

New York City
November 1980

1

Psychoanalysis and Social Science: Possible Partners?

How do you put a whole
society on the couch?

Was du ererbt von deinen Vätern hast,
Erwirb es, um es zu besitzen.
(What thou hast inherited from thy fathers,
Acquire it, to make it thine.)
                    Goethe, *Faust*, Part I

CHAPTER ONE

The Problem and the Prospects

"It can't be done." So say many sociologists. So say many anthropologists. So say many psychoanalysts. The "it" is the integration of psychoanalysis with the social sciences, specifically with sociology and anthropology, into a coherent psychoanalytic social science.[1] Some sociologists say sociology has its own job to do, to understand society, to analyze social structure, social conflicts, and social change; and that these are all social processes, not to be reduced to psychological processes, while psychoanalysis has a different task entirely, the analysis of the internal process of individuals, which are irrelevant to understanding society. Some anthropologists speak in a similar vein: anthropology is the overarching science of man, concerned with analyzing culture and cultures, and society and societies; the tasks of psychoanalysis are different and irrelevant, being concerned with the intrapsychic processes of individuals, not the cultural processes of whole cultures. Many psychoanalysts take a parallel separatist position: we can psychoanalyze individuals; we cannot psychoanalyze groups much less whole societies. Let each stick to his last.

Many social scientists claim that it is impossible to be both a social scientist and a psychoanalyst at the same time: that these are separate and even contradictory pursuits. Many psychoanalysts agree with that view, though often for different reasons. Some social scientists claim that to introduce psychological conceptualization into analysis of social process amounts to reductionism, a cardinal sin for the scientist. Some would say that it is even more blameworthy if the psychological variables being introduced are what are, in the minds of such sociologists, abstractions or undemonstrable entities such as unconscious processes or forces, or hypothesized mental structures, or imaginative fantasies such as the Oedipus complex.

To such social scientists, society is one thing, individual personality is another. Trying to explain a social process like the rise of capitalism by appeal to personality factors constitutes reductionism. Some psychoanalysts would respond that it is equally absurd for social scientists to claim to "explain" what is bothering people who are suffering from emotional disorders, by arguing that they are suffering from the contradictions of capitalism, or from the alienation of people living in a competitive market society.

With the many in several fields who say integration cannot be done I disagree. The aim of this work is to demonstrate that it can be done. An integrated psychoanalytic social science can be done. Not only that. It should be done. And it is being done. We not only can have but we need to have psychological propositions to explain what is going on in society and in culture, and these should preferably be in a psychoanalytic vein.

I shall develop the meaning of these terms. I believe that psychoanalytic psychology, for all its imperfections, is the best viable psychological underpinning for this task. I also believe that it needs to be enriched by understandings from the social sciences, more specifically sociology and anthropology, and that together these three fields can constitute an overarching social science that neglects neither the intrapsychic depths of individuals nor the complexities of interactive and interpersonal processes in society, nor the intricate symbolic processes of culture. I argue that anthropology cannot be truly the overarching comprehensive science of humanity if it does not encompass in a comprehensively integrated fashion the insights and knowledge, derived from psychoanalysis, of the details of the psychic unity of mankind (a phrase unfortunately long out of fashion) through its unity in evolutionary origins and ontogenetic developmental universalities of human experience. The intricacies of the latter have been the major subject matter of psychoanalysis as a scientific field, and the knowledge thus derived is directly linkable—and should be linked—with anthropology's otherwise derived evolutionary knowledge of the human species and its knowledge of the myriad cultural variations. The emphasis in psychoanalysis on universalities of human experience, including most signally the universalities of the unconscious and its ever-repeated manifestations in the symbolisms of the hundreds of cultures of the world, links psychoanalysis to the universalistic emphases in anthropology, and to those in sociology. The latter appear in those sociologies which emphasize universal social processes, universal contingencies and requisites applying to social order and social change.

Some psychoanalysts have been influenced by certain aspects of recent work in sociology and anthropology, but more prevalently by those aspects that emphasize *differences* among societies and subsocieties, and differences among cultures and subcultures. Some have thereby been misled into imagining that psychoanalytic ideas could not properly be applied to people growing up within a different subculture in modern society, e.g., that of lower-class blacks, and that they certainly could not be valid for different, for example exotic, societies, such as tribal ones anthropologists have studied, particularly if the latter do not have a nuclear family structure like that of the modern Western world. We believe such emendations of psychoanalysis are unsupported by the empirical data, are an unjustified dilution of powerful insights and explanatory ideas, and a short-sighted adoption of the least valuable positions from within the array of contemporary social sciences to the detriment of more adequate and more apposite perspectives from these same social sciences. Similarly, some social scientists have adapted watered-down versions of psychoanalytic ideas to their social-scientific analyses in a manner satisfactory to neither the social-scientific nor the psychoanalytic community. Some of the ways each side has used partialized aspects of the other, in an unsatisfactory manner, will be examined in more detail later in this chapter.

Within sociology, there are some perspectives which are more amenable than others to articulating linkages with psychoanalysis, that could lead in the direction of a psychoanalytic sociology. For example, what Ritzer (1975) refers to as proponents of the "social definition paradigm" in sociological theory, could be more readily connected with psychoanalytic propositions. Social definitionist theories have in common (despite their many differences) their basic paradigmatic position that "society" is an abstraction to refer to ways people commonly and similarly *define* the social world. (By contrast, a "social facts" paradigm has as a basic assumption that "society" is a reality *sui generis*, and so is social structure; so are social institutions, and the like, regardless of how individuals define their social worlds.) For social definitionists, how people *subjectively experience* the social and cultural and interpersonal world around them, constitutes the crucial material of sociology.

Psychoanalysts would answer, fine, that is what we are constantly dealing with. Social definitionist types of sociologists, such as those of the "labeling" persuasion (see Howard S. Becker 1963; Edwin Schur 1971; and others) would, however, be unlikely to include *unconscious* subjective processes among those they consider relevant and necessary to understand, in order to interpret, what is going on in the social world. By contrast, a truly psychoanalytic sociologist would do so. And interestingly, some sociologists, whose theoretical position could be classified as social-definitionist, and who do this within the framework of phenomenological understanding, such as Peter Berger (1963) and Thomas Luckmann (see Berger and Luckmann 1967), are among the most vociferous opponents of psychoanalytic ideas in sociology.

"Social-facts paradigm" sociologists emphasize what they see as an "objective" social reality, such as the class structure of a society, which has a reality of its own regardless of what kinds of subjective social definitions individuals in that society may make. People within a society may, for example, grossly underestimate the extent of class differences in that society, and in that be quite mistaken about the reality of class in that society.

The social definitionists would then reply: the very fact of having such a mistaken conception is itself an aspect of the social reality that has to be analyzed and understood. For example, if the evidence shows that the misperception is a distortion of thought produced by ideology, the subjects can be said to have what Marxists call a "false consciousness."

The psychoanalytic sociologist would go further, and seek into the unconscious psychic mechanisms, e.g., projections and displacements, that contribute to such misperceptions of social reality. In order to deal adequately with such phenomena, we need to understand the intriciacies of human thinking, feeling, and willing, in all their depth. That requires getting beyond obvious conscious levels into preconscious and unconscious dimensions. Of course, analysis of preconscious and unconscious processes is not all that psychoanalysis is about, but it is the crucial aspect that distinguishes a psychoanalytic view from other psychologies. And it is also, in the same way, the crucial way in which psychoanalytic thinking about how people make "definitions" of their social world differs from the ways in which social-definitionist sociological social psychologists conceptualize these processes. To the latter, for example, defining oneself as a "failure" and acting on that definition in such a way as to bring about a self-fulfilling prophecy of "failing" in life may be a set of propositions made by a sociological social psychologist of G. H. Meadian persuasion (see Mead 1934).

A psychoanalytic-sociological view would go much further and ask what intrapsychic dynamic processes are involved in the self-definition as "failure" and how these processes are set in motion within the personality in the context of crucial social relationships in infancy, childhood, and later in life.

THREE WAYS: SEPARATIST, IMPERIALIST, AND INTEGRATIONIST

There are three possible ways in which the relationship of psychoanalysis to the social sciences may be conceptualized. These could be called the separatist, the imperialist, and the integrationist.

Separatists

In the *separatist* formulation, each of the disciplines is seen as having its own distinctive set of problems, of methods, of theoretical formulations, distinct and separate from those of the other disciplines. This is the viewpoint represented by the kind of sociologist referred to above, who sees sociology as concerned with social structure, and psychoanalysis with personality dynamics, and neither as in any way related to or interconnected with the other. As Wallerstein and Smelser (1969) have pointed out, the increasing specialization of all fields of knowledge in the recent period has led most practitioners of any of the disciplines to take essentially this kind of view. The separatist position in psychoanalysis is represented by those psychoanalysts and psychoanalytic theorists who insist on the separation of psychoanalysis from sociology and anthropology as a necessary element in the development of this discipline. Such psychoanalysts tend to denigrate or abhor efforts of some psychoanalysts to make forays into the arena of social and cultural analysis, which produces, in their minds, amateur social science and "wild analysis" unwarrantedly extending into the social sphere propositions that logically and properly belong in the sphere of individual psychology. At the extreme, such analysts would point out that you can put an individual patient on the couch; you cannot put a whole community, much less a whole society, or a whole culture on a couch. Similarly, anthropologists who see their task as the analysis of culture reject any kind of psychologizing—and perhaps most particularly, any of a psychoanalytic kind—as an unwarranted·intrusion of a theoretically irrelevant set of variables, and an unwarranted mixture of levels of theoretical analysis. Such sociologists and anthropologists may or may not regard psychoanalysis as an untenable psychology, but the question is irrelevant for their kind of internal professional concern. And they find themselves in agreement with separatist kinds of psychoanalysts at least on this point, that the different disciplines should go their separate ways. In sociology, those following a "social-facts paradigm" (Ritzer 1975) are most likely to insist on this separation. In anthropology, those following Leslie White (White

1949, 1959) in insisting on the *sui generis* distinctiveness of culture as a phenomenon in its own right (by implication independent of any psychological functioning of definite individual human beings who "carry" that culture) would also be the more extreme example of social scientists insisting on the separateness of their discipline from psychoanalysis or any other psychology. However, many other kinds of sociologists besides those of the social-facts persuasion, and many other kinds of anthropologists besides Whiteans, tend also to share the specialization perspective in arguing for the separateness and distinctiveness of each of these disciplines, from each other, and (pertinent for our purposes) from psychoanalysis. For example, Bendix (1952) argues that sociological propositions have a distinctly different orientation and content from propositions in "psychiatry" (presumably psychoanalysis) and it is a reductionist error to attribute such sociological phenomena as group cohesion or widespread compliance with cultural symbols to psychological attributes of individuals.

Imperialists

A second way of relating the two fields, social sciences (sociology and anthropology in this case) and psychoanalysis, is the imperialistic approach, which can take the form of psychoanalytic imperialism, of sociological imperialism, or of anthropological imperialism. The imperialistic position holds the view that these fields are intrinsically connected, in the manner that one's own discipline is the overarching one that subsumes the other or others. Thus sociological imperialism would argue that psychoanalysis and all other psychologies are simply subbranches of an overarching sociology that is a general social science including all kinds of studies of man in society, taken both individually and collectively. It would not deny the relevance of psychological "factors" or "forces" in the functioning of human beings in groups and in society generally, but would subsume these as part of a general sociology. Similarly the cross-cultural studies of tribal and other societies that have been the hallmark of much of (at least social and cultural) anthropology are seen in this perspective as simply "comparative sociology"—that is, the study of varying social structures. Most contemporary sociologists do not explicitly take this kind of position as a theoretical stance, but something like it is implicit in many general sociology testbooks, which, in an effort to be comprehensive, bring in cross-cultural materials from anthropology and also treat the "economic order" and the "political order"—the subject matter of economics and political science where these are separate disciplines—as aspects of the social order that properly come under the scope of sociology. Some such books also bring in socialization studies, some using a psychoanalytic viewpoint as part of the subject matter. Usually in such work the extent of the integration of psychoanalytic concepts and modes of analysis is quite limited, sometimes little more than a brief nod in the direction of Freud's salient concepts, with emphasis on id, ego, and superego and minimal recognition of the psychology of the unconscious. The same applies, but usually less so, to some general texts in anthropology. For a major theoretical perspective that could be regarded as social science imperialism, we have to go back to classic masters of the nineteenth century, among whom Marx comes close to a full-scale articulation of such a position. Of course, there was at that time no depth psychology any social theorist could rely on, let alone absorb into his system, but the discussions of "alienation" and related concerns of the early essays and philosophical manuscripts (e.g., Marx 1844) provide what are in effect sketches for a psychology that would be subsumed into the general theoretical framework of the dialectical materialistic approach to society. In our own time, the work of Talcott Parsons comes close in some respects to a sociological imperialism in the sense intended here. The part referred to is that in which he uses and "translates" psychoanalytic concepts and propositions into his sociological framework. (See T. Parsons 1951, 1964, 1967.) However, much of that work might well be regarded, instead, as an integrationist approach, and will be discussed in that context later in this chapter.

Anthropological imperialism is abundantly evident, at least at the verbal level, in a great many general works in anthropology (see Kroeber 1948; Kluckhohn 1949; Beals and Hoijer 1953, 1959, 1965; Hoebel 1966; and almost any general textbook in anthropology). Here anthropology is presented as the master science of man, theoretically at least claiming that this discipline subsumes all other fields of study that in any way relate to the study of human beings, human behavior, human action in society and in culture, in any and all of its variations through time and space anywhere on this planet. Thus sociology as the study of one particular kind of society—the modern industrial ones—is but a specialized sub-branch of the more general study of human society and human societies. Thus economics that focuses on the economic systems of modern market societies is but a specialized sub-branch of the more general science of man that includes the study of all varieties of economic systems in all kinds of societies from the most technologically primitive tribal ones through more complex herding, agricultural, patrimonial, feudal, and many other kinds of societies. Similarly, political science would be seen as a specialty focusing on political systems of complex nation-states, as compared with the more generalized studies of political processes in the whole range of types of society that anthropology (theoretically at least, again) would be addressed to. Similarly, the variety of intrapsychic underlying personality patterns of individuals participating in various kinds of cultures would be one factor in the study of culture, to be subsumed under others or under the total pattern of culture and society generally. In that respect, where psychoanalysis is relevant in understanding such patterns, it would be as an adjunctive set of concepts within the larger framework of the more over-arching science of man. (In practice few anthropologists actually operate this way; while those who do take seriously the relevance of psychoanalytic perspectives are more likely to be "integrationists"—in terms of my present categories—than imperialists, and the more important of these will concern us in chapter 3.)

On the other side, we come to psychoanalytic imperialism. In this viewpoint, psychoanalysis, not sociology or anthropology, provides the framework for comprehensive analysis of not only the inner functioning of individual personalities, but also of societies, cultures, and of human history. Few psychoanalysts today take this kind of position. (For one who does, see the works of Reuben Fine 1975a, ch. 14, 1975b, 1977. Fine believes psychoanalysis is *the* unifying science of all aspects of humanity.)

But Freud himself, in some of his works (though not consistently throughout), did articulate positions that suggest such an imperialist model. In the *New Introductory Lectures*, 1933b, at one point he wrote: "For sociology, too, dealing as it does with the behaviour of people in society, cannot be anything but applied psychology. Strictly speaking there are only two sciences: psychology, pure and applied, and natural science" (1933b:179). Elsewhere, however, he sometimes wrote about culture as a phenomenon *sui generis* (see Rieff 1966:7). The imperialistic vein is particularly evident in the formative period of psychoanalysis, from 1899 onward. There was a great flush of enthusiasm for the apparently enormous scope of applicability of psychoanalytic ideas to culture, symbolism, mythology, art, and literature. Ultimately, Freud thought, psychoanalysis would be the basis for a kind of master science of human life. It would be the key to understanding history, civilization, the evolution of the species in its cultural aspects, the mythologies and religions of the world. In four major works, he showed his version of how psychoanalysis could provide such illumination: *Totem and Taboo* (1913), *The Future of an Illusion* (1927), *Civilization and Its Discon-*

tents (1930), and *Moses and Monotheism* (1939). Most psychoanalysts of today refer rarely and with embarrassment to these works, or avoid them entirely, implicitly or explicitly regarding them as unwarrantable speculative extensions of psychoanalytic ideas into areas on which psychoanalysts necessarily lack any requisite expertise.

Freud himself did not always hold consistently to this kind of psychoanalytic-imperialist position. Like many another scientist of genius, he was frequently self-contradictory and changed his mind on many important points of theory at many times in his carreer. True he did hold to the main points of *Totem and Taboo* until and through his last work, *Moses and Monotheism*—points that most of even the most devout Freudians have found untenable or fantastic, such as the hypothesis of an original primal parricide and incest by the sons of the powerful father of the horde, which Freud adduces as the starting point of all civilization, with its universal twin taboos of incest and parricide. Though from an integrationist position such as the one I shall take and elaborate in the rest of this book, there is much to object to in the implied imperialism of these works of Freud, one must also point out the merit of Freud's being strenuously serious about the truths he had uncovered and therefore tracing their sequelae to their farthest implications. The danger of such single-mindedness is, of course, monomania and fanaticism—but those seem more characteristic of Freud's more "orthodox" but less imaginative disciples than of Freud himself.

Integrationists

By contrast with both separatists and imperialists of any persuasion, there is a variety of scholars and practitioners who try to use psychoanalysis and social science in some combinative way. Some attempt a definite integration of the two fields of approach in their work. Some work from within the framework of one particular discipline, and use frameworks and findings from the other discipline(s) in a more or less systematic way in their analyses. Some work as a practitioner of one discipline in collaboration with a practitioner of the other discipline. There are a great many ways in which professionals have made such combinative efforts, and they differ widely among themselves, in some cases being barely in communication with others doing combinative work in a different vein. There are anthropologists who work systematically with psychoanalytic ideas, some, like Róheim and Devereux, actively combining anthropological research and writing and psychoanalytic clinical practice. Others work systematically with psychoanalytic ideas, without doing analytic clinical work, e.g., LaBarre, Anne Parsons, Arthur Hippler, Warner Muensterberger. Others have mined the anthropological sub-field called "personality-and-culture," with some influence of psychoanalytic ideas, though the latter are not necessarily systematically integrated into their work. Sociologists in general have not been as much influenced by psychoanalytic ideas, and many of them are outright hostile to the use of any Freudian conceptions in sociology, e.g., Peter Berger (1963). Still, many have used psychoanalytic ideas, or at least showed receptivity to the influence of psychoanalysis, in one or another manner, and a few have attempted some kind of systematic articulation of sociology and psychoanalysis in their work, either at the theoretical level or in substantive studies of particular social phenomena. There has been sociological or socio-cultural interpretation and analysis *of* psychoanalysis and its impact on modern society and culture, e.g., in the work of Philip Rieff (1959, 1966), Sherry Turkle (1978), some of the essays of Benjamin Nelson (1954, 1962, and others), Edith Kurzweil's essays on Lacan, Althusser, and other contemporary French thinkers (Kurzweil 1975, 1980). These works are not exactly psychoanalytic sociology in the sense I am using it, i.e., of systematically linking psychoanalytic and sociological modes of analysis, either theoretically or on specific substantive questions. But they are relevant background reading for working in this integrative field. (Of course, these names are but the beginnings of a list, and I make no effort to be comprehensive here.)

There are also a number of sociologists who have made incidental use of psychoanalytic ideas in their work. For example, Arthur Vidich and Joseph Bensman use concepts derived from psychoanalysis in discussing adjustment mechanisms of various elements of the population of *Small Town in Mass Society* (1958). Bensman and Rosenberg in a general sociology textbook (1976) use psychoanalytic ideas in discussing socialization. So do Hans Gerth and C. Wright Mills in their work *Character and Social Structure* (1953). Some of the work of Alex Inkeles (1954, 1959) would also fit in here. And there are incidental but clearly knowledgeable references to psychoanalytic ideas in the *Critical Sociology* of Norman Birnbaum (1971) and sporadically (far from systematically) in the writings of Richard Sennett (1970, 1977).

Also relevant in this connection are aspects of the work of the critical sociologist Jurgen Habermas (1968), who, although not dealing with the substantive propositions of psychoanalytic theory of personality, extols the *method* of psychoanalysis as akin to the processes of de-mystification in critical-sociological analysis.

There are some sociologists, and one sociologically sophisticated historian, for whom psychoanalytic ideas are more than incidental in their work, though not in all cases systematically integrated into their sociological analysis. Here we can refer to the work of sociologist Dennis H. Wrong (see essays collected under the title *Skeptical Sociology*, 1976) and the social historian Christopher Lasch, who in two recent books, *Haven in a Heartless World,* 1977, and *The Culture of Narcissism,* 1979, uses psychoanalytic ideas in his analysis of recent family patterns and of widespread cultural patterns of the 1970s.

Some sociologists have been attempting some more or less systematic *theoretical* articulation of sociology and psychoanalysis: Talcott Parsons and his followers, anti-Parsonian critics like Dennis Wrong, scholars who started as students of Parsons, e.g., Neil Smelser and, in a different vein, Philip Slater, the historian-sociologist team of Fred Weinstein and Gerald Platt; some of the "Frankfurt School" social scientists attempting an integration of Marx and Freud (e.g., Horkheimer, Adorno, Marcuse, and more recently Schneider); and the theoretical part of the work of Nancy Chodorow. Some of the essays of Hendrik Ruitenbeek (1962, 1963c) and of Jerome Rabow (1977, 1979) are also relevant in this connection, as is part of Endleman's earlier work (1967).

Addressing particular substantive questions from perspectives combining psychoanalysis and sociology, we find the work of Lewis Feuer on student rebellions (1969), Chodorow on mothering (1978), Michael Maccoby on business executives (1975), Endleman on student rebellions (1970a, 1970b, 1972), and on kibbutz (1967, 1977a), Slater on small-group processes (1966), and Michael Schneider on post-capitalist society (1973).

Some of these sociologists have (in effect) followed the lead of such psychoanalytic anthropologists as Róheim and Devereux in actively pursuing work in both fields, i.e., sociological research, teaching and writing, and psychoanalytic clinical practice; some of them (e.g., Endleman) arguing that such combination is essential for doing integrative psychoanalytic-social-scientific work. Sociologists who have this kind of double professional identity include Ernest Van den Haag (see Ross and Van den Haag 1957, Van den Haag 1963, for samples of Van den Haag's more psychoanalytically oriented work); the tireless compiler Ruitenbeek (1962, 1963a, 1963b, 1963c, for a sample); Jerome Rabow (1977, 1979), Jon Snodgrass (1979), Michael Maccoby (1967, 1975); and myself (see bibliography). Each of these has combined these two areas of activity in different ways, and there is no consensus on a single viewpoint on how to do this kind of integrative work. These integrationists are more likely to regard doing actual psychoanalytic clinical work as an essential requirement for integrative work. The argument here is that the personal psychoanalysis and the constant process of re-evaluation and re-discovery of oneself in the countertransference involved in doing clinical work with patients constitute the special and absolutely necessary kinds of empirical exposure for utilizing psychoanalytic concepts and insights (see Endleman 1975a). One pair of integrationist theorists, Weinstein and Platt (1973), not only doubts the necessity of psychoanalytic clinical work, but even of the personal psychoanalysis, which most other psychoanalytic sociologists or anthropologists who have expressed an opinion on this, would regard as surely a minimal requirement (in addition to scholarly knowledge of the psychoanalytic literature), even if clinical work is not.

On the psychoanalytic side, a number of psychoanalysts in recent times have ventured into the territory of addressing sociological and cultural questions from a psychoanalytic perspective, one combining psychoanalysis with some version of sociological or anthropological analysis. Here would be included some of the early work of Wilhelm Reich, particularly on fascism (1933b), the work of Erich Fromm (e.g., 1941, 1955), Erik Erikson (see bibliography), Alexander and Margarete Mitscherlich (1963, 1975), Robert Liebert (1971), Alan Wheelis (1958), Joel Kovel (1970), among others.

Some of the integrative work is being done by collaborative teams of a psychoanalyst and a social scientist: the husband-wife team of psychoanalyst L. Bryce Boyer and anthropologist Ruth Boyer (1967, 1972, 1976); psychoanalyst Donna Bushnell and anthropologist John Bushnell on California and Mexican Indians (Bushnell and Bushnell 1971, 1977). Other team productions involving anthropological field work in tribal societies are reviewed in Boyer 1978. On the theoretical level sociologist Neil Smelser and psychoanalyst Robert Wallerstein (1969) have articulated the convergences and divergences between these two fields, and the difficulties of integrating them.

The recently burgeoning field of psychohistory should also be mentioned here, although most historians do not consider themselves social scientists and, with a few important exceptions, do not connect themselves with sociology and anthropology. For many reasons, I shall not attempt to draw upon or deal with their work in any comprehensive way in this book. Their work is variably indebted to or built upon psychoanalytic ideas, in some cases used in so diluted or transmogrified a form as not to be acceptable to practitioners of psychoanalysis. Some of the work in this field is inspired by Erik Erikson's excursions into psychoanalytic biography of major historical figures (Luther and Gandhi 1958, 1969) and much of it today revolves around *The Journal of Psychochistory*, edited by the indefatiguable Lloyd De Mause (see his works 1974, 1975, 1979). Notable figures in this field include R. Binion (1968, 1977): Glenn Davis (1977); Henry Ebel (see De Mause and Ebel 1977); Peter Loewenberg (1971); Bruce Mazlish (1963, 1972); Arthur Mitzman on Max Weber (1970); Helm Stierlin (1976); Robert Waite (1971a, 1971b); Fred Weinstein and Gerald Platt on modernization (1969); Victor Wolfenstein on revolutionary personalities (1967); Benjamin Wolman (1971); Joseph Dowling on millenialism (1977); Howard Stein on ethnic group fantasies (1978b, 1979).

The more important of the social-science-psychoanalytic integrative efforts will be discussed in greater detail and more critically in chapter 3.

First, it is necessary to set out in more systematic fashion the desiderata for a good and useful integration of psychoanalytic and social-scientific analyses, and then to consider some of the major difficulties such efforts at integration encounter.

THE DESIDERATA FOR AN INTEGRATION: PSYCHOANALYSIS AND SOCIAL SCIENCE

The fundamental propositions are these: 1) Any social science requires an underlying psychology of the individual human being, essentially a psychology of the nature of human nature; and 2) Any adequate psychology of human beings also requires an understanding of social processes and of the patterns and processes of culture, and how these in turn affect the individual human personality.

The requirements for an adequate psychology of the individual human being can be enunciated briefly and succinctly as follows:

—It should relate to the nature of the human animal as a biological species; it should articulate what are called (in that odd, redundant, yet useful, phrase) the *species-specific* characteristic of this kind of animal organism;

—It should take into account the probable evolutionary origin of this species; the particular evolutionary dilemmas that it faced in evolving toward and into its evolutionarily present biological state and how the species has "solved"—or left unresolved—those problems and dilemmas;

—It should address itself to the continuity of the human personality over the life history of the individual;

—It should deal with the individual personality as an *integrated* being, i.e., as distinct from a collection of separate functions (as some psychologies do); it should pay attention to the quality or cohesion in the personality; and conversely, be able to account for the absence of such unity or cohesion;

—It should be able to account for both processes of harmony and processes of conflict within the personality;

—It should address itself to the human being as a *social* animal having relationships with significant other human beings;

—And it should look at human beings as participants in culture and as makers of culture, and modifiers of culture;

—It should deal with both the inner processes of the individual and his relationships with the external social world;

—It should make access to aspects of psychological functioning not ordinarily accessible to conscious awareness; and be able to delineate and explain the variations in accessibility to consciousness, and how these in turn may change with situations and circumstances and stages in the life process of the individual;

—It should enable us to differentiate between universal characteristics of human beings and other characteristics that are variable;

—It should enable us to identify and explain variations between different groups of individuals (such as social groups, communities, and the like) and variations that are more idiosyncratic from one unique person to another; it should therefore have a definite sociological dimension;

—It should also include dealing with differences among cultures, thus would have to include an anthropological cross-cultural-analytic dimension, alongside the emphasis on universal characteristics of all human beings.

The call here for a well-articulated underlying psychology of human nature is clearly in opposition to a Durkheimian view prevalent in twentieth-century sociology. It would be well to explain briefly why we reject such Durkheimianism. Sociologists who follow Durkheim (1895, 1897) on this point take up his argument that there is a reality that can be called society. Society in this view is a reality *sui generis*, not to be reduced to psychological facts. For example, if you want to understand the *rates* of suicide—not the separate individual cases—i.e., the total number of cases per some unit of population, such as 100,000, in a given place and in a given unit of time (e.g., a year)—that is a social fact that can be explained only by other social facts, like the degree of integration, or the extent of anomie. In this viewpoint, trying to understand the individual suicide case psychologically would give you no understanding of the social phenomenon. The two fields, sociology and psychology, must be kept separate.

Integrationists would argue in response that that whole style of thinking, in Durkheim and in later followers, is defective. In discussing such elements as "social integration" or "anomie," Durkheim in fact found it impossible to do so without invoking *subjective* definitions that people make, though Durkheim did not openly acknowledge that he was doing so. In effect, he was smuggling a psychological viewpoint back in. For example, when we examine the major sociological propositions Durkheim developed, they look something like this: Suicide rates are higher where there is more of a sociological state Durkheim called "anomie," that is, normlessness, or breakdown of norms. The connection between anomie and suicide is that individuals in a state of anomie—i.e., deregulation by the usual norms—experience an absence or loss of social cohesion, and therefore are more likely to commit suicide. Durkheim claimed that though of course the individual psychological state is of interest in reference to any particular individual suicide, it is not relevant for sociological analysis. But, in fact, for Durkheim to make his propositions about anomie and suicide (and their connections), he does have to refer to individual psychological states, such as not feeling support from a cohesive community. In fact, his propositions can best be understood if restated as follows: "Suicide results from unrelieved conflicts, stresses, and anxieties in individuals. Social cohesion would provide psychological support for people subjected to such stresses. In the anomic situation, such supports are lacking." This is, of course, not the way Durkheim himself formulated it in *Suicide* (1897), but it is implied in his analysis, and that analysis is persuasive only if we supply the missing implications. Thus, while explicitly rejecting any psychological analysis, Durkheim had to, in effect, sneak it back in.

Would-be integrationists of sociology with a psychoanalytic psychology would say, therefore, that it is preferable to get the psychology in, in the first place, and that the relevant psychology is psychoanalytic.

It can be argued that there are non-overlapping concerns of sociology and psychoanalysis, with sociology being necessarily concerned with overt conduct and its ramifications on the functioning of social order, while psychoanalysis can be described as being concerned with intrapsychic functioning, without direct concern for the functioning of society. Certainly one can think of macrosociological studies of whole societies that would require little if any attention to individual psychological states. Examples of such macrosociological work would be trans-historical and trans-societal studies of economic-political orders such as capitalism and socialism, or traditional versus modernized societies. Similarly one can think of certain aspects of population studies that descriptively trace population trends in particular societies in given historical periods, and possibly correlate these with shifts in macrosocietal structures, e.g., degree of industrialization, and of urbanism, and the like. Possibly a separatist position in such cases may be defensible. Also, in such cases, an imperialism from a psychological side that would attempt to explain such sociological trends entirely by reducing them to psychological factors would be an *indefensible* stance. From the other side, in psychoanalytic studies, it is conceivable to postulate certain studies that are focused entirely on *intrapsychic* problematics with, implicitly, some kind of relating of different elements all of which are on the intrapsychic level, and asserting that a sociological dimension in the analysis would be irrelevant and unnecessary. A possible candidate would be analysis of dreams, in which their dynamics and even part of their symbolic content are universal and transcend cultural differences. Similarly, such analysis would strenuously resist any kind of sociological reductionism, such as uninformed claims that such processes are only a response to certain social conformity pressures in a particular society.

If one does focus on such non-overlapping areas of work in the two (or more) disciplines, insisting on the separateness of the disciplines where they do not need each other, this then strengthens the case for integration where the two disciplines do need each other, and where neither should be reduced to the categories of the other, as tends to happen in imperialistic approaches. Thus, many aspects even of what has been described as macrosociological study such as the specialties mentioned can be demonstrated to *require* a psychological dimension. For example, studies of the shift of whole societies away from traditionalism toward modernization would still, in certain respects, require inquiry into the *motives* of persons who abandon specific traditional practices for modern ones, thus contributing to the modernization process— and any study of motives requires an adequate psychology, therefore, in my view, a psychoanalytic psychology. And demographic studies that, for example, trace declining birth rates, cannot be adequately explanatory if they do no more than correlate these with median income levels, or measures of degree of industrialization or of urbanism, just as Durkheim's "explanation" of certain suicide rates by "anomie" is inadequate without getting into the psychology of *how* people become de-regulated from social norms. Similarly, on the other side, it is hard to see how one can carry out completely intrapsychic studies totally without regard to the social context of these processes, to the kinds of social relationships this person has and has had with important other persons from earliest infancy on, and how these in turn are imbedded in socio-cultural matrices.[2]

The only psychology of human nature that comes at all close to filling all of the requirements outlined above is, of course, psychoanalysis. LaBarre (1968) has neatly and briefly delineated the special qualities of psychoanalysis as a viewpoint and mode of investigation of the human personality. These qualities make psychoanalysis uniquely the psychology that can be articulated with approaches to society, to social processes, to social interactions, that have been the primary subject matter of sociologists, and can be articulated with approaches to culture, to cultural universals and cultural variabilities, that have been the work primarily of anthropologists. For contrary to those detractors of Freudian psychoanalysis who criticized it for being "too biologistic," the psychoanalytic view is distinctly (though not always explicitly) a *social* psychology, a psychology of the social relationships of human beings with one another. The intrapsychic processes that are so distinctively the subject matter of psychoanalysis are all meaningless without reference to the *social* ties that people have. These are the ties of the infant with the mother and other caretakers. They are the ties with other specific persons of other kinds, with other kin-related and non-kin-related "significant others." They are the life-long ensuing social connections of the child, the adolescent, and the adult with all the other human beings who make up his world. Such statements may appear to some to be simplistic truisms, but they need re-asserting here in contradistinction to frequently heard misguided adverse commentaries on psychoanalytic thought.[3]

It is often pointed out that Freud's work was carried out in a particular time and place, in a particular cultural milieu, with a particular kind of scientific ethos. (The same has to be said about any scientist, of course.) Some critics draw from these facts the allegation that therefore Freud's work is parochially culture-bound. In fact, however, Freud's work had the special genius of focusing on the *universalities* of human experience in ways that transcended the temporal and cultural-spatial limitations of the immediate context in which this work was being done. (see LaBarre 1954, 1968, 1970, 1978a, for elaboration of how Freud's view articulates with evolutionary biology and anthropology in ways that make psychoanalysis culture-*transcendent* and the potential starting point for critical evaluation of any particular culture. On this point see also Devereux—works cited—and an illuminating recent article by Howard Stein and Soughik Kayzakian-Rowe (1978) in a psychoanalytic-cultural exploration of hypertension, biofeedback, and the myth of the machine in American culture.) Freud was referring not only to babies in late-nineteenth-century upper- and upper-middle-class Viennese families, but to all human babies. They are all born by exactly the same biological processes anywhere in the world, anytime in human history. They all arrive in the same premature, helpless, dependent state, with the same bodily and psychological needs. They are all the same neotenous infantilized ape with a peculiar combination of under-development at birth and enormous maturational potentialities. All have the same sexual dimorphism combined with bisexual psychological potentialities. All have the same dilemma of absolutely having to connect with caretaking/parenting figures, adults of two different sexes, one necessarily the same as the child's, the other the opposite. All have the same potentialities and propensities for symbolizing and for the acquisition of and participation in cultural heritage. Freud was dealing with those characteristics that make us distinctively human, distinct from other animals, and all in certain fundamentals basically alike. Though the evolutionary anthropology of the day was (by present-day standards) inadequate for the purposes at hand, and misled Freud into the creatively howling misconceptions of his audaciously fantastic *Totem and Taboo*, his central point was sound. That was that the human animal has his roots in evolution (as Darwin told us) and that we needed to understand this evolution to portray and analyze the species-specific characteristics of the human animal. These characteristics include his mysterious and often baffling psyche with its mix of gross irrationalities and enormous rational powers. True, Freud's knowledge of anthropology was sketchy, second- and thirdhand, and from sources already becoming partly invalidated by that time (1900). Also true that that anthropology was woefully inadequate by the standards of later-twentieth-century anthropology with its amassing of huge amounts of direct field observations of "primitives" and "savages." Nevertheless, Freud extracted from his readings in that anthropology, and from his knowledge of history and mythology, crucial kernels of truth about the *universalities* of human experience, and particularly of human psychological functioning. He could see that these human beings from many parts of the world, many periods of history, many different cultural levels and styles of culture, all had in common not only the same animal anatomy and physiology, but also universal psychological and psychosocial problems and processes. Where anthropologists were impressed with the strange *differences* among the peoples of tribal societies, and between them and people of advanced civilizations, Freud was impressed with the striking *similarity* between certain ways in which "savages" experienced and acted in the world, and certain ways of neurotics or psychotics of our supposedly "civilized" society. He also saw similarities of both to ways in which the child experiences the world, in whatever society. Building on these Freudian psychic universalities, psychoanalytic anthropologists starting with Géza Róheim have been able to construct the cornerstones of a psychoanalytic social science. Now they could combine detailed empirical investigation of a large number of different societies, indepth study of the intrapsychic process of individuals in each of these societies, and cultural-psychoanalytic analysis of the symbolic structures of these societies, such as myths and folklore, religion and art. The deeper into the unconscious one moves, the more alike is all mankind (Róheim 1950).

Somewhere around two to possibly as much as four million years ago we find identifiably human animals appearing on this planet. While the fossil evidence indicates a number of varieties of this animal type for the earlier period, by the time of the disappearance of the last major variant, the Neanderthals, in the late Pleistocene age, we have indications that only one version survived, namely what we can call geologically modern man, Homo sapiens, and all human animals we know anything about from that time onward are members of one and only one species. The anthropological studies demonstrate how these are all alike in species characteristics, and these characteristics apply to all human beings that have been born and lived on the earth since that time. Psychoanalysis portrays the dynamics as universal for all human beings, and the articulation with the physical and physiological that is an essential part of the grounding of psychoanalytic psychology connects it with the anthropological-evolutionary views. Thus an integrative unity of perspective is possible.

Anthropologists and others of a culturally-relativistic mind, by contrast, emphasize *differences* among the hundreds of cultures of the world, and, correspondingly, the differences in personality patterns that will appear in these different societies.

Psychoanalysts (at least those in the Freudian mainstream, to be defined below) and along with them psychoanalytic anthropologists and sociologists, emphasizing universals, argue in response that the variations the relativists refer to cannot be more than within a rather finite range. They would argue also that such variations are more likely to occur at the relatively *superficial* aspects of personality, like the style of self-presentation, and not to any substantial extent in basic underlying *mechanisms* of personality process, such as the typical modes of defense, of anxiety-coping, and of adaptation.

Where the relativists would emphasize that each cultural milieu will foster certain kinds of configurations of both surface and deeper-lying features of personality, universalists emphasize that the range of variability of such configurations is not likely to be large. Relativists would emphasize that the way the psychological mechanisms are selected, arranged, and organized, even though chosen from a finite possible repertoire, can be substantially different in different societies or subsocieties. Universalists would emphasize the finiteness of this possible range of variations.

Besides specifying the desiderata of an adequate psychology for the projected psychoanalytic social science, we also need to do the obverse: to specify the relevant *sociological* questions that must be addressed. We need an analysis of the social and cultural forces that impinge on the individual personality. Such a sociology would have to deal with the following basic questions:

1. How is social order possible?

2. To what degree can a society tolerate turmoil and disorder and still maintain a viable existence?

3. How is social conflict generated, and when it is, how is it handled?

4. Is social conflict inevitable? Or is it possible for some societies to avoid or prevent it completely? Under what conditions?

5. To what extent is social order built on consensus, to what extent on constraint, or on some combination of both?

We are arguing that in order to develop and build a psychoanalytic social science, the practitioners must be able to handle both sets of questions, the psychological about the basic personality mechanisms and processes, and the sociological about the processes of society and culture, its mechanisms of order and disorder, of conflict and consensus, and the combinations of these.

CHAPTER TWO

Obstacles to Integration

The difficulties of carrying out this integrative task are enormous. Most social scientists are insufficiently versed in psycheanalytic theory and conceptions to be able to apply them well. Most psychoanalysts are too poorly grounded in the requisite sociology and anthropology. The psychoanalysts and social scientists I have referred to above as integrationists (or would-be-integrationists) are exceptions.

The difficulties include the following:

1. Proponents of each discipline (here considering psychoanalysis as one discipline, and sociology and anthropology together as one discipline) tend to *sterotype* the content, concepts, methods, and findings of the other;

2. Each discipline tends to *exaggerate* the degree of consensus (theoretical, methodological, conceptual, substantive) within the other.

3. The same or *similar vocabulary* is *used with* very *different meanings* or connotations in the two disciplines;

4. What are for one discipline *parameters*—boundary assumptions that refer to the content of a nearby discipline—are for the other discipline *variables.*

Related to #4 are the following:

5. What one discipline takes as *given*, unproblematic, the other regards as open to *question*, definitely problematic, requiring further research;

6. Each discipline tends to regard the other as carrying on a set of tasks necessary for someone to do, but *one's own discipline's tasks are of* more *central importance.*

Stereotyping

Psychoanalysts not otherwise well informed about social sciences tend to think sociology is concerned only with group or collective phenomena, and anthropology only with the study of tribal societies. Similarly, many sociologists and anthropologists think psychoanalysis is concerned only with psychopathology, or that psychoanalysis attributes all personality characteristics to the effect of the first five years of life. As Boyer (1978) points out, many anthropologists were repelled by culture-and-personality studies because they stereotyped psychoanalysis essentially as stuck in the topographic model of the early Freud (concern with levels of consciousness) and ignored the advances of psychoanalysis after the structural model (of id, ego, and superego) became the central part of the psychoanalytic paradigm and was developed further in the "ego-psychology" of Hartmann and his followers, with emphasis on adaptation and on conflict-free portions potential in the ego. (See Modell 1975 for important theoretical discussion of the problems of psychoanalytic ego psychology in the 1970s.)

Some sociologists stereotype psychoanalysis as a clinical discipline that is concerned only with adjusting patients to the existing social order no matter what, and therefore reject psychoanalysis out of hand from a "radical-sociology" perspective (see Skolnick and Currie 1970 and similar animadversions against psychoanalysis in Skolnick and Skolnick 1971 and later editions). Needless to say, this is a major distortion of the outlook of most psychoanalysts as practitioners, and certainly of the value positions held or implied by psychoanalysis. To summarize, psychoanalytically, there can be very psychopathological forms of conformity and very psychologically healthy forms of rebellion, from the institutionalized norms of society, just as there can be the reverse.

Exaggerating Consensus in the Other Field

Sociologists are likely to consider psychoanalysis as an essentially integrated and homogeneous field in which there is a basic consensus on a core body of theory and a set of main propositions. Thus a sociologist might ask, "What is *the* psychoanalytic view on this question?" And anthropologists may assume there is some basic unity and homogeneity within psychoanalysis. Similarly, psychoanalysts are likely to attribute to sociology, or to anthropology, a certain unity of purpose and approach, and a core set of theories and propositions. In all cases, they would be wildly off the mark. A psychoanalytic audience need hardly be reminded of the great diversity of viewpoints even within what might be called mainstream psychoanalysis, the stream from Freud, through Hartmannian ego psychology to current object-relations theory. Nor can we help but be reminded of the near-chaotic state of psychoanalytic theory today, the pervasive assaults on the basic Freudian metapsychology, the anarchy of terminology revolving around the clinical phenomena different from the classical obsessional and hysterical neurotic syndromes. (See Schafer 1976 for one thoroughgoing attack on classical Freudian metapsychology—one of many currently going on—and Kohut 1971, 1977, and Kernberg 1975, among the major figures involved in the currently raging controversies regarding narcissism and borderline conditions. See also Giovacchini's trenchant critique of Kohut's version of narcissistic pathology, 1979.)

Outsiders, such as sociologists and anthropologists, may exaggerate the extent of consensus in psychoanalysis on such basic questions as the Oedipus complex, its genesis and significance in psychosexual development, the differences in its forms and functions in boys compared to girls, and so on. Yet, in fact, within psychoanalysis itself there is little consensus on these matters. There is the basic split of those psychoanalysts who can be called "revisionists" or "culturalists," who take overseriously the words or the implications of certain anthropological studies to mean that many societies or subsocieties may not have an Oedipus complex in the personalities of their members at all. They therefore argue that the Oedipus complex is culturally determined and not universal, as Freud and many psychoanalytic anthropologists, such as Róheim, LaBarre, Devereux, and myself, are likely to maintain. The revisionists in the directions of the "neo-Freudians' of the 1930s and thereafter, in particular Fromm, Horney, Kardiner (1939, 1945), most of the Sullivanians, and to some extent Erikson, generally tend to take this position. (For example, in the Bieber group's classic psychoanalytic study of male homosexuality—see Bieber et al. 1962, and discussion of this in Part 4 below—the "culturalists" among the psychoanalysts concerned tended to regard the Oedipus complex not as universal nor even as generally found in this society, but rather to appear only in a certain kind of psychopathological family constellation within this society.) Even a psychoanalyst in the mainstream (and collaborator in psychoanalytic anthropology), such as Boyer, finds the question of the "cultural determination" of the Oedipus complex still open to question. Psychoanalysts and social scientists who reject its universality have generally based their position on Malinowski's study of the Trobriand Islanders, discussed on this question in *Sex and Repression in Savage Society*, 1927. From that work Malinowski concluded that the Oedipus complex was absent in the Trobriand Islanders, and probably also in many other societies that lacked a patriarchal nuclear family system such as prevails in the Western civilized world, and that it is therefore not universal as Freud alleged or assumed. For what I regard as conclusive refutation of that misperception by Malinowski, see Róheim 1950, Anne Parsons 1964, and Endleman 1967. Basically what Malinowski—and other anthropologists focusing on the matrilineal clan structure of such societies as the Trobriands— missed was that in all of these societies there is in fact a nuclear family consisting of mother, father (her mate), and children, and that the father— not the mother's brother—is the sexual possessor of the mother, therefore the sexual rival for the mother, to the boy. Similarly, with father and mother possessing each other, exclusively, in the girl's sexual longing for the father, the mother is obviously the crucial sexual rival. Thus there will inevitably be oedipal triangles. And most societies do in fact have such nuclear families, as the norm as well as the practice in most cases, or as the norm and ideal even where not existent or not prevalent in practice. The maternal uncle as authority figure for the boy in matrilineal systems does not appear on the scene—in Trobriands, and usually in other cases too—until the boy is past the age of five or six—i.e., *after* the age at which the oedipal crisis has appeared and been dealt with. Therefore, it is reasonable, as Jones argued in response to Malinowski (see Anne Parsons 1964 for detailed analysis), that the hostility of young males toward the maternal uncle is, in fact, a displacement from the original rivalry-hostility toward the father. Anne Parsons recognized that the precise nature of the primary nuclear-family conflict experienced by the child, revolving around something like oedipal themes, could, of course, vary in relationship to the specific nuclear-family structure, its relationship to wider elements of the kinship system, and the precise details of the relationships of each of the parents to boy and girl children.

Similarly, psychoanalysts may think of sociology as basically a unitary field with basic consensus on central themes, concepts, theoretical positions, and methods. In fact, the discipline is far from consensus or homogeneity on any of these matters. On theoretical orientations, one sociological critic, George Ritzer (1975), finds that, in fact, sociology today may be described as lacking any one reigning paradigm, but as split among at least three distinctly different ones. These three have very different and often mutually contradictory basic assumptions about the world and about the nature of sociology as a science for understanding the social world. There are followers of a "social facts" paradigm, split themselves among structural-functionalists and conflict/dialectical theorists. Then there are "social definitionists," also split into warring factions, such as symbolic interactionists, labeling theorists, dramaturgic theorists, phenomenologists, and others. And there are "social behaviorists," paralleling, basically, behaviorists in psychology.[1]

Followers of a "social facts" type of paradigm assume "society" is some kind of reality in itself, rather than an abstract term. Among these there are cleavages among structural-functionalists, following (more or less) Malinowski, Durkheim, Radcliffe-Brown, and more recently Talcott Parsons (Malinowski 1944; Radcliffe-Brown 1935, 1952; Durkheim 1895; Parsons 1951, 1967) and conflict theorists like Gouldner (1972), Coser (1956), and neo-Marxists like Birnbaum (1969, 1971), Bottomore (1965, 1966), and others. (Ritzer is aware that classifying all of these into the "social facts paradigm" is at least partly arbitrary.) "Social definition" paradigm followers have in common rejection of the idea that society is a thing in itself, insisting the term is an abstraction. What is real to these sociologists are human beings engaged in subjective processes of definition (of the social and natural world) and reactions to these definitions. They share an acceptance of the theorem first enunciated by W. I. Thomas (Thomas and Znaniecki 1918ff.; also Thomas 1928, p. 572; Thomas 1951) to the effect that "if people define something as real, it is real in its consequences." Among these sociologists, however, there are major factional battles among symbolic interactionists, dramaturgic sociologists, ethnomethodologists, phenomenologists, as well as many variation on any of these. Symbolic interactionists, probably the most widespread and influential of the sociological social psychologists, take off from the work of the philosopher-psychologist-sociologist George Herbert Mead (1934)—who was, incidentally, the important influence, sociologically, upon the neo-Freudian psychoanalyst Harry Stack Sullivan (1953). These emphasize that the social world, and the individual person's self, for that matter, are all social constructions, products of the definitions human beings make in their interactions with significant other human beings. (For contemporary examples, see Manis and Meltzer 1972 and Shibutani 1961.) A special variant of this kind of work is found in the original writings of Erving Goffman (1959, 1961, and other work), which take the dramaturgic analogy—"all the world's a stage . . ." to farther and thought-provoking conclusions. Another variation are sociologists who have come to be labeled (or label themselves) "labeling theorists." Prominent among them are Howard S. Becker (1963) and Edwin Schur (1971), who have applied this approach especially to the study of social deviance. They insist that the labels attached to persons or situations by persons in significant positions determine what is the social reality in a particular society at a given moment in history. Still another variation in the social-definitionist perspective are the social phenomenologists, who argue that all reality, including very importantly, social reality, is a matter of "social construction." Major proponents of this view are Peter Berger and Thomas Luckmann (Berger 1963, Berger and Luckmann 1967), and they have a host of followers. An offshoot of this kind of phenomenological position, derived from the philosophical work of Alfred Schütz (Schütz 1964, 1970, 1971) is the work of Harold Garfinkel (1967) and his followers, which has been called ethnomethodology. In the third paradigm category, "social behaviorism," we find the work of George Homans (1961), who is in effect the Skinner of sociology, emphasizing the view that the central reality is not social structure, or social definitions, but social *behavior*.

These are but a few of the divisions among contemporary sociologists. These are at the theoretical level. Not necessarily entirely corresponding to these theoretical differences, there are major methodological cleavages among sociologists: first the major one between macrosociologists, concerned with whole societies and social structures, including those doing comparative studies of whole civilizations, and on the other side microsociologists who focus on more microscopic aspects of social process, social interaction, labeling and its consequences, and the like. Macrosociologists are more likely to rely on broad descriptive and historical accounts, documentary sources of many kinds, including governmental data on populations, work-force participation, incomes, and other economic-political material, as well as the whole array of demographic data. Microsociologists are more likely to utilize questionnaire and personal-interview methods of various kinds, or anthropological participant-observation studies "in the field." Social factists are more likely to be macrosociological in methods, social definitionists more likely to use one or more microsociological methods, and/or introspective subjective observational methods. Ethnomethodologists have developed a series of strategies more distinctly their own, involving a kind of experimental manipulation of everyday social scenes. Dramaturgic studies rely heavily on the special idiosyncratic observational talents of the sociologist doing the work—in fact, few if any of the imitators of Goffman have produced work that comes anywhere near his special artistic insights. Sociological behaviorists tend to mimic psychological behaviorists, attempting, where feasible, experimental methods.

The diversity, in short, is enormous. From the viewpoint of an outsider to this discipline, such as most psychoanalysts, the insiders are engaging in "the narcissism of small differences" (as Freud put it). The outsider psychoanalyst, by contrast, tends greatly to overestimate the degree of consensus and homogeneity within a field like sociology.

As for anthropology, the diversity within this discipline is if anything even greater than one finds within sociology or within psychoanalysis. For a beginning, the discipline consists of five rather different sub-disciplines; cultural anthropology, ethnology, physical anthropology, archaeology, and linguistics. Some would count six, considering social anthropology—the comparative study of social structures—as distinct from cultural anthropology, the comparative study of cultures. (Many sociologists would count comparative study of social structures as part of sociology, of course.) Relatively few anthropologists continue to be well informed about any of the sub-disciplines other than their own, at least after some years after completion of their graduate training. What unifies these subdisciplines (if at all) is the overarching idea that they all pertain to the study of the human species, in all its aspects, evolutionary, historical, cultural, and social (many would add psychological, as, for example, those anthropological imperialists mentioned above.) Physical anthropology itself includes at least three branches, tracing the evolutionary history of the species in relation to other animal species, studying the physical diversites of human beings within the same species, and human biology. Archaeology involves digging up the remains of long-gone cultures of the distant, mostly prehistoric, past, and connecting that with the evolution of the physical species and its later infra-human variations. Linguistics involves the comparative study of language and of languages, that crucial dimension of human culture. Ethnology involves the attempted reconstruction of the historical movements and connections of peoples over the face of the earth, using both archaeological and contemporary (or recently historical) cross-cultural descriptive data on the hundreds of tribal and more complex societies now anthropologically known. Within social and cultural anthropology, the sub-discipline most relevant here, there are also a great number of conflicting schools and viewpoints. Culturologists like Leslie White (1949) insist on the *sui-generis* character of culture as a phenomenon in itself, not reducible to psychological characteristics of individual persons—a view parallel to the social-factism of followers of Durkheim in sociology, who argue the reality of society, and of social structure. There are also neo-cultural evolutionists, like Sahlins, Service (1960) and company.

Then there are structuralists, followers of Lévi-Strauss (1962), where "structure" is used not in ways of sociologists of "social structure," but rather as referring to basic structures of human mentality underlying all human cultures. (This kind of universalism shares some elements with the thinking of Freud, but is significantly divergent from Freud in important ways. Lévi-Strauss even uses a concept of "unconscious" mental processes, but not in a way congruent with psychoanalysis. See Edith Kurzweil 1975, 1980, for a penetrating analysis of this.)

And within cultural anthropology, while the prevailing emphasis in cross-cultural studies of different societies (mostly, though no longer exclusively, tribal ones) continues to be that of cultural relativism, there are others who are more likely to emphasize the universal features of all cultures. For example, we find universally in all cultures, some forms of linguistic and symbolic communication, some kind of kinship structure, some version of family, some form of sanctioned mating, primary incest taboos, some form of secondary incest taboos, some kind of distinctive patterning of life-cycle stages and transitions, some status distinctions on the basis of age, sex, and kinship position, sanctioned reactions to conduct considered disruptive or subversive of the social order, some modes of expressive patterning in terms of art, mythology, folklore, and the like, some version of "religion" (in the sense of ultimate values, belief in extra-human forces, some kind of patterned relationship of human beings to these forces, etc.) some system of moral codes, some patterned ways of handling the ever-potentially troublesome feelings of sex and aggression.

Similar Vocabulary Used With Different Meanings

Communication—let alone integration—is often difficult between two such disciplines as psychoanalysis and sociology, because some of the same terms may be used in both realms of discourse, but with quite different meanings, or at least connotations.

For example, in psychoanalysis the term ego (used by the English translators to render Freud's "das Ich," literally "the I") has a particular cluster of specific technical meanings. The word was already widely in use in ordinary English before Freud's time, with a set of layman's meanings, one being an inflated sense of one's own importance, as in "he has a lot of ego," or "a big ego," or almost a synonym for self-esteem, as in "the prize was a boost to his ego." Self-esteem would, of course, be only one of the many functions of the structure psychoanalysts call ego, and inflated self-importance would more likely be dealt with as heightened narcissism, or narcissistic vulnerability, in psychoanalytic thinking, rather than by use of the term "ego." Some sociologists follow the popular usage. Others use "ego," or the adjectival forms "egoistic" or "egotistic," in ways following Durkheim's usage, which also antedated Freud's, as in Durkheim's concept of "egoistic suicide." Here the reference is to the person's wish, right, or even obligation to make individual decisions for himself as opposed to having them imposed by some collectivity or authority.

In both of these usages, the reference is usually to *conscious* psychological processes. By contrast a major part of the psychoanalytic exploration of ego functions deals with *unconscious* aspects. The ego's defensive mechanisms, as outlined in Anna Freud's *The Ego and the Mechanisms of Defense* (1937) and elaborated in the later "ego psychology" of Hartmann and followers (Hartmann 1939, 1964) are to be understood as largely *unconscious* processes.

Similarly, on the other side, some psychoanalysts use the terms "deviant" and "deviance" in ways which clearly imply a value judgment on the behavior of the person so described. By contrast sociologists studying deviance attempt to use this term in a value-neutral manner simply to refer to action which the people in that society regard as a violation of some norm accepted by that society.

In a variation on this difficulty, a term may be used in one of these fields which practitioners in the other field find far too diffuse and undifferentiated. Such a case is the psychoanalytic usage of the phrase "external reality." Sociologists would find this term much too crude and undifferentiated. If pressed on this point psychoanalysts would say, of course, external reality means the physical environment and the social environment of the individual. "Social environment" in turn would be regarded by most sociologists as itself too diffuse and vague a term. The sociologist would refer to the persons with whom the given individual has some kind of definite relationships. Among these he would differentiate persons with whom the individual has some highly important kind of relationship, the "significant others" (in symbolic-interactionist terminology); others related in a definite but not so significant a way; others in an impersonal affectively neutral relationship (e.g., bureaucratic officials); still others as part of an amorphous crowd or collectivity around him. Thus the psychoanalyst's "external reality" or its subdivision the "social environment" is to the sociologist a complex differentiated world.

Parameters for One Discipline are Variables
for the Other

One major difficulty in integration of psychoanalysis with sociology-anthropology is the fact that what are for one discipline parameters[2]— i.e., boundary matters, assumptions about what is thought to be understood in the neighboring discipline—are for the other discipline *varia-*

bles to be subjected to study. This difficulty has been well articulated in a thoughtful collaborative paper by the psychoanalyst Robert Wallerstein and the sociologist Neil Smelser (Wallerstein and Smelser 1969:697). "Each [discipline] assumes as givens, parameters, what are variables of the other behavioral science(s)." Thus sociologists studying social mobility may assume a psychological motivational *given*, e.g., that sons will seek to surpass their fathers, which for psychoanalysts would be a variable: how differently different sons handle the problem of oedipal rivalry with the father. We can consider how differently we might sociologically study social mobility if we assumed instead that sons will, ordinarily, seek to follow in their father's footsteps. Similarly, psychoanalytic formulations of an "average expectable environment" (Hartmann 1939, 1964) set such an "environment" (a term too gross and undifferentiated from a sociological viewpoint, as already indicated above) as a kind of parameter within which one then proceeds to examine the variables of intrapsychic functioning, of conflict and defense, of struggle and adaptation, etc. But what if an "average expectable environment"—implying a certain social-cultural stability, uniformity, consensus, and orderly consistent structure—is not the usual state of affairs in a society at a particular period of time—or perhaps of *any* society? What if the parameter were, rather, an expectable state of constant social tension, conflict, turbulence, and change? Clearly, the problem for psychoanalytic study would then be adaptation to such a vastly different social world. In reality, of course, most of the time we find neither consistent orderliness and stability, nor consistent and persistent turmoil, turbulence, and change in all aspects of life. Still, if there is a great deal of the latter—as has generally been true of all modern societies of the past few centuries, as well as of many others at all different technological levels in many periods of the past—the meaning of "adaptation" in both content and mechanisms must surely be quite different from what it would be for a stable and traditional society with very little change. Still, psychoanalysis would alert us to the high probability that the nature and range of the psychological resources potentially available to persons would still be basically the same for all human beings, or vary only within a finite and knowable spectrum.

"Givens" of One Discipline are the "Problematics" of the Other

Very broadly, psychoanalytic writing that focuses on the individual personality tends to take the social and cultural world as given, or as ground to the figure under scrutiny, the internal dynamics. Conversely, social scientists, where they recognize internal psychic dynamics at all, tend to take them as given, or in a certain sense as ground, while what for them is the figure, the social and cultural structures and processes, are seen as problematic and full of complexities to which one needs to devote exacting attention. Even social scientists who are somewhat attuned to psychoanalytic ideas may use these ideas or concepts in ways which neglect or elide the problematics psychoanalysts would see in these terms. For example, Vidich and Bensman, in their very illuminating book about a small upstate New York community, *Small Town in Mass Society* (1958), use at some points some psychoanalytically-derived ideas about the citizens' use of certain defense mechanisms, such as denial and reaction-formation. These authors use these terms in an unproblematic way. Within psychoanalysis it would be much more problematic whether the instances in question really were what psychoanalysts would call denial or reaction-formation, as the case may be, in a strict psychoanalytic sense. For instance, in this case it is not clear whether the authors are referring to conscious or unconscious processes, or some combination of both, and if the latter, what is the evidence that that is what is psychologically going on? On the other side, psychoanalysts taking as given what for social scientists is problematic, many of the examples we have just given of other kinds of difficulties and misunderstandings between the fields would fit here as well: psychoanalysts, using the terms "environment," "status," "deviation," and the like, tend to ignore the problematics of all of these ideas in the social sciences.

One's Own Discipline's Tasks Are of Central Importance

In this viewpoint one may regard the other discipline as doing something important for *someone* to do, but "this is not *my* work." This attitude would of course be more extreme in those within any of these disciplines who take a separatist (as distinct from imperialistic or integrationist) stance on the relationship among these disciplines: "each to his own last." But even integrationists, persons attempting to integrate these different fields into some kind of unitary psychoanalytic social science, are likely to be faced with the fact that their primary professional identity is located in one of these disciplines. Thus, George Devereux, one of the foremost psychoanalytic anthropologists, who has practiced both psychoanalysis as clinical practice, and anthropology as anthropological field work, declares himself (primarily to anthropological audiences) as first and foremost an *anthropologist*, albeit one who is much more psychoanalytic than most. (However, Devereux has also published extensively, in psychoanalytic journals, on psychoanalytic topics and for psychoanalysts.) On the other side, a psychoanalyst such as Herbert Hendin presents himself as a psychoanalyst first, and does not pretend to be a sociologist, though most of his work constitutes forays into distinctly sociological territory.

IMPLICATIONS OF THESE DIFFICULTIES

The implications of the foregoing discussion are, of course, that the scholar who would attempt integrative studies combining psychoanalysis and the social sciences of sociology and anthropology needs to be well grounded in both areas. Efforts in such an integrative direction up till now have for the most part been done by either social scientists (sociologists or, more likely, anthropologists) who have some (though quite variable) grounding in psychoanalysis, or by psychoanalysts who have some (again quite variable) grounding in the relevant social sciences. Usually studies that are strong in the social science dimension are not so strong, or are sadly weak, in the psychoanalytic aspect. Conversely, studies that are well-grounded psychoanalytically tend not to be particularly sophisticated in their sociology or anthropology. Some integrative attempts find their authors attacked by some critics from both camps, as inadequate in their social science, and also in their psychoanalysis.

Here are some examples: Lewis Feuer's *The Conflict of Generations* (1969) is a massive cross-cultural and transhistorical study of student rebellions over the past century and a half. He is strong on historical detail and on sociological analysis of the contexts of these rebellions. His integrating theme is that these rebellions, disparate as they are, have a common psychological core, essentially an oedipal rebellion against the father and father-figures. Psychoanalytically this is a flawed work in that it uses an oversimplified, outsiders' version of the Freudian psychology of father-son relationships. (I am not suggesting Feuer was entirely wrong, for the evidence of the then current student rebellions indicated to me—see Endleman 1970a—that Feuer's formula did fit some of the students involved.) But where most of the social science critics of Feuer's work objected to his using psychoanalytically formulated explanations at all, I would fault the work for being *insufficiently* psychoanalytic and using psychoanalytic ideas in too oversimplified and too undifferentiated a manner. My own interpretations attempted to pay attention to the elements of conflict and ambivalence in the feelings of male student rebels toward their fathers and toward male authorities in the university and in the polity—particularly the police. Far from being absent, I believe the oedipal themes were present in abundance, but in a complexity of psychic context that is slurred in Feuer's analysis.

On the other side, we have work like that of the psychoanalyst Herbert Hendin. His recent work, *The Age of Sensation* (1975), attempts to portray contemporary college youth (or at least a small subsample at an elite college) in the sociological context of certain institutional trends of present-day American society. The clinical portraiture of the students involved appears to be psychoanalytically sophisticated and nuanced (though it will inevitably not please all kinds of psychoanalysts). The evidence in reference to intrapsychic processes appears to be rather good. Some of the students were patients in therapy; others were recruited to be paid for a series of psychoanalytically-grounded depth interviews. Granted, this kind of evidence is far short of what psychoanalysts usually require of themselves and their colleagues in clinical situations, in order to support particular clinical interpretations. Still, we can have a certain confidence in the empirical grounding for the psychodynamic interpretations Hendin offers of the intrapsychic processes of the individuals involved. However, when Hendin comes to discuss social trends, his arguments are much weaker, and the evidence presented rather flimsy and impressionistic, e.g., on the prevailing patterns of child-rearing in contemporary America. What comes across then is a professional psychoanalyst but an amateur sociologist. (In fairness, it needs to be said that, to my knowledge, no *sociological* works have adequately answered, with a convincing array of evidence, the kinds of questions on the sociological level, that Hendin alludes to, or that are germane to his arguments about prevalent childrearing trends and probable psychological sequelae of these at the intrapsychic personality level.)

Integrative psychoanalytic-sociological work that has drawn the critical fire of both psychoanalysts and sociologists is that of Erich Fromm. True, Fromm has many admirers in both fields, and a whole segment of "neo-Freudian" or "culturalistic" psychoanalysis has been derived from or influenced by his work. These evidently find his psychoanalysis acceptable and assume that the sociological side of his work is sound. However, in reference to his two main interdisciplinary works, *Escape from Freedom* (1941) and *The Sane Society* (1955), sociologists have found much to criticize, and so have mainstream psychoanalysts. What Fromm had to say in the 1941 work on the transformations of capitalism, many sociologists would find to be a watered-down and distorting rehash of Marx and Weber—and both of whom had done it better. On the other side, classical analysts can see little in Fromm's concept of the "authoritarian character" that marks any advance over classical psychoanalytic work on the sado-masochistic character, well delineated in a great deal of earlier psychoanalytic work. (See Fenichel 1945 and references therein to the substantial literature on this.) And concepts such as the "marketing orientation" (in Fromm's 1947 work, *Man for Himself*)—later influential on the work of Riesman, which is still less psychoanalytic—would be regarded by psychoanalysts in the classical tradition as a distortion and trivialization of the Freudian psychoanalytic conception of the anal character as formulated early by Abraham (1927) and elaborated by others in the mainstream psychoanalytic tradition. Psychoanalysts of this background may regard Fromm as passable sociology but poor psychoanalysis; social scientists are more likely to respond in reverse: passable as psychoanalysis, poor as sociology.

Besides Feuer and Fromm, other Marxists or former Marxists have made efforts of some kind, to coalesce Freudian views with a sociology along Marxist or neo-Marxist lines. Jurgen Habermas (1968), a leading critical theorist, though doing little with any of the substantive propositions of psychoanalysis, does in recent work show appreciation of psychoanalysis as a *method* of inquiry, a mode of acquiring self-knowledge superior to other psychologies which do not get into the *unconscious* level. It can thus be an aid in the process of the de-mystification of the world, a central task in critical theory. Sociological theorists of the "Frankfurt School" (many of them contemporaries and colleagues of Fromm in pre-World-War-II Germany) made various related efforts to relativize psychoanalytic views and connect them with a Marxist kind of understanding of society. Their major American effort was *The Authoritarian Personality* (T. W. Adorno and colleagues, 1950), which attempted to link racial and religious prejudice with authoritarianism in general social outlooks, and these in turn with personality dynamics, conceived in psychoanalytic terms.[3] This work educed major criticisms from both sociological and psychological directions. (See, for an overview of contemporary evaluations, Christie and Jahoda 1954.) Their conception of the "authoritarian personality" is clearly derived from Fromm's usage, and suffers from the same kind of superficializing of classical psychoanalytic concepts.

Wilhelm Reich, in much of his early work (pre-orgone), tried to fuse Freudian and Marxist ideas, often to the dissatisfaction of both camps. His *Mass Psychology of Fascism* (1933b) is the major work in that vein.

A more recent revival of attempts at Freud-Marx integration is the work of a young German scholar, Michael Schneider, *Neurose und Klassen-kampf* (Neurosis and Class Struggle), 1973; English translation by Michael Roloff, *Neurosis and Civilization*, 1975). This ambitious work attempts to "rescue" psychoanalysis from its alleged immersion in bourgeois values and assumptions, and also to defend psychoanalysis against misguided Marxist detractors. Schneider faults the psychoanalytic revisionists (neo-Freudians like Fromm, Kardiner, Horney) for encouraging a perspective in psychotherapeutic practice which *could* be used in justification of adjusting the patient to the existing social order, with the implication that he would be dissuaded from taking a more justified critical stance toward the surrounding society and particularly its forms of power.[4] At the same time he regards as correct the relativizing done by those theorists (and their allies in culture-personality anthropology) who deny the universality of basic Freudian propositions of psychosexual development, Oedipus complex, and conflicts between instincts and culture. (For example, Schneider, evidently relying on secondary sources primarily, manages to misread much of the culture-personality anthropological literature as having "proved" the non-existence of oedipal conflict in many primitive societies.) He thus, in my view, mistakenly rejects the crucial universalist elements in psychoanalysis and thoroughly psychoanalytic anthropology. Schneider's work will educe criticism from those within the mainstream "classical" psychoanalytic tradition for its too hasty and too easy relativizing. It will also elicit critique from the sociological side from any sociologists not convinced of the adequacy of the Marxist view of society.

Conversely, the general run of culture-and-personality anthropological studies (such as early Mead, and Benedict, Gorer, DuBois, Spiro, Kluckhohn, Honigmann, Kardiner-Linton, drawing mostly on simplified and watered-down psychoanalytic ideas, tended to be disparaged or rejected by other anthropologists on the grounds of being "too Freudian"—epithets like "piss-pot determinism" were hurled against this kind of work in the late 1940s. Meanwhile, from a strictly classical psychoanalytic view, they were seen as not psychoanalytic enough. Hartmann, Kris, and Loewenstein (1951) delivered a thoroughgoing critique of that body of anthropological work, from a psychoanalytic viewpoint. In the same period Róheim (e.g., 1950) was flailing this work for being grounded in an entirely inadequate psychoanalysis, and chastising its neo-Freudian foundation for rejecting the crucial biological baseline of Freud's psychology.

Róheim, in turn, being both a practicing psychoanalyst and a field anthropologist, often found detractors in both fields, each regarding him as an intruder who had wandered into their territory. (See Robinson 1969 for a sketch of the relevant intellectual history.[5])

Another work to be conisered in this context is Christopher Lasch's *The Culture of Narcissism* (1979). Lasch is a sociologically and psychoanalytically informed historian here attempting some kind of definitive socio-cultural appraisal of the perplexities of America in the 1970s. He purports to see the key to a whole range of cultural phenomena of that decade in the psychoanalytic concept of narcissism, which he claims to be the emblematic psychic disorder of our time, in the way that hysteria was for the period around 1900. This looks promising, and his chapter portentously entitled "The Narcissistic Personality of Our Time" (echoing Horney's appraisal of characteristic difficulties of the 1930s) does, in fact, show a sophisticated grasp of recent psychoanalytic writings on the nature and problems of narcissism. Lasch is aware of the controversies within psychoanalysis as to whether the narcissistic disorders are in fact far more prevalent today than in the earlier decades of psychoanalytic practice—as often asserted—or whether their apparently greater prevalence is only an artifact of changing conceptual baggage in the field and of changing and expanding patient populations.[6] Lasch thinks it is the former, though aware that it cannot be demonstrated conclusively with the available evidence. He sees broader cultural changes as consistent with such a shift, and as reflections of what can be deduced as changing personality dynamics widespread in the population. He regards the patients showing narcissistic personality disorders as but exaggerations of widespread trends in the society, and therefore as clues to stresses and difficulties appearing generally in the socio-cultural realm.

Lasch makes a number of illuminating cultural and social observations on the current American scene, particularly on the trendy elements in the self-awareness movements, the degradation of professional sports, changing ways of relating to demands for success, the collapse of authority in the family, and the like. However, most of the socio-cultural observation is only fortuitously if at all connected with the psychoanalytic delineation and scrutiny of narcissism. And as in Hendin's work, there is the persistent difficulty that generalizations about current changes as, for example, in family patterns, while plausible, are not backed up by any systematic empirical demonstration.

Where, then, do we find satisfactory integrative work? To that question we turn in the next chapter.

CHAPTER THREE

Integrative Work

Where then do we find satisfactory integrative work that will pass muster with both psychoanalysts and social scientists from sociology or anthropology? Since probably no work from within one discipline will satisfy all psychoanalysts, and no work will satisfy all sociologists or all anthropologists, in any case, it is most unlikely that any would-be integrative work will satisfy any substantial portion of the scholars in all three fields. What is to be judged a valuable contribution will, of course, depend on the particular assumptions and convictions ("prejudices" to those who do not share them) the particular social scientist or psychoanalyst holds. My own must be clear by now: mainstream psychoanalysis, i.e., the line from Freud through Hartmann to contemporary ego psychology and object-relations theory. It would include work such as that of Margaret Mahler and her colleagues (*Human Symbiosis*, 1968, and *The Psychological Birth of the Human Infant,* 1975), Edith Jacobson (1964), and others in that tradition cited earlier and later in this work. I do *not* include in my intellectual pedigree the early major dissidents Jung (1902 ff., 1958, 1959) and Adler (1927) and their followers; nor the later revisionists in the "culturalist" or "neo-Freudian" direction. By these I mean the later work of Horney (1937 and later), Fromm (1941, 1947, 1955, etc.) and Sullivan (1953) all of whom have thrown out too much of the baby (specifically the human *animal* infant with its psychosexual-developmental vicissitudes) with the bath water in their efforts (incorrectly, in my view) to sociologize the psychoanalytic perspective on the world. Nor do I include in my pedigree the later work of a different kind of revisionist of Freud, namely Wilhelm Reich, when he moved into the orgone theory—though the earlier version of his *Character Analysis* (1933a) was still in the classical psychoanalytic tradition and made an important contribution to it. His *Mass Psychology of Fascism* (1933b) belongs also to that, to my mind more acceptable, period of his work.

My biases within sociology-anthropology must also be clear by now: among the various reigning paradigms in sociology, the work I would find most congruent with a psychoanalytic social science must certainly fit into the "social-definition" kind of paradigm: one that sees the reality of the social world as existing in the subjective consciousness (and I would add, unconscious) of the real live individual human beings living in the world, making their subjective definitions, which in turn constitute the social reality in all of their consequences and ramifications. This would then reject the assumptions of either followers of a social facts paradigm, to whom "society," "culture," "social institutions," "social structures" are realities *sui generis,* rather than abstractions for the manifold consequences of human beings acting in the world and acting on the basis of their subjective feelings and cognitive definitions. It would also reject the "social behaviorist" kind of paradigm, which sees only behavior as the reality to be studied and consistently and ideologically rejects dealing with what to anyone psychoanalytically minded are the most significant aspects of human action, namely the level of subjective meaning in all its variations.

Within anthropology, my allegiances are with those who recognize not only the wide range of cultural variations from one society to another, but also see—and emphasize—the universals to be found in all cultures of the world about which we have any knowledge (and that by now is many hundreds of societies ranging from technologically extremely rudimentary tribal societies, through a variety of more complex ones, to the whole range of complex historically-known societies.) My allegiance is also with those who focus on the evolutionary unity of mankind, for it is in the evolutionary view, which traces the origins of this species in the particular ecological-geographic and climatic circumstances of East Africa in that late-Miocene period, that we have the important linkage between anthropology as the omnibus science of mankind, and psychoanalysis as the science of the psychic vicissitudes that plague and facilitate an animal whose extreme infantile helplessness is a crucial fact of lifelong significance. While my thinking on matters anthropological has been influenced by the whole corpus of anthropological developments of the twentieth century, certain strains in that development have been less congenial and would be points of major theoretical disagreement: namely the culturological viewpoint (White et al.) which sees culture as *sui generis* and independent of any psychology of human functioning, and the more extreme versions of cultural relativism which state or give the impression that the human being is infinitely malleable in the direction of any kind of cultural institutions whatever. I also do not find persuasive a cultural anthropology that evades the basic questions of the animal nature of the human animal.

HIDDEN STRUCTURES AND DYNAMICS

One important feature of integrative work that would bring together psychoanalysis and sociology/anthropology would draw on an aspect of both psychoanalysis and of sociology, that is, it would recognize and emphasize the underlying or hidden *structures*. A major theme of sociology since Marx, whether or not explicitly declaring this ancestry, is that there are underlying structures in society not obvious in the layman's view, and the task of uncovering and analyzing these structures is that of the social scientist. Marx declared that "history happens behind our backs." Latter-day sociologists such as Merton, combining in effect structural-functional with Marxist-type conflict theories, have pointed to the "latent functions" of social customs or social institutions, and refer to "unintended and/or unanticipated consequences of purposive social action" (Merton 1936, 1949). There are both structures and functions that are hidden from the view of the layman, including (perhaps most significantly) the participants in any particular pattern of social action. Merton (and others in his vein) drew on Max Weber's demonstration that Puritans following a Calvinistic view of the world sought salvation and (thereby, but quite unintentionally) produced modern capitalism. Similarly, superficial aspects of the main structures can change in many surface details, while the underlying structures remain the same. Thus capitalism can (and did) develop glosses over the moral ruthlessness of cutthroat competitors and "public-be-damned" industrial and financial barons of the past, and present a surface of public-mindedness and a rhetoric of "service" to the consuming public, as well as "humanizing" many aspects of industrial processes, without in any fundamental way altering the underlying structure of a capitalistic economic order.

Thus, thoughtful sociologists might well question whether changes in "life styles" in the 1960s and 1970s really constituted fundamental social change in the sense of significantly altering the structures of crucial institutions. (Note the absurdity of some of the claims of counter-culture enthusiasts of the late 1960s, e.g., Charles Reich in *The Greening of America* declaring bell-bottomed pants a "revolutionary" change in society. That certainly constituted mistaking fashion change for fundamental institutional change.) Perhaps it would be an exaggeration to think of *all* the changes of that period as nothing more than fads and fashions. Some would point to substantial changes toward greater acceptance of adolescent sexuality—considered to be radical to advocate only a few years earlier—as one of the significant cultural changes of that period, but one could still question what crucial institution has been fundamentally altered thereby, to the extent that we could say the basic structures of modern society have been basically changed.

Correspondingly, in psychoanalysis, the key understanding is that there are *hidden* structures and *hidden* processes, within the psychic functioning of the individual—namely, of course, unconscious and preconscious elements—whose discovery and analysis are the special task of this discipline, requiring a special point of view and particular specialized research and clinical techniques. It is by now a commonplace of intellectual history, though nonetheless significant and worth repeating in this context, that Freud ranked his own discoveries with those of Copernicus and of Darwin, in constituting a major shift in human thinking, of a kind inevitably wounding to the narcissism of human beings who like to think of themselves as the center of the universe, unique in creation and in command of their own lives. Where Copernicus devastated the geocentric universe and Darwin the anthropocentric conception of man's special place in the animal world, Freud saw his own work as the most narcissistically wounding of all, since the basic principle in the exploration of the unconscious is the recognition of a vast underground within each of us which is scarcely known at all to the individual involved, and even less understood, thus decimating the notion of human capacity for rational thinking, clear self-perception, and rational choice. That we are not—at least not fully—in command of ourselves—let alone of the social and political world around us—is certainly among the most challenging of the propositions taught by psychoanalysis. The part of this recognition that concerns us at this moment is the sense of underlying structures and hidden—but discoverable—dynamics within the personality. These structures and these dynamics have a persistence and continuity of their own, beyond superficial changes in personal style, self-presentation, and the like.

These underlying structures and dynamics have a pattern and persistence that needs to be understood in order to evaluate and see in perspective what may appear to be important changes in a person's life and way of dealing with the world, but which may, on closer inspection in relation to underlying structures and dynamics, prove to be relatively superficial shifts, alterations in cosmetics and costuming, so to speak. There is a tendency in some interdisciplinary work relating psychoanalysis and the social sciences to overestimate the capacity for and probability of major changes in one's life patterns at later stages in the "life cycle." Thus Weinstein and Platt (1973)—one of the major theoretical contributions of recent years, be it noted—take up from Talcott Parsons (e.g., 1964) and from their reading of Erik Erikson (1950, 1959) propositions to the effect that personality change, even major personality change——presumably of the dimension that can result from an intensive psychoanalysis——can and presumably regularly does go on at all stages of life, including maturity and old age. They do not, to my mind, present any persuasive evidence that this is the case. Examples they use include such things as a person changing from an intense ideological commitment to Catholicism to a comparable commitment to Communism. Can that really qualify as a major personality change—in underlying structures and dynamics—unless one is able to demonstrate that the underlying dynamics of the ideological position have in fact changed? My suspicion in most such cases is that there has been a change in ideational contents—in this case ideological—while the underlying dynamics of authoritarian submission remain the same. In fact, in that kind of politico-religious conversion, the attraction of authoritarian controls and thought control is common to both persuasions, and one can expect a person so converting to be changing only the surface conscious rationalizations, and not the underlying inner processes.

For example, a patient had been a completely gung-ho marine in the earlier part of the Vietnam war, and there accepted with fervor the authoritarianism that pervades that branch of the military. It did a lot for a confused and unsophisticated youngster of seventeen. Later, after his discharge from the military, he changed, following association with a peace group that included veterans and quickly became converted to their ideological position. From their point of view his "consciousness had been raised," and he then spouted their particular brand of radical rhetoric. But in his dealings with co-rebels in the peace group, he got to be known as now "a marine of the left"—i.e., he acted in a very authoritarian way, being very submissive to people he regarded as above him in the organization, and aggressively bossy to others he saw as below him. His colleagues evidently saw no change in his basic psychological orientation, only a change in the contents of his rhetoric. Before, he waved the flag. Now he shook his fists in "revolutionary" gestures. Revealingly, in his therapy, he said during a period of confusion about the direction of his life, "I'm not sure just what I want to do with my life.

At times I want to be a full-time revolutionary. Other times I think I might want to be a cop." At the time he left therapy, to set out on cross-country travels to "find himself," he was still not sure in what direction he was headed, to become a revolutionary or to become a cop.

He was thus reminiscent of the characters in Anthony Burgess' *A Clockwork Orange* who early in the story are, along with the hero, tough adolescent thugs and delinquents, and later turn up as the policemen who arrest him.

Work that aims successfully to combine sociological-anthropological social science and psychoanalysis needs to convey simultaneously an understanding of hidden social and cultural structures and dynamics and covert psychological structures and dynamics and the interplay between them. This is an extremely difficult task, and proponents attempting it have generally been either strong on the socio-cultural side while weak on the psychoanalytic, or the reverse.

EXAMPLES OF INTEGRATIVE WORK: SOCIOLOGISTS

Parsons, Parsonians, and Their Critics

At the theoretical level, in sociology, major connecting work has been given in the theoretical essays of Talcott Parsons (see especially 1964), which attempted to link, systematically, theoretical propositions developed by Parsons and his colleagues in the "theory of action" with relevant parts of psychoanalytic theory, particularly in those aspects linking internalization, socialization, acquisition of normative structures, their implantation into the personality structure, the relationship of superego formation to social structure and the structure of moral norms holding together society. The essays "The Superego and the Theory of Social Systems" (originally 1952, reprinted in Parsons 1964) and "The Incest Taboo in Relation to Social Structure and the Socialization of the Child" (originally 1954, reprinted 1964) are particularly seminal in introducing crucial points of articulation between sociological theory and psychoanalytic theory. See also the paper on "Social Structure and Personality" (1958, reprinted in 1964). These works and others collected in the volume *Social Structure and Personality* (1964) have had an impact on a number of other sociologists and social scientists attempting integrative sociological-psychoanalytic work.

On one major point Parsons diverges significantly from an important element in Freudian theory. Parsons claims that *all* structural elements of the personality are modifiable by cultural influences, and that would include not only the ego and the superego—which would be obvious—but also the *id*. If he were saying that forms of *expression* of id impulses, necessarily showing modifying influences from ego and superego functions, come under the influence of culture, no classically oriented psychoanalyst would quarrel with that statement. But to argue that the *id* itself, that reservoir of basic instinctual forces in the personality, is so modifiable, requires abandonment of crucial features of the Freudian structural theory, for which one must demand what empirical evidence Parsons has to offer for such a major revision of psychoanalytic theory. Clearly—not being an empirical sociologist—Parsons has none. If one thinks of the structural concepts of id, ego, and superego as, necessarily, abstractions, ways of conceptualizing certain functions of the personality, the concepts providing a way of differentiating these functions (which in empirical reality are all mixed together in actual cases) for clarity of representation, then it does major violence to the theory to see the id as susceptible to cultural modification, thus making it not clearly differentiable from ego and superego. Parsons here seems to be sharing, in some degree, the prevalent anti-biologism in sociology, finding it difficult to conceptualize, even, some biological substratum within the human animal-personality, which is clearly recognized and given theoretical articulation in Freud's instinct theory and his theoretical apparatus of distinguishing id from ego and both of these from superego. Parsons' assertions on this matter, given no empirical evidential foundation, serve to decrease rather than foster clarity of understanding. The effect is unfortunate, since it has also influenced later sociologists who have attempted to articulate sociological and psychoanalytic understandings, e.g., Weinstein and Platt, to be discussed presently.

An important critic of Parsonian sociology whose work is relevant here is Dennis Wrong. (See papers collected under the title *Skeptical Sociology*, 1976.) In his well-known article "The Oversocialized Conception of Man in Modern Sociology" (1961, reprinted in Wrong 1976 and many other places) Wrong correctly points out how the Parsonian kind of sociology of socialization, in emphasizing harmony between personality and society, errs in neglecting, omitting, or denying precisely what is central in Freudian thought, namely the *conflict* between instinct and culture. This conflict can be formulated as the opposition between instinctual drives and social conformity pressures. In Wrong's view, the

Parsonian version of the theory of internalization robs this psychoanalytically-derived concept of its original Freudian force; for in Freud, the
completeness of that process, in reference to social norms, is not to be
taken for granted, and in fact is eternally problematic. The emphasis
on internal psychic conflict in Freud—sadly missing in Parsonian theory,
as in much neo-Freudian thinking—is precisely what gives Freudian psychology its special appositeness in dealing with the conflictful and troubled nature of life in any modern society as complex as ours. Wrong has
also been among the few sociologists to argue forcefully for the rein-
troduction of the concept of human nature, and for recognition of its
biological substratum, as taught by Freud, in opposition to the prevalent
etheralizing of humanity that is implicit in much of the corpus of sociological work of recent generations.

Wrong is one of the major figures in recent sociology to take psychoanalysis seriously and to use insights derived from psychoanalysis in
critical commentary both on sociological theory and on various aspects
of contemporary societies. Not being interested in constructing grand
sociological theories à la Parsons, nor in programmatically setting forth
a systematic theoretical position, Wrong does not make it programmatic
in his writings to attempt an integration of sociological and psychoanalytic modes of analysis. Some of his essays, in fact, are quite separatist,
rather than integrationist (in the sense I give to these terms in chapter 1),
seeing certain areas of sociological work as distinctly sociological and
definitely different from the tasks psychoanalysis (as a psychology) sets
itself. He emphasizes, for example, that basically, as a distinct discipline,
sociology is concerned with conduct and its social effects, as contrasted
with the psychoanalytic concern with the inner dynamics of motivation
or etiology. For example, in reference to the psychoanalytic-sociological
comment I would share with Weinstein and Platt to the effect that action
that is socially-conformist may be either adaptive or regressive in intrapsychic functions, and so may rebellious conduct be, Wrong points out
that this does not amount to a criticism of the sociological view, which
is necessarily concerned with conduct itself, not its psychic sources.
(Wrong, personal communication; viewpoint reflected in many of his
essays in Wrong 1976.)

One important sociological student of Parsons, namely Neil Smelser,
has already been mentioned for his collaborative essay with the psychoanalyst Robert Wallerstein (1969). Smelser's part in this work is clearly
built on Parsonian theory. Smelser has also collaborated with his psychologist brother William in a thoughtful collection of readings connecting personality and social structure (Smelser and Smelser 1963,

1970). Their own introductory and connecting essays in these volumes make no pretense at going beyond basic orientations to the problems essentially derived from Parsonian thinking.

In *The Theory of Collective Behavior* (1962) Smelser applies psychoanalytically derived conceptions of anxiety to collective social phenomena. He shows how different kinds of socially induced stresses evoke anxieties, and thence beliefs of hysterical, wish-fulfillment, and hostile types, with correlative social behavior as panics, crazes, and antagonistic riots.

Another sociologist whose work can be accounted among the contributions to psychoanalytic sociology—at least some of his *earlier* work—is Philip Slater. His most signal contributions in this vein are a theoretical essay called "On Social Regression" (Slater 1963), and a provocative book on group dynamics in the Freudian vein called *Microcosm* (1966). (Unfortunately from the viewpoint of this present work, Slater's later work veered signally away from these orientations into counter-culture advocacy, support for what he would earlier have labelled "libidinal diffusion," later into mysticism and anti-scientism. Nevertheless the contributions of these earlier works remain.) In the essay "On Social Regression," Slater shows how three types of "libidinal withdrawal"—each analyzed in a psychoanalytic vein—constitute threats to an ongoing social order: they are familial withdrawal, as in violations of the incest taboo; dyadic withdrawal (as in love-couples' isolating themselves from all other institutional ties with the surrounding society), and narcissistic withdrawal, either in ego weakness or in forms of ego strength. In *Microcosm* Slater demonstrated how the basic Freudian themes of oedipal involvements and their transformations, infantile dependency strivings, cannibalism, and totem and taboo fantasies, appear and get structured in didactic groups.

Slater also wrote an essay on "The Social Bases of Personality" for a 1969 book edited by Smelser (see Slater 1969) that is continuous with his early work.

Weinstein and Platt. A major theoretical work in psychoanalytic sociology deriving largely from Parsons' thinking is *Psychoanalytic Sociology* by Fred Weinstein and Gerald Platt (1973). Though flawed in ways I have suggested, this is one of the more significant recent efforts coming from the side of sociology (Weinstein is a historian, Platt a sociologist, obviously a protégé of Parsons.)

In this short, densely written volume, these authors set out to develop a systematic theoretical framework for a psychoanalytic-sociological study of mass and group phenomena as well as individual behavior.

Their sociological orientation is taken directly from Parsonian structural-functional action theory. Their psychological orientation is a selective use of certain aspects of recent developments in psychoanalysis. It is not an empirical case study book, but rather a sophisticated updating of articulations between psychoanalysis and sociology in the Parsonian vein. Their basic sociological questions are: how is social order possible? and how do we account for social change? Answering these requires an understanding of individual personality motivations. Analyzing social cohesion and stability necessitates a psychology of the process of internalization, provided by psychoanalysis. This involves the vicissitudes of reactions to *objects* (in a broadened version of the psychoanalytic usage of that term, to include not only persons and representations of them, but also symbols, values, cultural modes, the building blocks of the moral structure of society). Significant also, in their view, are the vicissitudes of reaction to the various kinds of abandonment and object loss all human beings must at some time or another face. Internalization provides the psychological key to cohesion and stability; and reactions to object loss, particularly to loss of important *symbolic* objects like cultural values in the form of dissent from established patterns, violent challenges to authority, or violent efforts to re-establish a lost past, provide the major mechanisms of social change. These reactions may be regressive or adaptive or a combination of both.

Weinstein and Platt have selected certain aspects of recent developments in psychoanalytic theory to emphasize, in preference to (not entirely to the exclusion of) propositions and perspectives in the "older" psychoanalysis of drives and psychosexual development. There is little reference here to drive theory (except negatively), to libido, repression, regression, Oedipus complex, anal sadism, and the like. Rather the mechanisms of internalization, introjection, identification and processes of reactions to object loss, constitute the key conceptual apparatus being used.

Understandably, *some* selectiveness in reference to psychoanalytic theory would have to be practiced by any would-be integrationists attempting to combine psychoanalytic and sociological thinking, considering that it would be difficult to say there is today any one coherent psychoanalytic theory that integrates all the recent developments (even within the "classic" tradition) in ego psychology, object relations theory, analysis of narcissism, theory of the "self," and other special preoccupations of contemporary psychoanalysts, along with the developments elaborating earlier psychoanalytic theory on drives, psychosexual development, the topography of levels of consciousness, and the structural theory of id, ego, and superego.

Weinstein and Platt depart most from classic psychoanalytic formulations in devaluing propositions dealing with psychosexual development and resolution of the Oedipus complex, and the corollary idea of assigning determinative primacy to the early years of life. A proposition considered essentially bedrock within classical psychoanalysis is that orientations toward the world developed early in psychosexual development within the family of origin (or its functional equivalent), and related to the crucial persons therein, tend to become strongly established, and to become the models for relationships outside the family later on, often in complex, convoluted ways, involving reaction-formations, repressions, regressions, projective identifications, and so on. These tend to influence intensely, though not necessarily totally to determine, later object choices and reactions to them, in crucial areas of work and love, and also in any other institutional domains.

Weinstein and Platt cast doubt on such propositions. They choose to support statements by Parsons and other social scientists that are unsubstantiated by any clinical evidence, and to interpret Erikson to fit their purposes, to assign to later institutional influences upon the individual determinative influences just as compelling as those of the early years. In contrast to the massive clinical evidence within the psychoanalytic literature that supports the enormous consequentiality of determinative influences in the earliest years of life, statements of Weinstein and Platt to the contrary, like those of many neo-Freudian "revisionists" before them, tend to remain at the level of mere assertions, important perhaps to buttress a general theoretical position.

Still, for all its shortcomings, this work does display two among the very few sociological social scientists of the current period who do take psychoanalysis seriously, and who do take seriously the value, in fact necessity, of forging the links between psychoanalysis and social science.

Weinstein and Platt are also valuable in their level-headed recognition that, contrary to the ideological viewpoints of new leftists and their supporters, there is no intrinsic connection between psychoanalysis—either as theory or as practice—and an ideology of adjustment to the established order no matter what. It is simply not true, they point out—quite correctly—that psychoanalysts as therapists are committed, in the nature of their clinical work and of their theory, to getting their patients to conform to the established normative order of the whole society around them, regardless of what that requires. "From a psychoanalytic point of view, there are obviously very dysfunctional forms of conformity and compliance, and very syntonic forms of rebellion."

As a work of theory, this essay by Weinstein and Platt does not make any pretense at serious analysis of particular empirical situations.

Nancy Chodorow

Probably the most important recent new work combining psychoanalytic and sociological perspectives is Nancy Chodorow's *The Reproduction of Mothering* (1978). Raising the question of why it is always women who mother babies and young children, and not men, Chodorow proceeds to answer this sociological question about the nature of the gender division of labor in reference to parenting activities by a carefully worked out psychoanalytic account of how differently girls develop compared to boys in ways that lead to both the capacities and the motivation for giving the kind of intimate psychological and physical care human infants have to have. Her account draws rather more on recent "object-relations" psychoanalysis of the "English school" than on classical psychoanalysis emphasizing libidinal processes and ego development, though she does draw to some extent on those traditions as well. If babies are mothered by women, and not by men, or not by both women and men together, girls will have systematically different infantile and childhood experiences in relation to the crucial parent, the mother, than will boys; and so will they have different relationships with the father. Chodorow treats both libidinal and object-relational aspects of these processes. Girls will be pushed much less toward separation-individuation from the mother and will to some extent retain important aspects of the early infantile infant-mother fusion on into later phases of development, including adulthood. Therefore they will retain, much more than boys and men, capacities for empathic connection, nonlinguistic communication, intuitiveness, and responsiveness to the psychological states of the "other," all of which are important, even essential, in mothering babies. Hence women will want not only to have babies, but to take care of them as well. By contrast, males' psychological development leads, typically—that is with female mothering—in different directions, so that they enter the later stages of infantile sexuality and other aspects of later infancy and childhood development very differently from girls, and later as men are much more cut off from the kinds of psychological attunement that women typically have and that connect with mothering. Hence both sexes will be likely to re-constitute substantially the same gender division of parenting, "reproducing" the mothering pattern in the next generation, which in turn will create offspring who will reproduce it again the next generation after that, and so on indefinitely.

Chodorow connects this psychoanalytic account with a sociological view of how this gender division of labor fits in with other institutional processes and changes that have been going on in modern society. And she is particulary good at demonstrating how inadequate are the usual sociological explanations that are given for the gender division of labor and its social-psychological supports that are couched in terms of simple role-learning. Such theories, Chodorow argues (quite correctly), tend to assume a simple direct transfer of conscious teaching (e.g., little girls are to play with dolls and become mommies when they grow up, boys to play with trucks, etc. . . .) into the psychic functioning of the child; tend to work mainly at the level of conscious processes, and to focus predominantly on aspects of role learning that occur mainly at the school age (psychoanalytically, latency), neglecting the vast, complex, and crucial processes of intrapsychic development that have gone on before that time in the centrally significant infantile and early childhood development.

Unlike Weinstein and Platt, Chodorow does see and accept the central psychoanalytic view of the crucial significance of infancy and early childhood.

Since all psychoanalytic social scientists must make their own selection from among the many strands and approaches within the psychoanalytic tradition, it is pertinent to note how Chodorow specifically makes this selection. Though not excluding the strains of classical psychoanalysis that emphasize drives and libido, she does emphasize the perspectives of the "object-relations school" (or "English school"). The major figures there are Michael and Alice Balint (M. Balint 1965, 1968; A. Balint 1939, 1954), W. R. D. Fairbairn (1952), Harry Guntrip (1971), and D. W. Winnicott (1958, 1965, 1971), and there are numerous others in Britain, America, and elsewhere. [1] Where for Freud and the Freudians, the basic instinctual drives—sex and aggression—are the driving forces in human personality and these drives are a biological given of the human animal, for the object-relations theorists, the center of attention is on the way the infant and growing child relates to the crucial external *objects* in his world, first the mother, later others, and to his own internalized versions of these objects. Thus, external and internal objects, and the relations with these objects, are at the center of concern, and are seen as the main determining forces. Not that drives are left out entirely, but where Freudians emphasize the vicissitudes of the libido, these theorists work on the vicissitudes of the object-relations of the child. This emphasis Chodorow finds more compatible with making the linkage to sociology.

While sexuality is as important for the objects-relations theorists in analysis of the early development of the child as it is with Freudians, the accent is different. They (implicitly or explicitly) reject the Freudian idea that there is a biologically determined built-in maturational sequence in which different zones of the body are crucial at successive stages of the development of infantile sexuality. Rather than the zonal dominance (of a particular stage) determining the central problems of object relations at that stage (essentially Freud's view), these theorists see it almost turned about: the object-relations dilemmas and vicissitudes of a particular period conduce to the use of particular body zones as vehicles for particular kinds of object-relations striving. Similarly, problems of the oedipal period are analyzed with focus more on the nature of the object-relationship between the child and the two parents and their respective inner object representations in the psyche of the child.

This conception of "objects" is taken directly from the work of Freud himself, and moved from an associated part of the analysis in Freud to center stage in these theorists.

That psychoanalysis is a *social* psychology, concerned with the relationships among human beings, and between any particular human being and other individuals, groups, and society at large—a viewpoint more implicit than spelled out in Freud—is here more evident, with its focus on the exploration of the connections between persons at the level of their deepest intrapsychic processes. (In that it is a superior psychoanalytic psychology to that of the "interpersonal"—Sullivanian—variety of culturalist psychoanalysis, who also appear to be concerned with interactive processes, but often at the sacrifice of the intrapsychic.)

Chodorow's work has the merit of recognizing the superiority of an object-relations perspective to a culturalistic-psychoanalytic one for articulating the connection between psychoanalytic and sociological analyses of particular phenomena. It also shares the defects of such virtues in its aversion to the biological grounding in Freud's work, with the result that, while there is much reference to libidinal matters, it lacks any clearcut grounding of such processes in recognition of the human animal as an animal. So though not as extremely as in the culturalists, this object-relations usage does tend to etherealize basic psychoanalytic truths.[2] (There is an endless tendency in all kinds of workers with the Freudian ideas to recoil from those more gutsy, and very fundamental, aspects of the Freudian vision, which need, not such avoidance, but rather confrontation and incorporation into a more comprehensive bio-psycho-social view of man, such as I attempt in the following chapter.)

EXAMPLES OF INTEGRATIVE WORK:
PSYCHOANALYTIC ANTHROPOLOGISTS

Major integrative work that is both theoretically sophisticated and backed up by strong empirical studies comes from the main psychoanalytic anthropologists. Of these, the major figures, as already mentioned are (were) Géza Róheim, Weston LaBarre, George Devereux, and Anne Parsons. *Some* of the work of Margaret Mead would also fit in here. To be included here as well should be the work of the psychoanalyst Bryce Boyer and his anthropologist wife Ruth Boyer on tribal groups like the Apache (Boyer and Boyer 1967, 1972, 1976; also Boyer 1964), and the creative work of a team of Swiss psychoanalysts, Paul Parin, Fritz Morgenthaler, and Goldy Parin-Matthey on two tribal groups in West Africa, the Dogon and the Agni (Parin et al. 1963, 1964, 1971). Current productive anthropologists working the strictly psychoanalytic vein in the legacy of Róheim and Weston LaBarre are Arthur Hippler on Eskimos, Athabaskans, and Australian aborigines (Hippler 1974, 1977, 1978; Hippler, Boyer, and Boyer 1975), and Howard F. Stein on Slovak Americans and ethnicity in America (Stein 1974, 1978a, 1978b, 1979).

Here we shall concentrate on works of Róheim, LaBarre, Devereux, and Anne Parsons, as the outstanding exemplars.

Géza Róheim

Róheim (see works already cited) studied a number of tribal societies. His work emphasizes the universality of both cultural and depth-psychodynamic themes that recur in all of these, and in all societies, in fact. All deal in one way or another with the same basic human vicissitudes and dilemmas. They all deal with the relations between the sexes, the processes of reproduction and its socio-cultural definitions. All are concerned with the same basic psychosexual developmental phases, with children living in some kind of kin unit including significant adults of both sexes, with the child's having to deal with the mated adults' sexual relationship. All deal with universal dilemmas of growing up. All have some version of the nuclear family consisting of a mated pair, man and woman, and their offspring, sometimes as part of a joint or extended family, sometimes cross-cut by a unilineal clan organization. (The existence of these wider or different kinds of kin organization does not refute the universality—and psychologically, the crucial nature—of the nuclear family. Róheim also emphasized the universality of the basic incest taboos (those within the nuclear family, i.e., mother-son, brother-sister, and father-daughter) and correspondingly the basic psychological problems facing all human beings (in one form or another) of the oedipal conflicts and the necessity of their resolution.

One of Róheim's major assertions was the universality of the unconscious. The deeper into the unconscious you go, the more similar are all human beings. This can be seen in both individual dreams and in the culturally stylized dreams of collective fantasy products of art and mythology.

For example, here are two dreams: (1) "I have an argument with father. He wants to shoot a boar. Then father has small eyes like a pig. The boar chases me up a tree and threatens to cut the trunk of the tree with its tusks." (2) (Another dream, another dreamer): "A pig chases me and I climb a tree. It's a (name of a domesticated pig) but it is also a bush pig, it has tusks." The first dream was dreamt by an upper-class male New Yorker, a patient in Róheim's psychoanalytic practice of that time (1940s). The second dream was dreamt by a chief of Kebebeku on Normanby Island in Melanesia. The latter's elaboration of and associations to the dream are these:

> The place is my own garden. It is my own pig. I am growing it for a feast (in reality) but it is also like a bush pig, it has tusks. My mother was very good to me. She always told me and my brother not to go far because the sorcerers would get us. I dream this very often. Once it is a black pig, then a red one. . . . Sorcerers send supernatural pigs to kill people. (He talks about incest, real and mythological, and about his many triumphs with women in his premarital love life.) . . . It is evident [to Róheim] that the pig in the dream represents the threatening Oedipal father. (Róheim 1950:15)

Róheim's point here is that there is potentially universal symbolism here. No cultural features of these two entirely separated and extremely different cultures could explain the near identity of these two dreams, but the basic unconscious processes, the basic intrapsychic oedipal conflict and fear of the father's punishing the son for his oedipal wishes, are the same in both. The same or very similar dream symbolism recurs in countless cultures widely separated in time and space, and of no demonstrable culture-historical connection with each other.

One of Róheim's special contributions on this matter was to *not* follow the postulate of a universal racial unconscious implied in Freud's most Jungian (and therefore, in this respect, least satisfactory) book, *Totem and Taboo*, or explicitly stated as a central axiom in the work of Jung in order to explain these striking transcultural commonalities, but rather to adduce what he called an "ontogenetic theory" (as opposed to a phylogenetic one) of culture origins. This theory argues that each successive generation of human beings has to face the same life-developmental problems, with the same essentially limited and finite repertoire of psychic capacities, and deal with a finitely variable geological, geographic, climatic and plant-and-animal environment on the same planet. The phylogenetic aspect is there, of course, for we have to face the same problems as infants and young children, because we are all one species that has evolved in a particular way at a particular time and place in the life of this planet. (See Róheim 1943 for elaboration on this point. We shall take up in the next part of this book the question of the evolutionary history of mankind and how recent anthropological formulations of it can be articulated in a more satisfactory manner with psychoanalytic understanding.)

Róheim was particularly vitriolic in attacking the prevailing ideology of cultural relativism that dominated anthropology for the period of roughly the 1920s through the 1950s (and still to a degree today). That viewpoint became the central perspective in the inter-war period, in the work of Ruth Benedict, Margaret Mead, Melville Herskovits, Clyde Kluckhohn, and many other students and intellectual descendants of Franz Boas. Róheim insisted that their message of extreme, even infinite, variability of cultures—and correspondingly of personality patterns culturally molded—was greatly oversold, considering the species characteristics of the human animal, his probable evolutionary history, and the commonality of basic psychological-developmental problems facing all human beings. To be sure, he demonstrated how differently the basic developmental and psychodynamic vicissitudes could be negotiated and culturally resolved in such different societies as the Central Australian aborigines, the matrilineal people of Normanby Island in Melanesia, various Amerindian tribes, and various large-scale societies of the modern world. But to make sense of each of these, he had to use a psychology of universal dimension, that is, psychoanalysis. In all of these analyses, not only is the prevailing personality pattern in a particular society a socio-cultural product, but also the prevailing cultural patterns are themselves the product of certain types of resolutions of basic psychodynamic problems faced commonly and similarly by all the persons of that society.

Also, as already noted, Róheim thought that the general run of culture-personality studies in anthropology were built upon an entirely inadequate psychoanalytic conception, particularly one that in its neo-Freudianism and relativism, had lost the crucial biological baseline and psychosexual-developmental propositions derived from Freud. He raged against those who praised that kind of culture-personality work as having accepted diluted wine and trashy imitations, when full-strength good wine and real works of art, that is *really* psychoanalytic-anthropological work, namely his (later that of certain followers), was readily available, but "too strong stuff" for people who find vulgarizations more palatable. (I agree with his judgment on this, though, not surprisingly, his exaggerated, dogmatic, and polemical style and sometimes paranoid-sounding phrasings put off many scholars who could have benefitted from his work.) He particularly objected to the relativism of these studies which suggested (often stated) a *tabula rasa* conception of human beings as infinitely malleable into any kind of psychosocial forms whatever.

Róheim's approach was taken up by Weston LaBarre and George Devereux in particular, as well as a number of other anthropological scholars such as Warner Muensterberger, Anne Parsons, and Arthur Hippler.

Róheim had the distinction of being the first scholar actively to pursue careers in both fields, psychoanalysis (including clinical practice) and anthropology (including detailed empirical field work). In this he set a model for a number (still a small number) of other psychoanalytic-social-scientists since his time.

Margaret Mead

Some of the middle-period work of Margaret Mead moved away from the extreme relativism of her earlier work, such as *Sex and Temperament in Three Primitive Societies* (1935) (much beloved of feminists today), into an emphasis which is much more psychoanalytic and much more universalistic in orientation, such as *Male and Female* (1949) and a thoughtful essay on "*Totem and Taboo* Reconsidered, with Respect" (1963). Whereas her earlier work has suggested that the nature of "masculinity" and "femininity" were (at least potentially) infinitely variable according to infintely variable cultural emphases from one society to another, *Male and Female* (built, evidently on much more psychoanalytic understanding) suggested that biologically determined differences between the sexes would limit such variability, making it more likely that there would be great similarities among all males across myriad cultural differences, and among all females transcending such cultural differences, such that the differences between the sexes, in psychological-developmental problems and possible resolutions of these problems, would probably be greater than the differences for one sex among the different cultures of the world. (Significantly, this later work of Mead is now much less cited than the earlier one by ideological feminists within psychological and social-scientific fields.) In the 1963 paper Mead ventures into the area of evolutionary speculation, finding much greater plausibility in Freud's *Totem and Taboo* hypotheses than either she or other anthropologists had earlier accorded them, if one but amended the hypothetical time dimension for the events, or series of events, hypothesized by Freud. This provocatively speculative paper is distinguished from much of Mead's earlier work, not to mention from most other anthropological writing of the period, by its non-relativistic, even antirelativistic stance and implication. (See discussion of this work in relation to the general issues of the evolution of the human species raised by *Totem and Taboo*, and by anthropological work since that time, in part 2 below.)

Weston LaBarre

After Róheim the next major exponent of a strictly psychoanalytic anthropology (as contrasted with a "psychological anthropology" built on more eclectic, or more neo-Freudian, psychological foundations) is Weston LaBarre. Though not—as contrasted with Róheim and with George Devereux—a clinical practitioner of psychoanalysis, LaBarre's erudition is deeply rooted in classical psychoanalytic writings, particularly those of the first and second (intellectual) generations of Freud and his followers. Like Róheim's psychoanalysis, LaBarre is much more rooted in the classical psychoanalytic work emphasizing psychosexual development, the topography of consciousness, and the economic and dynamic elements in the Freudian metapsychology, and less influenced by Hartmannian and following ego psychology and later "object-relations" emphases in psychoanalysis. His major models in psychoanalysis are clearly Freud, Róheim, and Ferenczi. In addition to a number of significant theoretical and synoptic essays, he has published two major works that should have an enduring influence in this field, *The Human Animal* (1954) and *The Ghost Dance: Origins of Religion* (1970). The earlier work is a remarkable synthesis of physical and cultural anthropology, psychoanalysis, and linguistics, linking contemporaneously available evolutionary reconstructions of the history of the human species, understanding of man's animal nature, his psychodynamics rooted in the perennial infantilism of the human species, and understanding of the cultural diversities and universalities discernible in the vast ethnographic knowledge available to modern anthropology. A major contribution of this work is to extend the psychoanalytic understanding of irrationality in the individual human personality to the collective scene of a whole culture or subculture, demonstrating in innumerable cases how "twenty million Frenchmen *can* be wrong . . ." and why. He sees a culture as not only a set of collective adaptations to difficult external reality, but also as a set of collective illusions and culturally stylized regressions that are not necessarily (and usually not) in the service of higher ego adaptations.

Such themes are elaborated in much greater detail in the *magnum opus* on religion, *The Ghost Dance*. This work in effect does for Freud's *The Future of an Illusion* (1927) what Róheim had earlier done for *Totem and Taboo*, that is, it extracts the kernel of insight into the basic process involved and develops it in the context of the enormous wealth of anthropological scholarship lacking in Freud's time, as well as, in this case, an intensive historical knowledge of the great religions of the world. The universal existence of *some* kinds of religious (or magical) beliefs and practices in all the known cultures of the world demonstrates, for LaBarre, not the existential "truth" of religious doctrines, but rather the universality of certain kinds of psychodynamic problems faced by human beings, for which magical and/or religious practices and beliefs provide some kind of "solution." Religions are seen as consensually validated systems for dealing with collectively experience anxieties, in each case of a particular kind and with specific kinds of origin in the experiences of the people of that particular society and that particular era. Thus, too, religious functionaries of either the shamanistic or the priestly variety (or, commonly enough, some combination of both) are consolidations of particular kinds of character adaptations to infantile or childhood psychological problems commonly experienced in that tribe, in a form that sufficiently resonates with the corresponding intrapsychic needs in the relevant public or clientele. Shamanistic versions of such functionaries display adaptations to early infantile omnipotence and narcissistic problems, while the more priestly versions function in reaction to and adaptation to dilemmas more of the oedipal stage of development. In more recent papers (LaBarre 1978a, 1978b) Labarre has elaborated further on the connection between the animal ancestry and nature of the human species and pan-human religio-magical preoccupations that cut across the cultures of the world.

Evidently, like Róheim, LaBarre's emphasis is on the universals of human experience, and of human cultures, that can be discerned above and beyond the obvious cultural variations.

George Devereux

George Devereux is, as already mentioned, one of the few psychoanalytic social scientists who has combined active work in both psychoanalysis (he was for many years a practicing psychoanalyst, having been trained at the Menninger Foundation) and social science, in his case anthropology. His empirical work has embraced field-experience-based studies of the Mohave Indians (Devereux 1937, 1939, 1961, and references thereto in many of his other writings), of a tribe called Sedang-Moi in Vietnam; analysis of psychodynamic-cultural patterns of ancient Greece (e.g., most recently, Devereux 1976); and on a number of specific aspects of contemporary modern advanced societies, e.g., the problem of charismatic leadership and problems relating to crime and delinquency. He has also produced one of the most important works of psychoanalytic-social-scientific epistemology, *From Anxiety to Method in the Behavioral Sciences* (1967). (Compare his more recently published work, 1978.) One of his first major theoretical contributions is the paper, "Normal and Abnormal: The Key Problem of Psychiatric Anthropology" (1956, in English; much expanded in the French language version, 1970b). This provides one of the most sophisticated models for a genuinely *trans*cultural (as distinct from cross-cultural) psychiatry or psychoanalysis, resolving most of the dilemmas raised by a simple-mindedly, culturally relativistic anthropology. His insistence on making a clear analytical distinction between deviance (norm-violation) and psychopathology is a major contribution. And his distinction between basic psychological *processes*—which can be evaluated as relatively more adaptive or relatively less so, as more regressive or less so—and the *content* of behavior, ideation, and cultural forms is crucial: the former follow lines of a distinctively finite repertoire of all human beings, while the latter can be widely variable: the former may therefore be the baseline for evaluating the relative health or pathology of any of the latter. This is a far cry from the value-judgment refusals of the extreme relativistic position.

As in Róheim and LaBarre, a fundamental emphasis here is on the psychic unity of mankind, abundantly documented by the psychodynamic similarities of human beings in all of the apparently widely differing societies of the world.

(See elaboration of implications of these themes in part 5 below.)

Anne Parsons

Another major exponent of integrative psychoanalytic anthropology was the late Anne Parsons. (See the posthumously published collection of her most important papers, A. Parsons 1969.) Her work combined theoretical sophistication and assiduous attention to empirical detail based on intensive field work in the best tradition of modern anthropology. She devoted herself to the central themes of classical psychoanalysis, particularly the Oedipus complex, and eonnnected these with anthropological analysis of culture and social structure, with special emphasis on the symbolic systems of a culture. Her major empirical research was in a working-class section of Naples and a study of patients in psychiatric hospitals there. Her most important paper, for our purposes, was entitled, "Is the Oedipus Complex Universal? The Jones-Malinowski Debate Revisited, and a South Italian Nuclear Complex" (originally 1964, reprinted in several places, including Parsons 1969.) In this paper she re-evaluated the debate between the anthropologist Malinowski (who disputed the universality of the Oedipus complex on the basis of its alleged absence in the Trobriands) and the psychoanalyst, disciple of Freud, Ernest Jones, who disputed Malinowski's analysis of his own data, and reasserted the universality of the Oedipus complex (almost as though it were the central article of dogma in the Freudian faith. (See Jones 1924; also counterarguments against Malinowski in Róheim 1950 and in Endleman 1967.) Anne Parsons brought to bear later developments (i.e., post-1920s) in both anthropology and psychoanalysis, especially in the theory of symbolism, to argue that both Malinowski and Jones were wrong, Malinowski for being insufficiently psychoanalytic, and Jones for overextending the Freudian theoretical scheme to make oedipal involvement responsible for the whole cultural institution of matrilineal kinship (then called "mother-right"). Parsons showed that the case (of the Trobriands) is more complex than either Malinowski or Jones presented at that time, and that indeed brother-sister incestuous feelings could well be connected with the particular kind of intense uncle-nephew ambivalences (that Malinowski emphasized) both similar to and different from those of father-son relationships in the kind of kinship structure familiar to Freud and to Western societies generally.

The second part of that paper is devoted to a psychoanalytic-sociological study of working-class family life in Naples as of the mid-twentieth century. Parsons shows it to develop a "nuclear complex" of a kind still different both from that of northern Europe (significantly influenced by the Protestant Reformation, as major parts of Southern Europe were not) and from the matrilineally organized tribal peoples of Melanesia such as the Trobriand Islanders of Malinowski's study. Do the working-class Neapolitans develop an "Oedipus complex" of the classical Freudian variety? Not exactly, says Parsons. True, they do encounter psychological difficulties revolving around a triangle of son-mother-father for the boy and of daughter-father-mother for the girl, but the details of these, reflecting a different familial social structure, are different from those posited in Freud's classical statement of the Oedipus complex, which can be seen as reflecting a more patriarchal organization of society and of the family. Southern Italy—of which the Neapolitans Parsons studied are one version, sharing much in common with the rest of the region, and in fact with circum-Mediterranean cultures generally that were untouched by the Protestant Reformation—presents patterns of family organization rather distinctive compared to northern Europe. Significantly, for this analysis, they retain a much more Mary-centered—therefore mother-centered—version of Christianity, linked with a particular kind of matricentrism in the family, persisting alongside or within the prevailing official pattern of patriarchal control. At the socio-cultural level, her analysis is built on finely tuned social and psychological observation, fine detail in the best traditions of anthropological field work, and acute theoretical analysis. At the psychological level, if we ask whether her analysis is derived from a sufficiently strong set of pieces of evidence of the kind parallel to that found in the clinical situation of the psychoanalyst, in quantity and detail comparable to what a clinician requires to back up interpretations, the question is hard to answer, because the answer depends in part on how well persuaded the reader is, in advance, of the plausibility of the theoretical propositions. Certainly she indicates a wealth of observation of what typically goes on within families, reflections on the focal concerns that appear in popular literature and drama, observations of typical conflict scenes among family members, as well as symbolic materials indicated in the kind of language used in various situations, typical joking patterns and the like, judiciously analyzed for their symbolic significance. This reader found her analysis persuasive. Others might not be so convinced. But then again, within psychoanalytic work itself, one analyst's interpretation of his case material before a professional audience may be and often is disputed by other analysts looking at or hearing the same case material. I suspect that the degree of consensus on interpretations within psychoanalysis is probably less than one could find among different sociologists looking at the same data.

My assessment is that Anne Parsons' work was among the best integrative psychoanalytic-social-scientific work that was both theoretical and empirical being done in recent times. It certainly ranks with the best of the work of psychoanalytic anthropologists such as the three major masters of that genre, namely Géza Róheim, Weston LaBarre, and George Devereux.

Any of these demonstrate that it can be done, and also that there is no one standard way to do it. Each of these scholars is or was distinctive and unique—an acceptance and fostering of idiosyncrasy and eccentricity more likely in anthropology than in sociology—and each defied much in prevailing canons of how to do certain kinds of study of human beings. Comparable examples within sociology are even rarer, and again there, there is no formula. Certainly no scholar immersed in one standard way of doing sociological research comes close to any of these kinds of questions, nor to research procedures at all relevant or apposite for this kind of integrative work. It is probably to the advantage of this elusive "field" to be as little structured and formalized or formularized as it is. The really generative work in this field shares certain central perceptions: of the human animal who is still an animal, with all its overlay of culture, who has an evolutionary as well as a cultural and personal history, certain universal mechanisms for defense and adaptation, pan-human developmental problems in many guises, and impressively (though by no means infinitely) varied modes of adaptation and development in a great variety of social and cultural climes.

Part 1

SUMMARY AND CONCLUSION

An integrated psychoanalytic social science, embracing psychoanalysis, sociology, and anthropology, is a difficult but essential task. Social science needs an adequate underlying psychology; psychoanalysis is the best such available, connecting as it does to man's animal heritage and nature, and exploring at all depths the totality of psychological experience, and articulating readily with analysis of social structure and culture. Conversely, psychoanalysis needs the infusion of the perspectives of sociology and anthropology, in order adequately to locate the psychodynamic processes it explores in their social and cultural context. The integration presents manifest difficulties, not least the skepticism and hostility of scholars or practitioners who insist on the separation of these fields, and the opposite tendency in some others to assert an imperialism of their own discipline as subsuming the others. The difficulties also include the tendency of practitioners in each discipline to stereotype the other, to exaggerate the consensus in the other, to use the concepts of the other in distortingly oversimplifying ways, to consider as "given" what in the other discipline is "problematic," and to regard one's own discipline's concerns as central while those of the other are peripheral. Integrative efforts that have been made so far include some from within each of these disciplines; many tending to be relatively stronger on one side, e.g., the social-scientific, weaker on the other, e.g., the psychoanalytic, and in many cases to find themselves assailed or rejected by both disciplines, Works like those of Feuer, Hendin, Fromm, other Freudian-Marxists, and culture-personality (mainly neo-Freudian) anthropologists are considered in this connection. Turning to more adequately or successfully integrative work, we considered the theoretical contributions of Talcott Parsons, Smelser, Slater, Weinstein and Platt, and Chodorow, from sociology, and the work of psychoanalytic anthropologists who follow the classical Freudian line of work (rather than the neo-Freudian), namely Róheim, Labarre, some of Margaret Mead, Devereux, and Anne Parsons, noting how the diversity and divergences of these several important contributors indicate that there is no one standard way to do this kind of interdisciplinary integrative work, and the positive value of this rather loose and unstructured situation. Common threads in all of these works are the recognition and unraveling of hidden structures and dynamics in both sociocultural processes and individual psychodynamics, and the attention to the universalities of human experience through time and space.

It is to one aspect of the latter, namely the evolutionary history of this species and its implications for the psychosexual developmental patterns of all human behavior, that we now turn to in part 2.

2

Human Origins: Biological and Social Sciences and Psychoanalysis

In the prolonged symbiosis of the child with his parents we have the reason why human beings live in families and in this prolonged co-existence of two generations we have the biological basis of social life.

L. Bolk, *Das Problem der Menschwerdung*, 1926:20

The peculiar availability of the [psycho-] analytic psychology for this purpose [a consistently naturalistic view of man] is based on the fact that alone among psychologies it has taken seriously the human body as a place to live in, as it has been alone in taking seriously the symbolic content and purpose of thought.

Weston LaBarre, *The Human Animal*, 1954:xiii

Sections of this part constitute a revision and updating of an earlier publication (Endleman 1966).

CHAPTER FOUR

Human Evolution:
Some Recent Theories

Anthropologists in recent decades have been making great strides in accumulating the fossil and other evidence for human origins and interpreting this evidence in reconstructive schemes that try to trace the evolutionary history of this species, in a degree of detail impossible to Darwin a century ago. What needs to be done now is to link our present tentative understanding of the human evolutionary history with psychoanalytic understanding of the working of the human psyche, and both of these with understanding of the working of society and of culture.[1] The evolutionary history illuminates the psychic evolution: the questions of how we got to be the kind of animal we are, the characteristics this animal shares with other mammals and with other primates, the features that are distinctively human, at least in degree if not in kind.

And how do these connect with the basic problems of human psychology that psychoanalysis has dealt with—the basic drives of sex and aggression, the particularly human kind of life-cycle developmental pattern, the peculiar dynamic organization of conflicting or potentially conflicting forces within the personality, the structuralization of the personality, and its adaptive capacities and those forces interfering with adaptation? Each of these fields helps to illuminate the other: the evolutionary history helps understand the peculiarities of the human psyche, and understanding the psychic forces can help us reconstruct the evolutionary history with greater psychological plausibility.

THE HOCKETT AND ASCHER
HUNTING REVOLUTION THEORY

I will start with one reconstruction of this evolutionary history presented a few years ago by Charles Hockett and Robert Ascher (Hockett and Ascher 1964) called "The Human Revolution." It is the work of two anthropologists, one an anthropological linguist, the other an archeologist. Hockett and Ascher put together a theory of human origins drawing on the rapidly accumulating evidence of fossil finds that had been made during the period between the end of World War II and the early 1960s. These finds, particularly those in Africa, had filled out to a considerable extent the range of evidence anthropologists had available to deduce the line of descent of the human species from other forms of primates known to exist in earlier ages.

The period Hockett and Ascher refer to is the geological period called the Miocene (meaning a minority of recent life forms). Geologists date it as somewhere about 28 to 12 million years ago. This is, of course, some millions of years before the earliest date at which we can reasonably deduce that more or less clearly identifiably human ancestors appear on earth, tha date being—depending on which of the conflicting current authorities you credit, either about four million years ago, or perhaps about two million years ago. (The estimate varies also according to what characteristics you choose to define a distinctively human, as distinct from proto-human in some approximation.)

Physical anthropologists have uncovered a large number of different kinds of fossil remains of different human-like animals that are more advanced, evolutionarily, than any of the present-day ape cousins of man like the chimpanzees and gorillas, but less advanced than what we call, in this context, "modern man," i.e., *Homo sapiens*. These include a variety of types that have been called the Australopithecines (or South-African Man-Apes) which may date back as far as four million years, or by a more conservative estimate, two million years.

Then from the early to middle Pleistocene (previously thought to go back about one million years, now thought—by some—to be possibly more) and on from there through the four ice ages, there is a great variety of types which some anthropologists think could be generally classified together under one genus, *Homo*, and one species, *erectus*—for the erect posture. (These are to be distinguished from specifically modern—geologically modern that is—man we call *Homo sapiens*, in a number of ways, but compared with the Australopithecines, they are much closer.) They include the types earlier called *Pithecanthropus erectus* ("erect ape-man of Java") and Sinanthropus ("Peking man" of China) and other close variations on these; and would include, according to some (but not all) specialists, the type called Neanderthal Man, of which we have a large number of skeletal remains as well as rich associated cultural evidence, coming fairly close to geologically modern times, i.e., about the last 100,000 years or even more recent, and overlapping in time, with types that are distinctly modern man, i.e., *Homo sapiens*, such as the Cro-Magnon man in Europe and comparable modern types evidently of our own species, but with regional variations in detail, appearing in Africa, in the Middle East, in the Far East, and in Java. These latter are all fairly recent developments, probably dating back 40–50,000 years at most. After that we have no more indications of Neanderthals or other *Homo erectus* types, and all the *Homo* types are distinctly *Homo sapiens*.

There is, of course, far from complete agreement among anthropologists as to how to classify the whole range of fossil remains of human or close-to-human animals, but the categorization just presented does seem to have fairly wide acceptance, and should serve the purposes of the present discussion.

The Australopithecines would be dated as late Pliocene (the geological period during which a majority of "modern" forms of life first appeared) and the *Homo erectus* types to the more recent period, the Pleistocene (meaning "nearly all of the recent forms"). The Hockett and Ascher reconstruction starts considerably farther back in time, in the period before the Pliocene, called the Miocene, and the putatively ancestral species they refer to are still far from human or "close-to-human" in type.

We can summarize the main features of the Hockett-Ascher reconstruction as follows:

From geological and paleontological evidence scholars can deduce that in East Africa during the Miocene age a major long-term climatic change occurred: it was getting drier, and areas that had previously been heavily forested were therefore changing to grassy savanna land. This produced an ecological crisis for the animals living there, which included small tree-dwelling primates (the category of mammals that includes monkeys, apes, and man). These primates are considered to be probably ancestral to both the modern apes and to man. With this kind of ecological change, the species existing in a particular environment, in this case forests, must compete for a diminishing supply of life support. This competition will go on between different species, and within the population of any one species. In this case, it was a competitive struggle for the forested area among the bands of these primates ("apes" or "protohominoids"). In this struggle, weaker bands were forced to the edges of the forest groves. From there they had to migrate across open grassy savanna land in quest of other forest grove territory in which to carry on their accustomed arboreal and vegetarian life. As the forests receded further, and other forest groves to which they might migrate also became overpopulated in relation to food supply, the migrants had to trek over progressively longer and longer distances of savanna land to try to reach other forest groves. Presumably many of them never made it. They could be preyed upon by large carnivorous land mammals already occupying the savanna territory.

This may sound like a classical Darwinian struggle for existence, with only the fittest surviving. But it was not exactly that. Evidently the "fittest" from among the tree-living apes—i.e., "fittest" to stay and hold that tree territory—survived to continue living in the trees, and later to evolve into the other tree-living ape forms such as we can find in geologically modern times, like chimpanzees, gibbons, and orangutans. But the ones that went on to evolve into human beings included those who were "weaker" or "less fit" to stay in the trees, who in effect got kicked out by their stronger siblings and cousins. In other words, the out-migrants were those "least fit to survive" in the competition for the *past* territory, but some of these later underwent evolutionary changes which made them better able to survive in a land environment.

As the grove-to-grove treks that these "rejects" or "expellees" had to take became progressively longer, so did there develop an increasingly greater need for these apes to develop a more fully two-footed mode of locomotion. Tree-living primates have, in effect, four *hands*, and though they could on occasions where necessary walk on the two hind limbs, it is not a comfortable mode of locomotion for them (as is the case for chimpanzees and gibbons today). To be able to do this regularly and with ease, the animal had to develop *feet*. Since the body was already vertical (in adaptation, ages earlier, to tree life) the most likely direction for further evolutionary change was toward walking on two feet ("bipedal locomotion").

Evolutionary selective processes thus led to the development of the distinctively human foot, the only important human bodily *specialization*. (This was an irreversible evolutionary change that very consequentially marks off the humanoid or human versions of primates from the other primate relatives.) Related to this bipedal locomotion was the evolutionary shift to fully erect posture, a definitive qualitative break from all of the non-primate mammals, and a quantitative one from the vertical but only partially erect one of the other primates. Bipedality and fully erect posture were adaptive not only for locomotion, but in two other significant ways as well. They could now see potential predators over the savanna grasses. And the upper limbs, still ending in hands, would be free to do things other than assist in locomotion. The hands were already prehensile in the tree-living primate ancestors. Now they could be used to carry things like tools or weapons.

We know from studies of live primates of today that tree-living primates can and do fashion rudimentary tools out of materials at hand. What Hockett and Ascher postulate is that such tool-making and tool-carrying, occasional in tree-living primates, become in the land environment a necessity, and there is a selective premium on the development of the anatomical and behavioral elements in the capacity to do this. Using hands to carry weapons also moves from their use first as instruments of *defense* against larger and more powerful mammal predators, to their use as weapons of *offense*, a crucial development in the emergence of the hunting style of life, which is what Hockett and Ascher mean by "the human revolution."

With hunting, the former tree-living, apelike primates, were on the way to evolving into human beings. Hockett and Ascher call them, at this stage, "proto-hominids."

With hunting comes also a major change in diet. Tree-living primates of today are—and presumably these tree-living ancestors also were— largely vegetarian. The proto-hominids who were their descendants, adapting in evolutionary terms to the grassy savanna land life and be- coming hunters of large mammals, became carnivores, or, more pre- cisely, switched to a diet that was no longer vegetarian, but omnivorous.

These changes in turn set the stage for the development of language and speech. Major evolutionary changes in the anatomy and physiology of this animal were required, and it must have taken many hundreds of generations. The connections are complex and lead simultaneously in many different directions.

Hunting of larger land mammals, made possible by the carrying, first of ad hoc, then of deliberately manufactured weapons, in turn requires social cooperation and coordination. It is unlikely that the earliest waifs to venture out onto the strange savanna grassland, after having been ejected by stronger or fiercer conspecifics, could have survived in that territory in any numbers unless they had migrated in *groups* in the first place, and it is reasonable to hypothesize that they already had the rudiments of some kind of group formation while still in the trees (tree- living primates of today do have it).

The descendants on the ground needed group formation even more desperately. The competing mammals on the land were larger, stronger, and faster: therefore singly or in very small groups, these small primates would be easy prey for such carnivores. But in larger groups and with better cooperation and coordination, they could protect themselves, and with further evolutionary development—which included larger and better brains—they could become not only defenders, but also aggressors, against the larger (but stupider) land mammals.

Social cooperation and coordination require communication, and in that environment much of that communication has to be over some considerable distance. Hand-signaling for communication is not suitable beyond a limited distance, nor at night, and is also impeded if the hands are busy carrying things like weapons or food. Visual attention is focused on the prey and on other hunters. Therefore the most feasible form of communication must be *auditory*. There are predecessors for that in the tree life, where such primates probably already had some kind of *call* system of vocal communication, which could have been somewhat along the lines of the present-day gibbon, which has been found to have something like seventeen different, distinct vocal calls, each carrying a distinct message such as "Danger!"

So, Hockett and Ascher hypothesize, the now ground-living apes continue their call system, but now it has to become much more complex, because by this time the hunting arrangement of social groups has itself brought about a more complex social organization. This has been necessitated by more complex and collective food getting by hunting, with groups of cooperating adult males, and more elaborate food *sharing*.

This set of hypotheses by Hockett and Ascher leads in the direction of a theory of the origins of speech predominantly along the lines of *vocal-auditory* communication. (There have been, of course, other kinds of theories advanced about the origins of human language, many others, in fact, as will be discussed later in this section.) More complex cooperative food getting, by hunting, and more elaborate group sharing of food require more complex social organization, and more mutual socialization of the members of the band. The bands would have to have been in the range of at least ten to thirty members to ensure survival chances. We can make intelligent guesses about how such bands lived in such an environment by looking at present-day tribal groups living at the technologically most rudimentary level, that is the level of hunting food animals and gathering wild food plants, particularly those in land areas similar to what East Africa must have been during that drying-up period of the later Miocene. What we find in such groups today is groups of adult males cooperating to carry out such hunting, while the adult females (assisted by juveniles) gather wild food plants, usually not far from a camp base, a kind of "home-base" that is the center of relative safety for the whole band. Such patterns of territoriality may go back to the tree-living ancestors, whose counterparts today have such a territorial pattern: a safe "home-base" area surrounded by a not-clearly-bounded good-getting territory.

These elements are related to the development of language and speech in a number of ways. We can come at it from several directions in the evolutionary story. One is anatomical: the human foot, enabling bipedal locomotion, involves a fully erect posture, for which there is clearly a selective evolutionary push for these animals. That in turn brings about a whole series of changes in what could be called the engineering design of this animal's body, in the direction of becoming human. The head changes to a less prognathous and less flat-topped shape—the jaws recede because much of what was earlier done by the teeth and jaws is now done by hands. The head becomes more dome-shaped to accommodate a progressively larger and more convoluted brain. That brain in turn becomes capable of more complex operations and connections, particularly those involved in human speech and human language.

The evolutionary process involved is both biological and cultural simultaneously. This proposition is a significant departure from the picture given or implied in much earlier anthropological writing on the evolutionary emergence of the human animal. In that earlier work, one gets a picture of an animal that first evolved into a human form in a biological sense, and then, only after having completed that anatomical and physiological evolution, started to develop culture. The Hockett–Ascher reconstruction (sharing in this respect a viewpoint now generally consensual among anthropologists) declares such a disjunction unlikely, arguing instead that it is much more likely not only that both biological and cultural evolutionary processes were going on hand in hand, and simultaneously, in the same evolutionary period (several million years), but that they were mutually interdependent: the more complex social organization both promoting and being promoted by the more complex physical nature of the animal. All of these in turn, as will be discussed shortly, connected with the significant *psychological* developments, and with the development of cultural formations interdependent with the development of a more distinctively human body, and particularly, human brain.

How speech-language developed starting from something like a primate call system, Hockett and Ascher hypothesize as follows:

Each call in a call system is a discrete vocal *signal*—not a symbol—

communicating the total *Gestalt* of a situation, e.g., "food here," "danger here," "I am here." The first step toward language would be the blending of two different calls into a new composite, e.g., a new call indicating both food and danger, using one constituent element of each of the old calls. While such blending must have occurred fortuitously thousands of times in the earlier tree life, without being taken up and transmitted throughout the band, the new and socially more complex savanna life would put a premium upon such innovations. Blending then brings about a process of building composite signals out of separate meaningful parts. Linguists call this changing a *closed* system into an *open* one. This opening up must have taken thousands of years. Once accomplished it is revolutionary.

For now, communication demands detailed *conventions* that cannot possibly be transmitted through the genes—presumably the mechanism of earlier systems—but must be *learned*. Therefore there is natural selection for greater learning capacity, and hence for the bases in brain structure for such capacity. Thus the physical evolutionary changes are interconnected with the changes leading to more complex *culture*.

Opening up the vocal-auditory communication system now involves *displacement*: that is, it makes it possible to talk about something not in sight at the moment, or about something in the past or expected in the future, or something purely hypothetical, or imagined, or mythical. Such capacities become more and more necessary in the more complex social life of these developing animals.

(Parenthetically, this lingust's use of the term "displacement" is not to be confused with the psychoanalytic usage of that term, though they are not entirely unrelated.)

The use of displacement (linguistically) has a parallel psychologically with carrying a weapon for which one has no immediate use, involves thinking about having used it in the past, yesterday, or last month, or last year, and also the possibility of thinking about using it again at some time in the future. In other words, what we call memory, and foresight. Tool and weapon *manufacture*—as distinct from carrying things that are used only as tools or weapons—would certainly involve such mental capacities and operations. The memory and foresight psychological operations involved work along with and reinforce, and are reinforced by, the operations involved in using proto-language displacement processes, those involved in thinking and communicating about things or events not present here and now, events past or future or hypothetical. Linguists call such a system, where it is still a blending of calls, "pre-language."

As this process is going on, the physical shape of ape-becoming-human body is changed: the brain, the head generally, the face, the vocal apparatus, are all becoming something closer to what we find in modern man. Use of blended-call pre-language also increases the innervation of the vocal tract, and enriches the cortical representation of that region. This process probably took hundreds of generations. This is still not human speech-language, however.

The next stages would go something like this: The number of different call-blends keeps increasing. Eventually it reaches a point where it becomes hard to distinguish some of these combinations from others which are similar. Then, by mutation, some individuals appear who start to listen to and articulate these call-gestalten not as total units, but rather in terms of smaller constituent elements, discretely produced and heard, in varying arrangements. They thus begin to make a crucial distinction: the distinction between sound units—called "phonological components" or "phonemes" in linguistics—and a collection of sound units that has a minimum unit of meaning—linguistically, a "morpheme." Making that distinction constitutes the great step forward: at that point we have true language. If we consider tool-making and language as critical criteria of humanity, then at that point the ape-like ancestor has evolved into man. By "human being" we mean, in this context, a generalized primate with one physical specialization—the human foot—with fully erect posture and bipedal gait, stereoscopic and color vision, very complex hand-eye-brain coordinations, a large, very convoluted brain with a highly developed cortex, great learning capacity, the use and manufacture of tools, and speech. It is also an animal in which the period of immaturity and dependency of the young has been prolonged, compared to all other animals lower on the evolutionary scheme. (We shall elaborate anon on the interconnections of these latter features with the psychological features of human beings that psychoanalysis has concerned itself with.)

Hockett and Ascher postulate that this evolutionary process was essentially completed by the beginning of the Pleistocene period, i.e., roughly about a million years ago. (Other anthropologists differ from this estimate, some in each direction. Some think it was largely completed by the time the Australopithecines appeared, going back perhaps as much as four million years; others place full language development as not having been completed until much more recent times, essentially, with *Homo sapiens*, and therefore perhaps not earlier than 40–50,000 years ago. For immediate purposes of tracing connections between the postulated evolutionary history—its main outlines and sequences, rather than specific dating—and psychoanalytically based conceptions of the development of the specifically human psychology, these discrepancies about the probable duration and timing of this physical and cultural evolutionary process are probably not very important. More on this later. For now we shall stay with the Hockett-Ascher hypotheses and their significance for making the psychoanalytic-evolutionary connections.)

Prolongation of infancy and subadult condition is a significant part of these evolutionary changes. Prolongation of infancy is made both possible and necessary by the other changes. Greater security, which came with the combination of hunting and food-gathering and fending off of predators, makes possible a longer period of maternal care of infants. And a more prolonged infancy is made *necessary* by the evolutionary changes Hockett and Ascher are describing: life has become more complex; there is a great deal more that members of the species must learn, and that can be taught to them only by other members of the species, rather than transmitted through the genes. What has to be learned, by human communication and interaction, includes, pre-eminently, language and conventionalized symbolism. This goes far beyond what could have been carried in the genes of the ancestral primate that had call systems. The greater complexity of band organization with the emerging hunting-gathering economy, and the greater security with interdependency, would also necessitate a longer period of immaturity and malleability available to learning. This latter does, in fact, happen for the animals that become human. Thus we have the phenomenon of "neoteny," or "infantilization," some implications of which we shall discuss as they connect with psychoanalytic understandings.

One important by-product of this whole evolutionary process, Hockett and Ascher point out, is the shift from an exclusively dorsal to a predominantly frontal position in sexual intercourse. Presumably the enlargement of the gluteus maximus produced by the shift to bipedal erectness made the old primate dorsal coital position awkward or impossible, fostering the invention of the frontal position.

Thus, then, the gist of the Hockett-Ascher reconstruction: a combined bio-physical-cultural evolutionary development initiated by climatic-ecological crises necessitating some of the tree-living primates to descend to the ground and adapt to a grassy savanna ground environment, developing means and capacities to defend themselves against larger and fiercer land-mammal predators, learning to take the offensive against some of these and develop a hunting life style; developing a more complex social organization in order to accomplish this, along with a more complex culture, and particularly, a communication process that moves from calls, to call-blends, to linguistic combination of sound units with conventionalized (therefore learned) symbolic referents, all this enabled by the more complex brain deriving in turn from body changes attendant on bipedal locomotion and completely erect posture, prolonged infantile dependency and helplessness opening up the possibility of each generation learning (from the older ones) complex cultural skills, symbolic communication, language, and transformative capacities qualitative far beyond the rudimentary cultural capabilities of tree-living primates of then and their descendants of today.

IMPLICATIONS OF THE HOCKETT AND ASCHER THEORY

The implications of this analysis ramify in many directions. First we need to reemphasize that the process as postulated by Hockett and Ascher is both bio-evolutionary and cultural-evolutionary at the same time. In this view, man did not become human first in a physical sense and *then* start to develop culture. He started to develop culture in the process of becoming physically human, and started to become more distinctively physically human in the process of, and due *at least in part* to the process of becoming culturally more adept and more complex, in developing the capacities using complex hand-eye-brain coordinations, utilizing memory and foresight, developing that brain to become more effective at all of these. Individuals or bands with greater or more advanced linguistic development, thus greater communicative capacities, had a greater chance to survive, both in struggle with predators and other species, and with less developed conspecifics; and surviving they developed even further the linguistic and other cultural forms.

With a higher level of culture than their tree-living ancestors, they could afford a longer infantile dependency period, which also means a longer period in which the young can learn the culture of the tribe, therefore more of such culture, and more complex culture, can be passed on in this way, and cultural transmission becomes the preeminent means of learning how to survive and how to live in the world—as compared to mechanisms more intrinsically or more nearly exclusively dependent on the genes. With more culture and more complex culture to be learned, there is then a selective pressure toward the survival of those better able to handle it, and lesser survival possibilities for those less well endowed— therefore a long-term selective movement toward the more complex human animal we know today.

Infantilization

Next, consider the implications of *neoteny*, or *infantilization*. These terms are used with a number of different but interrelated meanings. One is the prolongation of infancy (and by extension of juvenility) in this species, as compared with related mammal and other animal species, as just mentioned. An aspect of this is that some aspects of infancy, in feeling and reacting, in thinking too, are carried over (not unchanged, usually) into later stages of life—a feature of human psychology that is central to our psychoanalytic understandings. Another meaning is that in the human animal, individuals retain into adulthood traits or attributes that are to be found in the infantile, or in the embryonic form, of other mamals, but not in the adults of those species. (E.g., an embryonic chimpanzee looks much more like a human being than does an adult chimpanzee.) The catalogue of such traits reads very much like the catalogue of characteristics that mark us as distinctively human (as compared to our nearest primate relatives, the great apes): orthognathy (i.e., the jaw not protruding the way it does in the apes); the position of the foramen magnum (opening in the skull that accommodates the articulating neck bones at the top of the spinal column); loss of pigmentation in the skin, hair, and eyes (comparatively); the form of the pelvis, and *relative* hairlessness of the body. (See Róheim 1950 and LaBarre 1954 and other writings cited in part 1 above, for fuller discussion of these phenomena.)

Neoteny is part of a whole evolutionary process. In the evolutionary development from other mammals to other primates to man, there are certain progressions: the duration of gestation increases; the typical number of offspring per birth declines; the period from birth to sexual maturity increases; and even more dramatically, the period from birth to full adult growth increases. And the long prenatal period and the protracted and helpless infancy are prerequisites for the ultimately high development of the nervous system and the mental capacities of the human animal. This is rather standard anthropological knowledge.

What needs to be added at this point is a set of ideas about how neoteny came about that are not so standard a part of the anthropological literature. Róheim (1950:400–2), summarizing the anatomist L. Bolk's evidence for the infantilization of man, argued that if a fetal quality becomes gradually permanent, there must be an inhibitory factor that prevents the (otherwise "normal") process of ontogenesis (i.e., development of the individual, as distinct from the species). Bolk assumed that the cause must be endocrinological. In turn, such endocrine changes could come about through a change in *diet*. Now we can connect that idea with what we are hearing in current evolutionary reconstructions such as that of Hockett and Ascher: i.e., that there was, in fact, in the transition from tree living ape to ground-living proto-hominid, a change of diet of major proportions: from the largely herbivorous one of the arboreal apes to the carnivorous, or omnivorous, one of the land-living hunters. Here the pieces of the puzzle start to fit together.

There is another aspect of infantilization. Compared to the neonate of other primate species, the human infant is born prematurely, i.e., at a time when its embryological development has not reached as far as that of corresponding new-born apes, or the neonates of other mammals. This is a kind of accidental by-product of other evolutionary trends. Walking upright led to the development of a narrower pelvis, adapted to holding the guts in position. However, the head has now evolved to a larger size and vaulted shape to accommodate a much larger and more complex brain and to relate to the flatter and more frontally oriented face. As a result, since the head is proportionately a greater part of the total embryo's body than it is later of the child or adult, and this more so in humans than in other mammals, we arrived in evolution at a dilemma: the danger that the head of the fetus would not be able to pass through the birth canal of the mother. In fact, if fetal development were to continue in the human to a point corresponding to what it does in other primates, it would definitely not be able to get through. The result is a kind of engineering compromise: the baby has to be born earlier.

Shifts in Sexuality

There is another, related change involving sexuality: the shift from periodic estrus in the female to nonperiodic continuous sexual receptivity. One way it could have happened is this: in the Australopithecines of about four million years ago, the female, about four feet tall, weighing about seventy pounds, had an estrus cycle of say twenty-eight days, making her receptive to the males for about eight days of the cycle. We have the rudiments of a hunting-gathering economy, the males doing the hunting, the females the gathering of wild food plants. Male chimpanzees and gorillas in the wild will share food with *estrus* females. Suppose the Australopithecine males did the same. The males come back from hunting with meat food. Only females in estrus get some. Some females get smart and pretend to be in heat a few days before or after their estrus cycle, thus artifically extending their receptivity period. Jane Goodall has observed a female chimpanzee who did just this—faked estrus receptivity to advance her interest. A female chimp Goodall called Flo, having just finished her estrus period, became jealous a new female chimp who was getting too much male attention, and began to show the pink swelling of estrus all over again (Goodall 1971).

Suppose, then, that the hominid ancestor females—the smarter ones among them—began extending their estrus periods by several days at a time, from eight days, to ten, to twelve, and so on. These smarter, sexier females attract more male attention, become pregnant more often, produce more and smarter offspring. The brain enlarges by this kind of selective breeding. Also involved would be a change in the nature of female sexuality, from being nearly entirely under the control of instinct to becoming partly under volitional cognitive control.

There could be other mechanisms, involving the usual evolutionary process of genetic variation. While the receptivity period might be on average about eight days out of a twenty-eight-day cycle, there could be variation from this to as much as ten or eleven days on the upward end, and down to six or five on the lower end. It would be the upper end that interests us: those with a longer estrus period would have greater mating probabilities, therefore greater chances of passing on this characteristic to their daughters. That process, however, would not be associated with the evolution toward greater *intelligence*. The hypothesis of faking it would.

If the females evolved to something closer to constant month-long and year-long receptivity, the males would then be faced with a strange new situation: many receptive females at any one time, which could be something of a dilemma. Why?

Suppose the evolving hominids had some kind of dominance hierarchy among the males, comparable to that found in many of the present-day primates, and that the more dominant males had first choice of the available receptive females and had to protect these females in heat. With the expansion of the number of females in heat at the same time, the amount of time and work the dominant males would have to spend protecting these females would increase. How could they devote themselves to hunting and other food-getting activities? We can hypothesize that the dominant males open the ranks and allow less dominant males to have some innings with the receptive females. This would not be too difficult, since there would be more to go around at the same time. The implications of that kind of change would be enormous. It would mean a modification of dominance hierarchies on the part of the males and a decrease in the force of instinct in their lives too. They would have not only less need of automatic dominance over females, but also of dominance over lesser males.

This process connects with brain size. Brainier females were extending their receptivity periods. Brainier males were increasing their capacity to modify what had been earlier, instinctively acquired dominance behavior and moving, with *foresight*, to more cooperative patterns.

This whole complex connects with the earlier birth of the human neonate—bigger brains, bigger heads, necessity for premature delivery. Therefore, much of the head and brain growth has to go on after the baby is born. (The brain doubles in size in the first year, and reaches 90 percent of its final size in three years.)

The result is a female, the mother, increasingly handicapped by all this progress. She now has a baby that is the most helpless mammal neonate ever. And it is also an infant that is unable to cling to her adequately. Primate babies have four hands, so they can use the lower pair—the ones that humans have replaced with feet, to cling to the mother. The cost of our developing that specialization, the human foot, necessary for erect posture, bipedal locomotion, is to make the big toe no longer an opposable thumb, and the whole limb extremity unfit for grasping. Not only that, this human neonate is not even capable of holding up his head or lifting his chin. Thus we have a human infant in extraordinary need of maternal, or generally parental, care. Add to that, what we see from the viewpoint of the mother: This mother, perhaps with a new infant every year or two, has to come up with some more reliable means of protection for herself and her offspring. There would be a premium on her attaching herself for more than temporary periods to one particular male who would provide food and protection for her and her babies. There would be a premium on the female changing from a more or less promiscuous estrus-heat primate pattern to a more selective and eventually monogamous pattern.

The "prematurity" of human birth is a crucial point for connecting psychoanalytic with anthropological understanding: for this is a major reason why the human infant is so extraordinarily helpless and dependent. (It is also a demonstration of an important feature of evolutionary process: not all evolutionary developments toward a particular species are necessarily harmonious with one another, or entirely adaptive in all respects.)

The extreme helplessness connects with how crucial we (as psychoanalysts) see the earliest mothering contacts to be in the development of the child's personality, and how vulnerable the infant is to deficits in early mothering.

Other connections between neoteny and man's human nature also refer to sexuality. Man is highly infantile in many respects. But also this peculiar human sexuality is in fact quite *precocious*. Again we have non-harmonious, even opposite, types of processes going on side by side. Here an animal that is highly infantilized, with a very prolonged infancy, and a long period between infancy and full adult growth, nevertheless has a sexuality that starts extremely early, in fact in certain respects immediately at birth. The sexual pattern is present in infants before the gonadal hormone is produced in adequate quantities. The female ovum is practically fully developed at age five years. Róheim (1950) called this Soma lagging behind Germa. LaBarre (1954) elaborates on this point. With man's reproductive economy, heightened by cultural advancements, precocious and lifelong sexuality far surpasses reproductive necessities. There is thus "surplus" or "discretionary" sexuality. This is very significant for the social life of man. How so? Freud taught us that social ties are essentially *libidinal* ties—frequently transformed in many guises.

Another element in human sexuality, alongside of and associated with its non-seasonality and its precociousness, as well as its polymorphous potentialities, is the associated conflict between promiscuity and more or less stable monogamous pairings. The theory just propounded—not Hockett and Ascher's but not in conflict with it—of the female's turning to long-term pairing, for protection and security, to one particular male, would show the origins of relative monogamous fidelity on the part of the female. We can see what advantage there is for the male that she limit her sexual favors to him. But what is in it for the male to cease being promiscuous (if he does)? We would answer as follows: If most or nearly all of the females are receptive at any time, this leaves sexual opportunity for most or nearly all of the males rather than only the dominant few. If clear-cut dominance patterns decline as a means of settling which males have access to which females, we have a new situation which has both greater abundance of sexual opportunity (from the viewpoint of the males) and greater potential for inter-individual (male) fights over potential sexual partners. This then ties in with the Hockett-Ascher and related theory: relatively permanent monogamous unions reduce fighting among males for females, fostering cooperation in hunting. Otherwise phrased: there is a trade-off; any particular male renounces promiscuous access to many females in favor of more or less exclusive rights to one of his own. This way even males who would be low-ranking in a dominance hierarchy would be assured of access to a mate on a fairly regular basis. This constitutes an aspect of the domestication of the hominid species—particularly of the males of the species. Against this many males have been rebelling ever since. It could be argued that the males got forced into such domestication against their wills. To this day when they—or some of them—rebel against this, they may scheme to get away from their wives for a spell, in the company of other men, for hunting for example. (See Lionel Tiger, *Men in Groups*, 1969, and Tiger and Fox, *The Imperial Animal*, 1971.)

The domestication of the males, as well as the females, leads to the pattern of *food-sharing*, an essential aspect of group survival. It would work at the level of the family built around a monogamous pairing, and extend from there throughout a territorial band. The female sharing food with her offspring is ancient in the animal world, appearing not only in mammals but in birds as well. The *male* sharing with his own particular female and their offspring, and the further extension of that to others outside the family, is an aspect of human domestication. The evolutionary changes in the female and in childbirth have to be accorded their proper place in this process. It is also a process in the direction of increased cooperation, altruism, and social feeling for justice. (There is a whole tradition of thought that sees all of these as more highly developed in human females than in human males. See discussion in chapter 9 in the context of Freud's contrary idea of the weaker female superego.)

Both points can be made: that the human female has ancestrally and to the present day always lived closer to the biological realities of day-to-day, month-to-month, year-to-year life, than the male: and *also* that her connectedness with child-bearing and child-rearing made her the forerunner of those trends toward social cooperation and altruism through which human communities came into being, expanded and prospered, and developed more complex cultures. She thus in these ways stands closer to both primeval instincts and the more evolutionarily advanced aspects of human existence.

This kind of reconstruction would put the origins of monogamous marriage and of the nuclear family as far back as the Australopithecines, perhaps as much as four million years ago.

Frontal Coital Position

Discussion of this precocious, nonseasonal, and lifelong human sexuality can also be connected with another evolutionary change: from the dorsal to the frontal coital position. True, one can occasionally observe a frontal position used by orangs in the trees; and true, humans use other positions besides the frontal one. But what I mean is that this position is a specifically human development, is found nearly universally in human societies, and is (nearly) a human monopoly in the animal world. This position fosters and reinforces a more frontal approach to the world in general. Such a frontal approach is already begun in the relative verticality of the tree-living primates.

It is pushed much further in the human species. The frontal coital position puts the adult male mate in a position to the adult female similar to that of a suckling infant, and can thereby enhance the diffusion and complexity of sexual feelings. That would indicate a break from the seasonal quality of sexuality of arboreal primates ancestral to man. (Present-day tree-living primates, where copulatory behavior was observable, have been found to be quite seasonal in this, contrary to what primatologists had earlier believed—Devore 1965.) Thus nonseasonality as well as frontal coital position appear as specifically human developments. (Being exclusively human is not crucial to the present argument in any case; what is essential is that they are *pan*-human, and have developed in evolution, probably in the context of the kind of evolutionary history here being postulated.)

Implications of the change to the frontal position include the following: human beings take a more frontal approach to the world generally, and specifically in sex. This means, among other things, that all relationships, mate-to-mate as well as parent-to-child, are now essentially face-to-face relationships. This is probably an important determinant of what could be called man's peculiarly polymorphous *sexual sociality*.

Infantilization means a much greater continuity in the human species of infantile (even embryonic) processes and attachments throughout life than in infra-human animals. So there is a connection again with infantilization or neoteny. This means a greater diffusion of sexual-social feeling throughout the whole range of interindividual relationships. That would be another way of referring to the polymorphousness of infantile sexuality persists (in the unconscious, if not overtly) throughout life. Add to this the convergence of mother-infant and mate-mate sexuality produced by the change to the frontal coital position, and we have the basis, in evolution, for the great extensiveness and displaceability of sexual-social ties that Freud saw in the human species.

It could therefore also bear upon the bases for the phenomenon of *regression* in man. In the psychoanalytic sense, that means going back to an earlier developmental stage in some aspects of one's psychological functioning—not necessarily in all—in reaction to great stress, frustration, major object loss, or other depriving experiences. Róheim, following that idea, claimed that we are all of us—all human beings—in basic respects babies crying out in the dark.

Lest we not be understood, we are not arguing that the frontal coital position alone produces the frontal approach to the world that makes more, or most, or all, of human relationships much more like face-to-face relationships, but rather that the frontal position is one among a number of determinants in the "frontal pattern," which can be seen, psychoanalytically, as "over-determined" (more precisely, as multiply-determined). A frontal approach to the world has connections with many other phenomena besides those involved in sexuality. For example, with the development of language as a cultural pheonmenon, and with how it is acquired in individual life experience.

ELAINE MORGAN'S AQUATIC THEORY

A very different theory of human evolutionary origins that also has important implications for psychoanalytic inquiry is Elaine Morgan's *The Descent of Woman* (1972). Morgan points out that there is a huge time gap between the late Miocene period (when the ape like ancestors were supposed to have come down from the trees), which ended about twelve million years ago, and the appearance of the Australopithecines, about at most four million years ago, at the early part of the Pleistocene. That constitutes a whole geological age, of about eight to ten million years, unaccounted for in terms of any fossil remains of creatures in process of evolving from a more ape-like ancestor into something more like *Homo sapiens*. That age was the Pliocene, which was marked by great heat and droughts throughout the parts of Africa that had been forested jungle before. Morgan argues that those ancestors that came down from the trees—small, rather defenseless primates not yet adapted with erect posture and bipedal gait—could not have survived, on the *ground*, through that whole period to evolve into what we find much later as the Australopithecines. They would have been easy victims of mammalian predators such as large cats (ancestors of tigers, leopards, etc.).

She also argues that the hairlessness of humans compared to our ape relatives could not have come about in the way the male theorists like Desmond Morris (1968) have hypothesized, i.e., by adaptation to a hunting pattern on the ground. For why then did the *females* lose body hair more than did the males? They were not, according to that theory, the ones doing the hunting, and in fact their retaining body hair would have been a boon for clinging babies.

So what is Morgan's answer? They took to the *water*. She argues that they had to escape the terrible heat of the Pliocene droughts and also the predators who were bigger, stronger, and faster than these small apes. The solution: jump into the sea. She hypothesizes that our ancestors must have survived on the seashore, partly in the water (near the shore), and on the shore. They must have done so in a manner similar to that found in a number of other sea mammals, but without total adaptation to the sea. This theory, she claims, would explain all those aspects of the evolution of the species, from the time of the descent of the arboreal primate ancestors to the ground in the late Miocene or early Pliocene, up to the much later time when the Australopithecines, near human, are evident. For example, the relative hairlessness of humans is better explained by positing an *aquatic* period of nearly ten million years or so, as other aquatic mammals have also become hairless. Similarly, the important development of pendulous—not orb-like—breasts in the human female—absent in our primate relatives—giving baby something to hold on to either in the water or when sitting on mamma's lap on the shore.

Morgan got the idea of this aquatic theory from a then little-noticed paper by Sir Alister Hardy in *The New Scientist* in 1960 ("Was Man More Aquatic in the Past?").

Where Morris had argued that the human female had evolved "orb-like" breasts as a mode of sexual attraction of the male, focusing him on her frontal orbs instead of the dorsal ones (her buttocks) to encourage the frontal coital position, Morgan scoffs at that as a typically androcentric theory. Human female breasts in the mature adult are rarely "orblike" or "hemispherical." Their evolution has to do not with her mate but with her baby, since that is who they are for. Whatever mate-mate erogenous function they may later have acquired. Morgan argues that they were developed in evolution in the first place for the baby, and elongated breasts rather than orbs would be better for baby to cling to.

The aquatic theory would explain why we have uncovered no fossil evidence of any forms intermediate between the tree-dwelling primate ancestors of the Miocene and the Australopithecines. We have no fossil remains of any hominid animal for that whole period of the Pliocene. If they had been on the ground during those eons, why did they leave no fossil evidence? In the sea, or on the seashore, they would not leave such remains.

As for other elements of human evolution: erect posture, bipedalism, larger brains and therefore larger heads, Morgan claims, are better explained by positing a combined aquatic and seashore adaptation during the Pliocene, rather than a ground-dwelling hunting pattern. Upright posture would be encouraged by the need to get as deep into the water as possible to escape land-mammal predators (who are not aquatic) holding the arms, including perhaps a baby, over one's head. Hairlessness would be a water adaptation, not one for land life in a torrid climate. The aquatic theory would also explain the development of a layer of subcutaneous fat in the human species—more developed in females than in males—which would have been quite maladaptive on land in the Pliocene heat. It is found also in other aquatic mamals. The food supply would be plentiful in the sea and on the shore. Its animal component would consist of forms of life smaller, slower, and less fierce than the primates, in contrast to the larger, faster, and fiercer land mammal predators. She could catch small shrimps, baby crabs, birds' eggs; he could crack shells of mussels, lobsters, and the like with his strong canines, and she would learn to crack these with a pebble used as a tool. So we would have the beginning, in this female activity, of humanlike tool-using, to be followed later by tool-making. A hunting land primate could not have discarded fur or body hair to become cooler and at the same time developed a layer of subcutaneous fat which would make him hotter; both developments together would make sense in a water environment.

The evidence Morgan adduces for this theory comes from comparison with other sea mammals and study of how they differ from their closest land-living relatives. The female dugong (sea-cow), for example, is reported to suckle her infant while she is floating upright in the water. Another mammal, the rhytina, has two well-developed pectoral breasts and, like humans, usually produces only one infant at a time. In another such species, the manatee, the female has one breast under each flipper, where it joins the body. Also the human is one of the few species that sheds salt-water tears. The only other animals that do are all aquatic. Water-living crocodiles do; land-living crocodiles do not. Aquatic lizards, yes, terrestrial ones, no. The distinctively human development of the buttocks, and their being larger and more protuberant in the female, are also explainable by postulating a sea-and-seashore period. The typical apelike rear—with the vaginal opening highly exposed and scarcely any fleshy protuberance—would be very uncomfortable for the female sitting on the seashore, for example, nursing her baby; she also has three orifices there that need protection. The male's buttocks would be less highly developed, and have a smaller layer of subcutaneous fat than hers. But, for both, the development of the muscles in that region would be adaptive for swimming. (Critics of this theory argue that the functional necessities would not apply any more in the water than on the land, where bipedal locomotion with upright posture would adequately explain the development and value of the buttocks.)

In reference to the "invention" of the frontal coital position, Morgan points out that practically all land mammals use a dorsal position. The one exception is another primate, the orangutan, which *sometimes* has been observed using the ventral position, with both partners hanging from tree branches. And practically all aquatic mammals, like the sea-living rhytina, whale, and manatee, as well as the freshwater beaver, copulate frontally. This, says Morgan, strongly suggests a long aquatic period in our ancestry. As the female's buttocks got larger and the vagina shifted forward and inward, rear entry for the male became increasingly difficult or awkward, especially if he still had only an average primate-size penis, which is a lot smaller than the penis of the average human male. (Erect posture is assumed, bringing the angle between leg bones and spinal cord from about 90 degrees to something closer to 180 degrees. This could happen in either a sea or a land environment. Therefore frontal coital position does not argue inherently more for either one of these theories. Morgan's point is that it is not inconsistent with postulating about ten million years in an in-the-sea and on-the sea-shore environment.)

Morgan then hypothesizes that as the climate later changed these hominid ancestors came back onto the land permanently and adapted to a terrestrial life. (Had they not done so, they would have evolved into just another sea mammal.)

Therefore, proponents of a theory like that of Hockett and Ascher could reply to Morgan that the adaptation story from then on—i.e., from the time of getting back onto the land after the aquatic experience—would have to follow essentially the patterns postulated by their land theory. Perhaps the timing of when, specifically, these developments took place in the whole cycle would have been different, i.e., later. By the land theory, one would expect the Australopithecines to be farther along in evolution by the time they appear on the scene, about three to four million years ago. In fact, the fossil remains and associated cultural artifacts indicate an erect bipedal tool- and weapon-using animal with a fair size brain, probably not yet with human speech. By the aquatic theory, these developments would have awaited the return to the land. Hunting and land-food-gathering would not, by the aquatic theory, have developed till the Pleistocene (in contrast to the land theory which sees these developing through the Pliocene.) We don't have a clear consensus among specialists about how long any of these developments took to evolve. Some think the human foot took hundreds of generations to evolve; others that it could have come about rather quickly under certain environmental pressures.

Morgan adduces the aquatic theory to explain several aspects of our sexuality: loss of estrus, shift to frontal coital position, enlargement of the male's penis, and more drastic changes in the female sexual anatomy. The vagina shifts forward and upward, making the dorsal position awkward or impossible, considering the simultaneous development of the large female buttocks. These implications ramify in many directions.

This is how Morgan theorizes the frontal coital position was invented: An enterprising male hominid tries the then usual dorsal position; it doesn't work; he forcefully turns the female over, "attacking" her in both senses of that term. Then he has to inhibit his "stop the action" response to her submission signals in order to go ahead and effect intercourse. Thus he links male sexuality with aggression, and she links sexuality with submission. Morgan sees this change developing in the aquatic period, in the sea or on the seashore. She points out it is comparable to the frontal position used by other sea-living mammals (and not by their terrestrial cousins). Males best able to inhibit previously programmed reactions of withdrawal (to the female's subsmission signal) would have more sexual success, produce more progeny, and by generations of selection, lead to the establishment of this pattern.

Why did this process have to have happened in or near the water, as Morgan hypothesizes? Why would it not have been just as likely on the land, if we assume prior development of the upright posture, bipedalism, larger buttocks? If they were developing the frontal position in the water, as Morgan says some aquatic mammals do, it would not require much physical force by the male to turn the female around, but then, in the water she could probably escape more easily, assuming she could swim as well and as fast as he could. And there is good reason to believe she could. In fact, Tiger (1969) points out that the one physical sport or activity in which human females excel over males is long-distance *swimming*. Morgan, noting that, takes it as further support for the theory that our ancestors took to the sea.

We are, in fact, one of the few present-day land mammals that really enjoys going back into the water, and human infants, given the opportunity, can learn to swim even before they learn to walk. Many do in Melanesian tribes where the village houses are built directly over the water; and so do some present-day Californians. The female ancestor probably learned to swim better than the male to assure not only her own survival, but also that of her infant. This combination, therefore, suggests that the shift to the frontal position must have occured on land, and if it happened during the postulated "aquatic" period, it must have occurred on the seashore, not in the water. In that situation, the female, turned around to a supine position, would in fact be more vulnerable and less able to escape unwanted sexual attentions.

From the viewpoint of connections with out psychoanalytic understanding of human psychology, the differences are not very significant between the Hockett-Ascher theory of human evolution on the land, with hunting as the crucial change, during the whole long period from late Miocene to early Pleistocene, and the Morgan theory, which hypothesizes a roughly ten-million-year-long period on the seashore and in the shallows of the sea before the hominid creatures returned to the land. The hunting-revolution processes postulated by the land theorists would then still have to go on, but at a considerably later period than those theorists have hypothesized. Both kinds of theory postulate the emergence by the time of the Australopithecines—perhaps as early as four million years ago—of an upright biped with large head and large brain, possibly with speech or something close to it, use of more than rudimentary tools and weapons, a year-long nonseasonal sexuality, sexual division of labor, socially defined and perpetuated patterns of cooperation and control over both sexual impulses and aggression as a prerequisite for minimally peaceful group life. Both would also lead us to an animal with a sexuality that is complexly interfused with its sociality, and an animal with the most helpless mammal neonate ever, requiring massive amounts of maternal and other adult-female nurturant care, and psychological help in dealing with its huge vulnerability, combined with greatly enlarged learning capacities in that larger brain, and vastly and increasingly urgent dependency on the process of human culture.

CHAPTER FIVE

Language Origins
and
Related Developments

THEORIES OF LANGUAGE ORIGIN

The Hockett-Ascher reconstruction of the probable evolution of human speech-language appears to me to be ingenious and provocative but incomplete, as I have outlined in an earlier publication (see Endleman 1966). After all, language is an oral activity, most intensively developed in fact-to-face contacts—in contrast to a call system, which operates primarily at a distance. LaBarre, in comments on the Hockett–Ascher paper (LaBarre 1964), notes that there is a puzzling difference between calls (e.g., gibbon calls, or a human's "piercing" scream) and ordinary speech language. The pitch of calls is in the frequencies around 3,000 cycles per second, near the top of the range for the human ear and the range to which the human ear is most sensitive. (Calls at this pitch can be heard over longer distances than lower-pitched ones of the same amplitude.) By contrast, ordinary human speech is mainly in the range below 1,000 cycles per second. LaBarre asks: "Whence the massive flatting of speech-frequencies in man? Or did speech not arise out of "closed" primate call-systems after all, but rather from the lower frequencies of feckless play-chatter, where speech has remained ever since? (LaBarre 1964:150).

But why the either/or in Labarre's questions? Why must language have developed exclusively from a call system, or exclusively from what LaBarre calls "feckless play-chattering?"If we keep in mind the general principle of multiple determination (in Freud's language, "over-determination") and apply it to language and speech, we can hypothesize that many different kinds of influences went into the development of distinctively human speech and language. Existing presentday species of infra-human primates show both call communication and that kind of "feckless play-chattering" just referred to, mothers with infants and juveniles at play, not to mention adults in all kinds of playful situations. We would probably be justified in assuming play chattering in the putative ancestors of human beings, in the protohominids on those grassy savannas. The term "play" in this context is significant: by that we suggest that it was not only in the "serious" and utilitarian contexts of the need for more complex communication in hunting and related activities (those of adult males primarily), but also in the emotive and less utilitarian contexts of more intimate human contacts that some part of the origin of speech-language is to be sought. These more playful situations, we can postulate, must have also contributed to the origin of language. Communication in these situations—even in modern human beings—is often sub-linguistic, i.e., "phatic"—essentially nonverbal and not symbolic in the verbal sense. Pre-linguistic billings and cooings of mothers to infants would be a good example. And adult lovers may lapse into a kind of "baby talk."

We can elaborate further on the implications of considering play as part of the context of language origins. Play can provide the context for innovations in human communication, parallel to the blending of call elements and their eventual analysis into conventionalized phonemic elements. Hockett and Ascher in their paper refer to "generations of chattering . . . increasing the innervation of the vocal tract." Now "chattering" is clearly not the same thing as "calling." But it is the sort of thing mothers do with infants, and juveniles (and often adults) do at play. (For adults, listen during any cocktail party.) How is play involved? Play can include "playing around with" elements that are already given, trying them out in new combinations and sequences. Play may also involve body contact, as in fighting or sexual play. And a major context for play is the mother-infant relationship. Róheim (1943) defined speech as "orality coming to terms with reality." and what is more oral than infancy?

The progressive lengthening of infancy and heightening of dependency of the infant and the juvenile involved in the evolution to humanity is certainly relevant in this context too and it must have heightened the significance or Eros and play in the mother–child relationship. That in turn would encourage a greater variety of vocalization, which must have led to new combinations. Such combinations must have occurred or been invented more or less fortuitously thousands of times in the primate past. But now they would have an evolutionary significance. There would be a premium upon preserving such new combinations as an aid to communication in the now more complex life of the emerging hunting-and-gathering economy. There must also have been greater complexity in interpersonal relationships, not only of mother and child, but also of juveniles to one another. Add to that the mate–mate relationship, which becomes emotionally more involved when coitus becomes a face-to-face matter in the frontal position. Greater face-to-face contact also means greater *oral* contact—critical for the development of speech—and greater vocal communication. Then LaBarre's point about the low-volume and low-pitch vocalizations characteristic of face-to-face and intimate situations is relevant here. That is, chattering—at low volume and low pitch—in these situations must have provided one additional context for the development of new combinations and arrangements of vocal sounds, in the direction toward pre-language thence to language proper.

But, we can ask, how can we talk about juvenile play vocalizations being at *low* volume? Anyone who has been around children at play can tell you that the noise level is very high indeed, in volume and in pitch. That part of it does seem to be more like a *call* system of communication, rather than a chattering one. What I am postulating here is not that it was play-chattering *rather than* calls, from which speech-language evolved, but rather that *both* must have been part of the process, and both must have made contributions. Juvenile play, with call-like, high-volume, high-pitch vocalizations, must also have made its contribution to the development of language. Modifications, additions, and new combinations of vocal calls must have come about not only for the "serious" utilitarian purpose provoked by the instrumental demands of the emerging hunting economy, but also out of play involving juveniles, and probably play involving adults as well. Play is often an imitation of "serious" instrumental activities, and in such an imitation there is more room for introducing innovations and combinations.

The reader may now object, are we not now hearing yet another highly speculative theory about the origin of language, and what would make this set of hypotheses any more plausible than any of the many other theories that have been propounded in the past? There has been a great variety of theories of the origin of language. In fact, the anthropologist Gordon Hewes (1971b) has put together a whole bibliography of books and articles on the topic of language origins. Some of these theories are the following:

One theory argues that language came out of prelinguistic vocalizations that are imitative of sounds heard in the environment, the sort of thing we have in onomatopoeia, sometimes referred to as the "bow-wow" theory. Another traces language from emotive ejaculations a human—or primate evolving into a human—may make in any kind of intense emotional state, what we still have left in the language when we say "ow!" "wow!" "yikes!" and the like. This has been called the "pooh-pooh" theory or the "ai-yai-yai!" theory. There is also one called a work-chant theory, referring to sounds made to physical exertion, the "yo-ho-ho" theory. Another alleges that language originated in exclamations people make in exultation over a successful feat, what could be called a "ta-ra-ra-boom-de-day!" theory. Yet another has been called the bab-ble-luck theory: according to this one, associations are made between babbling sounds spontaneously made by infants and some feature of the external environment. Related to that one, there is yet another that at-tributes it to mouth gestures, what has been called the ta-ta theory, i.e., the mouth parts imitate the movements of hands, arms, or other parts of the body. While we're at the mouth, we need to mention yet another, referring to sounds that infants make at the mother's breast. That one has been dubbed the "chew-chew" theory.

We could add to any of these a whole repertory of nonlinguistic sounds and exclamations any animals at all resembling a human being might make in carrying out any of the body processes: eating, eliminating, copulating, scratching, rubbing, body-grooming, fighting, or mock-fight-ing. All of these theories—pooh-pooh, bow-wow, ai-yai-yai, chew-chew, ho-he-ho, ta-ta, and babble-luck—refer to the kinds of vocali-zations out of which later combinations and conventionalizations could have been made, leading in the direction of speech language.

There are also other theories that focus not on what kinds of vocal materials must have been later combined, but on the *conditions* under which such developments take place. There is an instinctivist theory, which argues that language appears at a certain level of *cognitive* evo-lution and is inborn thereafter. That one would, of course, not explain why or how it appeared at that level.

Then there is a conventionalist theory, according to which individuals deliberately agree to create language in order to improve their social life. Such a theory of the origin of language would appear too rationalistic and improbable. It would presuppose that the beings in question had some-thing like language to communicate with in the first place.

There is also a theory which attributes the origin to chance mutation. In this one, language origin is attributed to a random biological event. That there could have been only *one* such event sounds wildly improb-able. However, a series of mutations, affecting the neural organization of the brain and the whole vocal apparatus, especially the supralaryngeal tract, would be a necessary part of the theory I am here adducing, drawing on Hockett-and-Ascher and on psychoanalytically oriented emendations of that theory discussed above and to be elaborated in the following.

There are still other theories of language origin. Hewes indicated twelve different ones. Some of these probably most anthropologists and other social scientists of today would not even begin to take seriously. One is the divine or miraculous origin theory, claiming language is the gift to man of the Creator.

One other theory does need to be taken seriously, however. That is the contact theory. According to that, language is a natural outcome of man's social communicative needs. This sounds like something close to part of the theory I am expounding. Social communicative needs would certainly be part of the conditions for the development of language. These needs can be seen as becoming more intense as the once-arboreal ape-like animals became ground-dwellers, more crucially interdependent and in need of each other's cooperation, especially as they developed a hunting mode of life.

The critic impatient with the plethora of theories of language origins, each apparently as speculative and possibly plausible or implausible as the next, may feel we should simply once again call a moratorium on the formulation of such theories. That is, in fact, what the Paris Linguistics Society tried to do in 1866. They found themselves swamped with proposed papers on the origins of language, each as speculative as the next and each as devoid of firm grounding in empirical observations as the next. In response, the members of the society declared the subject taboo and called a moratorium on any more such papers. (Obviously this would not stop speculative scholars and others from formulating such theories; but the Paris Linguistics Society would no longer provide a forum for their presentation.) The society felt that none of the proposed theories was either provable or disprovable by any empirical evidence available at the time.

We might wonder if that argument could not just as cogently be made today. Why revive interest in the origins of language at this time? Are we in any better position in 1980 than we were in 1866 to back up any speculative theory?

In answer we can say, yes, we do now know a great deal more about what our probable ancestors as far back as a few million years ago looked like, and how and where they lived. We also know a good deal more about the probable sequence of evolutionary development in man's anatomy and physiology, partly from embryological knowledge on the basis of Heckel's postulate that ontogeny recapitulates phylogeny. And we are starting to know a great deal more about our nearest present-day primate relatives, the great apes and some of the monkeys, from which we can make more intelligent guesses about what they were like, those primates that were probably ancestral both to these presentday ape cousins and to ourselves. We also know more about what the more immediate precursors on our own evolutionary family line were like.

Therefore, the theories of today can attempt to piece together information from a great many different fields of study: physical anthropology, primatology, archaeology, embryology, comparative anatomy and physiology of different existing species, as well as linguistics and the cultural anthropological study of contemporary primitive tribes living at the most rudimentary technological level. And we may add, here particularly, that the picture derived from linking up information from these many different fields can be further developed by the infusion of psychoanalytic ideas.

If all of the earlier-formulated theories of language origin are lacking in one way or another, what is there to recommend the theory I am here expounding? None of the theories that focus on only one kind of pre-linguistic vocalization, like chew, bow-wow, or yikes, can be adequate because it leaves out all the others. What is being suggested here, by contrast, is that *any and all* of these kinds of vocalization, from chewing or sucking sounds, to babbling, to onomatopoeia, to long-distance high-volume high-pitch calls, could have, in fact must have, contributed to the repertory of sounds of proto-language. Many of these sounds must have been important parts of the content of vocalizations in subhuman play. With an animal that is cortically increasingly complex, play activities would then allow innovative elaborations of such "raw material," expansion of the repertoire, and then the chance for playful recombinations of the elements.

Add to such recombination or blending, the process of conventionalization, and the animal is on the way to language. Conventionalization means that a particular sound comes to be conventionally associated with a particular referent. At first there may be a close affinity between the sound and the activity or thing being referred to. But later, when such phatic elements are blended and recombined in ever more complex ways, the relationship between the sound combination and the thing or event referred to becomes "purely conventional." That is, there is no longer an obvious connection, and the association of the sound and referent—now arbitrary—has to be *learned*.

This theory of language origin then claims that there must have been *multiple* influences leading to the development of human language. It would be a parallel in the cultural sphere for what Freud called "over-determination" in the sphere of the psychology of the individual. ("Multiple determination" is probably a more precise term.)

There is yet another variant theory of the origin of language that deserves consideration here. That is the *gestural* theory, most recently revived in the work of the anthropologist Gordon Hewes (see Hewes 1971a, 1973). This work we shall take up in more detail later in this chapter. Basically, Hewes theorizes that the proto-human ancestors developed a language-like communication system first in the form of gesture language, and only later developed vocal language, transferring the same earlier capacities from the manual-visual sphere to the vocal-auditory one. Hewes acknowledges a whole list of predecessors who formulated one or another version of such a gestural theory, though he grounds his own formulation on evidence only now available in the late twentieth century. Predecessors include the Abbé de Condillac, Lewis Henry Morgan, Alfred Russell Wallace, George Romanes, Wilhelm Wundt, Richard Paget, and Alexander Johanesson (see Hewes 1973 for references). The earlier versions were weaker because they lacked the kinds of supporting evidence Hewes sees as now available, particularly the recent studies of language capacities of chimpanzees, to be discussed shortly.

For the moment let us briefly note that this gestural theory does not preclude the combination of call-blending (à la Hockett and Ascher) and of play-chatter-blending as a contribution to the beginnings of vocal language in humans that we are hypothesizing in this chapter. We shall later discuss this point in more detail.

Hockett and Ascher postulate that there was some selective advantage, in a utilitarian sense, of blending elements of calls. In other words there was some "need" to have this more complex kind of communication system. We can now ask what would be the push or the need to move toward blending of elements of sub-linguistic vocalization in the intimate mother-child and other juvenile situations? We can answer that mammal teaching of the young is usually direct, behavioral, immediate in the situation involved. Consider a cat teaching her kitten how to catch mice, for example. But, as life becomes more complex, there is need for more of the teaching to be *anticipatory* rather than contemporaneous with its uses. There is thus more need to communicate about things past, future, or potential. Anticipatory vocal socialization requires displacement, in the linguistic sense. (Probably the same kinds of psychological capacities are involved here as in what psychoanalysis calls "displacement.") Psychoanalytically, language means (among other things) that symbol replaces object. We reinvest objects with libido by the meaning of words.

The question arises, then, does this not imply the absence of *direct* cathexis of objects? I think it does. And this suggests a transformation of the animal's direct erotic relationship to the world through a medium that holds out long-range potential for enormously greater mastery of the world. Language in this context, then, stands between the animal, in this case the human, or proto-human, and the object. That would account for the magical quality of words, and magic is an essential aspect of infantile development. Language can be said to be bound up with repression, and thus be regarded as one of those great compromise formations, at the cultural level, which advance the cultural evolution of mankind, and permit much gratification of Eros while damming up other aspects.

We need to clarify here just what we mean by saying language is bound up with repression. A point of connection between them is the phenomenon of *negation*.

A call system can include a call which signals "danger!" This can imply, "Do *not* come near!" But by its nature, the call system communicates only *positive* statements: "Here's food," "Here's danger," or "Here I am, over here!" and no negative ones. Blending of call elements, however, introduces the feature of negation, Hockett and Ascher argue. It can do so as follows: Suppose a call had elements A B C D and signified food. Suppose then that another call, signifying danger, had elements E F G H. Now suppose a new situation including *both* food and danger and an individual wants to communicate both these elements simultaneously in one call. He makes up a new call that is a kind of compromise between the two other calls, and it comes out with the elements A B G H. Now A B C D no longer means only "food," it means "food and no danger." And E F G H no longer means only "danger," it means "danger and no food." In that case, they could invent yet a fourth signal, with the leftover elements, C D E F, which would now mean "*no* food and *no* danger." Thus the concept of negation has entered the signal system. Once a blend such as A B G H has occurred and then been accepted and diffused throughout the community of primates using this call system, it *can* logically lead to the conceptualization of negation. But will it do so? Or under what conditions will it do so?

We can postulate that there would have to be certain *psychological* developments as preconditions for this conceptual one. Freud argued in his paper "On Negation" (1925b), since the concept of negation does not appear in the unconscious, negation must be tied up with the process of repression. Repression is the primal act of negation. At the same time, the *conscious* use of negation makes it possible to deal with the repressed material, so long as it is denied. Therefore we can deduce that the process that Hockett and Ascher describe could be carried to its logical extension of "CD equals NO danger" only by an animal that has learned how to repress, that is, an animal that is human, or close to human.

Norman O. Brown, in *Life Against Death* (1959) hypothesizes (p. 321) that "formal logic and the law of contradiction are the rules whereby the mind submits to operate under the general conditions of repression." Could that hypothesis not be extended to include all of language in general? We think it could. Then we could formulate it that language can arise only in an animal that has learned how to repress. If we ask then, what would account for the *need* to repress, in the postulated proto-human primate of those Miocene savannas, we have to answer, precisely the conditions we have just been describing: a new and challenging environment requiring more elaborate inter-individual dependency and cooperation, including the need to control intra-band aggression and sexuality. We can also include the developments in sexuality we have just been dealing with, which produce a conflict between parental— mother-infant—and mate-mate sexuality. Also, we need to point to the heightening of libidinal attachments and their prolongation with the in-creasing infantilization of the human animal. This would require repres-sion as a major mechanism because sexuality in this new context be-comes more problematical and more fraught with the possibility of conflict, both internal psychological conflict and interpersonal social conflict. It would include internal psychological conflict because of the competing claims upon the female from her mate and from her infant. And interpersonal conflict surrounding sexuality would be constantly potential in the potential competition among the males for sexual access to the available females. Such competition could seriously disrupt the solidarity of the adult male group, where cooperation is essential for the group-organized hunting activities. So in all of these respects we can postulate that mechanisms for blocking off at least some aspects of the experience of feelings of sexual arousal and gratification, and certainly for blocking off certain avenues of expression of sexual feelings, would be a necessary condition for the maintenance of some minimal level of group solidarity and cooperation necessary for these extremely vulnerable proto-hominid primates to survive under terrestrial conditions. Hence the need for repression as the primal mechanism for such control. An animal that has learned, thus, the technique of *repression*—essentially, pushing down and aside and forgetting, then forgetting that one has forgotten— is more capable of developing and expressing the concept of *negation*. The necessity of repression for any kind of organized social life is, of course, not a new discovery here. The notion is well developed in Freud's gloomy essay, *Civilization and its Discontents* (1930), a signal expression of the Freudian tragic view of life. Here we are elaborating on those views, as applied specifically to the conditions we postulate existed in the evolutionary phase of our ancestry during which formerly tree-living primates had come down to the ground but had not yet developed into a fully human form.

LANGUAGE, REPRESSION, AND PLAY

However, if language is built on repression, and repression seems to work in directions opposite those of play, it would appear that play is antithetical to language and not supportive of its development as we have been hypothesizing. The difficulty we typically have in seeing play elements or origins in "serious" customs or institutions (see Róheim 1943) is a mark of that repression characteristic of well-scoialized human beings. And one function of play is to evade such repression. In play we have the excuse, "It's not serious, we don't mean it, we're just playing around." In a playful situation a portion of the repressed content can be expressed, usually disguised, but especially in some innocuous-looking form. Freud has much to say about such phenomena in *Jokes and Their Relation to the Unconscious* (1905a) and in *The Psychopathology of Everyday Life* (1901). Play is also the assurance that the repression of unconscious forces is never quite complete, so that channels are open to reach those layers. Play is thus the particular opportunity for creative forces of the unconscious to assert themselves, as they do in art (see Kris 1952 and Endleman 1967, ch. 5). We can allow it, repressed human beings that we are, on the pretext that it is separate from things that "really matter."

Play in that context then, is seen as *antithetical* to language in that it undoes or compromises the processes of repression which are essential to the development of language. In this context, we are thinking of language as constituting a formal system of constructs and categories that constrain and channelize any confrontation with "reality." Anthropological linguistics shows that any particular language constitutes a certain arbitrary codification of reality that makes it difficult even to think in terms of any other categories. For example, Indo-European languages make it difficult to think about *time* except in *spatial* metaphors. It also makes difficult, if not impossible, certain kinds of playful verbal elaborations or recombinations. That is where poetry and myth come in. These major cultural inventions, in effect, come to the rescue of unconscious content that is obscured or prevented from reaching consciousness by the codifications of the language of that particular group. They are never entirely successful in this rescue mission. But they do serve as preservers of pre-linguistic and nonlinguistic play dealings with reality, by putting forth verbal structures that defy the laws of logic, especially the law of contradiction, in ways analogous to those of the dream, that ever-renewed resource of the unconscious. In other words, playful use of language can preserve much of the quality of what psychoanalysts call "primary process." Thus play is in many ways antagonistic to language, for language as codification is certainly an expression of secondary process.

However, earlier we discussed how play may have contributed to the *origins* of language. Are we not here faced with a contradiction? The answer is both yes and no. Yes, but contradictions are built into the essence of being human—as infants we are both utterly helpless and megalomanically omnipotent. We react one way with our intelligence and an opposite way with our feelings. We are often a battleground of Eros and Thanatos. We may have loving-sexual and aggressive-hostile feelings toward the same person, even at the same time. And so on.

And no, play as supportive of the origin of language and play as antithetical to language are not necessarily in contradiction: both conditions are true; both obtain; and they can have a kind of dialectical relationship to each other. They are in a constant state of tension. Language needs to formalize, i.e., to constrain, repress, and sublimate the forces of play. Still, it needs play for constant renewal and revitalization, and for breaking through the rigidities of formalization, especially those involved in the process of negation, and in the linkage of language with the rules of formal logic.

The need for an element in language that allows for a breaking out of formalization and the like would also suggest why formally constructed artificial languages that are intended to be universal, like Esperanto, have been such dismal failures, even though they would seem to be so reasonable as solutions to the tower of Babel of the hundreds of languages spoken and written in the world. It would also count as a factor in the difficulties of having language-translating machines.

We may ask what is the relevance of all of this in understanding human beings in relationship to society? The reply is that if we want to know what qualities are universal for all human beings, specific to this species, it is useful, in fact necessary, to understand where we came from in evolution and the particular kind of animal we became through the particular historical accidents of our evolutionary development. We have to note, of course, that these "accidents" were determined by other conditions.

The drying up of the forested areas of East Africa during the later part of the Miocene age was determined by other conditions, but was an accidental circumstance from the viewpoint of the evolution of particular species. So was the presence of particular types of arboreal primates in that environment at that time. So was the presence of particular kinds of large land-living mammal predators on the savannas in that period. We need also to point out that it was not a smooth evolutionary development, all harmoniously in one direction. The discrepancy between the pelvic development of the female, with its relatively small pelvic opening, and the increased size of the fetal head to accommodate the larger brain, resulting in the necessity for premature birth of the human infant, therefore its extreme helplessness and extreme malleability—these are all in a sense fortuitous developments. And they are fatefully consequential for the nature of the human species.

LANGUAGE NOT UNIQUE TO HUMANS?

These developments are related to the specificity of the *way* human beings have language and have culture. For long it was thought that this was the only species who had culture, and who had language. Now we know that this is not true. For culture: we can see all kinds of rudiments of culture, of ways of doing things that are passed on by deliberate teaching and learning, that are not determined by some kind of genetic code, in many other animals. This is certainly the case for our closest relatives among the primates that exist today, namely the chimpanzees, orangutans, gorillas, and gibbons. For long many thought anything chimpanzees in human captivity, such as in zoos or in circuses, can do that looks at all human has been taught to them by humans. But recent studies, such as those of Jane Goodall (1971) of chimps in the wild, indicate they will fashion a stick to a length and shape to stick into a termites' nest, then after the termites have crawled onto the stick, the chimp will pull it out to eat the termites. This is certainly tool-making and learning, rudiments of culture.

As for language, though none of the other primates have *speech*, chimpanzees at least have now been demonstrated to have a communication system that qualifies as language. Allen and Beatrice Gardner and their colleagues have taught infant chimpanzees to communicate gesturally by the American sign language for the deaf (Ameslan). The chimpanzees communicate in this gesture language not only with their human mentors but also with each other. (See Gardner and Gardner 1969, 1971, and an excellent popular book on this subject by Eugene Linden, *Apes, Men, and Language*, 1974.) Though psycholinguists like Roger Brown have challenged the claim that these chimps were learning and using language, arguing that what they were doing was only making *signs*, not manipulating *symbols*, that criticism has been disputed.

If we go back and reconsider what we really mean by language as a communicative system, we need to turn to what anthropological linguists such as Charles Hockett have set forth as the criteria for language. One of these is *displacement* (used here in a linguistic sense, not a psychoanalytic one—though the two are not unrelated) as has already been discussed in considering the Hockett–Ascher 1964 theory of human evolution. Displacement involves being able to use a communicative element in a situation other than the one in which it has originally been learned, or in which it has a direct bearing on action. This capacity is necessary in order to be able to talk *about* something, not just to communicate an immediate situation like danger or food, or an immediately present feeling like ouch! Only with this capacity can we talk about something that happened in the past, or will or might happen in the future, or something that's conditional, or something entirely hypothetical or fantasized.

Regarding this fundamental component of language, the Gardners' and others' research indicates clearly that the chimpanzees under study have this capacity and do in fact use it. A chimp learns a gesture sign like the one for "out"—as in go out, come out—or a sign for "ball," and then later uses this sign in other situations, communicating both ways with human interlocutors and also with other chimps. Hockett, in an earlier, general book on linguistics (1958), set forth a list of seven criteria for language, stating all must be present. One is displacement, as just discussed. The other six are: duality, productivity, arbitrariness, interchangeability, specialization, and cultural transmission.

Duality means the communication system is patterned in two ways: it has a phonological system—a set of different sounds—and a grammatical system, i.e., a set of rules for the ways the sound combinations are put together to constitute units of meaning. *Productivity* means the animal can generate and understand an infinite number of messages put together from a finite number of meaningful units which in speech are called morphemes. (Blending, mentioned earlier, of smaller constituent elements into new combinations, is one of the methods by which we get productivity.) *Arbitrariness* means there is no obvious similarity between a plereme and its meaning. (A plereme is the smallest meaningful unit combining a number of building blocks of communication, which in speech would be a morpheme, combining the sound elements called phonemes.) *Interchangeability* means that any organism equipped to send a message must be able to receive one. *Specialization* means that the behavior triggered by any particular communicative behavior is not directly related to the physical consequences of the message. And *cultural transmission* means just what it suggests, that the transmission of the communication, to qualify as language, must be carried out by teaching and learning on an inter-individual basis, and not through genetic codes and the like.

Hockett had earlier credited the present-day apes with possessing, in the wilds, the rudiments of cultural transmission, displacement, interchangeability, and specialization. Roger Fouts (in work reported by Linden 1974) has trained chimps in gestural sign language at the Institute for Primate Studies in Oklahoma and claims his trained chimps' use of a gestural sign system satisfies the conditions of duality, productivity, and arbitrariness. The sign language itself has the property of duality of patterning; it is evidently arbitrary; and the already trained chimps do use the signs and elements productively, e.g., using the sign for dirty as a cuss word, and inventing new signs like the combination of "fruit" and "drink" for watermelon, and those for "water" and "bird" for swan. Fouts (as of the time of Linden's writing) expects to be able to show that the already trained chimpanzees will teach the "language" to other chimpanzees that have been introduced into the chimp colony, and that as trained females like Washoe, the first one, have babies, they will teach this language to their young, thus demonstrating cultural transmission decisively.   '

Thus, if the Gardners, Fouts, and Linden are right, we can no longer continue to think of language as an exclusively human attribute, as has long been believed and as has been a basic assumption in all of Western thought.[1]

However, even if this new evidence challenges the notion that language is a distinctively and exclusively human attribute and capacity, it does not necessarily challenge the hypothetical process of human evolution that we have postulated earlier. For that process refers specifically to the development of human *speech*-language.[2] Also, if we are arguing that a particular set of attributes is a *universal* characteristic of all members of a species, it is not logically necessary to be able to say it is found *only* in this species and in no other.

However, the evidence of the gesture-communicating chimpanzees does raise questions about the validity of the hypotheses expounded above, about the relationships between the development of speech-language, in the evolution of man, and other psychological characteristics that make us distinctively human. Central here are cognitive capacities, which have been thought until now to be distinctive of our species and are hypothesized (in the theory developed above) as being closely linked to the development of speech-language: namely, the thinking capacities of memory, foresight, negation, interrogation, and conditionality. One can raise the question whether these capacities can be associated with a purely *gestural* kind of communicative system such as the Ameslan that the Gardners' and Fouts' chimpanzees have learned.

One interesting aspect of this is the question of *negation*. In the theory expounded above, we link negation as a cognitive capacity with the phenomenon of repression, hypothesizing that only a distinctively human animal, or one very much on the way toward becoming human, utilizes this most elemental of defense mechanisms. What then about the "talking" chimpanzees? Do they indicate evidence of the capacity for negation? The answer is evidently yes: these chimpanzees have learned a sign for negation, and use it appropriately. They can and do say "no" in answer to sign questions like "Washoe want fruit?" and they can use the sign for "no" as a modifier in "two-word" or "three-word" declarative sentences.

Now of course we do not know anything about these apes' unconscious; they have not yet started telling the human companion-mentors their dreams. Therefore we have no way of knowing whether they "have no negation in the unconscious" as Freud argues for humans. But they certainly do have in their conscious communicative behavior. We also do not know (and probably will not be able to find out) if they have therefore also experienced the phenomenon of repression as a precondition for their being able to use the concept of negation in their communications, in contrast to an ostensibly purely affirmative message process used in a pure call system. They might very well have such psychological complexity. Chimpanzees are, after all, not representative of our putative *ancestors*, but rather our cousins, who have had a long evolutionary history of their own, probably from common ancestors (to ours), probably even earlier than the arboreal period of the ancestors of humans who later came down from the trees. The phylogenetic development of the chimpanzees may well have involved some processes rather parallel to those of the human beings.

HEWES' GESTURE THEORY

The evidence of chimpanzees like Washoe has been used by another anthropologist, Gordon Hewes (1971a, 1973), to back up a theory of the origin of human language quite different from the one argued by Hockett and Ascher. Basically Hewes theorizes that our ancestors first developed language in the form of a *gesture* system and only much later in the vocal-auditory form of a speech-language.

Hewes argues from the fact that the archaeological and fossil evidence on proto-human ancestors like the Australopithecines—there is doubt as to whether they had *speech*, though it is likely they could *sing*—indicates tool-using and tool-making. (As Goodall saw, contemporary chimpanzees are capable of both.) These capacities indicate use of visual-motor channels of the brain. The visual, kinesthetic, and cognitive pathways employed in tool-making and tool-using coincide with those which would have been required for a gestural language system. These are not the same as those involved in speech, which utilize the vocal-*auditory* channel. This latter implies surmounting a neurological barrier, namely associating visual stimuli with sounds. Manipulation of the hand in using things such as stones that are ready at hand, and later in deliberately making tools, can be described as using the hands *propositionally*— as distinct from simple bodily reaction to the immediate here and now, to the stimuli coming right at this moment from the environment. Then, as life for this proto-human animal became more complex and demanding, pressure for propositional communication mounted. Then it would be natural for this animal to exploit the same ability that was used in propositionally employing the hands in making and using tools, to program motor actions in gestural communication.

We can ask if there is supportive evidence for these hypotheses; for the theory that gestural communication language preceded vocal language. For example, if phylogenetically one feature or capacity appeared earlier in evolution than another, one could expect this to show also in the ontogenetic development of the individual. In fact, we find that both deaf human infants and chimpanzees such as Washoe of the Gardner-Fouts studies learn their first gestural sign long before normal human infants say their first word. This suggests that human beings are equipped ontogenetically—and therefore we may deduce phylogenetically—for gestural language before we are equipped for speech. Also at birth, the normal present-day human infant's supralaryngeal tract—which is believed to distinguish a primate who can speak from one who cannot— more closely resembles that of the Neanderthal Man than it does that of an adult modern man. (The supralaryngeal tract is the area of the vocal apparatus necessary for the generation of consonants and vowels.) The Neanderthal's supralaryngeal tract is different from that of modern man in a way that leads researchers to believe that the Neanderthals could not generate the full range of sounds possible for modern man. Perhaps, Lieberman and Crelin 1971 speculate, this inflicted upon the Neanderthals a competitive disadvantage relative to the more capable—and fully modern *Homo sapiens*—Cro-Magnon contemporaries. We can therefore speculate that since the Neanderthals already had a fairly complex culture, they must have been able to make symbolic manipulations and would, therefore, most likely have had some kind of communication system, which, if not fully vocal, must have been gestural. So reasons Hewes. Neanderthals were, or course, relatively late in the fossil history of man, i.e., late Pleistocene period. Much earlier hominid types, either ancestral to or collateral to *Homo sapiens*, show definite evidence of tool-making and tool-using. These were the Australopithecines (or South-African Man-Apes) with definitely associated tools. And later, all the varieties of types current anthropologists call *Homo erectus*, like Pithecanthropous Erectus (Java Man) and Sinanthropus Pekinensis, or Peking Man, and so on. Their supralaryngeal tracts suggest that they probably did *not* have speech. But their tool-making and tool-using suggests capacities that could have been expressed in gestural language. Another line of evidence in support of Hewes's theory is that *terrestrial* primates (as contrasted with arboreal ones) inhabiting savanna territory today do seem to communicate more by gesture than their jungle counterparts, according to Altmann (1967).

How would this gestural theory of language origins relate then to the Hockett and Ascher reconstruction? In the kind of hunting economy Hockett-Ascher postulate our ancestors developing on the East African savannas, it is conceivable that some gestural communication was used. But it would not for long be adequate. There is a limit to the distance over which hand gestures would be visible, let alone decipherable. Silent gestures would, it is true, excel over vocal calls where the hominids did not want to reveal their presence, or scare away the game, but there would be a distance limit. They could also not be used at night. Additionally, there is an obvious conflict between using hands to carry or throw weapons and using them for gestural signals. Hewes, in presenting this theory, admits these limitations. He also indicates another one: that a sign lexicon is likely to have a rather limited number of items, i.e., gestural signs, far less than the items in a spoken language.

It is open to speculation whether the ground-living emergent hominid hunter of the savannas had a range of vocal calls first, or a set of sign-gestures first, or was developing both simultaneously. The general line of development was toward the freeing of the hands and therefore the snout, therefore the flattening of the whole contour of the face, therefore room in the skull structure for a more vaulted dome holding a larger more complex brain. That whole line of development would suggest a movement in the direction away from elaborating hand gestures and toward the elaboration of vocal calls and other vocal messaging.

However, the recently studied chimpanzees demonstrate that an animal at this evolutionary level can have a gestural communication system that qualifies by certain criteria as language, without having speech language. But we know no instance of an animal having a speech language without gestural communication or at least the capacity for it. That suggests a certain sequential pattern. The Australopithecine and the Neanderthal evidence, as well as the use of gestures in a linguistic way by deaf human infants and by chimpanzees earlier than normal human infants' use of vocal language, all point in the same direction.

Still, the limitations on the use of purely gestural communication for the emerging savanna hunters just referred to would put a selective pressure on this animal to develop more adequate communication devices. That would necessitate development of the vocal-auditory direction. That is what Hewes hypothesizes for the *later* stage of development. How much later, and when, is still a matter of controversy. The Hockett-Ascher theory postulates the transition to speech-language as having been completed by the beginning of the Pleistocene, i.e., at least a million years ago. Other anthropologists contest that date, arguing it must have come much later. Hewes hypothesizes that the whole cultural complex in reference to tools found in the Lower and Middle Paleolithic—Old Stone Age—hand-axe traditions, could have been accomplished *without* spoken language, and with only imitative learning and perhaps gestural language. The Neanderthals, coexisting with *sapiens* types till quite late, probably did not have the anatomical apparatus necessary for the production of speech. And the various *Homo erectus* types had brains substantially smaller than *sapiens*, and probably without the elaborated development of the right hemisphere that makes possible speech and the symbolic manipulations using it. Therefore it is argued that there is a good case for postulating that speech language was achieved only in geologically recent times, perhaps 50,000 years back. By this argument, the rapid appearance and multiplication of modern man (*Homo sapiens*) roughly about 40,000 years ago, can be seen as an adaptation to spoken language, which in turn would explain what comes across as a quantum jump in human biological *and* cultural evolution at that time. It would also explain why *sapiens* displaced the Neanderthals and other *Homo erectus* types everywhere, beating them out in the evolutionary struggle, though it is possible there was interbreeding between those more primitve and the more modern types.

According to Hewes' theory, as that later stage developed, the gestural language did not simply disappear. Rather it remained and developed in certain aspects of this animal's communicative functioning. Hewes sees Upper Paleolithic art—e.g., the cave paintings—as "frozen gestures," and also notes that Chinese and Egyptian hieroglyphics—of a much later period—had many representations of arm gestures. Hewes hypothesizes that the two channels—the earlier visual-gestural and the later vocal-auditory—went into a kind of division of labor.

The gestural-visual still is the mode for advanced propositional communication in higher mathematics, physics, chemistry, and biology. Examples are flowcharts, molecular structure diagrams, maps of all kinds, and any device we use to represent the interplay of complex variables that cannot easily be portrayed by the linear medium of speech.

On the other side, the vocal-auditory channel is the medium of close interpersonal communication. Hewes sees it in song, poetry, drama, religious ritual, and political discourse. One would have to note, of course, that not all of these are close interpersonal face-to-face communication. Prior to the development of modern electronic media, the participants would, however, be physically present.

Hewes thinks this kind of division of labor developed only under much later conditions, at a time long after speech developed into full-scale language. It would take a long process before speech could become completely conventionalized and removed from technological and gestural roots.

The complexities of the relationships between a Hewes gestural theory of language origin and a vocal one such as that of Hockett and Ascher suggest that it is unlikely that any monistic theory of language origin will be entirely satisfactory. We can argue that there are bound to have been a variety of different communicative techniques developing in the hominids that were on their way to evolving into human beings. Gestures would be inadequate over long distances or at night. Calls work at a distance but are unlikely in intimate face-to-face communication. Much interpersonal communication must have been phatic, as much of it still is today. Such communications include both vocalizations and body language, whether intentional or unconscious (see Birdwhistell, *Kinesics*, 1970). Seeing language development as adaptive in an evolutionary sense (i.e., it had to serve some functions for the organism developing it) is correct but incomplete, since it suggests that communicative behavior is all utilitarian. We must consider play, as having had a part in the origins of language. Some of the evidence about the recent gesture-language-learning chimpanzee is suggestive here. Washoe uses a sign like that for "tickle" to ask her human interlocutor to engage in roughhouse play with her. Chimpanzees in the wild certainly engage in a lot of play. (We don't know how much of this is connected with gesturing activity.) And the "talking" chimpanzees Washoe and Lucy playfully combine gesture units in new combinations. Washoe invented a sign for "bib" on her own. Lucy invented one for "radish" combining signs for "cry" and for "hurt."

LANGUAGE AND PLAY

We suggest that the relationship between language and play is a dialectical one. Play must have had a part in the origins of language. Also, any developed language constrains the free flow of fantasy from the unconscious and preconscious and necessarily limits the particular ways in which perceptions and affects may be organized into thoughts expressible linguistically. Therefore, in these respects, language is antithetical to play. It is antithetical to the freedom which is crucial to play. These two contradictory statements are both true. They are dialectically connected. Like myth and language, or art and language, play and language are in a constant state of creative tension with each other. Each strains at and constrains the other. Each, in so doing, infuses the other with something more. Language needs to formalize. It must have a structure. (And, if we are to believe Chomsky and his associates, all languages have a common "deep structure" that is a pan-human universal.) In having structure and formalization, it needs to constrain the forces of play. It must use repression and sublimation in opposition to play and in taming it. Still, it constantly needs the infusion of play as a force of constant renewal and revitalization. Free play is one of the major forces in the constant process of linguistic change. A language changes as its speakers and users playfully recombine its elements and invent new locutions, or recombinations of old ones, or new sense to old words and phrases, misspeak and thus transform its grammar and syntax. Play breaks through the rigidities of formalization, particularly those involved in the process of negation, and in the rules of formal logic.

It certainly seems likely that the playful-erotic situations of mothers and infants were at least part of the context in which vocalization developed in the direction of speech-language. (They could also have been part of the context for the elaboration of gestural elements into a gestural-language system.) If the mother's hands are busy holding the infant and her body busy giving it suck, her mouth and ears are free for other kinds of communication, and this would be vocal communication. So too for the play-erotic situations of adult males and females together. Evolutionary reconstructions that concentrate only on utilitarian-adaptive functions are incomplete. We need to include as well ludic situations.

LANGUAGE AND SEX DIFFERENCES

Regarding playful-erotic situations between men and women: It is legendary among travelers to foreign lands that the best place to learn a new language is in bed. Perhaps this can be applied to theories about the origin of language.

The female's world of communications includes both her mate-mate sexuality with her man and her mother-infant sexuality with her children. Thus it can be said that the female lives more of her life closer to the phatic body communications that go back farther in human evolution than the development of speech language and the formalization of thought in logical structures, which in many respects have been more the property of the world of adult males. A related observation is the fact that the physical dimorphism between males and females is greater in the human species than in most of the related primates and most other mammals, in fact. (There are racial variations in this, of course.) The down-from-the-trees reconstructions suggest that the development of the hunting economy favored such dimorphism as a correlate of the emerging sexual division of labor, the adult males hunting large game animals, the females and juveniles collecting wild food plants and catching small game animals close to a home camp. Such an economy would put selective pressure on the animal to develop differential body specialization in the two sexes to adapt to these different roles and, along with that, differential psychological and behavioral attributes. These would include differential approaches to language learning and use. Speech language must have developed both by elaboration and blending of distant call elements (Hockett–Ascher view) and by elaboration and blending of close interpersonal vocal elements associated with phatic ties. These two avenues differentiate, basically, according to sex: the line from calls from the world of adult males and that from vocal-phatic cries, that of females and children. Many languages of today still have different forms, indicated, for example, by different inflections for when a female is speaking than for a male speaking, and some have almost distinct dialects for the two sexes. Such developments are probably later elaborations of an evolutionarily much earlier bifurcation along sex lines.

Still, one may ask: If the line from phatic vocalizing to speech-language emerges from the world of adult females *and children*, and since half of the latter would be males, does this not mess up the theory? In reply, we can say: it would, if we were arguing that the language worlds of males and females are entirely distinct and apart. They never are. Nor are other aspects of psychological functioning of females and males. Because as children they were part of the world of "women and children" (still true today in the vast majority of cultures of the world) the males grow up never being entirely foreign to the linguistic reflections of that world of body-feeling of the women's round of life. This is both essential for, and makes possible, cross-sex communication at all levels. In referring to differentiation, however, we are pointing to *relative* emphases. The world of Logos has been predominantly a male world, and has probably been so in all cultures where it is highly developed. Correspondingly, the world of body-feeling has been predominantly a feminine world. To the extent that this is true, we may be dealing here with a very deeply rooted psycho-biological difference between the sexes. (Further implications of this argument, and the counter-arguments made against it by modern feminists, will be discussed in the next part.)

Certainly cultures differ on this point. They may either deemphasize or accentuate this fundamental difference. However, it is unlikely it can be eliminated entirely.

MORE THOUGHTS ON FRONTAL COITUS

There is more to be said about the relation of the invention of the frontal position in sexual intercourse to the evolution of human sexuality. This position has fundamental implications for psychosexual development. As noted, it fosters assimilation and diffusion of mother-infant and mate-mate sexualities. The context is neoteny, therefore prolongation of infantile responses to the world, as well as the constant, precocious, ubiquitous, and polymorphous qualities of human sexuality. All of these in turn are adaptations to the problems of that evolutionary period that saw the emergence of humanlike animals.

This diffusion of the two types of sexuality, where the mother is sexually connected both with her infant and with her adult male mate, must certainly promote all kinds of father-child rivalries and animosities. Hence some of the roots of major aspects of the *father's* side in both kinds of oedipal triangles. Additionally, mother-child animosities and rivalries would be involved. For the female in coitus, the male is similar in many ways to a suckling child. But so, in a sense, is the female to the male. She, like a suckling infant, is receiving, through an erogenous body orifice, life-giving substances from a protruberance of the face-to-face partner's body. Thus we have the breast-penis equation of infantile sexual fantasy, as elaborated long ago by Freud. In fact, in this specific respect, *she* is more like a suckling infant than *he* is. Psychoanalysis teaches us about the re-arousal of unconscious infantile sexual fantasy in the sexual activities of human adults.

The point here then is to show some of the *evolutionary* roots of these phenomena and to emphasize how their rootedness in human evolution gives them a pan-human universality. This is not just mammalian behavior, but the behavior of a very special primate. The universality of primary incest taboos—mother-son, brother-sister, and father-daughter, and their homosexual coordinates, and of oedipal phenomena, ignoring their minor variations with social structure—is also illuminated by this evolutionary perspective. (On these universalities, and refutation of the counter-arguments of some anthropologists, see chapter 2 above; also Endleman 1967:34; Anne Parsons 1964; Róheim 1950.) This evolutionary view also puts a different light on the phenomenon of *repression*, the major defense-mechanism concept of psychoanalysis. (Whether this is an exclusively human phenomenon has now become more controversial, since gesture-language-learning chimpanzees indicate they can deal with and utilize the concept of negation; it is doubtful that we shall be able to find out the intrapsychic meaning of that phenomenon in that species.)

For humans, we can certainly say this: repression is the mechanism that an infantilized human ape with a burgeoning polymorphous sexuality imposes on himself. He has the aid of those giants, the nurturant and often terrifying lover-haters, the parents. And this repression is in the service of regulating the potential chaos of intermingling and potential fusion of infant-mother and mate-mate sexualities, and the need to have some kind of boundary-maintaining mechanisms within the potentially explosive situation of a close nuclear family or its surrogate. It also arises from the need for adult males to maintain a solidarity of cooperation in hunting, which sexual rivalries could destory. And we could extend the argument to the need for solidarity among a group of cooperating adult females too.

Language flows from this process (among others) and helps to consolidate it. Play helps in the development of language, and also works against it and against repression in the service of polymorphous, mostly unconscious libidinal forces. Repression is critical for the resolution of the Oedipus complex and for internalization of the incest taboos, while play and its derivatives in poetry, art, and myth repeatedly break through these constrictions. Repression makes possible the whole complex of mastery on which man embarked by changing from dinner to diner on the Miocene African savannas, and the peculiarly "crazy rationality" by which he has constructed a whole world around himself, substituting his man-made environment (culture) and the constrictions of Logos, for instinct and the predation conditions of nature.

CHAPTER SIX

Totem and Taboo **Again?**

Freud argued in *Totem and Taboo* (1913) that resolution of the Oedipus and imposition of the incest taboos, which are obviously two parts of the same thing, are the essentials for human beings to develop any kind of civilization (Freud's term for what anthropologists call "culture"). The evolutionary reconstruction I here propound may be taken as a revised version of *Totem and Taboo*.

That work of Freud's has been subjected to scorn by most anthropologists, and to neglect or indifference as "speculation" by many psychoanalysts. It is therefore useful to reconsider it in some detail here.

First, a brief summary of what Freud actually wrote in that work. On the basis of hypotheses of Darwin and of Robertson Smith, Freud assumed that the social organization of primeval mankind was a Cyclopean family consisting of a totally dominant father monopolizing the females and of submissive and subordinate offspring. Freud studied secondary sources derived from the then available anthropological accounts of totemism in existing primitive societies. He was impressed that its crucial elements consisted of powerful taboos on the eating of the totemic animal and on sexual relations between a man and a woman of the same totem. Noting the psychoanalytic discovery of totemistic fantasies in children in modern societies far removed from primitive beginnings, Freud argued that the phobic reactions of a child toward the particular animal that had the most fantasy significance for the child could best be understood as symbolic displacement from feelings and fantasies toward the *father*. He also accepted Robertson Smith's hypothesis that the sacramental meal, eating the totem animal, is an essential part of the complex of totemism. He then brilliantly put together these different lines of evidence and speculation and put forth his famous hypothesis about the origin of human culture.

It was this: that at one point the sons got together and finally rebelled against the tyranny of the father and his monopolization of the women, and in concert killed the father and ate his body. Then, however, the other side of their typical filial ambivalence toward the father came to the fore. Since they also loved and admired him, they now felt an overpowering remorse. Their guilt then made the father in some ways more powerful in death than in life. For the sons now instituted the primal taboos of totemism: thou shalt not kill the totem animal (symbolically; the father) and thou shalt not have sex with the women of the totemic group (i.e., the mother and the sister). Basically, these correspond to the two taboos of the Oedipus complex, against incest with the mother and against killing the father. Thus is begun human civilization.

Freud insists in this work that this must have been an actual *deed*, and that the memory of it and the consequent guilt and expiatory taboos have been carried down in the biological inheritance of human beings ever since that time. Thus Freud was accepting a Lamarckian assumption that acquired characteristics, in this case a complex psychological pattern, can be inherited.

(Parenthetically be it noted that Freud here explicitly departed from the perspective he arrived at in relation to "remembered" sexual seductions which he had earlier thought to be the starting point of his hysterical patients, which he later concluded were most likely not actual events but *fantasies,* and that it was these fantasies that had had such powerful psychological effect. According to many commentators, this revision marks the beginning of psychoanalysis proper, turning, as it did, the attention from external events to intrapsychic functioning, a key element in psychoanalytic psychology. Here, in *Totem and Taboo,* Freud explicitly rejected the hypothesis that the parricide and incest of the story were *fantasies*, rather than actual events, in a manner which seems to most psychoanalysts inconsistent with what he himself developed as the essential spirit of psychoanalytic inquiry.)

Anthropologists have been almost unanimous in criticism and rejection of this work. (Important exceptions will be discussed anon. See Derek Freeman for careful review of the whole controversy—Freeman 1967.) Some, in a more charitable vein, say that Freud could not have known any better, given the state of anthropological knowledge at that time. They find no substantiation for the Darwinian hypothesis that early man had a social organization like the one Darwin thought was that of gorillas. Recent research on gorillas (e.g., Schaller 1963) contradicts what Darwin thought to be the case. Second, all the recent work we have been referring to, connecting paleontological evidence with ethological studies of existing primates, suggests that early man did not have anything like the intense dominance hierarchies that this part of Freud's hypothesis presupposed. Another point is that anthropological research since Freud's work contradicts the idea that the sacramental meal is an essential and typical feature of totemism (Freeman 1967).

Then there is the Lamarckian hypothesis that memories of any such events have been transmitted genetically over these thousands of generations. Modern genetics (see Dobzhansky 1962) finds no evidence whatever that any phenotypical changes in individuals, in physical characteristics that have been environmentally produced, can be genetically transmitted. If that is true for physical features, how much more unlikely that any *psychological* characteristic, such as Freud postulated, has been passed down in this way (Freeman 1967). Of course, it is unnecessary at this late date to beat this phylogenetic issue to death, since all responsible scholars, including psychoanalysts, find Freud wrong on this Lamarckian line.

If we ask, then, what is left of the *Totem and Taboo* speculations, the answer comes from Róheim. Róheim pointed out that the phylogenetic assumptions were unnecessary, and that *Totem and Taboo* has much to teach us if we replace the phylogenetic formulation with an *ontogenetic* one. That is, the oedipal issues and the great twin taboos against incest and parricide continue to be alive in succeeding generations not by genetic transmission but rather because the same dilemmas appear again and again in the individual growth and development of each human being.

As for the theory of an actual primal parricidal deed, one may wonder how Freud could have imagined that others would accept his formulation of this as a literal event. Most psychoanalysts find this an unfounded speculation, and one that is irrelevant to an appreciation of Freud's clinical insights. Freeman (1967) and others have noted that in the same work Freud himself offered an alternative hypothesis along the lines of *fantasies* rather than deeds. Freud wrote that when we inquire into the behavior of neurotics,

> We find no deeds, but only impulses and emotions, set upon evil ends but held back from their achievement. What lie behind the sense of guilt of neurotics are always *psychical* realities and never factual ones. What characterizes neurotics is that they prefer psychical to factual reality and react just as seriously to thoughts as normal person do to realities.
>
> May not the same have been true of primitive men? We are justified in believing that, as one of the phenomena of their narcissistic organization, they overvalued their physical acts to an extraordinary degree. Accordingly,

the mere hostile impulse against the father, the mere existence of a wishful phantasy of killing and devouring him, would have been enough to produce the moral reaction that created totemism and taboo. (Freud 1913:159)

Freeman points out that that theory would be entirely acceptable and tenable in the light of modern knowledge (Freeman 1967:19), for it is in accord with basic psychoanalytic knowledge about the power of fantasy. In the light of Freud's own prior development of fantasy theory, it is surprising to find him, some years later, insisting on the reality of the *deed* as an actual historical event. Freeman devotes a major part of his essay to an exploration of *why* Freud made such an insistence, in terms of Freud's own history and particularly his relationship with his father.

A different answer to the question about the status of the events Freud postulated as deeds comes from a provocative paper of Margaret Mead called "*Totem and Taboo* Reconsidered with Respect" (Mead 1963). Perhaps, Mead asked, Freud in insisting these were deeds, not fantasies, was right after all, except about *time*. What if this kind of event *had* happened, not in the shadowy past of our own species, but rather at some much earlier evolutionary period? Suppose this had happened at a time before this species developed the "distinctively human growth curve with its early spurt toward apparent maturity, and then the long slow plateau of latency followed by a second spurt at adolescence"? (Mead 1963:193). Might it not be, Mead asks, that the Oedipus complex goes back to a real situation in which sons at puberty, reached at an age of seven or eight years without the long latency period, were as big as their fathers, who were then already declining in vigor and unable to withstand the sons. The "primal crime" would have been, then, deeds, committed over and over for hundreds of thousands of years, until the evolutionary changes transformed these prehumans into humans, by bringing in the latency delay, a characteristic peculiar to man among the primates.

Such a reconstruction, of course, leaves out something that for Freud was critical: the sons' later remorse, guilt, and establishment of penitential institutions. In Mead's version, the later changes that put an end to the generationally-repeated killing of fathers by pubertal sons, would have come about by the shift to latency, and the changed growth pattern, such that boys of six to eight or so would be physically much smaller and weaker than their fathers. Hence they would be unable, feasibly, to carry out the parricide. One could think of a transitional period in which the period of latency was in process of becoming longer, and during that era, some kind of ancestral memory of earlier parricidal acts would be maintained. Then the parricide would later be renounced, with the rationalization that sheer physical strength was not up to the task.

AN UPDATED TOTEM AND TABOO

We are here propounding a kind of revised updated version of *Totem and Taboo*. This verion would avoid the criticisms that were levelled at Freud's version of earlier in this century. It would do so, first, by being built upon up-to-date anthropological knowledge both of presently existing primitive societies and of the evidence for early man and his immediate ancestors that is vastly more adequate than that available to Freud at the time he wrote. We also have vastly better information on other living primates collateral in the evolutionary line to man than was available six or seven decades ago. Second, we do not require Freud's Lamarckian phylogenetic hypotheses. We can rely instead on Róheim's ontogenetic theory, which explains more of the available facts. Thus we can explain both the origins and the persistence of the Oedipus complex and incest taboos as fundamentals of human civilization that have been persistent through all that we know of human history. The Oedipus complex, and the necessity of its resolution in each individual in each generation, and the incest taboos and the taboos on parricide, are rightly regarded by Freud as the foundation stones for human civilization. (On that point Freud's *Totem and Taboo* is still a monumental work.)

I take it as given that the Oedipus complex and the incest taboos are in fact essentially universal. These universalities are in turn connected with other features of our evolution already touched on: the frontal coital position; its consequence of diffusion and confusion of mate-mate with mother-infant sexualities, the necessities of control of genital sexuality within the family and of control of sexual rivalries among cooperating males.

The lengthening latency period is multiply significant here. It lessens the extent of sexual drive in growing-up males, making it less likely they would attempt to challenge the sexual possession held by the father, a challenge physically dangerous while the sons are far from full body growth. Chance and Mead (1935) have suggested that in an ancestral primate-hominid band those young males whose sexual drives overcame them before their physical prowess was sufficiently developed and their bodily strength great enough to enable them to challenge mature males successfully would have been driven off or killed. In either case their genetic potential would be lost. Therefore only those able to restrain themselves would father the next generation. Therefore there would be a long-term selection for the capacity to delay genital gratification. The long-term evolutionary process would then be a combination of genetic selection and cultural institutions. Culturally defined controls in the form of the incest taboos would be supported by bio-psychological processes that are summarized in the term latency. Psychoanalytically, the meaning of latency is the maintenance for a period of about seven or eight years of the results of the resolution of the Oedipus complex, with repression as the primary psychological mechanism, and the toning down of the whole sexual drive during this period, allowing the completion of body growth and the use of that period for the acquisition of the basic utilitarian skills of the culture.

However, some observers may at this point raise the objection that the latency period may not in fact be a universal feature of mankind. Some anthropological studies indicate that children in the age range between five and puberty may have quite an active sex life, including genital contact, at least with other children. Malinowski's celebrated account of the Trobriand Islanders of Northwest Melanesia certainly indicated that. And for a number of other tribal societies there seems to be a good deal of sexual play in that age period. It also seems to occur in some segments of modern industrial societies.

In answer some psychoanalysts have shifted their statements about latency. Rather than referring to a complete cessation of sexual activity in that phase, they refer to a shift in the *relative* strength of the sexual drive during this phase as compared with the pre-genital sexuality of infancy and early childhood up to the oedipal phase on one side, and the powerful strength of the sexual drive from the onset of puberty on.

If sexuality is originally as potentially polymorphous and constant and lifelong as Freud has—I think correctly—claimed, it is not inconsistent with the theory of latency to allow for the possibility in some societies of *playful* and relatively polymorphous expressions of sexuality in the age period from five years to puberty. The Trobriand accounts certainly look like play rather than consequential genital object relations. In fact, in that tribe, the adults look upon such sexual play as precisely that, and when it includes attempts or even successes at actual coitus between a boy and a girl of that age range, the adults look at it with amused toleration, commenting on the absurdity of children thinking they are grown up. Also, interestingly enough—since their culture provides no theory of a connection between intercourse and conception—they laughingly dismiss such juvenile erotica as unimportant, since "nothing can come of it," presumably meaning the girl could not get pregnant.

It is also significant that in all the tribal cases where the children of that age have coital relations, it is only with other children their own age, all pre-pubertal, and not with post-pubertal youngsters or adults. There is an exception, however, where such sexual contact is *imposed* on the pre-pubertal child by a perverse adult male. In these pre-pubertal contacts, there also seems to be strict observance of brother-sister incest taboos, as well as their extensions to clan brothers and sisters, such as, for the boy in a matrilineal clan, his mother's sister's daughter.

There is also work on the Australian aborigines which suggests that in some of these tribes at least there is plenty of sexual activity among children in this age range (see Róheim 1950). Margaret Mead noted that finding in Róheim's work. She commented as follows:

> It is latency [Mead meaning here the growth plateau in the period between age about five and puberty] that has given mankind time to utilize the cultural complexities he has invented. Róheim claimed that the Australian aborigines had no latency—in the familiar sense of absence of sexual preoccupation. Might we not say instead that the Australian aborigines did not *use* the period of latency, did not use the oedipal crisis, to free children for a period from their preoccupation with sexually mature adults? Australian aborigines would then be seen as . . . Homo Sapiens like ourselves, who had physically attained, but failed to make social use of the strange prolongation of the growth curve that makes a human youth mature at sixteen instead of at eight or nine. (Mead 1963:194)

This is to say that latency in one aspect is a biologically determined phase, which might or might not be utilized as a way of handling psychosexual development by taking the youngsters away from conscious sexual preoccupation and overt sexual activity. Interestingly, Mead's point also implies, as she elsewhere states more explicitly, that culturally *utilizing* this delay period in suppression of sexual activity and preoccupations is a mark of more *advanced* cultures. By this reasoning, the technological primitiveness of peoples like the Australian aborigines would be connected with this lack of cultural institutionalization of latency as a period of reduced sexual activity and preoccupation.

Freud had already hypothesized something along these lines in his *Autobiographical Study* (1925a) where he wrote:

> The period of latency is a psychological phenomenon. It can, however, only give rise to a complete interruption of sexual life in cultural organizations which have made the suppression of infantile sexuality a part of their system. This is not the case with the majority of primitive peoples.

(Parenthetically, that places Freud among those giving a culturally variable interpretation of the psychosexual stages, contrary to what his ill-informed critics believe to be his entirely *biologistic* orientation. Freud was, of course, always aware of cultural factors, even if he did not always place them at the center of his attention.) However, his saying here "the majority of primitive peoples" is probably not entirely accurate in the light of present-day anthropological knowledge. Not all of the present-day tribal peoples have the kind of sexual free-for-all in that later child-hood period that Malinowski described for the Trobriand Islanders and Róheim for Australian aborigines. From a psychoanalytic viewpoint, it is also oversimplifying to see sexual interruption during this phase as correlated directly with suppression of infantile sexuality. We would nowadays, with the influence of the ego psychology of Hartmann and others, see a great many other factors involved here.

(Parenthetically, again, thinkers following or influenced by the extreme versions of cultural relativism in anthropology of, roughly, the interwar period, will probably take exception to our here referring to some cultures as on a higher level of development than others. That extreme of cultural relativism tried to convince people that cultures may be different but are all equally valid as possible ways of dealing with the basic problems of human beings. It also pushed anthropologists to abandon the useful term "primitive" and even such a term as "preliterate" to refer to such tech-nologically unadvanced tribal societies, for fear of committing the dread sin of making value judgments. In some latter-day versions of this kind of simplistic thinking, it was even considered as bordering on "racism" to point out the technological primitiveness of tribal peoples who practice a hunting-and-gathering or early-horticultural way of life. Compromisers may emphasize that the differences being referred to are all concentrated on *technological* levels without implying that the technologically more complex is necessarily superior. However, there is at least implied a judgment that capacity for higher levels of technological development is connected with higher levels of ego development, and greater usage of resources within the generally human repertoire. That *is* a value judg-ment, and many would argue there is nothing objectionable about it. A mud hut is not the same as the Sistine Chapel. It is always dangerous, of course, to question liberal shibboleths such as the relativistic notion that all cultures are equal.)

On latency, present-day psychoanalysts no longer tend to use the term to mean that this period is completely devoid of sexual urges. There is a good deal of evidence in the clinical literature indicating the persistence in this period, in modern societies, of pre-genital sexual feelings ex-pressed in masturbation, in voyeuristic and exhibitionistic activity, and in sado-masochistic activities. And these, unless in extreme degrees, are not necessarily now seen as indicators of pathology. As Blos expresses it, in his sensitive book about adolescence (Blos 1962), there is no new sexual *aim* in this period. Rather what changes is the growing degree of ego and superego controls over the basic sexual drives.

Cases like the Trobriand Islanders do not necessarily contradict that formulation. Their adherence to brother-sister incest avoidance rules and lack of child-adult relations certainly suggest the maintenance of ego controls, even if the degree of freedom of overt sexual activity, including imitation of adult intercourse, is vastly greater than typically found in modern societies. Also the fact that the sexual activities are among the children themselves and do not include adults supports the hypothesis that a function of this stage is to prevent a physically immature sub-adult from challenging the adult males' sexual possession of the adult females. It would also help explain why, where adult-child intercourse does occur, it is much more likely to be between adult male and juvenile female or, in the incestuous case, between father and daughter; also why father-daughter incest is behaviorally much more common than mother-son, and why the father-daughter incest taboo is usually less stringent and less intensely internalized on the part of the child than the mother-son incest taboo.

Father-daughter incest involving a juvenile female would not be likely to challenge the de-facto distribution of sexual power in favor of the adults—specifically the adult males—in the way in which son-mother incest would, or in fact any sexual contact between a juvenile male and an adult female. Anatomically, of course, coitus of adult female with juvenile male is simply that much less feasible, compared to that of adult male and juvenile female, to say nothing of the question of relative strength. In one sense, we can say that the resolution of the Oedipus complex in the boy, with his giving up the mother as a possible sexual object, serves as a protection against the potentially devastating blow to his narcissism that would be incurred if he attempted coitus with her and was simply too small. We also know from clinical evidence that the earlier castration anxiety includes such fantasies as being engulfed and swallowed up in the mother's large sexual organs, or the more terrifying fantasy of the *vagina dentata*, a fantasy that appears overtly in the myths and folklore of many tribal peoples.

The period of development of infantile sexuality and the Oedipus complex is one of rapid physical growth (see Comfort 1963). So is the period just preceding and culminating in puberty. Relatively, the period in between—the latency period—is one of diminished growth rate. If we conceptualize infantile sexuality and the Oedipus complex as rehearsals for pubertal and post-pubertal sexuality, the latency stage can be seen as one necessitated by the danger of competing sexually with adults during a phase at which the juvenile has yet to reach adult size and strength. Comfort takes that argument further: he likens the Oedipus complex to a temporary organ. He sees it occurring on a sensitive part of the curve of general bodily growth. At such a point, a small change in rates contributing to the total could produce a very large change in the duration of the organ by moving the end of existence all along the length of the plateau. Thus, under some circumstances it might continue to persist throughout the whole of the period we call the latency phase. In the normal course of modern human ontogenetic development, this is not what occurs. Comfort suggests that the evolutionary development of the unconscious appeared as a response to the need not to have the castration anxiety associated with the Oedipus complex—preceding it in the girl, following it in the boy—carry over at the conscious level throughout the latency phase. Comfort suggests that the same necessities contributed to the development of speech. It connects with the phenomenon of neoteny, i.e., infantilization, of the human species. That goes hand in hand with its apparent opposite, precocity. The sexuality of human beings seems precocious, as suggested in the phrasing of the infantile sexuality as a kind of rehearsal of puberty. While man is not the only animal where you find premature appearance, at least in fragmentary form, of physical or behavioral characteristics which can serve a definite function only at a much later stage of development, it is more extreme in the human species than in other animals.

It is, of course, an exaggeration and simplification to say that infantile sexuality is a rehearsal of pubertal and post-pubertal sexuality, at least it is not so in a simple straightforward way. Psychoanalysis is often accused by its critics of reading adult forms of sexual feeling and response back into very young children, even infants. That is an unfortunate impression an outsider might get from reading some of the Freudian literature. We have to qualify the picture. We do know a lot about infantile sexual fantasy, and there is no question that it does continue to play a role in the adult sexuality of all human beings, but usually in ways considerably transformed from the infantile forms. A main area of difference, of course, is that the infant and pre-pubertal child does not yet have the ego capacities clearly to distinguish fantasy from reality. His ego is far less structuralized than it will be later, and his superego undeveloped or archaic. All of this is different from the normal pubertal youngster and the later adult. Also the infantile sexuality is more directly and openly polymorphous, as contrasted with the subordination of oral, anal, and phallic modes and elements in the adult under the primacy of genitality. However, we still have to emphasize that there is a *continuity*, and to speak of the infantile as "rehearsal" of the pubertal and adult is one way of referring to that continuity. The intensity of libidinal feelings of the infant and pre-oedipal child, combined with limited internal controlling capacities and the necessity of several more years of soma growth, requires some devices to delay the full flowering of adult sexuality.

This connects with the need for time and freedom from countervailing internal or external pressures for the growing animal to acquire the basic elements of culture, which in humans means a very complex body of knowledge and skills (even in the simplest of hunting-gathering tribes), which can be passed down only by cultural transmission, by conscious or unconscious learning from intended or unintended teachers and models, and is not available by genetic transmission.

The *capacity* for such learning is of course genetically acquired. The anatomical basis for such capacity includes, specifically, features of the brain: its sheer size—compared to lower primates and to hominid ancestors—and the development of the neo-cortex and, specifically, the lopsided left hemisphere that includes the areas for speech. In fact, according to one theory (Krantz 1961) earlier hominids may not have attained a brain size adequate for speech (he and others estimate the minimal volume as 730 cc.) in individual development until the stage of nearly full adult growth and of sexual maturation (puberty). By this hypothesis, in the evolution toward the modern human, that development moved farther and farther back into childhood and infancy, now being reached in the human infant at the age of one year or so.

Thus, both the attainment of a brain size sufficient for symbolic thought and possibly for speech, and the development of sexuality have receded—in ontogenetic development—from puberty to an early stage of infancy (see A. E. Mourant, "The Evolution of Brain Size, Speech and Psychosexual Development," *Current Anthropology*, 1973). Mourant states that the onset of speech (in the individual) became dependent on psychosexual events "arising on the one hand from the evolution of 'built-in' responses, and on the other from the supply by cultural means of symbolic material for these responses to use." This is a cogent linkage of psychosexual development with the development of speech and symbolic thinking. This line of analysis connects well with the whole evolutionary-developmental picture we have been constructing in this part.

Mourant's analysis also provides another line of understanding of how and why the *sapiens* types of hominids displaced the other variants (Neanderthals and *Homo erectus* types), so that after about 40,000 years ago, none of the latter were left on the earth:

> Those communities where there was the best correlation between physical and cultural evolution were the ones which prospered and tended to survive in the course of natural selection, because they could devise better tools and the individuals composing them could spend more years learning to use them in the arts of winning food, finding or making shelter, and probably killing members of rival communities. (Mourant 1973:31)

RELATIONS TO SOCIOBIOLOGY

One may query at this point the connection between the line of analysis I have developed in these chapters and the recent revival of interest in the connections between sociology and biology in the work of the sociobiologists such as Edward O. Wilson (1975) and Pierre Van den Berghe (1978a, 1978b). That work is attacked by most sociologists as being guilty of reducing social phenomena to biological ones, or of attributing to genes what should properly be attributed to culturally transmitted learning.

This appears to be a new version of the old environment-versus-heredity controversies. It should be evident by now that neither side in such controversy can be entirely right. Nothing in human behavior could be the product only of environment, or only of genetic predispositions. These must always intersect in many ways. The sociobioloists, in their drawing on *ethological*-animal studies, however, seem to see human behavior as considerably more determined by built-in species characteristics, biologically derived, than do most sociologists who have been trained to think in terms of sociological-environmental forces as the primary determinants.

From the perspective I am developing here, however, the sociobiologists are to be criticized not for what has been perceived as their biological reductionism, but rather for trying to link the two levels, biology and sociology, without taking into account the crucial intervening level, that is, of course, the psychological, and in this case the psychoanalytic-psychological. Psychoanalysis is *the* psychology that is best equipped to make the linkage between the biological on one side and the socio-cultural on the other. More than a bio-sociology, we need a bio-*psycho*-sociology.

Earlier efforts to link sociology with biology, specifically with evolutionary theory, led in the nineteenth century to Social Darwinism, adapting what these theorists conceived to be Darwin's ideas about the survival of the fittest to sociological schemata. It was, of course, partly the blatant ideological bias of the social Darwinists that gave that version of bio-sociology a bad name for later sociology. The theory served as a justification for the dominance of the elites of advanced industrial capitalism in terms of a putative biological superiority. (Obviously, if they were surviving best, they must be the fittest people of modern society.) Therefore, so the social-Darwinist theory ran, any efforts to alleviate the dismal conditions of the people at the bottom of society were misguided, since such people were obviously the least "fit," and must be so on a biological basis. Therefore helping them would only impede the evolutionary progress of the whole society. Variations on such ideas saw different races of mankind as being on different levels of superiority or inferiority on a biological basis. The past association of versions of bio-sociological thinking with ideological class or racial bias led egalitarian-minded sociologists and other social scientists to avoid any kind of connection with biology entirely. A similar cast of mind leads some sociologists or students of sociology to react very negatively to the idea of meritocracy, i.e., some kind of stratification of society based on differences in ability levels, some aspect of which is probably determined by genetic inheritance. By implication, those offended by this idea seem to think that to consider that there could be anything genetic at all in individual human differences marks one automatically as a racist or worse.[1]

The situation is somewhat different in anthropology, with its claims to be *the* comprehensive study of mankind, in all his dimensions, therefore obviously including the biological. However, there is some tension between the egalitarian ideological predilections of most culturally relativistic cultural anthropologists, and the interest in biologically based racial differences as well as bio-evolutionary work of physical anthropologists. This is sometimes glossed over by the argument that what racial differences exist are entirely in nonessential or superficial or "cosmetic" features of human beings that have nothing to do with basic pan-human capacity for culture or any of its symbolic forms. In fact, that last statement is more an article of liberal faith than of demonstrated scientific fact, since we have in truth little in the way of conclusive evidence either for or against that proposition.

Part 2

SUMMARY AND CONCLUSION

If we are going to view human beings in all their dimensions and in all their complexity, we need a psychoanalytic psychology and a socio-cultural analysis built on the works of contemporary sociology and anthropology. A holistic view of mankind must also take adequate account of what man is like as an *animal*; therefore we cannot avoid the biological aspects of this species. One part of that is to trace the evolution of this species through the kinds of evidence provided by a number of inter-related disciplines, several of which are more or less located within the concerns of anthropology, i.e., study of the fossil remains of animals probably transitional between primate ancestors and modern man, associated cultural artifacts studied by archaeologists, and the comparative study of living related primates, particularly the closest relatives, the great apes. This gets us into linguistics and the controversies about the probable origin of human speech and human linguistic communication, and a reconsideration of what had not too long ago still been considered a basic truth, the idea that only the human species had language. That proposition is no longer tenable in light of the demonstration of gestural language in chimpanzees, as well as many kinds of not too distantly related communication systems not only in primates and other mammals, but in other realms of the animal kingdom as well. We are still far from having thoroughly assimilated the implications of Darwin, as well as those of Freud.

Reconstructions of the evolutionary history of man are necessarily speculative, and necessarily require some kinds of imaginative leaps in bringing together the implications of many different lines of research in many different fields. Such extrapolative jumps are the essence of scientific change (or advance); not merely new data, but new ways of looking at existing data, or of bringing together the data from a number of different areas of research which are commonly quite separated from each other.

My interest here is reconstruction not only of the anatomical and physiological evolution of the species, but also of the behavioral and the psychological. For that we need to bring together what has been done on biological evolution, with psychoanalytic insights into the nature of human sexuality, human pairing and parenting, and all of the problems about unconscious mental functioning and its relationship to human growth and development, and the vicissitudes of psychic conflict and suffering common to human beings. The psychoanalytic view and the evolutionary view illuminate each other. The bio-cultural evolutionary reconstructions which have been burgeoning in recent anthropology are enriched by psychoanalytic ideas about the connections relating to body shape, the physiology of pregnancy and childbirth, the peculiar help-lessness of the human neonate, the physical dimorphism of the sexes as connected with the evolution of man through the hunting revolution. And on the other side, psychoanalytic understanding of the continuity from infancy and childhood through all of adulthood of the peculiarities of human sexuality is enriched through tracing the evolutionary origins of this peculiarly human body and experience.

My reconstruction draws on Hockett and Ascher and others empha-sizing the "hunting-revolution" approach, with side references to the divergent aquatic theory of Elaine Morgan. It also takes into consideration Hewes's gestural theory of language origins, and reports and commentary on the demonstrations of chimpanzees' capacity for learning gestural language, and provides psychoanalytically based commentary on these. It runs, briefly, as follows: Climatic-ecological crises of the Miocene period in East Africa forced some of the arboreal primate ancestors down to the ground, requiring an adaptation to a grassy savanna ground en-vironment with threatening large mammal predators. Thus developed the hunting-gathering mode of life and simultaneously the anatomical-phys-iological and behavioral evolutionary developments toward the human animal: upright posture, the distinctively human foot, increased verti-cality, freeing of the hands, recession of the snout, development of larger brains and a head adapted to contain them. Contemporaneously the cultural development included development (of necessity) of more com-plex communication, developing both gestural and vocal-auditory modes, and the latter specifically in the direction of speech-language, with its qualities of displacement, duality, productivity, arbitrariness, interchangeability, specialization, and cultural transmission. Evidence from a variety of angles suggests gestural communication developed phylogenetically earlier, but was of necessity in time supplemented and later partially supplanted by vocal-auditory communication which in turn developed into full-scale speech language. In this process, both the elab-oration and transformation of high-volume high-pitch call systems (pri-marily in the context of distance communication of adult male bands) and the transformation and elaboration of low-pitch low-volume feckless play-chattering and related vocal phatic communication in the context of mother-infant, mother-juvenile, and inter-juvenile play and other intimate associations, must have played their roles in this crucial cultural development. Play, in its association with erotic connecting and intimate contact, is a crucial element in this pattern, alongside and in opposition to the practical-utilitarian adaptive elements in this evolutionary process. Play and Eros operate in a dialectical relationship with work, reality principle, and Logos, in the development of human language and symbols, in the development of ever more complex human culture. The evolutionary bodily developments leading to erect posture, modification of the pelvis, enlargement of the brain, enlargement of the head, together work toward the dilemma of human mammalian childbirth, with the result of the "premature" birth of the human infant. This, in turn, results in the extreme helplessness of the human neonate, its extremely prolonged dependency on adult care for physical survival, and emotional responsiveness of the mother and other mothering persons to the infant and young child, as crucial prerequisites for human infantile growth and development. Along with all of this, the transformation of sexuality in this human animal to its lifelong, nonseasonal, precocious, and endlessly peremptory character, bringing the complexities of the vicissitudes of human psychosexual development that are distinctive of this species. Connected with these processes, in turn, is the distinctively human phenomenon of neoteny or infantilization, by which characteristics that are infantile and later outgrown in other related mammalian species, are in this species retained and persistent in a variety of ways throughout the whole cycle of growth and development and the adult life course, giving to human early psychological development a degree and kind of consequentiality unequaled in other species.

Further connected elements are the distinctive human phenomenon of latency and that of the frontal coital position, probably invented by proto-hominids in our ancestry. Latency as a slowing down of the growth curve during the phase from age about five till puberty, and a corresponding diminution of the force of sexuality as a major drive (which might or might not be culturally utilized), marks a distinctively human phenomenon. Latency enables the acquisition of complex culture and the consolidation of ego and superego capacities that are necessities for participation in ever more complex culture and civilization. Latency promotes the forging of workable adaptations connecting the life of the drives with internalized controls and reality-perception and adaptation capacities of ever more intricate kinds. The frontal coital position, in

turn, adds special dimensions to human psychosocial sexuality, facilitating the diffusion and confusion of mate-mate and mother-infant sexualities, connecting these with the generally more frontal approach to
the world and its facilitation of ever more intricate and internally conflicting kinds of intimate communication. The bimodal development of
the dual (mate-mate and mother-infant) sexuality of the female, alongside
the single (mate-mate) sexuality of the male, both complicated by the
lifelong persistence (through myriad modifications and transformations)
of the polymorphous sexuality of infancy, works toward the dimorphism
of the sexes not only in biological, anatomical, physiological, and functional terms, but also in behavioral and psychological attributes. These
divergences are, of course, never absolute, and may be either accen-
tuated or minimized by the cultural pressures of a particular place and
age, our present one being one emphasizing their minimization. Their
being rooted in the evolutionary development of the species in simultaneous biological and cultural aspects in the survival-dictated emergence of the hunting-gathering economy on the Miocene savannas, as our
proto-hominid ancestors were changing from dinner to diner and evolving
into complexly communicating precociously and nonseasonally sexual
human-like beings, would indicate the limitations on modification of this
deeply embedded difference between the sexes.

In thus in effect rewriting *Totem and Taboo*, we are eschewing Freud's
Lamarckianism, and his positing of phylogenetic transmission of acquired
memory traces of hypothesized oedipal revolt and remorse, and relying
instead on the better grounded Róheimian ontogenetic theory of cultural
origins and cultural intergenerational transmission. The endlessly repeated power of oedipal phenomena and necessities for the basic incest
taboos as foundation stones for culture can be well understood in terms
of the same kinds of basic developmental and psychological events re-
curring in each generation as each undergoes the same human processes
and dilemmas of life from one generation to the next, each in the same
kind of human body, each with the same kind of repertoire of potential
human psychic devices and adaptational mechanisms, all built upon the
same evolutionary history of the species, and each dealing with intense
complex relationships to at least two crucial adults of the two different
sexes in the ever-repeated fundamental triad of late-infancy life and its
tragic dilemmas. Where neoteny is derived (in part) from the dietary
change from herbivorous to omnivorous in the new ground-dwelling life,
and repression and control of sexual rivalries is necessitated by the requirement of group cooperation of the hunting band of adult males, these
converge in the psychosocial crisis of the oedipal situation and the necessity for its resolution and the ushering in of the humanly distinctive

and crucial latency period. In evolutionary terms, greater survival chances went to hominids with this kind of sexuality, language capacity built on the combination of repression and play, capability to arrive at and thence to resolve the Oedipus complex, to enter latency and self-imposed delay of sexual gratification through that crucial juvenile learning phase. So too the capacity to render major aspects of experience (especially of early infantile experience) into the unconscious, maintain repression as a major psychological defense device, and develop the whole human repertoire of the ego's unconscious mechanisms—projection, introjection, displacement—in the service of an equilibrium that serves the maintenance of some—and in many cases very advanced and complex—civilizations.

Much of this theorizing, especially on human sexual dimorphism, and on differential psychosexual development between males and females, and the sociocultural implications of these differences, leads into the thorny territory of controversy raised by contemporary feminism on these and many related issues. This requires much more extended discussion. To that we turn in Part 3.

3

Sex Differences: Feminism Confronts Psychoanalysis and the Social Sciences

The little girl has only to wait for something inside herself to unfold, for her to become a woman; the boy must actively do something, be active and assertive, achieve some mastery, to prove and validate his adult masculinity. . . . This difference is found in all cultures.

Margaret Mead, *Male and Female*

BIO-EVOLUTIONARY BACKGROUND: RECAPITULATION

In Part 2, I traced a reconstruction of the bio-psycho-cultural evolution of the human species. In it I pointed to what appear to be very fundamental bio-psychological differences between males and females in the human species, rooted in the evolutionary processes deduced from paleontological, physical anthropological, linquistic-anthropological, and psychoanalytic lines of evidence. Much of that reconstruction involves human sexuality which is distinctive in the animal world by its precocity, polymorphousness, lifelong continuity, nonseasonality, and its peculiar bifurcation between the dual sexuality of the female (mate-mate and mother-infant) alongside the single (mate-mate) sexuality of the male. Tracing of communications also indicates a divergence of female from male in important ways: the female living more of her life close to basic body phatic communications that go back farther in evolution than the more recent developments of speech-language and the world of Logos, which is a more predominantly masculine world.

Several of the changes in the bio-evolutionary history of the human species have special bearing on the female and on differences between females and males. The change from estrus to a non-seasonal sexuality changed the dominance patterns, particularly among the males of the species. The shift from dorsal to frontal coital position effected a mix-up in the signals of dominance-submission with those of sexuality, confounding and interfusing sex and aggression in this animal ever since. The change in the body architecture of the female in connection with upright posture and bipedalism required premature birth of the infant, resulting in the most helpless mammal neonate in evolutionary history, and hence a requirement for an amount and complexity of maternal (or generally, parental) care of both physical and psychological kinds for the neonate for a period far more prolonged than in other mammals. This has profound implications for the psychosexual development of both sexes, and particularly for the requirement of a development in the female of psychological mechanisms favoring such maternal behavior. Also, the change from a relatively free-for-all promiscuity of the ancestors to more distinctly regulated mating, probably largely along monogamous lines, along with some kind of household arrangement approximating the nuclear family, implies the domestication of the human animal and particularly the domestication of the male, never entirely complete, and from which he has been rebelliously trying to escape ever since, freer as he is from the impediments of pregnancy and infant care. There also thus evolved a female closer to basic body-phatic communication along with its associated intuitive-empathic qualities, and also more evolved in patterns of cooperation, altrusim, and concern for social justice, compared to the male. Sex differences in aggression and its probable lines of expression were probably also established in this ancient evolutionary development, completed perhaps as early as four million years ago, and at latest about a million years in the past.

These bio-evolutionary background considerations are essential as we turn now to the heated controversies raging today on the questions of the differences between the sexes, their roles, actual and putatively normative, and the battles over equality or equity between the sexes that have been stirred (anew) by the revived women's liberation movement of Western countries of recent years. In these struggles, embattled protagonists have drawn on or are fighting against viewpoints presented on the basis of empirical evidence or of theoretical interpretation by the social sciences and psychoanalysis, and vocal minorities within each of these fields are voicing challenges to prevailing viewpoints in their own and related fields. The context of these struggles is a whole series of related changes in modern societies which have unsettled (in many cases overthrown) traditional patterns of a near or distant past, and promise (or threaten) much more drastic changes in the prospective near future.

In this part, I propose to look at some of the issues raised by the women's movement from a combined sociological and psychoanalytic viewpoint. I first outline a schematic of the conflicting sets of norms operating in modern society on these issues, what I call the "traditional" and the "vanguard" norms. I then raise questions about the difficulties facing the possibility of full implementation of the vanguard norms. First, the difficulties from a sociological viewpoint: are these sociologically viable? Then from a psychoanalytic viewpoint: psychologically and psychodynamically are such norms grounded in propositions about the nature of psychological differences between the sexes, grounded in both biology and in psycho-sexual-developmental processes that differentiate between the sexes, resulting in systematically different sexual personalities and gender identities? I raise the question of how susceptible to change such processes could be, given the kinds of psychodynamic processes we learn from psychoanalysis. Finally, we make a foray into a sociological-psychoanalytic analysis of the women's movement itself as both a sociological and a psychological phenomenon, utilizing processes and mechanisms familiar in reactive and mitigating mythologies that develop in intense ideological struggles of various kinds.

CHAPTER SEVEN

"Traditional" vs. "Vanguard" Norms on Sex Differences

Particularly striking in the current scene in advanced technological societies of today is the plurality of norms that are operating simultaneously in reference to gender differences. For purposes of heuristic simplification, however, we can reduce that plurality to two identifiably different sets of cultural norms: a traditional one that is largely patriarchal from the Western past and an emergent one that could be called "vanguard," which is much more egalitarian between the sexes. The latter, while having many other roots, is most vocally expressed by the feminist movement of today.

Parenthetically, let us make it clear at this point that we are dealing with *norms*, which refer to the standards of what people think they *should* do or *should not* do, or the ways people think they *should* feel or *not* feel, given certain situations, or *should* think, or *should not* think. The norms are not to be confused with the reality of how people actually do behave, feel, or think. Nor are they to be confused with what psychoanalysts may think is "normal" as distinct from psychopathological; nor are they to be confused with what one could discover is empirically the average or usual kind of behavior, feeling, or thinking in a particular society at a particular time. (See chapter 15 below for more exhaustive discussion of the interrelationships among these different conceptions of "normatively required," "normal" in the sense of psychologically healthy, and "normal" in the sense of usual, ordinary or average.)

The norms and the system of norms (or normative system) are, of course, a major element in any sociological analysis. We need to be clear at this point also that in sociologically analyzing the norms themselves—and their relationships to behavior, feeling, thinking—we are basically *reporting* and *analyzing* the norms that exist, and not making an ideological judgment one way or the other on whether we personally subscribe to these norms, or hold by them, or challenge them with some other set of norms—all such evaluative processes are outside the arena of what we are here concerned with.

TRADITIONAL NORMS

The discussion here of "traditional" gender norms follows rather closely from a distinction I made in another connection, in a paper of a few years ago, on "dominant vs. subterranean" cultural traditions of the West (Endleman 1973). That paper drew from the work of Weber and Marx, and from David Matza's excellent analysis of "Subterranean Traditions of Youth" (1961). On one side, we there distinguished a "culture of rationality," a set of norms emphasizing rational ego processes, instrumentalism, mechanistic use of time, secondary psychodynamic processes, ego and superego strengths, etc., while on the other side a set of "subterranean" traditions in opposition to the former normative system; in the latter we find emphasis on primary process, on intuition (as against logical thought), on expressiveness, on a more "organic" and "flowing" approach to time, etc. These polarities, interestingly enough, also define a set of gender role differences, according to the long-prevailing "traditional" norms of the Western world.

On one side you have a person who is supposed to be rational, logical, objective, anti-emotional, disciplined, self-disciplined, controlled, calculating and instrumental, more related to objects than to people, more interested in mathematics, "hard" sciences, and the applications of these in technology, and relating to mechanical clock time. By contrast, an opposite set of norms favors a person who is less rational, who is open to non-rational and irrational aspects of life, not always very logical, frequently inconsistent, changeable, subjective, attuned more to persons than to things, not highly disciplined, therefore more open to momentary emotion and enthusiasm, more interested in humanistic pursuits and the arts than in science and technology, not rigidly calculating, more expressive than instrumental, more intuitive, empathic, emotionally labile, personalized in relationships, often illogical, highly subjective.

According to the traditional, essentially patriarchal cultural norms of the West, the former configuration refers to the norms of how *men* should be, act, behave, feel, and think; the latter, to how *women* are expected to be. To carry the dichotomy further: a man is supposed to be oriented to time in a more objectified way, oriented to clock time, to think in terms of time progressions from the past through the present into the future. He is supposed to be masterful over his own body and its more wanton impulses, not imprisoned in his bodily self and its functions. He is supposed to be attuned to a morality of abstract principle. He is supposed to seek achievement, and to be aggressive, physically and otherwise, and to be tough-minded and unsentimental.

By contrast, according to those traditional norms, the woman is supposed to be oriented to time in terms of organic processes and periodicities, to be emotionally volatile, to lose self-control in difficult situations. She is supposed to be attuned to a morality of personal self-interest or personal loyalties. She is supposed to be more attuned to her own biological processes, her own body.

In reference to work, by these traditional norms, the man is supposed to be strongly oriented to work, to make work a central part of his life, to derive his satisfactions and his social status from his work and his achievements. Work is to be an intrinsic aspect of his masculine identity. He is supposed to place a high value on his work, if necessary a value superseding that on relations with wife and children. He is supposed to be independent, self-reliant, competitive, where feasible domineering, and above all, not passive but active.

By contrast, according to these traditional norms, the women is not supposed to be invested emotionally in work; and certainly not to have her feminine identity attached to work; rather she is supposed to be personally most invested, emotionally, in her relationship to her man and to her children. If, for economic reasons, she *has* to work (as a large percentage of the female population has had to do since the industrial revolution) then the traditional norms would *allow* her working, but still say that she should if at all possible be at home devoting herself to husband and children. She should also, according to these norms, be dependent, relying on her man, initially her father, later her husband; and noncompetitive, submissive, and passive. If she does go to work in the labor market, she is to limit herself to fields of work traditionally defined as "feminine"—teaching, caring for others' children, nursing, social welfare work; in other words work involving traditionally "feminine" emphasis on nurturance. Preferentially her work should be the boundaryless labor of keeping a household and caring for the needs of her mate and her children. Career work as a central part of life would be allowable—though still not positively valued—only for those "unfortunate" women lacking husband and children.

For the man: sex he is supposed to regard as primarily for his satisfaction, not as a means of relationship and *her* satisfaction, if relevant at all, is to be considered primarily as a mark of his prowess. As a child he is to engage in vigorous, aggressive, even dangerous physical play and games, and never display fear, anxiety, or hurt in these contests. Even, to some extent, he is to resist female authority. As a grown man, he is supposed to dominate over women, children, servants, and other subordinates. Toward women, he is to temper this with chivalrous attention that emphasizes his strength and her weakness and inferiority.

For the woman: she is to regard marrying a suitable man, staying married to him, having children and taking care of them and the household, as her primary goals in life. She is supposed to be supportive, meek, subordinate, submissive, unassertive. In sex she is supposed to be non-initiatory, passive-receptive, focusing more on giving her man satisfaction than on getting it herself. And in sex, *relationship* is supposed to be more important than physical gratification.

These then are the traditional or patriarchal gender role norms. They are sharply differentiated and clear-cut. Persons following these norms would know just what is expected of them in the way of behavior, of feelings and thoughts, and reactions particularly to the opposite sex.

According to these, the rationality-work-discipline complex that makes possible modern technological market societies is essentially an ethic for men, while women are to follow the way of the more irrational, intuitive, empathetic, and illogical approach to life.

VANGUARD NORMS

By contrast, the more newly emerging norms in modern society would do away with nearly all the differentiations between the sexes that are built into the traditional norms.

The ideal woman by these norms would be the potential if not actual equal of the man in rationality, logicality, precision, organization skill; in mathematics, physical sciences, engineering, technology, business, and all the rest of the "masculine" fields. She should be the equal of any man in independence, self-support, decision-making capacities, assertiveness, and power. She should seek achievement and success on her own, by her own talents, which should be given as much encouragement and training as those of any boy or man. Her status should be what she personally achieves by her work and accomplishments, not a reflection of her husband's, and not a derivation from her father. In sexuality, she should meet the male partner as an equal, both being able to take active and passive roles as the spirit moves them, and she should certainly never cede sexual dominance to the male. She should be insistent on her own sexual gratification as well as in pleasing her partner. She should also be ready to dispense with men altogether for sexual pleasure, if that suits her.

As for marriage and children, under these norms: she should be ready to dispense with them entirely if she wants or to regard them as an option which she may or may not want to exercise. As for children, with overpopulation the way it is already, according to these vanguard norms, there is no good reason to expect every woman to have children. Those who want to, and who enjoy having and taking care of babies, may do so, and either take care of them themselves, or have someone else take care of them. Even if she does decide to try to combine career and marriage-cum-children, she should still not be expected to make the children the center of her life.

In another version of these vanguard norms and expectations: she should combine career with marriage and children, to be in effect superwoman, adept at all of these roles—high-powered career woman, wife, mother to her children, hostess, chauffeur, household-organizer; adept at the personal relationships of family, friends, associates, competitors, and everyone else with whom she has to maintain personalized relations, and at the same time capable at the hard-headed activities of business or profession, their norms of objectivity, composure, and competence. In work, she is not to limit herself to the traditionally "feminine" fields, but should be free to venture into any of the traditionally "masculine" preserves, such as business manager and executive, into physically tough jobs, such as mining and construction, or dangerous ones like police work or firefighting, the military, and professional sports, all on a par with the man. In all of these she is to insist on being given equal opportunity for training, apprenticeship, promotion, remuneration, and advancement, to be evaluated entirely on the basis of talent and ability, not on gender.

On the division of labor in the household, if the wife is also out of the house on a career job: the emerging norms are already fairly clear. The work is to be divided flexibly, according to talent, inclination, and circumstance, e.g., in relation to their different work schedules, rather than strictly according to gender.

The vanguard norms also include a new set of expectations in relation to how daughters are raised. The little girl growing up is to be raised as the equal of the boy. If she wants to engage in rough physical activity or aggressive play like her brothers, she should be allowed, even encouraged, to do so. She should be encouraged to be assertive and have a mind of her own, and to resist the attempts of any male to make her passive and submissive. She is to be taught that her mind is just as good as any boy's and that there is no such thing as any natural inferiority of girls to boys in mathematics and the like.

So far, we have been dealing with vanguard norms for women. When we ask, then, what are the vanguard norms for men, we find a more complex situation. From some perspectives, the traditional gender role expectations have not changed nearly as much for men as they have for women, Yes, one can point to greater permission for men to be emotionally expressive. Men can even cry in public now. (Though it can still be a political liability, as it was for Senator Muskie in 1972.) And the macho ideal of physical aggressiveness is certainly no longer in undisputed ascendancy and, in fact, is regarded as something of a joke by many men as well as women. One could also note the trend to allow young men to be much less committed to career achievement and success without having to feel their masculinity is suspect.

In one version, males should not only share equally with females in household work, but should, as an essential, share baby and child care. Nancy Chodorow (1978) and Dorothy Dinnerstein (1977) both see this as essential. Both want complete de-differentiation of gender roles.

Some feminists want men to be "liberated" too, acquiring the positive qualities (empathy, intuition) now associated with femininity, in effect totally erasing psychological differentiation between males and females, each acquiring what are now seen as the "positive" qualities of both genders.

Many who favor feminist norms do not include an expectation that males cease to regard work as essential for masculine identity.

The outline just presented is deliberately over-simplified and schematic, to serve as a heuristic device, a point of reference for looking at actual situations where some variations of one or the other set of norms is actually being adduced.

There are indications that many men, including very young ones, will *state* agreement with some aspects of the vanguard norms—e.g., giving women equal job opportunities—while at the same time expecting the actual women in their own lives to follow traditional gender-role norms in reference to household and child-rearing responsibilities. For example, Mirra Komarovsky's *Dilemmas of Masculinity* (1976) found that Columbia College undergraduates (necessarily all male) basically subscribed to most of the traditional norms regarding gender division of labor, centrality of career for the man and not for the woman. While in line with the "liberal" atmosphere of their sophisticated ivy league college milieu they supported, *in the abstract*, equality for women in pursuing careers, they still expected the women they personally would marry to stop work and raise the kids. They also indicated that the essentiality of work and supporting a family is still strong in the norms of male youth of today, at least those represented by such a college sample.

Many who would support, in principle, the norm of sexual equality in educational and employment opportunity would still not go so far as to want to make it a norm that women *should* seek careers, and subordinate marriage and children to that. Some would say career and family should be combined only by segregating them in time, career in early adulthood, then marriage and children and concentration on the children until the youngest is well into the teen years, and then resumption of career in the middle and later years. Also, many women who accept some feminist norms would nevertheless continue to value *some* of the differences the traditional norms refer to, e.g., more personalized relationships and greater intuitive capacity in females, both very positive features in favor of the women over the men.

There are clearly class differences in normative conceptions of gender roles. Members of the working class are more likely to adhere to traditional norms. Komarovsky's earlier study, *Blue Collar Marriage* (1962), demonstrated that in those working-class families sex role segregation in marriage was very strong, patriarchal patterns were maintained in the marriage relationship (husband dominant if not supreme on major marital decisions). A more recent study with a more limited sample by Teresa Donati Marciano (1974) finds that working-class husbands, even at an income level that would qualify as "middle class," still maintain basically the same traditional patriarchal norms, and both husbands and wives continued traditional differential socialization of their children according to sex: boys to be tough, aggressive, emotionally unexpressive, slightly wild, sports-minded; girls to be gentle, domestic, quiet, tractable. The wives were slightly more open to communications reflecting vanguard or feminist norms (partly coming specifically from the middle-class social scientist woman researcher), and perceived such shifts, however slight, in their awareness and expectations as threatening to their husbands. Another exploration of current working-class families, Lillian Rubin's *Worlds of Pain* (1976), also shows persistence of traditional gender norms. In the area of freedom for exploration of sexual variation, the women are, if anything, more traditional than the men, being much more uncomfortable with media-disseminated notions of sexual experimentation. Far from being in tune with sexual-liberationist feminists on the expectation that women should expect and demand full sexual satisfaction on a par with the men and that women should be just as initiatory in sexual relations as men, these women at most submit passively to their husbands' requests for sexual variation (cunnilingus sometimes, fellatio rarely). (Rubin does note that such responses are not limited to working-class women, though impressionistic evidence elsewhere would suggest that among younger women—say under 35—this would be less frequent in middle- and upper-class levels, than in the working class whom Rubin studied directly.)

Aside from this working-class bastion of maintenance of traditional norms and resistance to vanguard innovations, the picture elsewhere in modern societies seems to be extremely varied and confused and internally inconsistent. Many may support at least some aspects of feminist norms for women, but not particularly any complementary changes for men, especially in the "last bastion" area of sharing household and child-caring responsibilities, and the critical issue that work and, if possible, career should be an *essential* of masculine identity, and not an *option* as it may for many women.

It is evident that the newer norms involve a lot of conflict and internal inconsistency, especially if there are not matching and complementary norms for men. Add to this that men are conflicted and ambivalent within themselves and among themselves about how much of the vanguard norms they should be making accommodation to, and in what spheres. Many will support, for example, the general idea of equal employment opportunity for women, but only up to the point where their own jobs could be threatened. People of both sexes tend to support traditional norms in some respects, vanguard ones in other respects. But the combinations are different from one individual to another. The result is great profusion and confusion of mixes of norms that people hold.

This is very much in contrast with a traditional society, such as most tribal ones studied by anthropologists. There, where there are distinct norms governing differences of gender roles and differential temperamental expectations of the two sexes, the set of norms—no matter how arbitrary to an outsider—does make sense of the complementary and reciprocal position of the two sexes. There the masculine gender role definition is supportive of and complementary to the feminine one. For example, if he is expected to bring in economic support and she is expected to take care of the household and the children, each has a clear-cut and obviously mutually necessary and valuable contribution to make. Each is dependent on the other making her or his contribution according to the normative roles. If he is supposed to be dominant and she subordinate, then the two fit together; similarly for active-passive, and any other complementary sets.

By contrast, in the present-day modern world, we are far from having any such clear-cut pattern. Instead we have a great deal of normative confusion. The traditional set of norms as a total package is becoming increasing unviable. But the vanguard package is itself almost impossible of realization, even if both sexes agreed with it entirely, and especially so where one sex is more interested in it than the other. The effect, then, is an approximation of a state of *anomie*, a lack of norms, or a state of normative disruption. On almost any particular item of the norms, there is far from consensus; and neither is there on either set as a whole. It is, therefore, little wonder then that so many people are angry and upset.

Example (real event): Scene: John and Marsha at a mod party. John starts to light Marsha's cigarette. Female liberationist confronts Marsha: "How dare you let him light your cigarette? Don't you see such chivalry means his male supremacy?" Later: Marsha offers John a cigarette, starts to light it for him. Liberationist number two accosts her: "How dare you light his cigarette? What are you, his slave?" What to do? John light his own cigarette, Marsha hers, each in splendid equal isolation? Or each at exactly the same moment, light the other's? (Simultaneous mutual combustion?) And thus enrage both types of liberationist?[1]

Serious feminists might well answer that this is a ridiculous example, calculated only to make a mockery of feminist ideas, picking the silliest manifestation of a line of thought and making it look as though it were typical of the whole movement. But the incident actually did occur and does illustrate what is likely to recur repeatedly when people challenge existing norms on small aspects of everyday behavior. Such challenges can result in absurd situations in which the usual custom-built lubrications of social intercourse fail. Then everybody is uncomfortable because there is no one universally satisfactory set of norms to fit the situation. That is a trival example of what is meant by *anomie*. And that small instance is as nothing compared to the much larger difficulties that men and women are now finding in arriving at comfortable intimacies with each other. There may never have been a time in history when the "game of the sexes" has been harder—for both—to play, and when the so-called perennial "war of the sexes" has been more the reality for greater numbers of people.

We see many of the repercussions of this in our therapy practices today. It is hard enough, given the divergent paths of psychosexual development of males and females. Add to that the recurrent contemporary uncertainty about how one is supposed to feel, think, and act in any particular kind of contact with the opposite sex, and we have most certainly compounded perennial problems.

DIFFICULTIES WITH THE VANGUARD NORMS: SOCIOLOGICAL AND PSYCHODYNAMIC

There are two main problems with the vanguard norms as a total set: they are sociologically very difficult to effect, and they are psychodynamically based on questionable ground assumptions. The latter refer to assumptions about psychic reality and psychic development, particularly as these relate to differences between the sexes, that are on a shaky foundation from the viewpoint of psychoanalytic understandings of psychosexual development of males and females.

CHAPTER EIGHT

Difficulties with the Vanguard Norms: Sociological

Sociologically, the demand for all but total de-differentiation of gender roles ignores the sociological necessity for *some* kind of division of labor and the necessity for socially defined role provision to assure reproduction and care of offspring. There are serious limits to how far any society can go in de-differentiating the sexes, as our society is in the process of trying to do at the present time, being pushed particularly by the feminist movement. It is simply not true that males and females are exactly the same, and to pretend that they are, and therefore to reject whatever kind of sexual division of labor we have had and to demand in its place *no* sexual division of labor at all, is bound to be unrealistic and to have strong negative consequences. Systems are strong where participants are playing *different* and complementary roles. They become weaker to the extent that such differences are erased. On the issue of reproduction and child care, it can be argued that it is simply not viable to have, following feminist demands and goals, every woman engaged in the labor force while at the same time having babies. *Someone* has to take care of children.

Feminists reply: who says it has to be women? And who says it has to be the children's own mothers? What about communal or other society-provided means of meeting these needs? Shulamith Firestone (1970) carried this argument to its *reductio*: she objected to women having babies at all, on the grounds that it was messy nasty business and interfered with a woman's freedom. At something less than that extreme, women can simply argue that they have a choice: they can choose to have babies or not to have babies. Technological means of contraception are by now sufficiently reliable so that this is a basic option. However, once a woman does go ahead and have a baby, the baby has to be taken care of, and one could certainly argue that it is irresponsible for a woman to bring new life into the world and then object to taking care of that baby or providing an adequate surrogate for such mothering care. Psychoanalytically there is a great deal to be said today on the question of the essentiality of good mothering for the child's personality development. We shall return to that question later in the chapter. Here we would simply point out the evolutionary aspect: this human neonate is born the most premature, the most helpless and vulnerable mammal neonate ever.

It is quite possible now for any woman who does not want to have babies to choose not to have any. Particularly if she finds caring for a baby abhorrent, she should be supported in the choice not to have any. We are now in modern society in a position to have differentiation _among_ women (as well as between women and men) on this basis. Other women find having a baby fulfilling, and a fuller realization of their feminity. _They_ can then have the babies. They are probably sufficiently in the majority in any case that we need not be worried that relying only on them the population would not reproduce itself.

On an evolutionary basis, the human neonate up to the age of at least a year (in many ways beyond that) needs an extraordinary amount and quality of physical and psychological care. Many observers believe that care should be given by on consistent primary caretaker; that this caretaker should be female; and the obvious candidate is the mother herself. (Of course, in many circumstances a surrogate may be necessary, or advisable, or accessory.) Without what Winnicott calls "good enough mothering," psychological development can be badly impaired. (See Selma Fraiberg's eloquent case for mothering in her book, _Every Child's Birthright: In Defense of Mothering_, 1977.) She shows that constant, consistent, loving, body-contact care by one consistent mothering person is an essential for full human psychological development; and without it such neglected, damaged children become antisocial delinquents and psychopaths, problems for society.

It is practically impossible for a woman engaged in the market workplace all day to give that kind of care to an infant. In practically all modern countries, day-care facilities cannot provide such care: caretakers there are impersonal, not affectively involved with the children in their care, and have too many at one time. The only possible nearly adequate surrogate would be a full-time nurse-caretaker in a one-to-one relationship with the infant, becoming in effect psychologically that child's mother. Such an arrangement is feasible for only the wealthiest (and it has long been a mark of highest-status women, to hand over infant- and child-care to such a surrogate).

Yes, there are class variations in the organization of parenting, as well as trans-historical and cross-cultural differences. But the basic functional problem remains: the society has to have a way of assuring biological reproduction and care for the offspring. The variety of ways this can be done is not infinite by any means.

Some feminists have raised an even more fundamental question: why does it have to be *women* who do the mothering? Why not men? or a sharing between women and men?

In all known human societies so far, there has never been one in which men are the exclusive or even primary caretakers of infants and young children. There are many societies, both tribal and complex, where fathers do take a tender concern with children and some where, as in the Arapesh tribe of New Guinea (see Mead 1935, 1949) the men are extremely "maternal" and take a considerable role in the care and rearing of infants and young children, but even there, as in other tribal cases reported, *women*, usually the mothers, along with other female helpers, are still the primary baby caretakers and child-tenders. And the evolutionary history we reconstructed in Part 2 tells us how the association of females with child care and nurturance and maintenance of the household came about in the phylogenetic ancestry of our species.

Feminists may well respond that just because this is the way it has been in human history, or how it came about in our evolution, does not absolutely require that it continue indefinitely into the future; that the conditions of modern advanced industrial society and post-industrial society make many of the older imperatives obsolete, or at least subject to radically different solutions.

Nancy Chodorow takes up this question in her recent book *The Reproduction of Mothering* (1978). Why do women, not men, mother? She answers with a psychodynamic-developmental account showing how "mothering" by women gets "reproduced" from one generation to the next. Girl babies and little girls grow up in relation to having a woman for mothering and not a man in the typical family constellation with this asymmetrical pattern of parenting. (This pattern, by the way, is universal.) In this pattern, a basic gender division of labor prevails: women take care of babies and children; men provide material support, etc. This pattern is so prevalent and ingrained we rarely question it. Chodorow's insightful psychoanalytic-sociological account shows how it works and gets perpetuated: girls grow up wanting to have babies and take care of them, and have the requisite psychological characteristics for doing so.

Still, as a feminist Chodorow balks at the implications of her analysis, arguing that the pattern can be changed and should be. (This last I regard as an ideologically motivated nonsequitur to her analysis.)

There are several alternative ways a woman in modern society might combine childbearing and child rearing with some kind of professional career. They are all difficult, and each requires sacrifice of one side of the two, at least some of the time. She can segregate the two in time: work career in early adulthood and early part of marriage, followed by having babies and taking primary responsibility for taking care of them, opting out of work career for those years, then resuming the work career when the children are grown or nearly so. Or she can give primacy to her work career, having the children taken care of by surrogates, and losing out on primary maternal satisfactions. Nobel-Laureate physicist Rosalyn Yalow stopped her work as a physicist only very briefly to give birth to each of her two children and claims she has always kept a kosher home to please her physicist husband (seeing no detraction from her professionalism in doing so). (See journalist's interview with her, by Elizabeth Stone, 1978.) Her children evidently missed getting warm mothering from her but will not publicly criticize her for that (Stone 1978). Yalow certainly does not align herself with feminists, however, rejecting any notion that catering to her husband's needs and wishes in any way subordinates or oppresses her.

Many feminists would advocate, however, that two-career parents should also equally share all of the baby- and child-care and household responsibilities, and *both* make all the compromises with their career work that might entail. So far, very few men, however supportive of feminist demands for equal employment opportunities for women they might be, are willing to make *that* kind of sacrifice.

CROSS-CULTURAL VARIATIONS: TRIBAL SOCIETIES

In tribal societies, the kind of "good enough mothering" that psychoanalysts value appears to be the rule rather than the exception. Typically the women are expected to have the babies and to take care of the babies, and to derive a great deal of basic feminine satisfaction from doing so. However, it does vary. In some societies the women are more warmly nurturant than in others. There is another important feature of tribal societies: women help each other. There are the linkages in the maternal clan line, with mothers and daughters close to each other (physically and emotionally) and cooperating a great deal. Or there is a group of sisters or otherwise related kinswomen helping one another in the care of the children of all of them, as well as in the whole range of household tasks. Or there is a group of co-wives in a polygynous household who share one another's child-caring and domestic tasks. All of these traditional arrangements contrast sharply with the isolated modern urban or suburban housewife who has to do it all herself.

These are, of course, traditional societies, in which women typically—though not universally—have little or no role in what the *men* consider to be the "important" kinds of work in the society: major political and economic functions and warfare.

(Parenthetically: feminists who find it a matter of complaint and grievance that women do not have more of a role in the "important" work of the tribe—as defined by the *males*—seem to be identifying with the aggressor and assuming, for themselves, the patriarchally tinged values that follow an androcentric conception of what kind of work is more important and which less, rather than recognizing that it is just as feasible to regard what women do, in such a tribal division of labor—bearing and rearing children, as supremely important, and obviously more literally creative than what the men are doing. In fact, in many tribal societies, for all their bluster of self-importance in the kinds of tasks males do in the sexual division of labor, males do implicity recognize the *superiority* of women's central life tasks. For example, in those many tribes in Melanesia that have male initiatory cults, the basic underlying theme of these cults is that it is the females who hold the secrets of life: creating new life. As they see it, men's role in this is uncertain, undefined, and could possibly be unnecessary. The initiation rituals are an attempt magically to undo this critical discrepancy. It is clearly a compensatory symbolic action.) (See Margaret Mead, *Male and Female*, 1949:118/ 119.)

Anthropologically, we find in tribal societies, that what *men* define as the more important tasks and functions is in the hands of the *men*, not the women. This nearly always includes a predominance of the power holding and power wielding. Though there are some tribal societies with a somewhat more egalitarian division between the sexes, in influence and power, there are evidently none in which *women* are in the dominant position. Feminists may question: what about those ancient matriarchies that Bachofen wrote about in the nineteenth century? To that, contemporary anthropologists reply: that's mythologizing: there has never been any proof that any such matriarchies actually existed. No societies about which we have either historical or anthropological information have been ruled by women.

If one asks about the goddesses and other female deities worshiped in many ancient civilizations: do these not indicate women holding political power? The answer is probably not. Since religious beliefs are a projective system and not a photographic representation of actual power among the adults in the society concerned, it is much more fruitful to look at female deities as reflections of infantile feelings toward the first important power in the infant's life: the mother. To the infant she is all-powerful, and either beneficent or cruel—or in different versions, both of these, in some figures one, in other figures the other. We must not be misled into regarding these figures of imagination as representations of actual functioning political systems in those ancient worlds.

In traditional societies women can generally exercise a great deal of influence and control informally in the household situation, without being chiefs in a political sense. In some societies, however, women *past menopause* could exercise political office. This was so in the Iroquois tribes in America. Women of childbearing age could not hold such office. The distinction indicates the feeling by the people of such societies that childbearing and child rearing are the crucial feminine tasks, perceived as incompatible with holding political power.

Many anthropologists have noted the trend of male dominance in at least the vast majority of known human societies, if not universally. Generally the technologically more complex societies have more intensive male dominance than those at the more elementary technological level, that is the hunting and gathering societies. Kathleen Gough notes that "In general, in hunting societies, . . . women are less subordinated in certain crucial respects than they are in most, if not all, of the archaic states, or even in some capitalist/modern nations. These respects include men's ability to deny women sexuality or force it on them; to command or exploit their labor or to control their produce; to control or rob them of their children; to confine them physically and prevent their movement; to use them as objects in male transactions; to cramp their creativeness; or to withhold from them large areas of the society's knowledge and cultural attainments" (Gough 1971:767).

Nevertheless, even in hunting and gathering societies, women are always to some degree subordinated to men. They are less so, Gough argues, where women are important as food obtainers than where they are primarily processors of meat and other food supplies provided by the men. This would be true where gathering of wild food plants (always the task of women, or women and children, in the hunting-gathering sexual division of labor) is the more important source of the food supply. It would also be true where hunting is small-scale and intensive, rather than large-scale and extensive. In the former it may include a lot of work of women and children (catching small game), in the latter it is adult-male work.

Marvin Harris summarizes the evidence for the universality or near-universality of the predominance in males in political power in all societies we know of (1977). He offers a theory to explain it. He attributes it to the combination of intertribal and intersocietal warfare, and the need to prevent overpopulation. These together, he claims, lead to systems of male dominance.

Such dominance is indicated in these ways: In samples of human societies studied by anthropologists, the bride in 75 percent of the cases must move to her husband's family, while the opposite appears in only 10 percent. Descent is traced patrilineally (i.e., in the male line) five times more frequently than matrilineally. Even where it is traced matrilineally, boys and young men come under the authority of the mother's *brother*, as the male authority of the clan. In many cases he moves at puberty or later from the mother's to the mother's brother's household. Plural marriage is overwhelmingly more frequently polygyny (one man with plural wives) than polyandry (one woman with plural husbands). Bride price customs—the groom's family paying the bride's for the bride—indicate the acquisition by the former of a form of valuable. Women are exchanged among groups of men, very rarely men among groups of women. Male chiefs or headmen far outnumber female chiefs or heads. Shamans are more frequently male than female (though it must be pointed out that in some tribes women shamans may approximate in number the male shamans, particularly in Siberia, the land of the Chuckchees, from whose language we got the term shaman in the first place).

Harris also adduces the following kinds of evidence: Puberty ceremonies are much more frequent, more highly elaborated, and constitute more gruelling tests of strength and endurance as qualifications for adult status in one's own sex in the case of males compared to that for females. Most such societies go to great pains to segregate the women from these ceremonies. Women in such societies are also likely to be segregated during menstruation as unclean. Male religious and ritual secrets, male clubhouses, males menacing women and children, all of these can be seen (Harris says) as marks of male dominance. In the economic division of labor, women are typically given more drudgery work. In many societies getting a woman assigned as a wife or a concubine was a recognizably legitimate reward for a man for bravery and aggressiveness in battle. This pattern, often associated with polygyny, is another indication of male dominance. These combinations are likely to be more prevalent in societies actively engaged in warfare at the band or village level of organization, and warfare and such male dominance tend to go together.

Under conditions of earlier and still-contemporary traditional societies, where warfare is important, as is population control, the society will develop institutions that emphasize male dominance, and a high degree of divergence between masculine and feminine gender roles. The result in such societies is that, wherever hierarchy is concerned, males are more likely than females to seek and attain the higher positions.

Harris sees such conditions as having been prevalent in the past in societies that became complex like our own. But he does not see these trends as *inevitable*, nor as being required to continue in the future in modern complex societies. He envisages conditions in the future, already emerging today, in which the necessity for institutions of male dominance and a high degree of gender differentiation that used to prevail will no longer apply. (For reasons developed later, I disagree. I think Harris is here acceding to ideological pressure from feminists.)

Harris' argument may seem at first glance rather similar to that of Steven Goldberg in *The Inevitability of Patriarchy* (1973), a work that really exercises the wrath of feminists. Goldberg thinks male dominance ("patriarchy") is inevitable in any society on *biological* grounds: hormonal differences between the sexes make it inevitable that males have greater aggressiveness and greater drive for dominance and achievement of higher status. Goldberg claims men do have such drives, and that societies tend to institutionalize these differences by assigning the dominant and high-status roles to men, not to women, and to accentuate this difference by divergent gender-role socialization. Harris puts the causative element on social structural factors, therefore, potentially at least, changeable ones. Goldberg, adducing biology, argues no possibility of change.

Both of these sets of arguments have been countered in recent years by feminist women anthropologists. Eleanor Leacock, for example, devastatingly reviewed Goldberg's *Patriarchy* book (Leacock 1974, 1975). She argues that it is simply not true that females are never, at a societal level, in positions of authority and dominance. Many African tribes were, before the colonial conquest by Europeans, ruled by female chiefs or queens. Unlike European ruling queens who come to the throne only on condition there is no qualified male heir to he deceased monarch, these African queens, Leacock claims, came to the throne in their own right.

She notes that the English explorer Livingstone mistakenly gave formal greeting to a female Balonda chief's husband instead of to her, and that he had other run-ins with women chiefs (queens) who refused to be affronted in this manner.

However, her data do not indicate that women *generally* were in positions of dominance over men: only that women were eligible equally with men for royal ruling rank. (Her point, that the influence of patriarchically minded male European emissaries, traders, and later colonial rulers led to the decline of females being in chieftainship positions, is well taken, but does not alter the general pattern of male dominance in the non-royal population of these tribes. The queen being affronted by a foreign emissary addressing her husband rather than her, is, of course, paralleled by the affront Queen Victoria would have felt if such an emissary mistakenly addressed himself to Prince Albert instead of to her; but that does not make Victorian England a matriarchy, any more than the England of Elizabeth I or Elizabeth II.)

These African societal cases are also exceptional compared to other known nonliterate societies. Rarely are such roles *regularly* available to females (as distinguished from incumbency based on lack of a ritually qualified male).

Leacock makes the point that in many primitive societies, roles of men and women were *different* and reciprocal, but not hierarchical, i.e., without any clear-cut dominance pattern. True enough, but wherever there is a dominance pattern, it is always in favor of the males.

The Manus of New Guinea (Mead 1930, 1949) present an interesting variation. Mead writes about them:

> The Manus example is instructive because it represents a case where women do not enjoy being women, not because public rewards given males are denied them—influence, power, wealth are all open to women—but because the sensuous experience of the female role of wife and mother is so undervalued. (Mead 1949:110)

Mead also points out that when Manus children are asked to draw males and females, the males are drawn with penises, the girls with grass skirts. This, to Mead, indicates the downgrading of the female, compared to the male, sexual and reproductive functions.

The point here is that it is one-sided and arbitrary to focus on differences in power and authority, which seem to be the principal preoccupation of Western feminists, at the expense of the fundamental question of honoring the special qualities of each of the sexes, in this case the particular reproductive functions and the biologically based greater attunement of women to the world of body experience, which may or may not be highly valued in a particular society. Many feminists evidently do not value this very highly, and some deny that such a difference even exists.

A division of labor, in which *by and large*—but not necessarily inevitably—women follow certain kinds of occupations and tasks and men certain others, does in fact tend to provide orderliness and security in society. It does not, however, preclude the occasional exception, such as the particularly muscular and brawny woman who can make just as good a stevedore as any male stevedore. And the women who have come to political power by *achievement* rather than by dynastic ascription, such as Golda Meir, or by a combination of kinship and achievement, such as Indira Gandhi, are testimony to the capacities of such exceptional women, but they are and remain exceptions.

OTHER ADVANCED SOCIETIES: ALTERNATIVES?

What about other modern technological societies where women do have a greater measure of equality than in the contemporary West? What about the Soviety Union? China? the Israeli kibbutz?

The Soviet Union

The most striking thing about the USSR on this issue, more than sixty years after the Revolution and after a deliberate pursuit of sexual equality in the earlier stages, is that wherever you find women in great numbers in a profession we regard as high status (e.g., the physician), we find that in the USSR that profession has much lower status than it does in the West.[1] The physician also has lower status than such other professionals as research scientists and engineers, of whom the vast majority in the Soviet Union are men. (Theoretically these fields are equally open to women.)

A recent journalistic report states that though 69 percent of Soviet physicians are women, only half of the chief doctors and supervisors in hospitals are women (Whitney 1979). Thus, the Soviet Union does not qualify as a case for women in the highest status occupations with anything at all like parity with males. Steven Goldberg saw it this way: he argued that the most capable and most competitive males—if competition is valued as it is in all modern industrialized societies—would seek out occupations as high on the status scale as they could reach. In the Soviet Union that would not be medicine, i.e., medical *practice*, in which one is in effect a state employee as contrasted with the private entrepreneur physician in capitalistic countries. In the USSR medical research would be a different matter: that is prestigious work.

Similarly, women are rare at the higher levels of government. They make up only 24.7 percent of the Party membership, and less than 3 percent of the full members of the Party's Central Committee (8 out of 287 members). On the supreme political organ, the Politburo, there are no women at all.

Further, while women constitute 51 percent of the labor force, they tend to be concentrated either in what have become "traditionally feminine" fields like child care, nursing, school teaching, other kinds of service work, or in the more routine, monotonous, and unchallenging areas of factory or office or sales work. Whitney (1979) reports women make up 84 percent of retail sales workers, one of the lowest paying jobs. (For an excellent general brief summary and analysis, see Hacker 1976: 200–05.)

Also, while most adult women in the Soviet Union are employed in the labor market, domestically they are still expected to be the ones primarily responsible for the household and child care in their "off-work" hours. These are still firmly defined as feminine tasks. Until recently care of children of working mothers was frequently in the hands of the *baboushka* (grandmother—more commonly the father's mother), but now many of these *baboushki* themselves want to be "liberated," i.e., to work in the paid labor force (Whitney 1979). Day care centers are still far from universally available, and would not meet the needs if the child were frequently ill. (Even occasional short-term illness of the child, in the Soviet Union as in the West, results in a dilemma for the labor-force-working mother: *she* must take time off from work to care for the child; rarely will the father consider this equally his responsibility.) A result is that many women, if they want to continue their work careers, are simply not having any children—the "stark choice: career or children" of the title of Whitney's report. (Note in the word "stark" the feminist bias in the phrasing, as though it were any simple matter in the West or elsewhere for a woman both to have a career and to have and take care of children *at the same time*.) This is one factor in the decline in the birth rate, with a population growth rate in the USSR now estimated as less than one percent. Another indicator of persistent gender-role differentiation along male-dominated lines is this: when the national census, taken in January 1979, asked "Who is the head of this family?" many men were incensed at the question (Whitney 1979). (As of August 1979, the results have not yet been published.)

China

It is true that the position of women in the People's Republic of China today is vastly different from what it was under the traditional Chinese system that lasted over 2,000 years, till about the end of the nineteenth century when Western influence began to modify the whole socioeconomic structure of Chinese society. In between the decline of the traditional system and the establishment of Communism in China in 1949, there was a period of rapid transition under the influence of "modernizing" ideas and ideologies from the West. Under the old traditional system the Chinese woman was totally subordinated in practically all aspects of life to the man, first her father, then her husband, then after widowhood, to the oldest son. This was true, though differently, whether the family was of the gentry or of the peasantry. The peasant female lived her life in almost total servitude, was treated as chattel, could even be sold into slavery, had to endure back-breaking labor in the fields, and also produce and care for children and the household, and, of course, had no schooling. The gentry female was materially better off and might have considerable leisure and little drudgery work, but was psychologically totally subordinate to her men; put into an arranged marriage where she was also subordinate to her mother-in-law. The whole society was hierarchically structured, with older over younger, and men definitely over women. If anything, the gentry woman had less real freedom of action than the peasant or coolie woman. Footbinding designated her restricted position.

The transitional period, begun with Western contact in the mid-nineteenth century, brought challenges to all these traditions of subordination and segregation of women. Women started to move into the wider world, a feminist movement began, propagating Western ideas of sexual equality. The Ch'ing dynasty was overthrown and the Republic declared in 1911. The Republic made new laws changing the position of women: freedom of mate choice (as against the older arranged marriage system in which the bride had no choice at all), increased rights of divorce for women, elimination of foot-binding, concubinage, child labor, and female slavery. These laws were, however, not always actually or fully implemented in practice, but in effect they set the stage for the effort at more thoroughgoing transformation ushered in by the Communist Revolution of 1949. (See the excellent brief summary and analysis by Helen

Hacker 1976:193–200, to which I am indebted for the present section; and Goode 1970.)

The Communist regime started at once to proclaim a policy of complete sexual equality, trying to break all remnants of the ancient traditional obligations of women to men (as well as of young to old, of younger generation to older generation). Its ideological baseline, however, was not personal freedom (for women or anyone else) but rather dedication to the revolution and the creation of an independent mobile work force intended to build a prosperous socialism with more efficient agriculture and rapid industrialization. Women were encouraged to delay marriage and childbearing and to work side by side with men in building the new nation. The sexual ethic was puritanical, not hedonistic. Abstinence prior to late marriage was put forth as the sexual norm.

Official *policy* looks enlightened by Western feminist standards: women are not to be regarded as sex objects nor subjected to a double standard of sexual morality, out-of-wedlock children may not be discriminated against, women are to have equal employment opportunities and equal pay for equal work, women are to move freely into many formerly "masculine" occupations at high skill levels. The Communist Family Law of 1950 abolished the old traditional family system.

Reality, however, differs sharply from the official policy in many ways. There is still a pronounced sexual division of labor. It is considered natural that women be the nursery and kindergarten teachers. In factory work, women are concentrated in the most monotonous and least mechanized kinds of work. Routine tedious tasks are considered more suitable for women, while heavy productive labor is still "masculine" work. Women do constitute half of the physicians, but, as in the Soviet Union and in contrast to the West, this is not a high-prestige occupation. Many paraprofessionals, such as the "barefoot doctors" are women, but again it is not a prestigious kind of work. By contrast, relatively few women are university teachers or hold positions in other more prestigious professions. The staffs of the few communal nurseries established for children of factory-working mothers, as those on rural communes, are all female.

Women hold very few of the leadership positions. In the Party's Central Committee, only 10 percent are women. Similarly, few women are in higher positions in the army, in industry, in the universities, in political committees, though theoretically and ideologically, these should be open equally to women and men. Also, women form an "industrial reserve army" (as in the West) and are the first to be laid off when employment declines. "Then, of course, as happened in 1962, the wife reverts to her traditional homemaking role" (Hacker 1976:197).

Communal nurseries and the like are available to only a tiny minority in the Chinese population. The result is that the typical Communist Chinese wife-mother of today has the double job of working in the public labor force and maintaining and caring for children and household, the traditional feminine responsibilities. As in the Soviet Union and on the Israeli kibbutz, and with a similar background, men do not deign to do "women's work." In China there is a further factor: he would lose face.

As Hacker points out, women, subject to greater work instability because of their simultaneous family and household responsibilities, cannot compete economically with men. Although through her employment (and the fact that the woman herself is paid directly, not as in the past through her husband), woman's marital power has been improved, the man makes no concessions to this in the form of taking on any of the housekeeping and child-care activities.

Alongside the oscillations of official Communist governmental policy in reference to women and the family, the actual position of women is one of a continuing sexual division of labor, of continuing traditional association of feminine work with childbearing, child rearing, maintenance of the household (or equivalent work, e.g., laundry, maintenance, in a rural or urban commune), with no move by men to undertake any of these kinds of work or assume these responsibilities. The discrepancy between the sexes in holding positions or occupations of prestige or power or influence continues. In other words, male dominance continues. (See Hacker 1976 and her sources.)

No more than the Soviet Union (or Western countries, for that matter) have the Chinese under Communism found a solution to the problem of how to combine complete equality of women's participation in the economy and the polity, with childbearing, infant- and child-care, maintenance of households, and provision of the basic affective needs of a family unit.

We may note that *Hacker* does not conclude from these experiences of the USSR and China (nor from the kibbutz) that sex equality is sociologically untenable, but, rather, adduces specific historical reasons in each case.

The Israeli Kibbutz

What about the Israeli kibbutz? Feminists might expect to find some comfort there in the egalitarian participation of women in these communal settlements. Interestingly, the answer is not at all. All the recent reports coming out of the kibbutzim, such as Yonina Talmon's (1972), indicate a definite division of labor by sex. One of the ideals of the original kibbutzim, when they were founded in 1909, was complete equality of the sexes in any fields of work. After a while, however, that revolutionary-idealistic phase passed. What we find now, about seventy years later, is this: men are concentrated in what the kibbutzniks call the "productive sphere": agricultural and factory work, and in political and economic management; women are concentrated in the "service" spheres: care of babies and young children in the communal children's houses, primary school teaching, laundry and kitchen work, communal dining-room work, clerical work, and the like. All committee offices, essentially the political roles of the community, are theoretically open to both sexes equally. In reality, however, women are rarely found in the crucial power positions of economic manager and general secretary (in effect, mayor) of the kibbutz. They are also more likely to be found on committees involving services, such as the education committee, or committees dealing with social or cultural affairs, rather than those involving production or general political power or the security of the kibbutz. They are also less active than men in the General Assembly of the kibbutz. Also, the higher the level of authority of an office or a committee on the kibbutz, the lower the percentage of women on it.

Lionel Tiger and Joseph Shepher in *Women in the Kibbutz* (1975) document in detail the sexual division of labor that has emerged in the kibbutzim. While in the early days of kibbutz history, more than half of the women worked for some time in production, the kibbutz moved gradually toward a much more polarized division of labor, with men now about 80% percent of the production work force. The second and later and kibbutz-bred generations are more sexually-polarized than the first generation, and younger kibbutzim more than the older. Advanced levels of education lead kibbutz women toward kindergarten and elementary-school teaching and medical nursing, while it leads kibbutz men into agriculture, engineering, economics, and management. Even in the army, into which Israeli women, like the men, are drafted, most kibbutz women (as well as other Israeli women) are working primarily in secretarial and service jobs. The women's army is essentially a substitute unit, providing back-up aid that rarely involves combat, even more rarely command positions.

Correspondingly, major recent changes in the kibbutzim are in the direction of greater familism, indicated by high and growing rates of birth and marriage, declining divorce rates, the problematic status of single persons, especially women, and mothers increasingly demanding and getting more time with their children. These changes have been pushed by the *women*, over the resistance of some of the men, but with the support of some others of the men. (Tiger and Shepher 1975, see particularly summary pp. 262–63.)

A major recent change on some kibbutzim is a changeover from communal children's houses as the sleeping arrangement for the children, to having the children sleep in their parents' apartments (see Endleman 1977a). This goes against one of the basic principles of the kibbutz, communal child-rearing. It works against one of the principal reasons for having the children in communal children's houses in the first place, that is, freeing the mothers for occupational work on the kibbutz. However, even on those kibbutzim where this change has been made, the children still spend their days in the children's houses. Thus communal childrearing is not entirely abandoned. And mothers do continue to do kibbutz work in the daytime. Only a minority of kibbutzim have thus far switched to such familistic housing. As of the early 1970s, I estimated about 30 out of about 280 kibbutzim had made or were in process of making this change (Endleman 1977a). All of these kibbutzim are part of the most so-called "liberal" federation, the Ichud. Tiger and Shepher make a somewhat different estimate, namely 20, for roughly the same period (Tiger and Shepher 1975:162).

Interestingly, in the very earliest kibbutzim, those founded by the Second Aliyah, 1909ff, when they did start having children, they had them sleeping in the parents' rooms or tents. Four of these early kibbutzim still had familistic housing in 1954 (Tiger and Shepher 1975:168) and still do today, the others having changed to communal children's houses. It was the kibbutzim founded under the Third Aliyah, with a still more radical socialist ideology, that insisted on the communal children's houses as a necessity for socializing the new human being the kibbutz system was supposed to produce. That became the standard for the kibbutz movement. For the most ideologically committed federation, Hashomer Hatzair, it is still considered an ideological essential of the communal system. There the resistance to the shift to familistic housing is most intense.

In the same direction is another innovation on kibbutzim where familistic housing has not been introduced. They call it *sheat hashava*, the "hour of love." It is a half-hour in the morning when the mothers take their children out of the children's houses to play or to walk with them. This innovation was pushed for by the *women* and is now legitimized, in spite of its going against the grain of the communal ideology and being considered disruptive by many men of the kibbutz. The change to familistic housing was also instigated by the women, with some support from some of the men. It was obviously intended to satisfy women's desires to be closer to and have more time with their children, even though it means more work for these women. With familistic housing, you need larger apartments, since the children must now have bedrooms, therefore more housework. It also involves more work for the mother getting the children to bed at night, getting them up in the morning, getting them ready, and taking them to the children's houses. Considering that the kibbutzim are (theoretically) so sexually egalitarian, one can ask why fathers do not do some of that work. Generally the men don't want to, feeling that these tasks are women's work. The women do want to do this. Also, the fathers usually have to get to their kibbutz work earlier in the morning than the mothers.

Besides the kibbutzim that have actually made the shift to familistic housing, there are many other kibbutzim where the women support such a shift for their own children. And there are, Tiger and Shepher report, many other indications of greater familism in the present-day kibbutzim. Compared to the rest of Israel, the kibbutzim have a higher proportion of people married, a lower divorce rate, and a higher birth rate.

On familistic housing, however, there are some interesting wrinkles. In the early 1970s, I found that different kibbutzim that had shifted to familistic housing did it differently in terms of the ages of the children involved. Some started with older children (age 7 and more), some with younger (age 3–6 years), but none included adolescents, who preferred to live communally and not sleep in their parents' homes. And most interestingly, none included infants up to the age of 3 years (Endleman 1977a). That seems strange. If it was a strong maternal impulse that moved these women to want to have the children sleeping in the parents' house rather than the communal children's house, one would expect it would be the infants the mothers would particularly want to have at home. When I asked women about this, the typical reply was: "Oh no, who wants to have to get up in the middle of the night with a crying baby when you have to go to work in the morning? Let the *metapelet* (nurse-caretaker) handle that." There thus appear to be some limits on the maternal side of the mother-infant bond.

Far from feeling "tyrannized" or subject to male dominance, these kibbutz women seem to be making a conscious choice for more of what we in the West see as traditionally feminine tasks and preoccupations, even in opposition to the overtly stated ideology of the kibbutz movement. All the moves in a more familistic direction have been instigated by women—sometimes with a fair amount of male opposition, sometimes and partially with some male support—certainly in response to the women's wishes and their own sense of needs. Since contraception is readily available to all kibbutz females from puberty onwards, having babies is clearly a deliberate conscious choice, and wanting to be more personally involved in caring for and socializing their own children than is possible if communal child-rearing were rigorously followed seems to stem from strong inner feelings of the women themselves.

Many kibbutz women are dissatisfied with their lot, but not in the ways Western feminists are dissatisfied. They are *not* complaining that they are being denied occupational opportunities. For example, you do not hear them crying that so few women are driving tractors. Rather they are complaining that they don't have enough time with their *families*, meaning their children, and secondarily their husbands.

How to interpret these trends has been the subject of diverse opinions. Tiger and Shepher emphasize that the trends are in opposition to explicit ideological intentions that are distinctly anti-patriarchal and shared by men as well as women of the kibbutz. One could hardly consider the increasing polarization of the sexual division of labor and the greater familistic emphasis instigated especially by the women as the products of a sexist plot by the men in support of a patriarchal world view. The self-selection of all adult kibbutzniks ensures that people strongly at odds with the egalitarian ideology would simply not stay on the kibbutz. Therefore, Tiger and Shepher argue, the actual developments—at odds with egalitarian ideology—must come from strong inner motivations of the members themselves, particularly the women. As Tiger and Shepher see it, the women are responding to a basic "bio-grammar" of the female of the species, which pushes her in the direction of wanting to have and care for babies even in opposition to conscious ideological convictions. (Some feminists would respond that this is just a fancier way of saying "maternal instinct," a concept many behavioral scientists regard as unfounded, the term "instinct" suggesting too great a fixity and rigidity.) Tiger and Shepher see some biologically grounded force as one precondition for the kibbutz developments here observed.

Others offer alternative interpretations. One such is to say the kibbutzniks were not in fact as revolutionary as they claimed from the very start. In response, others point out that in the economic-technological conditions of the earliest kibbutzim, physical strength was an important consideration, and it would have been unreasonable to shift some men from production jobs to service jobs. However, as later technological development made this strength difference between the sexes less relevant, one would have expected the sexual division of labor to become *less* pronounced. Instead, it has become more so. Thus, one can argue that the "insufficiently revolutionary" argument runs up against certain intractable realities of sex difference.

Determined feminists may claim that the sex differences that exist and persist on the kibbutzim are still all products of differential socialization; that the founding generation, though rebellious, had necessarily themselves been socialized in a more traditional sex-differentiated manner in patriarchal societies and could not be expected totally to overcome such socialization solely by an act of ideological will. Still, they were radical enough to reject other ideas and values they had been socialized into, in reference to private property, to competition, to religion, to urbanism, and many other things. If early socialization had made them so unalterable, how was it that they rejected *those* ideas and values, but not those in reference to sexual division of labor? Of course, as Tiger and Shepher point out, it is impossible to test any such theories on this matter. The kibbutz new-born are going to have to be socialized by *somebody*. It is impossible to tell how they might turn out in the second and later generations if they were socialized by people completely free of what feminists regard as male-dominated values of patriarchal societies, since such socializers are not available in the modern world.

Another interpretation of these findings is to argue that the men are keeping the women out of the more responsible and powerful positions— a kind of male-conspiracy theory. (The possible plausibility of such a theory is supported by recognition that men *have* in reality banded together in many aspects of work in modern societies to keep qualified women out of higher positions in business or the professions; and that political radicals—e.g., the "New Left" of the 1960s—were notoriously male-dominated.)

However, the argument does not hold up for the kibbutzim. All the founding-generation men were as sexually egalitarian as one could find anywhere in the modern world of the time (or since). And in more recent years, every effort to get women more politically involved in the affairs of the kibbutz or the federation has met with great resistance from the *women*. Women are very reluctant to take on the responsibilities and time demands of political office and have to be begged and persuaded to stand for office. They answer that they want more time with their families. And where they do get involved and active, as on the committees dealing with child care, education, and services—essentially, the kibbutz equivalents of H.E.W.—it is with a reluctant sense that, well, women should be doing these things, these are women's spheres. Kibbutz women told me, in the early 1970s, something like, "It's *natural*. What's the big question about it?"

How could one reconcile a male-conspiracy theory with the fact that all of the opposition to the "hour of love" came from the men, not from women? If men were so intent on keeping women in subservient housewifery and child-centered roles, why would they so object to this manifestation of familism that was introduced at the instigation of *women*?

Another possible theory is that the turn to greater familism and to more pronounced sexual division of labor can be viewed as a strategic *retreat* on the part of the women. When they saw that they could not get the more prestigious production and political jobs away from the men, they settled for intensifying their version of the domestic role. Helen Hacker in a keenly argued sociological analysis of gender differences in cross-cultural perspective (Hacker 1976) argues a variation of this theory: rather than a retreat from equality, the women engaged in a retreat from the ideal of women's doing "masculine" work. According to this view, the "equality" of the pioneering days was that of both sexes working at tasks in the productive sphere, i.e., the "masculine" work areas, and could be attributed to the struggle for survival crisis elements of that early settlement situation, which included a discouragement of having any children during that early phase. The development of the service aspects of the kibbutz economy came later, after survival security had been mainly achieved, and it became feasible, and later ideologically correct, to have children who then needed care and training. There seems never to have been serious consideration of having *men* function in those roles traditionally regarded as "feminine," and so seen by the men of the early kibbutz settlements as well as today.

Of course, there is an ideological presupposition in that word "retreat" in this context, which suggests that all reduction of sexual division of labor somehow automatically represents "progress." This does not seem to be the assumption of the kibbutz women, who at one of the federation meetings on this matter argued that what they wanted was simply that the tasks done by women should have the same prestige and respect as those done by men.

Another interpretation revolves around recognition of the fact that the kibbutz does not exist in isolation. It is part of a whole larger society which does not hold to all of the kibbutz's radical values. Therefore, this theory argues, outside influences pushed the kibbutzniks to a more traditional division of labor. The difficulty with this theory is that it does not explain why the kibbutzim today are even *more* familistic than the rest of Israel (see Tiger and Shepher's data on this) and have a division of labor that is even more polarized than the rest of Israel. Kibbutz women of middle age, who have siblings living in cities in Israel, told me, evidently proudly, that they felt *their* families (of procreation) were stronger, not weaker, than those of their urban siblings. (Unpublished field materials; general commentary on the findings appears in Endleman 1977a, and is consistent with trends seen by Talmon 1972, by Tiger and Shepher, and many other social scientific observers of the kibbutzim in recent years.)

If the "outside influence" theory were valid, how explain that the outside influences did not replace the internal socialism of the kibbutz with a move toward the capitalism that prevails as a major (though not the exclusive) feature of the Israeli economy? Or push the kibbutzim to restore private property, which they have not done? Why should outside influences work selectively only on sexual division of labor and on women's behavior and attitudes on reproduction and child care?

If one points out, as feminists do, that for women to pursue careers on a par with men, they must have adequate support in the way of economic security, child care facilities, and the like, the analyst has to respond by reminding one that kibbutz women are probably better off in these respects than women almost anywhere else in the world. The kibbutz automatically provides a whole series of supports that are lacking for working women, or any women for that matter, in other modern societies. Everyone on the kibbutz is assured of economic support. All children, whether with two parents, or only one, or none at all for that matter, can be assured of being taken care of and socialized in a circle of known and caring comrades, teachers, caretakers, and relatives. Education, at least to the end of secondary school, is assured for all. Whenever the mother is ill or incapacitated in any way, or has to be away from the kibbutz for a while, she can be assured that her children are being taken care of, and not just by impersonal day-care personnel or socially distant teachers, but by comrades of hers and her mate's, who are close kin ethnically, ideologically, and culturally in practically all respects. (See Endleman 1967, ch. 2; Spiro 1956, 1968).

No welfare system, no day-care arrangement, even in the most enlightened modern industrial society, can assure a support system of this kind. This gives the women choices. (True, the choices are not as infinitely wide as extreme feminists seem to be demanding, but neither are they anywhere else, nor can they be if a society has, as it needs, a structure that involves differentiation along gender lines.) The kibbutz women by and large have chosen to construct for themselves a life that is balanced between work and childbearing and child rearing and child caring in a way that is now tipped more toward the familistic than the ideology of the kibbutz earlier dictated.

Tiger and Shepher interpret this choice as one deeply rooted in bio-logical imperatives, rooted in the female's reproductive function. I think they are right to recognize a biological *component* in this. Where I differ from them, as I do from the sociobiologists, is in faulting them for missing that crucial intervening element, the psychological. This is not only a bio-social animal, but a bio-*psycho*-social one. What is missing in the Tiger and Shepher analysis is the psychodynamic dimension in the per-sonality development of kibbutz women. It is incorrect to translate di-rectly from the differing reproductive biology of the two sexes to the differentiated gender roles. In between are differing psycho-develop-mental histories in the two sexes. There we need psychoanalytic understanding.

In an earlier publication, I attempted such a psychoanalytic psycho-developmental reconstruction for the kibbutz personality development (Endleman 1967:127–78). Since that account was based on research and publications on the kibbutzim up to the early 1960s and thus is twenty or more years old, it is probable that some of that analysis is now out of date, and my more recent work on kibbutz (reflected in Endleman 1977a, based on field observations in 1970 and 1971) did not acquire sufficiently detailed developmental material. Thus, what immediately follows is conjectural and also needs the caveat that it is always difficult to generalize about "*the* kibbutz." That is so because there is much internal variation among the 280-odd kibbutzim, among the four major federations, and particularly between the more ideologically "pure" one, Hashomer Hatzair (which, for example, till recently, still resisted any possibility of familial housing) and the more "liberal" or "revisionist" federation, the Ichud, where familistically directed changes have been more prevalent, and where there is also greater intercommunity variation among the kibbutzim within that federation. However, even where in the minority of kibbutzim the children (of certain ages) do not sleep in the children's communal houses, they are still basically cared for and socialized in communal groups, and the *metapelet* (nurse-caretaker) is still the crucial caretaking and adult socializing agent. This still seems to be the universal practice in the kibbutz movement. Similarly, com-munal property and production, communal provision of basic services, and internal democratic socialism on each kibbutz are still bedrock fea-tures of kibbutz social structure and economy. And basic egalitarianism and the centrality of work in life are still the basic values of the kibbutz.

It is evident that neonates and infants of both sexes are "mothered" by a combination of the *metapelet* and their respective natural mothers. Each infant thus has two "mothers," and the crucial point for this analysis is that both are female. (No males take the role of *metapelet* for infants or very young children; and veteran informants in the early 1970s say they cannot remember there ever being any males in this role; there was one exception: one old-timer did remember a then-young man in the 1920s who said he wanted to take care of a group of kindergarten kids (age 4–7), adducing the ideology of sexual equality for his being so assigned; the arrangement, however, was short-lived; perhaps a few months. After that no other male even applied for such a position. The informant felt the male metapelet was subjected to just too much informal ridicule; "everybody felt this was just naturally a job for women." Endleman, field observations and interviews, 1971.)

Kibbutz mothers show an active desire to nurse their own babies, wherever possible. Work loads are much reduced for women in the late stages of pregnancy, cut to zero for the mother of the neonate, then only gradually raised back to two, then four, then to the standard (for females) six hours a day (compared to eight for men) as the baby goes beyond early infancy to the toddler state (see Tiger and Shepher 1975; Endleman 1967 and 1977a). There is no question that the kibbutzniks today, in particular the women, want a high degree of closeness of mother to infant. And the mother is with the infant when and because she wants to be, not because social pressure is forcing her. It thus appears that between the mother in her eager contact with the baby and the metapelet in her dutiful care to her job, the babies and children get plenty of what Winnicott calls "good enough mothering." This, of course, has a differential impact on the children of the two different sexes. For the girl, there is enough of a "good-enough mother" object to identify with, which in later development leads to the desire to become like the mother and the metapelet, by having and caring for babies herself.

Both the metapelet and the mother (both necessarily female) will react differently to boy babies than girl babies. The object-relations of the baby girl toward the metapelet and toward the mother will have certain similarities, predicated on the fact that each is also female, and will probably share features that typically appear in the infant girl's relations with the *mother* in our society: early sumbiosis and fusion, followed in the second year by difficulties in achieving separation-individuation, since the mothering female has a certain investment (emotionally) in maintaining the early mother-infant bond. Also, this mothering person, in each of her guises (metapelet and natural mother) confronts the little girl baby with her omnipotence, and each is frustrating to the child, though in different ways. Where the mother (as usually on the kibbutzim) nurses the baby, she is more likely to be the particular object of "fusion," but then she is frustrating in not being constantly with the child; the metapelet by contrast is frustrating in that she must divide her mothering among the several babies simultaneously in her charge—the number used to be about eight, nowadays more likely about five, but still enough to insure the lack of an exclusive claim by the infant upon her. The later infancy struggle of the child to free herself from the omnipotence of these two mothers is probably (as in our society) greater and more difficult for the girl than for the boy.

The boy's relations to the metapelet and to the mother will also share certain similarities and also will differ from those of the girl to the mother and the metapelet. Precisely because he is of the opposite sex, the metapelet will treat him differently than the girl babies in her charge; and so will the natural mother. Both are likely to encourage eroticizing of the relationship by the child, in a way they do not with girl babies. Both will also probably encourage stronger and earlier separation-individuation by the boy baby than by the girl baby, and also expect greater manifestations of aggressiveness in the boys than in the girls, thus fostering the boys' actual expression of this. (The differences may not be as pronounced as they had been in the past in our society.)

One could expect relatively clear-cut gender identification in the infant boys and infant girls at about the same ages as observed in our society, that is, before the end of the first year, and certainly well established by about eighteen months. Because the kibbutz.babies are always in groups, they will probably become aware earlier of the differences in the sexes, and will learn at an early age to connect this difference with the fact that both the important "mothering" agents are female.

There will also be identification with the metapelet and the mother, and these processes will necessarily be different in formation and consequences for the girl than for the boy.

The boy will shift his identification to the father and other adult males of the kibbutz, with whom the children have increasing contacts in early and later childhood.

The children clearly grow up in a two-sex world in which each will be pushed to identify with and anticipate participation as an adult of his or her own sex, and to associate such participation with the particular kinds of tasks the two different sexes perform.

Though fathers are warmly involved with their own children on the kibbutz, they are clearly more peripheral to the infant and young child than are the dual mothers, the metapelet and the natural mother.

Thus we have little reason to expect that the kinds of differences in object-relational attunement between females and males that we typically find in our society would be significantly different on the kibbutz. To the extent that this is true, we can expect females to want to be mothers, to want to mother their own children and/or participate in the mothering process for kibbutz children generally, in the function of metapelet, or nursery teacher, or primary school teacher, or in some other capacity defined as being in the "service" rather than the productive sphere.

RECAPITULATION:
VANGUARD NORMS: SOCIOLOGICALLY VIABLE?

We have been dealing with the question of whether, sociologically, the vanguard norms are a viable possibility in modern society. Cross-cultural evidence from tribal societies, though seeming to indicate some cases where women may hold the highest political office, as chief or monarch, do not seem to bear out a picture of female dominance generally in the society; some societies are gender differentiated but without a clear-cut gender hierarchy, but where there is some degree of hierarchy there seem to be no cases where it is not true that males are in the dominant position. We have considered a number of versions of attempts to explain this generality. Neither do we find historically significant exceptions to this general trend. Among contemporary societies that would appear at first look to suggest significantly different alternative patterns, neither the Soviet Union, nor mainland China, nor the Israeli kibbutz, each combining in a different way collectivism and an overt ideology of sexual egalitarianism, has in fact effected a social system that has totally de-differentiated the gender roles of females and males, or produced any close approximation of parity of women with men, in spite of ideological predilections toward such equality in each of these societal instances. The kibbutz has been considered at greater length, partly because it is much better documented by a massive amount of research along anthropological, sociological, and psychological lines, and because its current trends are so strikingly toward greater rather than lesser differentiation, in opposition to official ideology.

These lines of evidence all suggest there are exceptionally strong forces at work, which are probably a combination of biological, psychological, and sociological, that tend to maintain differentiation along gender lines. Frequently enough in complex societies this is in the direction of male superordination, or at least of important qualititative differences with no clear-cut hierarchy. Never do we find hierarchical differences clearly favoring the female.

Differentiation is a fundamental social process, as argued by countless sociologists from the "classical" nineteenth-century ones onward. Georg Simmel (1908ff) for example, analyzed how the interplay of social differences based on age, sex, social class, occupation, and any other social categories, as well as upon idiosyncratic personal differences, constitutes the very process of sociality. Complete equality of persons in society is thus an unrealizable ideal. Some thinkers go further: an *undesirable* ideal: approximations to its attainment would reduce the distinctive uniqueness of each individual and the diversity of such individualities, rendering life not richer but more sterile. Cynthia Nelson and Virginia Olesen (1977) devote a thoughtful essay to applying these perceptions to a critique of the concept of equality in feminist thinking. They argue instead for the value of a system like Islamic societies' *complementarity* of the sexes.

While differentiation into distinct social categories such as those revolving around age and sex, as well as instrumental functional roles like occupations, operates as at least a partial constraint upon individuals playing these roles, differentiation in the sense of recognition and encouragement of distinctive unique qualities in each individual operates also to limit the constraints of social categories, of which gender may be one.

Differentiation of gender roles, by providing clear-cut categories and expectations, provides a sense of security and facilitates orderly functioning of society. Along with other kinds of differentiation, it can paradoxically work in two seemingly opposite directions at once: constraining toward conformity to socially efined roles, and facilitating individual differences and thus personal freedom.

Feminist sociologists may ask, why does differentiation, even assuming its social utility, have to use ascribed status by sex as one of its forms? Why not simply differentiate individuals for roles by personal talents and inclination regardless of sex? We answer by turning to the other dimensions of the "powerful forces" just alluded to, i.e., the biological and the psychological. Biological elements have been dealt with in the preceding section on evolutionary origins. Here we now turn to the psychological, specifically the psychodynamic dimension, explored through psychoanalytic study. What is it in the ontogenetic psychological development of females that is distinctive from that of males, that would dictate, or at least cohere with, definite gender differentiation in society? What in these differing psychodynamic developments would vitiate the probability of attainment of the "vanguard" norms sought by modern feminism?

CHAPTER NINE

Difficulties with the Vanguard Norms: Psychodynamic

We earlier stated that aside from the sociological arguments, there are reasons for believing that there are psychological realities in the human condition, or better, bio-psychological ones, that would make it unlikely that the vanguard or feminist norms would, in fact, come into being as the predominant norms for the whole society. Let us now elaborate on that statement.

From psychoanalysis we now know enough about the differences in psychosexual developmental patterns of females compared to males. By and large these patterns diverge substantially according to sex. So much so that the probability of some version of our kind of society with complete equality of the sexes in all respects would seem to be very low.

Psychoanalysis is, of course, now being seen as a crucial "enemy" by many—not all—feminist critics. (For an important exception see Juliet Mitchell 1974.) Their antagonism tends to get focused on Freud and his views of women, or rather what they imagine his views of women to be, since many of the feminist objections indicate their makers have only a dim and third-hand notion of what Freud actually wrote. Still, even highly knowledgeable feminists, such as Nancy Chodorow, whose work (1978) is exceptional in its painstaking scholarly respect for and understanding of psychoanalytic theories, manage to fault Freud for patriarchal bias and other sins along rather standard feminist lines.

Feminists accuse Freud of being condescending, if not outright hostile, toward women generally, of not taking women seriously, of being both ignorant about them and yet pontificating erroneously and with malicious bias against them. They accuse him of believing women trapped in inferiority by biological destiny, of approving that inferiority, of generalizing about women from normative bias rather than empirical evidence. They claim he derogates their moral sense in his theory of their inferior superegos; that he accuses them unjustly of being vain, prone to jealousy, passive, and masochistic (there also in that sense inferior), irrational, lacking firm reality orientation, and being emotionally labile. They claim he draws from his biological determinism warrant for changelessness in women's inferior social status. They are particularly offended by Freud's theory of penis envy as central to female personality development.

Some of these criticisms stem, I think, from ignorance of psychoanalysis, some from only partial and distorted knowledge of it, some from ideological bias that refuses to countenance anything indicating important differences between the sexes, some from specifically antibiological bias. Some part of the criticism may well be justified, however, for there are certainly passages in Freud that could be quoted to demonstrate a strong patriarchal value position in his outlook. Much of the criticism shows its authors' unawareness of the substantial developments and changes in psychoanalytic theories about psychosexual development since Freud's work, changes in directions such that present-day psychoanalysis, even in its more classical versions, represents substantial modification of Freud's views. These changes derive particularly from the much more extensive and intensive exploration of the stages of personality, and specifically psychosexual development, preceding the oedipal stage, and taking us back to the earliest period of infancy, an era that was still largely a dark mysterious continent to Freud and his first-generation followers.

On many points of Freud's presentation of the path of female psychosexual development, latter-day psychoanalysis, in the "classical" vein, finds the picture requires *modifying elaboration* (though not rejection), introducing shifts deriving from the viewpoints of the latter psychoanalytic ego-adaptational psychology (Hartmann and colleagues) and from the "English school" or "object-relations theorists." We shall turn to some of these shortly.

(For an excellent compilation of major papers by Freud and later psychoanalysts on feminine development, along with thoughtful counterpointing essays to each of these by various present-day thinkers, see Jean Strouse, ed., *Women and Analysis*, 1974.)

On two points particularly, however, later psychoanalysis does declare Freud wrong about the female psycho-sexual-developmental pattern: these are Freud's idea that babies of both sexes are originally "masculine" in sexual orientation in the sense that both actively take the mother as sexual object; and second, Freud's view that penis envy is the central key to the whole later female psycho-sexual development, as well as being the major force leading the female to want to have a baby (symbolically the penis). Horney argued long ago (in opposition to Freud's picture of female development) that the little girl is feminine from the very beginning (Horney 1933). And recent research by direct infant and child observation indicates that distinctive gender identity is normally formed by at latest eighteen to twenty-four months of age, with rudiments going back to the first year of life (See Stoller 1977; Kleeman 1977; Galenson and Roiphe, 1977) considerably earlier than the "phallic stage" of Freud's construction, which would not be until the fourth year of life or later. As many critics have pointed out, it seems preposterous that the little girl at about four would have to change her sex.

On the other point, penis envy, probably no other aspect of psychoanalytic theory has aroused such intense hostility and vituperation from women, particularly feminists. Later psychoanalysis says Freud was mistaken in considering it *the* central force in female personality development, including her wish for a baby. Not that later psychoanalysis declares simply that penis envy does not exist. There is plenty of evidence that it does, that it does arise in the later-infancy early-childhood girl, and may possibly be universal in girls' experience.

Rather, the disagreement is on whether this experience is a central organizer and determinant of all later development in the female personality. That it could be the primary determinant of the female's wish for a baby seems improbable and also inconsistent with the evolutionary emphasis in Freud's psychology. If species survival depends on the female's wish to have babies, it is unlikely that it would depend so heavily or primarily on so compensatory a psychological process as penis envy. This is not to deny that there is, in fact, a symbolic equation of penis equals baby in the unconscious of human beings, as amply demonstrated in dreams, myths, and folklore, of so many cultures of the world that we have plausible reason to believe it is universal. Later psychoanalysis, however, demonstrates that this must be only an auxiliary determinant of the wish for a baby.

Psychoanalytically oriented child observation studies indicate little girls expressing (e.g., in doll play) a wish to have a baby from a very early age, long before the "phallic" stage at which Freud posits penis envy coming to the fore.(See research reported on in the volume edited by Blum, 1977, *Female Psychology: Contemporary Psychoanalytic Views*, which presents overviews of present-day classical, i.e., nonrevisionist, psychoanalysis on issues of female sexual and psychological development. Research reported therein indicates a quite early development, between twelve and twenty-four months, if not earlier, of a very primary sense of positive femaleness, and a wish for a baby at a very early age. long before any acute awareness of genital sex differences, or anything approximating penis envy.)

Janine Chasseguet-Smirgel (1964) analyzes how penis envy functions as a metaphor for the girl's envy and awe at, and wish for, masculine power *symbolized* by the phallus as a kind of compensation for the narcissistic wound she experiences in not having the attributes (that a boy does have) to oppose the mother and show independence from her. Penis envy is thus put in the context of revolt of the child (occurring in children of both sexes, but differently configurated in each case) against the omnipotent mother. (Nancy Chodorow picks up and uses to good effect this revision of Freudian thinking on this issue. See Chodorow 1978: 123.)

It would be well at this point to backtrack and present more systematically just what Freud and later psychoanalytic thinkers have had to say about female psychosexual development and personality development generally, to confront these formulations with the critiques that have come from thoughtful feminist theorists, and to suggest a reformulation that takes into account the sociological and cultural context for these personality developments. Not that Freud or later psychoanalysts have ignored socio-cultural factors, but, rather, it is rare, in the work of psychoanalysts to this point, to have them systematically integrated with the psychoanalytic account.

Very broadly, psychoanalytic work demonstrates beyond question that there are systematic divergences between female and male psychosexual development that result in associated differences in more general personality patterns. Of course, there are individual variations within each sex—and psychoanalytic clinical work has always focused a lot more on the idiosyncrasies of each individual case—so that, of course, there will always be some women who are psychologically more similar to most men, and some men who are psychologically more like most women than like most other men. But we are dealing with general *trends*, and these trends are different, in the nature of the case.

FREUD'S VIEWS

For the psychoanalytic account, taking Freud himself first: Freud's views on female psychosexual development were not unitary or entirely consistent throughout the whole long period of his psychoanalytic writings. His views date from the crucial *Three Contributions to a Theory of Sexuality*, first published in 1905 (1905b) with a whole series of important revisions in later years: 1910, 1915, 1920, 1922, and 1924. They are also developed in several later essays (Freud 1923, 1924, 1925c, 1931, 1933a, and 1940). Leaving aside complicated variations among these papers, the developed theory can be schematically outlined as follows:

Though human beings split into two distinct sexes, male and female, biologically, in reference to reproductive roles, all human beings are "bisexual" in a psychological sense, combining elements of psychological "masculinity" and "femininity" in varying ways. One meaning of "masculine" and "feminine" is active and passive, respectively. Other meanings are sociologically imposed by current conventions. (Note here that contrary to his critics, especially feminist sociological ones, and culturalist psychoanalysts like Clara Thompson, 1964, and Natalie Shainess, 1969, Freud was not at all unaware of how much of a role existing social customs and conventions played not only in people's sexual attitudes and overt sexual behavior, but also in the whole range of personality manifestations. He was constantly struggling with the question of how much of human sexual behavior, feelings, and attitudes to attribute to basically innate forces, how much to universal developmental patterns, and how much to varying socio-cultural conditions, and we are still struggling with these questions today, with no more definitive answers than Freud had in his time. Critics charging Freud with attributing everything to biology, or with seeing all personality manifestations as revolving around sex, have, of course, set up a straw man; neither of those statements accurately portrays Freud's thoughts.) Freud said that the equation of "masculine" with strong and active, and of "feminine" with weak and passive, is a *social convention*, embarrassed by the facts of actual psychological bisexuality in all human beings of both sexes.

Nor did he mean by "bisexuality" what has been attributed to him, or what is meant by those bisexual-liberationist activists who argue that it is limiting to the human's natural proclivities to have sexual relations only with the opposite sex, or only with the same sex. Such ideologists may try to thus trace their intellectual lineage to Freud, but that is not what Freud meant by the "original bisexuality" of all human beings. He did not mean that the "natural" state would be to have overt sexual relations with both men and women. He meant only that the potentialities are there, and that in the original sexuality of the neonate human being and of the very young infant, the libido is without any definite clear-cut objects, and therefore in that sense is not only "bisexual" but polymorphous, i.e., can potentially get cathected to any kind of object of either sex, of any species in fact, or even non-animate things, as well as relating to any part of the body. For further analysis on this question, and its relation to problems of homosexuality, see next part.)

Freud also meant by original bisexuality that any human being can identify with any other person of either sex, and in so doing present qualities culturally defined as either belonging to what we would now call his own gender, as well as qualities associated with the opposite gender.

To continue Freud's account: Human bisexuality is crucially involved in two phenomena: penis envy in the female, castration anxiety in the male, which are the obverse of each other. Because of the anatomical difference between the sexes, and the necessity to come to terms *subjectively* with this difference, the psychosexual developmental path for the girl will necessarily differ from that of the boy. (Later psychoanalytic writers indicate several other, additional, psychodynamic reasons why this divergence occurs. See later in this chapter.)

For the boy, the original object of libidinal desire, the mother, remains the sexual object. In the phallic stage, this desire collides with the father's sexual possession of the mother and his power as a punitive, potentially castrating agent. The oedipus complex—sexual desire for the mother and rivalrous murderous feelings toward the father—brings on fear of punishment from the father, the ultimate version of which would be castration. (Freud and later psychoanalysts use this term to mean removal of the penis, sometimes it implies removal of both the penis and the testes, in contrast to its "correct" technical meaning of removal of the testes. This "erroneous" usage has been pointed out by many critics, e.g., Chodorow 1978.) The fantasy that this could really happen is fostered by the boy's observation of other small human beings who are like himself except in this crucial respect, that they lack a penis, and an "obvious" theory to explain this is that they had one and have had it cut off as punishment: ergo, he too is in danger of being punished in this terrible way. The Oedipus complex thus leads in the boy to the castration complex, the dread of becoming castrated like the little girl. The boy therefore gives up the two primal criminal desires of mother-son-incest and parricide, dissolves the Oedipus complex, and identifies with the authoritative and law-giving father, develops his superego, and awaits physical maturity to pursue a substitute for the desired mother in women outside the family.

(Interestingly, some feminists seem to have little quarrel with this part of Freud's psychosexual theory, thinking that it accords with their experience of men as having this kind of "hang-up" about castration. It is when we turn to Freud's corresponding psychology about women that their hackles are raised.)

For Freud, for the little girl, the original libidinal object is the same, the mother. She is also the object of the earliest identifications. This relationship is ambivalent: it contains both love and hate. At the phallic stage, the girl discovers her lack of the penis. She envies males this precious possession, feels betrayed and cheated that she does not have one, and blames the most likely person for her "castrated" state: the mother. Thus, the "castration complex" for the girl is the conviction that she is already castrated. She therefore turns away from the mother as love object to the father, wanting his penis, and, by extension, a symbolic re-creation of the penis, a baby. The unconscious equates baby with penis. (This is only one of a number of related equations in primary process thinking, uncovered in dreams, psychosis, mythology, etc., e.g., body protrusions or extrusions: from mother's nipple, to penis, to feces, to baby; or body apertures: mouth, anus, vagina.) Desire for the father puts the girl in rivalry with the mother, intensifying already developed hostility toward the mother. For the girl, then, the sequence is reversed: castration complex comes first, that in turn ushers in the Oedipus complex. Since the father is a secondary (rather than original) libidinal object, and not invested with the intensities of both desire and hate originally directed toward the mother, the urgency to renounce and dissolve the Oedipus complex is not as great for the girl as for the boy. Nor is there so great a necessity for repression of its elements. It does, however, normally get resolved. The father is relinquished as libidinal object. The girl re-identifies with her mother, in her "feminine" attributes, including the wish to become a mother herself. Also, said Freud, the girl differs from the boy in superego development. Since unlike the boy she does not have to internalize a powerful and punitive father, her superego development will be weaker and less harsh than that of the boy. Because the girl's expression of aggression must be more systematically suppressed or repressed, her aggression gets turned back internally against the self. Hence masochism is an important part of normal female development.

Thus for Freud.

We need immediately to point out that much of this account has been brought into question, for modification, if not for outright rejection, by later work of psychoanalysts of both sexes.

MODIFICATIONS OF THE FREUDIAN VIEW

From the outset, many aspects of this picture were challenged or attacked from within mainstream ("classical" or "orthodox") psychoanalysis, and later from orthodox, from culturalists, from object-relations theorists, from adaptational ego-psychological psychoanalysis and, of course, in more recent years from responses to critics within the feminist movement. Modifications came from ideological shifts, from re-evaluations based on the usual psychoanalytic research base (i.e., direct clinical experience), from research in different but related traditions (e.g., most importantly, from direct child-observation studies, and from sociocultural studies in sociology and anthropology.)

To date, we cannot say that we have a fully rounded revision of the Freudian view within the classical perspective. Blum's introductory essay in his edited collection (Blum 1977) as well as the concluding essay in that volume, Peter Barglow and Margret Schaefer, "A New Female Psychology?" can be counted as good overviews. (See my paper, Endleman 1977b, summarizing the main recent psychoanalytic formulations; and the collection by Janine Chasseguet-Smirgel, *Female Sexuality*, 1970, for other papers within the classical perspective. Culturalist and object-relations variations are dealt with later in this chapter.)

Many important women analysts stayed very close to Freud's views, and have thought that their own clinical experience with female patients has largely substantiated these conceptions of female sexual development. Among these are Princess Marie Bonaparte (1951), Ruth Mack Brunswick (1940), Helene Deutsch (1925, 1930, 1944–45), and Jeanne Lampl-de-Groot (1928). However, two outstanding women analysts differed sharply from Freud on several of these issues, namely Karen Horney (1926, 1932, 1933) and Melanie Klein (1928, 1932)—note the early date of these criticisms, which are forerunners of criticisms by feminist theorists of a later period (1960s and 1970s). So in the same period, very early in this game, did an outstanding male psychoanalyst, Ernest Jones (1927, 1933, 1935). This topic was very hotly debated in psychoanalytic circles in the late 1920s and into the 1930s. Then it subsided from centrality of psychoanalytic interest for a long time, till it was re-awakened by the challenges of the revived women's movement of the 1960s and 1970s. Most of the challenges to the strict Freudian view that have come in recent years were already adumbrated in the dissenting voices of Jones, Horney, and Klein in the 1920s and 1930s.

Jones and Horney saw penis envy not as primary and normal, but rather as a regressive defense. Jones also argued that the girl's hatred of the mother long antedates the phallic penis-envy stage. Melanie Klein elaborated at length on the intensities of hate in the ambivalence the infant girl feels toward the mother. Also, where Freud saw the infant girl as striving in a "masculine" way toward the mother as object and later propelled into femininity in the phallic stage, Horney by contrast insisted the infant girl is "feminine" from the very beginning (Horney 1933). Researches of recent years bear her out (see above). They find evidence in direct child observations that infant females acquire at least a rudimentary core feminine identity in the first year of life.

Where Freud thought the vagina was usually undiscovered as a source of sexual satisfaction until puberty, Jones, Horney, and Klein all reported evidence of some vaginal stimulation and response during even early infancy. Recent direct-observational studies confirm this (see Galenson 1976 and other reports in Blum 1977). Later clitoral dominance would then be seen as a defensive operation, warding off anxiety about possible injury to the internal genital parts.

Later psychoanalytic work within the classical framework continues to substantiate Freud's emphasis that the influence of sexual-drive organization is special and important in the development of female sexuality and of female personality generally. (See, for example, Kleeman, in Blum 1977; Glenn as reported in Galenson 1976; Galenson and Roiphe, in Blum 1977; Roiphe and Galenson 1973; and Galenson 1976.) Penis envy and castration-complex phenomena do consistently appear, but in many cases considerably earlier than Freud had thought, shaping an already developing sense of feminine identity emerging from the relationship of the child to primary objects (Kleeman 1977; Galenson and Roiphe 1977). They also note that this development (of basic feminine identity) also has contributions coming to it from conflict-free areas of development. (Hartmann's ego psychology emphasizes that not all ego development stems from conflict; some of it develops autonomously, "conflict-free" (Hartmann 1939, 1964).

Much of the later psychoanlytic work modifying Freud's views of female psychosexual development derives from greater study and understanding of the pre-oedipal infantile stages and greater recognition and understanding of the relationship of the infant to the mother from the earliest stages of infancy. These shifts were started in the 1920s, contemporaneous with Freud's development of his female-sexuality theories. Lampl-de-Groot (though fairly "orthodox" Freudian) did nevertheless point out the crucial nature of the girl's relationships to her mother in the earliest infantile stages as determinant of her later psycho-sexual development. (This at least implicitly challenges Freud's idea that the castration complex and penis envy in the female—essentially phallic-stage phenomena—were "bedrock" (Lampl-de-Groot 1928).

Also, still within the classical psychoanalytic framework, Marjorie Brierley (1932) argued that the crucial determinant of a woman's psychosexual development is in the early infantile relationship to the *mother*. Brierley saw females differing from males in psychosexual development, not so much on any one specific point, but in the kind of *balance* of forces operating in the total constellation. For example, she saw a relatively greater role of *oral* fantasies in the total configuration of the normal female than in that of the male. Following Freud, she sees woman as having a dual sexuality, one in her mating relationship with the man, the other in her reproductive role and relationship to the infant. To fulfill both of these adequately, she must keep open two different series of symbolic equations deriving from universal human infantile and later sexual fantasies. One of these concerns body apertures: from mouth, to anus, to vagina; the other is from mother's nipple, to penis, to feces, to baby.

Pre-Oedipal Developments

Other modifications of psychoanalytic theories about psychosexual development of both females and males have come from work in the analysis of separation-individuation processes in early infancy (the major figures here are Margaret Mahler and her associates: see Mahler 1968; Mahler, Pine, and Bergman 1975, and bibliographical references to all of Mahler's work in the latter book), and from the English school of "object-relations" theorists (Fairbairn 1952; Guntrip 1971; Winnicott 1958, 1965, 1971; Michael Balint 1965, 1968; Alice Balint, 1939, 1954) and related work of John Bowlby (1969). Insightful synthesizing from these various sources is done by the sociologist Nancy Chodorow in her recent book on *The Reproduction of Mothering* (1978).

From these kinds of sources, we get the following modification of Freud's account, in reference to the preoedipal periods:

The neonate of either sex has a total dependency, physically and psychologically, on the primary caring person, usually the mother. This connection is both libidinal (Freud) and object-relational (Fairbairn). Infant and object are merged, fused. Mother serves as infant's "external ego" (Mahler). Cathexis is emotionally charged with this total dependence and fusion: the infant has "primary love" for the caring and gratifying object (Michael and Alice Balint). The infant's need is for contact, not only feeding. Gradually the infant experiences separateness from the mother. Differentiation-individuation begin. The mutuality with the mother is asymmetrical: baby's need is absolute: mother's is relative. The self develops by inner physical experience of one's own body and by demarcation from the object world. The early relationship with the mother is devoid of reality principle: the infant does not recognize the mother as a separate person with interests and relationships of her own apart from the baby. Reality principle starts to appear as the infant begins to see mother as separate. Anxiety, conflict, ambivalence develop. This enables the structuring of the ego. The baby internalizes parts of the mother object, splits off other parts (most likely negative ones).

Father enters the picture later and, as someone other than the primary caring person, can be used by the child to help individuation-differentiation. Father also represents society and culture (in contrast to the "pre-social" relation to the mother).

The quality of the early relation with the mother informs and interacts with all other relations during development and serves as the foundation-stone for all other love-object relations (Fairbairn). "Good mothering" means making total environmental provision, being the external ego, timing merging and separating precisely to the baby's emotional needs at that moment, total empathy for these needs, and extreme selflessness (Winnicott). Most healthy normal women are capable of this, and gratified by it as a unique incomparable experience, utilizing empathy, primary identification, adaptive regression, and non-rational intuitive capacities. (These are potential in both sexes, but more highly developed in females.) The female who has been so mothered herself becomes in turn a good mother. The specifically female experiences of pregnancy, childbirth, and nursing contribute to this process.

Gender differentiation starts early, and proceeds apace. The girl's relation to the mother is different from the boy's. It is critically important for her later development, is intense and ambivalent, and lasts through all three of the (Freudian) stages of infantile sexuality, affecting other attachments and developments. Her attachment to mother (unlike the boy's) remains pre-oedipal in important respects, because the mother, as the same sex, does not become for her a sexual object *in the oedipal sense*, as she does for the boy.[1] Mothers do much less pushing of separation-individuation to daughters than to sons.

By contrast, the mother experiences the infant boy as a definite *other*, opposite-sexed, opposite-gendered. The son's solution is differentiation buttressed by strong emotional investment. The mother may start early to push the son from a pre-oedipal to a more oedipal (i.e., sexual) kind of attachment—especially if the father is largely absent and the mother adult-deprived (Chodorow). While primary separateness is being established by the boy, issues of masculinity and genital differences become important. Phallic-masculine issues intertwine with object-relational and ego issues in the creation of a separate self.

Thus the boy and the girl move toward the oedipal phase from a background of pre-oedipal experiences that differ importantly in terms of the quality of the relationship to the primary care agent, usually the mother, and the secondary relationship with the father. These differences are both libidinal (as emphasized in Freud) and object-relational (Fairbairn, Guntrip, Winnicott, Balint, etc.).

We can note how this object-relations analysis of the relation of the mother with the infant girl and with the infant boy connects with the bio-evolutionary analysis we presented in the preceding chapter: The differential roles of females and males in the emerging techo-economic division of labor of the becoming human species of the East African savannas pressed this species to develop not only differential body specializations, but differential experiential and psychological ones. These include different approaches to communication, the men with greater emphasis on linguistic communication—hence Logos as predominantly a masculine world—the women with greater retention of prelinguistic phatic communication; and within language, differential usages as between males and females. (Many languages to this day have differentiated inflections for females speaking than for males speaking, and some have distinct dialects for the two sexes.) The bifurcation along sex lines that concerns us most at this point is the greater emphasis in the female on phatic forms of communication, in which body language, particularly in direct body contact, conveys a whole emotional atmosphere, or nuance of feeling ineffable to language. Females make this specialization in the context particularly of infant and child care. This then has differential impact on boy babies and girl babies, as outlined in the immediately preceding section. By greater fusion with the mother and greater retention of elements of this fusion into later developmental stages, girls acquire more of this feminine approach to the world than do boys.

Oedipal Period:
Later Classical Psychoanalytic Accounts

Departing from Freud, in some ways, Horney, Jones, and Klein, followed along these lines many years later by Janine Chasseguet-Smirgel

(1970) and Bela Grunberger (1970), formulate the girl's turn to the father as follows: the girl wants a penis (a man) *libidinally*, for sexual gratification, not *narcissistically* (as in Freud) for her own sexual organ. This wish expresses biologically given innate heterosexuality that develops spontaneously and is directed toward the opposite-sexed parent, the father, at this stage. It grows out of her primary awareness of her vagina. She moves from frustrated oral cathexis of the mother's breast, to oral cathexis of the father's penis, to genital cathexis of his penis, to oedipal desire for the father. The shift involves the obvious symbolic equation of mouth and vagina. *Narcissistic* penis envy comes later, and is a defensive maneuver, rather than a primary element as in Freud. It is a defensive flight from these libidinal oedipal desires. She makes such a flight because of fear of the consequences of any consummation of her libidinal wishes toward the father. These consequences are seen by Klein as maternal retaliation; by Jones, as extinction of her sexuality; by Horney, as internal rupture from the penetration (see Chodorow's discussion on this matter, Chodorow 1978:115–16). This account is significant in treating sexuality and reproduction as not inextricably and inevitably linked.

In analyzing the differences between the female oedipal situation and the male, it is useful to distinguish among three kinds of relationships: (1) heterosexual erotic attraction; (2) heterosexual *love* (deep emotional attachment); and (3) general non-sexual emotional attachment and its internalized object-relational counterparts (see Chodorow 1978:128). For boys the relationship to the mother in the pre-oedipal period is of type 3: it moves in the oedipal to a combination of all three types. The girl will probably retain type 3 attachment to the mother; and her turn to the father will involve type 1, but not types 2 and 3. The girl is still struggling to free herself from the omnipotence of the mother. Though the pre-oedipal relationship to the mother is doomed to eventual dissolution, because of its intensity, its ambivalence, and its prolongation, it involves a greater struggle on the part of the girl. The turn to the father is part of this struggle. The girl's oedipal involvement is thus not only a connection with the father, but a change in the inner-relational stance toward the mother. The girl has a "narcissistic wound" from which she seeks relief in the relationship with the father. "Rejection" of the mother is, in part, a defense against primary identification. The turning to the father is also enhanced by the father's own encouragement, his seductiveness, his positive response to elements of seductiveness in his daughter. But because of the factors just discussed, the father does not become the same kind of emotionally exclusive oedipal object for the girl that the mother does for the boy. Her father-attachment is more idealized and also less intense than the boy's attachment to his mother.

By contrast the boy's oedipal situation is less complex. The mother is the object of all three types of attachment. The central issues in this phase are the achievement of a personal masculine identification with the father, a secure masculine self, with the outcome of superego formation and its concomitant of disparagement of women. The boy's oedipal love for the mother is threatening to his masculine independence. The mother's intensity of emotional investment makes the boy's oedipal love too dangerous. In resolving it, the boy develops a more emphatic separation-individuation, and a firming of ego boundaries.

The girl does not need to repress her oedipal attachment as strongly as does the boy. Her major issues in this period revolve around the attainment of heterosexuality.

Her oedipal attachment is never as thoroughly resolved as the boy's. A major difference in outcome between the sexes is that the girl brings from the complexity of her connections with both the father and the mother a different kind of relational potential: greater continuity of elements of primary attachment, of fusion, of non-differentiation, of being more continuous with the external object world. All of these enhance and facilitate her own capacities and motivation for carrying on mothering as an adult. The boy has fewer of these capacities and less motivation. Transcendance of the oedipal (which may never be complete) may be prolonged, delayed till adolescence, where it may be accomplished when the girl reaches genital heterosexuality while at the same time maintaining much of the type 3 attachment to her mother (cf. Chodorow).

On the question of penis envy and castration complex, there is still a good deal more to be said. While their exact role is seen as more problematic by psychoanalysts of the classical persuasion today (than by Freud), they still regard it as definitely occurring in female children. (It is later repressed, made unconscious, so that "of course" adult women would not spontaneously remember having felt that way.) It may be a universal aspect—one aspect, not the whole—of female development. Many analysts think so. It may be determined in any of a number of ways, or any combination of these. It is probably "over-determined" (to use the Freudian phrase—"multidetermined" would be better). It may be an unconscious device of the little girl attempting to win, as her sexual object, the *mother* (assuming the latter's heterosexuality), as suggested in work of Alice Balint (1939, 1954), of Ruth Mack Brunswick (1940), and Jeanne Lampl-de-Groot (1928, 1933, 1952). This may be compounded with determinants coming from narcissistic injury (same authors). Ego issues: self-esteem, struggle for autonomy, may play a part (Chasseguet-Smirgel 1970). The penis may symbolically represent for the little girl independence from the omnipotent mother (Chasseguet-Smirgel 1970). Narcissistic penis envy (as distinguished from the wish for the father's penis as a heterosexual object wish) may be a reactive defense against fantasies of acting upon the sexual desire for the father and fear of the consequences of doing so (Horney, Klein, Jones, Chasseguet-Smirgel, as indicated above). The envy of the penis may derive from communications (possibly more unconsciously than consciously) coming from one or both of the parents that the male genital is better. And *additionally*, the penis may symbolize the social privileges and superiorities of males over females in the society (Horney, Thompson 1964, and other culturalist psychoanalysts).

Analysts think the penis envy phenomenon is probably applicable to all females growing up in Western societies, and some think it is probably universal for all human females. At least one anthropologist whose work is significant and relevant on such matters, Margaret Mead, presented evidence in *Male and Female* (Mead 1949) that would certainly suggest such phenomena in any of the tropical primitive societies she studied. Where little boys would run about naked till at least the age of seven or eight, and then wear only a flimsy pubic covering which certainly would not accomplish any goal of modesty, little girls began to be covered up in the pubic areas from the age of about four or five. The "explanation" given by the tribeswomen was that "she had something precious which must be protected." Since danger of physical harming of the genitals by tree branches or falling, for example, would appear to be more real for the boy than the girl in such circumstances, it seemed reasonable for Mead to conclude that the covering of the girl referred rather to shame on the part of females about her "damaged" or "incomplete" state. It could be, of course, that Mead, by this time in her career much more psychoanalytically minded than earlier, was reading castration anxiety into this situation, but one can wonder, what alternative explanation would be more persuasive? She points out that she found this difference in all the primitive societies where children go about naked or nearly naked in the earliest years. The Latin term *pudenda* (something to be ashamed of) had in the past been typically used to refer to the genitals—but most usually to the female genitals.

Mead concluded that she was confronting a pan-human universal matter of sexual difference, in response to the pride or shame one is to take about one's genital apparatus that would be applicable to New York or Mundugumor or anywhere.[2]

CHALLENGE FROM THE CULTURALISTS

From the culturalist school of psychoanalysis there came quite early their particular kind of challenge to the penis envy theories. Horney moved to more sweeping rejection of major Freudian positions. On penis envy, she wrote that it could be that the whole idea of penis envy in females was a male fantasy based on male infantile sexual theories, and accepted by others from Freud because of the male-dominated culture in which they lived (Horney 1926, 1932). The ideas of penis envy and the castration complex in women got accepted, Horney said, because they compensate *men* for their envy of females, of women's breasts, child-bearing capacity, and motherhood. Marmor, in an influential article, "Changing Patterns of Femininity" (1968), makes a similar point, emphasizing that it is men who envy women. In reply we have to say, of course, that certainly we know that males envy females. Margaret Mead (1949) documents a whole array of cultural patterns indicating "womb-envy," male envy of female functions, in many primitive tribes. Bettelheim, in *Symbolic Wounds* (1954), draws on this and other anthropological material showing how male puberty initiation rituals in primitive societies present a cultural manifestation of unconscious envy of the womb and of woman's reproductive apparatus and capacities. But the recognition that males envy females in no way invalidates the statement that females envy males.

Marmor argues that for so perceptive a man as Freud not to see male envy of females must have occurred because male envy of females was not so frequent an occurrence at that time, while female envy of males reflected a cultural phenomenon: females envied males' dominance and status prerogatives, not their genitals. As the status balance between the sexes has shifted in the past seventy-odd years, male envy of females has become more prevalent, Marmor argues.

That is not really a satisfactory argument. Bettelheim handles it much better. He says male envy of females was never absent, but in a highly patriarchal culture it must be more thoroughly repressed. In that kind of culture—which Europe of Freud's day certainly was—it appears "reasonable" that females should envy males, and therefore it is easier to perceive this envy. Mead (1974) makes a complementary comment: in many tribal societies, where the achievements of males—in the technological field—are modest indeed, the life-creating capacities of the females in reproduction are a matter of awe for young boys, and this awe is given ceremonial expression in rituals where males symbolically reenact female functions.

Clinical observations make it abundantly clear that there is male envy of female genitals and female reproductive capacities and functions. This and the cross-cultural material make it reasonable to assert that this phenomenon is a transcultural universal. It exists *alongside of* female envy of males, not as a contradiction to it.

Getting back to envy of males by females: it is a superficializing of psychodynamic insights given us by psychoanalysis to claim that such envy of males by females is *only* envy of superordinate social status and the like. Kleeman's and also Galenson and Roiphe's firsthand observations show little girls reacting to the genital differences between the sexes in the way the theory of penis envy postulates, especially on the matter of urination. The boy's different equipment enables him in both urination and masturbation to put on exhibitionistic display that is denied to the little girl. *He* feels in making this comparison that his equipment is superior. And so does *she*.

Freud did not say that the female *was* genitally inferior to the male, only that infantile subjective reactions and fantasies regarding the difference lead not only boys, but girls too, to *believe* that she is. Freud was grappling with the female's subjective sense of herself as damaged and inferior. As he saw it, identification with the mother, who at least unconsciously sees herself as inferior or defective, cannot but promote the girl's sense of her own defectiveness.

We can question whether little girls of about three can be much comforted by mothers or other well-meaning women assuring them that they have a uniquely valuable inner genital apparatus, and that with that, they can have babies some day, and that no boy has that or can ever do that. In the present-day psychoanalytic account, we pay attention to both elements: the little girl's narcissistic injury in perceiving herself as lacking the precious possession of the boy, and at the same time, her developing maternal wishes, the wish to have a baby, in positive identification with her own mother, and as a positive affirmation of her femininity—this also appearing from a very early age, long before the "phallic" phase.

Freud was also aware—contrary to assertions from many critics—of the *cultural* dimension in concepts of femininity and masculinity, and how culturally variable actual feminine development might be from one society to another, from one era to another. But he did consider that cultural pressures could not be the *whole* story, that they had to be built upon differences that were anatomical and physiological, and the subjective consequences of these differences.[3]

There has been much controversy within psychoanalysis about whether and, if so, when, the little girl "discovers" her vagina (See Freud 1925c and elsewhere; Horney 1933, among others). That there has been so much controversy is itself an indication of how problematical recognizing and being in touch with her genital apparatus may be to the little girl. There is no comparable problem about the little boy's discovering his penis. These are not only intractable anatomical differences, but they are bound also to have differential subjective correlates and consequences in the two sexes.

That is one of the meanings of Freud's phrase, "anatomy is destiny," which has become such a negative rallying cry for feminist detractors.[4]

FEMININE SUPEREGO

Another issue over which Freud has incensed feminists is his conception of female superego as weaker than and inferior to the male's.
What do we make of a passage like this?

> I cannot evade the notion (though I hesitate to give it expression) that for women what is ethically normal is different from what it is for men. Their superego is never so inexorable, so impersonal, so independent of its emotional origins as we require it to be in men. Character traits which critics of every epoch have brought up against women—that they show less sense of justice than men, that they are less ready to submit to the great exigencies of life, that they are more often influenced in their judgments by feelings of affection and hostility—all these would be amply accounted for by the modifications in the formation of their superego which we have inferred above. (Freud 1925c:257)

This certainly looks like patriarchal bias. It is also the kind of passage that leads feminist critics to argue that Freud was generalizing from normative bias, rather than from clinical or other kinds of evidence that would be required in the spirit of psychoanalytic inquiry that he himself created and supported (see Chodorow 1978 on this point). "Traits which critics of every epoch . . ." certainly does not suggest such concern for evidence, and implies that Freud himself agrees with these "critics" rather than asking if the allegations are in fact justified by the evidence. Score one for the feminist opponents of Freud on this one.

But these questions need to be raised: what is the context in Freud's developmental theory for *expecting* that the superego development of girls will necessarily (or at least probably) follow *different* lines from that of boys? how does later psychoanalytic work modify (or refute) Freud's superego theories? and third, is the *description*—leaving aside normative judgment—of feminine ethical stances actually so inaccurate?

If we translate from "the female superego is not as *strong* as the male's" to simply: "the female superego is *different* from the male's," do we really have grounds for rejecting this statement? In the context of the theory of oedipal development and its resolution, the masuline superego developing in the process of resolution of the Oedipus complex is a strongly punitive inner agent. This is built upon a need to identify with harsh punitive aspects of the father experienced by the boy as a potential punisher for the boy's oedipal incestuous and parricidal wishes. With that conception of the superego, it would follow that we could expect the superego development of the girl to move in a different and less punitive path. Since the Oedipus complex for the girl—in Freud's view— was necessarily differently arrived at and configurated than for the boy, and to the extent that superego formation is tied up with that complex and its resolution, the superego formation is bound to follow different paths for the girl. Since the father is not the first but the second love object of the little girl, and therefore not invested with the intensities of both desire and hate originally directed toward the mother, the urgency to renounce and dissolve the Oedipus complex is not as great for the girl as for the boy. (Later psychoanalytic formulations, including those within the diverging object-relations perspective, e.g., Chodorow, do not question the correctness of these propositions.) Nor is there as great a necessity for repression of its elements. Nor does she have the same necessity as the boy to internalize a powerful harsh and punitive father image in the development of her superego. Therefore, the superego is likely to be less harsh and unrelenting than in the case of the male.

On the next question, what does later psychoanalysis have to say on this matter? Within the classic tradition, the present-day picture is more ambiguous than Freud's, and without a very strong consensus (see essays in Blum 1977). There is, however, agreement that there is much more involved in superego development than what begins with the Oedipus complex and its resolution. Way back in the early writings of Melanie Klein in the 1920s and 1930s, there are reformulations of superego development going back to precursors in the earliest infantile experience. Klein, in fact, thought that the female superego could be even harsher than the male's, being built up of archaic elements of the bad mother object of early infancy. Glenn, in recent work (see Galenson's summary report, 1976), argues that the female superego development can, in fact, be quite strong, based on pre-oedipal precursors which combine later with oedipal fears of genital injury by penetration (thus parallel to boys' fear of castration). Others see the female superego as neither stronger nor weaker but as *qualitatively* different. It would use more shame than guilt reactions in its manifestations, be built more on fear of abandonment than fear of castration or injury. Such theorists (e.g., Kaplan, reported in Galenson 1976) see manifestations of this difference in girls' greater secretiveness, and greater tendency to lie, compared to boys, in latency and later.

And, drawing on a combination of recent mainstream classical psychoanalytic writings, and recent object-relations theorists, Chodorow formulates the superego differences between males and females as follows:

> Denial of a sense of connectedness and isolation of affect may be more characteristic of masculine development, and may produce a more rigid and punitive superego, whereas feminine development, in which internal and external object-relations and affects connected to these, are not so repressed, may lead to a superego more open to persuasion and the judgment of others, that is, not so independent of its emotional origins. (Chodorow 1978:169)

(Note that this formulation is not at all far from Freud's.)

Another variant formulation is this: since castration anxiety is more detached from problems of narcissistic injury than is fear of loss of love, it provides a more impersonal foundation for moral activity. This point is made in Roy Schafer's paper, "Problems in Freud's Psychology of Women" (Schafer 1974:464). Freud's conclusion was that women crave unconsciously to be loved, invaded, and impregnated, and therefore bend their morality all too readily to fulfill these cravings, overriding their otherwise cognitively held ideas of right behavior.

There are intriguing perplexities in Freud's conception of the intensely developed *masculine* superego. Its concentration on the maintenance of principle above all else, in isolation from effects on personal relationships, suggests a set of mechanisms that are primarily obsessional: use of isolation of affect; of intellectualization; the rigidity of moral stands built upon reaction-formations against anal sadism. Beneath this kind of morality one would expect to find ferocious and irrational unconscious guilt (e.g., the cleric in Somerset Maugham's story *Rain*). And persons with this kind of rigid morality are *also* likely to commit devious violations of morality and then either atone for these or magically undo them. Schafer in discussing this kind of superego formation (1974) suggests there certainly are no good grounds to consider this a "superior" morality compared to a feminine morality bent on fulfilling craving for love or arising from fear of loss of love. Superego, Schafer says, is not to be equated with morality in the sense of rational, adaptive, socially valuable moral codes. Rather is it "fierce, irrational, mostly unconscious vindictiveness against oneself for wishes and activities that threaten to bring one into archaically conceived infantile danger situations" (Schafer 1974). This is the demonic superego of Freud's formulation. And Freud conceived of the goals of psychoanalysis, in a patient where this kind of superego is especially strong, as the *reduction* of its ferocity and its sphere of operation, to be replaced by more rational and loving ego orientations. If the feminine superego is more likely to be lacking in these qualities of punitiveness and relentlessness, one may well question why it needs to be regarded as normatively inferior or worse in any way than the kind of masculine superego just described.

In chapter 7, in outlining the distinction between traditional and vanguard norms of differential gender identity, I pointed out that, in the traditional view, men were supposed to have a morality of abstract principle, and women were expected to attune their morality more to personal loyalties and personal emotional attachments. This is very close to the differences between the sexes we perceive in the psychoanalytic account. And the traditional norms have been prevalent in patriarchal societies for many centuries before Freud. To a great extent, these have been the traditional *norms* about morality in Western culture, and to some considerable extent still are. If men and women do more or less approximately conform in their actual personalities and behavior to such normative expectations in their real lives and in real reactions to moral dilemmas, why does anyone have to regard this difference as a derogation of women? The norms are *different*, but depending on one's value position, one could regard either as superior, or neither.

The whole history of civilization is full of ways *males* have followed an inexorable impersonal morality, for example, impersonal loyalty to the state and abstract principles of law, or religion, often into wars and persecutions, while the women are more skeptical of such impersonal forces and live much more in terms of personal emotional loyalties. Though there are cultural variations in this, one is hard put to name any society in which this difference is found in the reverse direction, i.e., males oriented to personal attachments while females relate to broad impersonal standards.

Here's an example of a difference in the predicted direction. It is from a tribal society, the aborigines of Central Australia: ''. . . in these tribes, the custom [of eating infants or fetuses] presents different aspects when we get our information from the men and when we talk to the women. *The men do a thing on principle, the women do it because they are hungry''* (Géza Róheim, *Psychoanalysis and Anthropology,* 1950; 61; my emphasis added). And in these same tribes, the initiation ceremonies for adolescent boys are saturated with moral teachings that are always formulated along the lines of general abstract principles. There is no corresponding training for girls (Róheim 1950).

But, one may ask, are not women more *religious* than men (at least in modern societies)? Isn't that devotion to impersonal moral standards? In fact, however, we find that the kind of religiosity displayed by women is more likely to be *personal* in quality, directed toward personal supernatural figures like saints and the Virgin Mary, rather than toward a more abstract impersonal concept of supernatural power as in Hebraic monotheism (no images, God is not man writ large), which must surely have been a masculine invention.

Culturalist revisions in psychoanalysis, in the work of Erich Fromm, the later work of Karen Horney, and the work of Harry Stack Sullivan (1953), and their intellectual descendants, emphasize the *socio-cultural* forces involved in superego formation in both boys and girls. In that formulation—much liked by non-psychoanalytic sociologists and social psychologists—superego is the individual psychological version of the cultural norms that people learn growing up in a particular society, internalized within the individual. From a classical-psychoanalytic perspective, however, that formulation is a distorting oversimplification. It makes it sound as though the child simply takes in the norms of the culture and makes them part of his own view. It also makes it sound as though the process were largely *conscious.* No doubt some moral learning, at later stages in childhood, is like this. But this is not at all what psychoanalysis means by superego as an internal agency largely unconscious in its development and functioning. More than that, the role of unconscious aggression, turned back against oneself, is an essential quality of the superego process. That is utterly neglected or bypassed in the kind of culturalist formulation just cited.

Proponents of a culturalistic psychoanalytic view point out that, in fact, the little girl in developing her superego does encounter different sets of norms for what is desirable in her as a feminine being, and what undesirable, than the norms the boy encounters, which are associated with concepts of masculinity. And femininity and masculinity in this context are clearly *culturally* derived conceptions, with no intrinsic relationship to given biological differences between the sexes.

Psychoanalysts of "classical" orientation respond that we do not really know that there are *no* intrinsic connections between conceptions of desirable feminine or masculine moral qualities and biologically given or developmentally determined sex differences.

No doubt the culture provides different conceptions of what is desirable in the female compared to the male, and these will go into the formulation of the superego. This however focuses on *contents*. It misses the question of the *dynamics* of how the superego develops as a structure. Most likely most women growing up in Freud's lifetime had communicated to them while they were growing up the ideas that the "good" girl and woman was to be yielding, submissive, noninitiatory, generous, giving, and devoted to the male, first father, then husband. These would be *contents*. There could be different kinds of processes, that is, dynamics, through which the girl arrives at conformity to, or deviation from, these contents. It is these processes that the mainline psychoanalytic endeavor is focusing on, from Freud on. Present-day work no longer regards Freud's formulations on this as adequate or complete. Newer work pays much more attention to *pre*-oedipal aspects of superego development (or at least its precursors). These include the role of identifications in infancy, with the mother and others, and how these are different for the girl than for the boy, on the basis of the nature of her body, her subjective experience of her body, her reaction to the mother's reaction to her body and to her femaleness. The mother's experience of herself as a female would obviously be of crucial importance in the little girl's identifications.

Clearly the superego *contents* for the female have changed considerably since Freud's time. The expectation that to be a good feminine person means she must be dependent and submissive, for example, would certainly not hold true today. Nor would the emphasis on *sexual* "virtue"—in much of the population at least.

Culturalists would therefore raise the question: if these contents—i.e., the contents of the norms—have changed, would not the dynamics have changed also? If girls are being raised differently today, by mothers who are much more attuned to norms of women's being active, autonomous, etc., compared to the passivity, submissiveness, and self-abnegation expected in an earlier era, would not the *processes* necessarily differ as well?

Classical analysts would respond, not necessarily, and probably not. Because most of what has just been said refers to predominantly conscious, surface manifestations, which might well cover over unconscious self-perceptions of mothers of today, of themselves as defective, damaged beings based on processes of their superego formation of a generation ago. Though the cultural forces of patriarchal institutions would be a factor in such self-perceptions, they cannot be the whole story, for we now know enough about the processes of early identifications and their unconscious elements, which have powerful and significant consequences for the later personality development. We seem constantly to have to make an effort to keep clear the distinction between superego, a largely unconscious distillate of intense affect-laden problems and dilemmas of the infantile period and the moral codes of a society or an individual—i.e., the *contents* that are available and operate at the conscious level.

Note that the psychoanalytic account of differences in superego formation between males and females is *not* arguing that women are more likely than men to violate moral precepts. Rather, that when they *do* commit offenses against the norms, they are more likely to do it from fear of loss of love, whereas men are more likely to do it from castration anxiety. Freud thought, I think correctly, that most people (of both sexes) are rather imperfect in their superego formation, and in the morality of their behavior, even in their own terms.

If we look at possible behavioral manifestations of gender-differentiated superego processes and consider the expectation of men following a morality built around abstract principles, while women build morality around personal loyalties and attachments, we find the inconvenient fact that women have participated prominently in such movements for social justice as temperance, anti-slavery, and equal rights for women. These are interesting "exceptions," in several ways. One is that the women who have participated have always been a minority (of women) and often considered a maverick minority socially defined as deviant, frequently evoking as much opposition from other women as from men. Second, their goals have been "humanitarian"—as distinct from technological, scientific, military, or narrowly political—and in that fit the "feminine" cultural domain. In pursuing justice for "underdogs" they both express envy and resentment toward the powerful of society and nurturance toward the weak and vulnerable, a classical maternal function. Significantly, they fit in with what has developed in women's participation in the occupational sphere in modern societies. The higher-level occupations most open to women are those associated with nurturance and caretaking: nursing, grade-school teaching, social work, and other "helping professions" (in the USSR, medical practice generally, as well), which in turn have become rather stereotyped as "feminine" occupations.

Relevant to the question of differential superego formation and functioning, Weinstein and Platt make this comment about the women's movement:

> . . . if women prove capable of organizing a social movement—as they now seem in the process of doing—and the movement is characterized by the same ego and superego qualities that Freud ascribed to men, the differences he identified could not possibly have been in the biopsychological factors. The differences would have to have been in social-structural factors. (Weinstein and Platt 1973:64)

Questions arise: *does* the women's movement utilize the "same ego and superego qualities that Freud ascribed to men"? And does the Weinstein–Platt conclusion follow, that this evidence must shift the understanding from "bio-psychological" differences between the sexes, to socio-structural factors? Certainly in reference to superego functioning, women's participation in the women's liberation movement may well be consistent with the more "feminine," less punitive, less inexorable kind of superego that psychoanalysis has described. Also, women's participation in such a movement may well be carried on in a psychological manner and style quite different from men's participation in comparable social reform movements. The women participating in such a movement may well, as already suggested, be a variant minority within the feminine minority. What looks like similar behavior in the two sexes may well have quite different psychological costs, concomitants, and meanings in the two cases—as, for example, the "maternal" Arapesh men of Margaret Mead's account (1935, but more importantly, 1949) have a rather different context and sets of functions in their infant-oriented behavior than do the women mothering these same infants. The empirical facts on such cases are sufficiently complex and multifaceted that we need to be wary of rigid either/or formulations, such as that it is either definitely a "bio-psychological" formation, or entirely a "social-structural-cultural" one.

There is, however, another figure of females in relation to morality, i.e., as the guardians of public morality, as upholders of abstract moral principles of honesty, probity, fairness, etc., as against the "corruption" of male politicians following an expedient morality built around personal loyalties. This would appear to be a difference in the opposite direction from the one above. However, these "personal loyalties" of men in the "dirty games" of politics are usually not so much personal in the sense of affectively laden love relationships (the standard feminine morality) but rather expedient bonding for purposes of self- and mutual-protection, self-aggrandizement, egoistic expansion, phallic assertion, and the like.

And relatively few women engaged in such battles show the kind of relentlessness associated with either male superego-dominated, abstract-principle-oriented behavior (or its other side in corrupt actions)—and these few are seen as having a "masculine," an "unfeminine" ferociousness, suggesting a need to outdo men in that kind of "masculine" game. (One thinks of the very few ferocious women radicals of the 1960s revolts, and their counterparts of earlier periods. See Endleman 1970a, 1970b, and related bibliographies therein.)

If crime statistics could be regarded as any kind of indicator of manifestations of the superego, one could argue that women have *stronger* superegos than men, since typically their crime rates are much lower than those of men. Interestingly, that discrepancy has been declining in recent years, in tandem with the increased opportunities for women in the marketplace, in the professions, and in many other occupations. There is also a *qualitative* difference. Women are more concentrated in certain specialties in crime: aside from prostitution, they are more concentrated in shoplifting, and in larceny by deception. Particularly bright ones may be involved in fraud by confidence games. They are rare in violent kinds of theft, in bank robbery, in extortion, or in crimes involving physical aggression generally—except, of course, for *crimes passionels* (the woman scorned, like whom hell hath no fury). That last type, however, fits perfectly with the picture of feminine resort to violation of usual morality in reaction to real or threatened loss of love. The other specialties seem to emphasize deception, sneakiness, lying, narcissistic theatrical performance (con games), all of which would fit with other gender differences we have been noting. And one kind of crime *only* women commit: stealing a baby to keep for herself: that one is entirely in line with what is distinctive of females' bio-psychosexual development. (On recent trends of women in crime, see Freda Adler, *Sisters in Crime,* 1975.)

OTHER FEMININE CHARACTERISTICS:
MASOCHISM, PASSIVITY, VANITY, ETC.

Feminists are also offended by other elements in the Freudian portrait of women: that they are masochistic, narcissistic, passive, submissive, vain, petty, jealous, irrational, not clearly reality-oriented. Freud certainly did in some of his writings indicate belief that these qualities were more likely in women than in men. Later psychoanalysis has somewhat modulated these views.

Regarding passivity: Freud himself said that the commonly held equation of active with masculine and passive with feminine is itself a cultural convention, not a matter of intrinsic connection with one's sex. True enough that the male has to be active, initiatory, and sufficiently aroused to have and maintain an erection in order for intercourse to take place, while there is no such necessity for the female. But beyond that, there is activity and passivity in both sexes, including within the heterosexual encounter.

Psychoanalytic work after Freud has elaborated on how activity is very much a part of female functioning, and obviously mothering a baby could not possibly be done by anyone who was entirely passive. Any of the main erotic orifices—mouth, anus, vagina—may be used in active as well as in passive-receptive ways. Erikson (1950) analyzed such variations in modes of using erotogenic zones, in his reformulation of Freudian propositions. A woman can be passive-receptive vaginally in intercourse—but she can also be actively grasping, vaginally. She can, of course, also be active and initiatory in other aspects of sexual encounter, as well as in any other aspects of behavior.

It is possible, of course, that women are *more* inclined to passivity than men. There may be a constitutional basis for this as was thought by Freud and some of his followers, e.g., Helen Deutsch (1925, 1944–45), or it may be primarily developmentally induced (or a combination of both). From an object-relations approach, infants of both sexes start out being the passive recipients of the caring ministrations of the primary caretaker, usually the mother. As the infant begins separation-individuation, the mother usually encourages the boy, more than the girl, actively to move out into the world and separate himself from her, or actively to take her as more of an oedipal than a pre-oedipal object. By contrast, she fosters the girl baby staying longer in the passive-recipient position associated with maintenance of the fusion or symbiosis of earliest infancy. (In addition, children of both sexes may *actively* seek the merging-fusion experience with the mother.) In the oedipal phase, the father may encourage the little girl's placing herself in a passive-seductive position in relation to him, and in various subtle or not so subtle ways reward her playing a passive-recipient "feminine" role toward him, avoiding the levels and kinds of obvious activity that mark a male child as more "masculine." He—and the mother as well—may encourage her to think of herself as someone who is *acted upon*, someone to whom things happen as distinguished from encouraging the boy actively to do things, to make things happen—the being vs. doing distinction which is strongly ingrained in culture as a feminine-vs.-masculine distinction.[5]

What about *masochism*, a way of turning aggression back against oneself? Analysts today agree that masochism occurs in both sexes, and has probably similar object-relational origins in each. However, it is still a question whether this is *more* likely in females than in males, and clinical experience of analysts suggests that it is. There is more control over aggression, i.e., overt expressions of aggression, imposed upon female children than upon male; and greater likelihood that rage experienced toward the disappointing and omnipotent mother may well have to be turned back upon oneself, rather than directed outward. Boys at the same stage are more likely to have many phallic outlets for aggression, and to be able to express such aggression in peer fighting with other boys, and in more sublimated form in sports and other vigorous physical activities. In our society until recently this kind of outlet was minimal for girls. Masochistic maneuvers in girls are also more likely to the extent that she identifies with a mother who is perceived as defective, weak, inferior, acted-upon rather than acting, and lacking in the same worth as a male. As masochism involves a posture that invites punishment from others, the implication is that there is a strong otherwise unrelieved underlying guilt. The source of such guilt in the girl may be rage against both the external object mother and the internal object mother. These pressures are stronger on average for the girl than for the boy.

Changes in sociocultural arrangements currently going on in advanced Western societies, according to which the little girl is given greater opportunity for expression of physical aggression, including rough physical activities and sports almost on a par with boys, may provide a shifting of the channelizing of aggression such that masochistic maneuvers become less prevalent and less psychologically necessary for the females. Impressionistic evidence at least suggests that this is already happening.

Narcissism is another of the qualities attributed to females as more typical of their character than of that of males. Again, psychoanalytic clinical evidence indicates it occurs in both sexes, and in certain of its elements is part of the developmental process in all human beings. One analyst, Heinz Kohut (1971), sees narcissism as itself a distinct normal developmental line alongside the libido, and makes a strong distinction between normal and pathological narcissistic development.

The "narcissism" that is attributed more to females than to males is presumably pathological narcissism, a disordered development of the "self." Again, it is not clear that this kind of pathology is any more prevalent in women than in men. If one focuses on the girl's feeling of "narcissistic wound" on the recognition of the difference between her genitals and the boy's, one would expect a primary area of difficulty to derive from this, and see such manifestations as enormous preoccupation with personal appearance, beauty, grooming, and personal adornment, as more distinctively feminine than masculine, and as indicators of narcissism, possibly pathological narcissism, then one might make a case for narcissism being more prevalent in females. "In our society as of this time" one would have to add.

And even for this society, it is questionable whether in fact females do really have much of an edge over males in concern with personal attractiveness. If theatricality—needing constantly to be on-stage, and center-stage, having others admire you—is one of the manifestations of heightened narcissism, then we'd have to say men are just as prone to this as women. Surely there is a cultural dimension here. Concern with personal adornment has in many cultures and periods been much more the province of men than of women, in others equally for both. One thinks of aristocratic circles in Europe in the eighteenth century where if anything the men outdid the women in this sphere. Margaret Mead reports of the Tchambuli tribe in New Guinea (Mead 1935, 1949) that it is the *men* who are concerned with art, decoration, elaborate hair styling, body decoration, theatrical ritual performances with elaborate costume, and the like, and who show the self-centeredness and "temperamental" quality associated with an operatic *prima donna* in our society—all indicators of heightened narcissism—while the women are brisk, managerial, with short-cropped hair, and show none of these indicators. Commonly in our society, however, men who act like that are regarded as at least a bit ridiculous—though sometimes "licensed" to do so on the grounds of being creative "artists"—and/or thought to be homosexual. That heightened narcissism is, in fact, associated with male homosexuality (though not in all cases—see discussion in next part), as well as with women—at least in this society, suggests that its manifestations are the defenses of people in an underdog or inferiority category, i.e., minority groups in the sociological sense of that term. (See discussion of women as a minority group—Hacker 1951, as referred to above—and corresponding discussion of homosexuals as a minority group in the following part.)

Vanity and pettiness would be character traits associated with or manifesting heightened narcissism. Jealousy would also be related, in that the partner's transfer of sexual attention and love from oneself to some rival, produces a narcissistic affront to the one abandoned. Envy, as distinct from jealousy, i.e., wanting to have something someone else has that you do not, but not in a context of rivalry where one getting it precludes the other also getting it (the jealousy situation), was also seen by Freud as more characteristic of women than of men, and he derived this from the primal envy situation, that of penis envy. (See insightful non-Freudian psychoanalytic discussions of these phenomena in Leslie Farber, *Lying, Despair, Jealousy, Envy,* . . . 1976, essay on "Faces of Envy.") Psychoanalysts today, whether in the "mainstream" or object-relations camp or interpersonal (Sullivanian), would all reject the idea of such phenomena being derived *only* from penis envy, and many would question whether they really are more characteristic of females than of males, or if so whether this may be an artifact of our particular culture. However, if women generally have a greater need to *be loved* (as distinct from *loving*) than do men—which would follow from the object-relations analysis of early mother-infant relations as they apply differently to the girl than to the boy—then one could expect a greater proneness to *jealousy* in females than in males. And if having something may be construed as being loved (and the "something" may itself *be* love), and someone else has the something, and you do not, and wish you had, and resent the other for that, then it would seem probable that women would also be more prone to envy than men. In all these cases, of course, these would be differences in degree, for certainly men are not immune to any of these feelings.

There is a current socio-cultural feature relevant to injured narcissism. If "liberated" women define as a prerequisite of their "freedom," being considered exactly identical to men, and insist *any* difference means female inferiority, then they will be constantly confronted with assaults to their self-esteem, to their narcissism, any time any difference between a man and a woman appears. Contrast traditional societies with a sharply defined and clear-cut gender division of labor, where women are more likely to feel secure in their feminine status and attributes—different from, never only inferior to, those of the male—and therefore have high self-esteem. If so, they are likely to pass on to their daughters, who identify with them, that kind of positive image of femininity.

Another relevant aspect of sex differences is in the relationship of adult coitus to the infantile relationship to the mother. I stated in chapter 5 that for the female in coitus, the male is similar in many ways to a suckling child. But it is also true that so is the female to the male. Like a suckling infant she is receiving, through an erogenous body orifice, life-giving substances through a protuberance of the face-to-face partner's body. Others have seen more of a discrepancy in the kind of replay experience adult coitus means to the female compared to the male, as replay of the mother-infant fusion. Balint (1956) sees the return to the experience of "primary love" (as with the mother) as the main goal of adult sexual intercourse. The male comes closest to that recapturing, coming nearest to a refusion with the mother: "with his semen in reality, with his penis symbolically, with his whole self in phantasy." By contrast, a woman, as herself, cannot relive her own infantile experience of merging. She can only identify with the mother with whom she was merged in infancy. It is thus easier for the adult male in coitus to entertain fantasy of re-merging with the mother. The partner is, after all, a female like his mother. But at deeper levels of unconscious fantasy, the woman may well be having that kind of experience as well, if she makes the uncon-scious equation of vagina with mouth, and of penis with breast, as sug-gested in my earlier discussion. True, in heterosexual intercourse, she will not be recapturing another *woman.* Thus, the male cannot have an exactly parallel function and meaning for the female partner in adult sexual relations as she does for him.

Note that these are intractable differences, built upon both biological and early-infantile-developmental factors.

SEX AND AGGRESSION,
AND SEX DIFFERENCES IN AGGRESSION

From a variety of lines of evidence there is good reason to believe there is a biologically given difference between males and females in aggressiveness, with an edge to the males.

Phylogenetically, the hunting-revolution ancestry of our species (see preceding section) puts a selective premium on males' having higher aggressiveness than females. Elaine Morgan (1972) presented an ingen-ious theory for how this came about in the invention of the frontal coital position. Protohominid males, in first forcing this new position upon reluctant and puzzled females (who thought they were being *attacked),* had to inhibit the previously phylogenetically ingrained "stop-the-aggres-sion" response to the female's submission in order to continue the se-duction. Thus, the dominance-submission signalling system got all mixed up with the sexual-response system, particularly for the males. According to Morgan, this has left its phylogenetic heritage in the species ever since: sex and aggression are all mixed up. This idea accords entirely with the psychoanalytic exploration of the complex relationships and interfusings of sexual and aggressive impulses in human beings, and how these mix-ings are more problematic for males than for females. Males think of "conquest" of the (possibly reluctant) female. Females learn to link sex-uality with submission to the aggression of the male. The shift to the frontal position makes the female more vulnerable. And this is the first species in which rape is possible. (See Susan Brownmiller 1975 for a rather paranoid elaboration of that point.)

For demonstrations of how old the fusion of male aggression and sexuality is in the history and prehistory of humanity, consider this:

> . . . a North African drawing leaves no doubt of this [the fusion of aggression and sexuality] since a line connects the hunter's weapon with his wife's pubic region; a wife's behavior at home affects the hunter's luck in a magic way; and the Indian hunter aims an arrow at a legendary deer only to find her turning into a beautiful woman. Sexual aggression and hunting, body image and weapon, are very early [in human prehistory] fused in the human-animal coition and hunt scenes of the ancient caves, as Leroi-Gourhan has shown (in *Préhistoire de l'Art Occidental*, Paris: Editions d'Art Lucien Mazenrod, 1965).

This is from the psychoanalytic anthropologist Weston Labarre, *The Ghost Dance: Origins of Religion*, 1970:169–70. The drawings and paintings referred to go back to Paleolithic times, a period in the early cultural development of mankind where hunting and gathering were the technological means of subsistence, hunting being a clearly masculine activity.

But have not the conditions under which this phylogenetic origin occurred, for human aggression and the sexual differences in it, long since disappeared for most of mankind? Two answers: one, the *ontogenetic* processes in which this develops in the life history of each human since that time continue to occur in the development of each human infant. Two: aggressiveness and its complications have continued long past the context of phylogenetic origin, and have become connected with a whole range of other aspects of human activity and development.

There is another feature of sex differences in aggression. Men bond together around aggression and its controls. Women bond together primarily around mutual caring and grooming and cooperation in nurturant tasks (Morgan again, 1972). Men bond in war and business (Tiger 1969). Women bond in nurturance. Sometimes, yes, women bond aggressively against what they see as injustice. Sometimes they pointedly exclude others they perceive as outgroups. This may take a particularly feminine bitchy form: e.g., a little girl of eight and her friends formed a club; what was it for? "It's a club against Nancy." Boys don't aggress in this way. Excluding, and fear of being excluded, with their relationship to abandonment fears and narcissistic injury, may be of concern to people of both sexes, true, but are more a focus in females.

Where women's organizations are aggressive, they are perceived by men as being aggressive in a qualitatively different way from that of men in organizations engaged in military or commercial combat. In the women it has a shrill hysterical quality (using that term in its popular rather than its technical psychoanalytic sense). It is the quality of people perceiving themselves as oppressed, or formerly oppressed, and as being at present still unsure of what power or influence they really do have in the world. Women will point out that according to men's definitions, when a woman is assertive, she's called "aggressive"—in this context a pejorative—or bitchy, a witch. When a man's assertive, he's called masculine, a go-getter, ambitious, a manly guy who will stand up for his rights. It's another case of in-group virtues being out-group vices.

Ontogeny of Aggression. In the intra-uterine state, the fetus is in a situation where all his needs are automatically satisfied. In fact, if we can imagine his mental life in that period, it would be one of *absence* of need. Ferenczi referred to this as a feeling of "omnipotence"—the feeling that one has all that one wants and that one has nothing else to wish for (Ferenczi 1951:218). With birth, the neonate embarks on a series of experiences which challenge and threaten that blissful feeling of omnipotence. The early infantile closeness to and oneness with the nursing mother carries over something of the womblike tranquility. However, from then on there is increasing pain in the problem of adapting to a reality which is no longer the bliss of the womb, nor the nearly equivalent bliss of infantile symbiosis with the mother's breast. With each *absence* of the nurturing mother the child is faced with frustration and the growing necessity of recognizing he is dependent on a power outside himself that sometimes comes when he wants, and sometimes when *it* wants. The infant is frustrated, therefore he feels aggression, is a formulation we used to use.

Now we have more subtle ways of describing this, in terms of object-relations theory in psychoanalysis, in the work of Margaret Mahler, of Melanie Klein, of Winnicott, and Fairbairn and Guntrip. Leaving aside the complexities and disagreements among these theorists, the essential point for our present purposes is this: when the child beings to be able to construct a sense of "objects" in the world (object used here in a psychoanalytic sense—i.e., of beings or forces outside of and separate from himself, but experienced internally within himself), these objects tend to take on a mental construction that is all in one extreme. It is either all totally good, or all totally bad. Thus the child constructs an internalized object of the mother as "the good mother"—here putting together all positive, gratifying, experiences the child has had of the mother. And another image, the "bad mother" may be split off, including all the negative, frustrating, threatening, dangerous things about her, which may then (later) appear in externalized fantasy images such as the bad witch or wicked stepmother of the fairy tales.

At this point for the child in the early infantile stage, the good mother and the bad mother are two entirely separate images, and the child does not integrate them into one developed and differentiated picture of a real human being who is the mother who is *sometimes* and *in some ways* "good," and at other times, and in other ways, "bad"—rather each of these images is absolute and separate. This will be so regardless of what the mother is actually like in reality to the infant, whether she is in fact a very warm, nurturant, comforting kind of mother, warmly giving most of the time, or in fact rather cold, distant, ungiving—that hardly matters, for inevitably there is bound to be a bad object because the child cannot have an actual world of omnipotence that he desperately and fervently wishes.

So *aggression* is experienced in the world outside and concretized in the image of the bad mother: dangerous, cruel, ungiving, painfully restricting the child. The greater the infantile fantasy of one's own omnipotence, the greater the rage at the disappointment and frustration of this omnipotence by the reality of the "bad mother" and other "bad objects." The reactive rage of the child who is not fed, or not fed quickly or adequately enough, is more than a matter of hunger: it is a threat to infantile omnipotence, to the infantile illusion of self-sufficiency. This rage in turn is projected onto the outside. Objects—people, animals, other forces—are then seen as raging dangerously against oneself. The world is full of aggression, much of it the aggression within oneself now projected onto the outside. (There are, of course, real dangers in the outside world, and real inadequate and frustrating or hostile mothers and fathers. But the infant does not realistically and objectively perceive them.)

Intrapsychic needs overpower any capacity to see outside reality clearly or objectively. The result is that the parents that actually were, were probably nowhere near as great or as awful as we remember them now. Rather they are idealized or demonized as the psychic needs of the child dictate. Thus there are universal psychic roots of aggression in the ontogenetic development of the individual. Some of this applies to both sexes. However, the hormonal input into the patterning of this aggression, and perhaps its intensity, may be greater for males than for females.

Sex Differences in Aggression. From a variety of other perspectives, scholars and researchers point to greater aggressiveness in males than in females. Hormonal researches indicate *androgen* is associated with higher levels of aggression (Money and Ehrhardt 1972, for review of relevant studies: see also Weitz 1977:15–19, for overview of the evidence). This is not to discount the role of socialization in *channelizing* whatever biologically-given differences already exist. Such socialization factors can only either accentuate or de-emphasize the already present difference in potential.

Judith Bardwick, in *The Psychology of Women* (1971), considers the difference as amply demonstrated. Even the anti-biologistic Chodorow concedes the possibility of biologically-based differences. Kagan and Lewis in *Change and Continuity in Infancy* (1971) report observations indicating male children showing more aggressive play than females at ages 8 months, 13 months, and 27 months. Eleanor Maccoby and C. N. Jacklin in The Psychology of *Sex Differences* (1975) also report consistent sex differences in aggression in the same direction.

Critics can argue that any studies of children beyond very early infancy could be reflections of culturally imposed differential treatment of boys and girls by mothers and other caretakers and socializers. (Therefore they might not be biologically based and could be changeable.) One study, at least, of neonates answers that charge. For the neonate, obviously, there has been very little, if any, time for socialization procedures to have had any effect. The psychologist Sheridan Phillips and her colleagues at Adelphi University directly observed human neonates during the first two days after birth. They expected to find no differences between the baby boys and the baby girls in activity levels of various kinds. Much to their surprise, they found instead that the boys surpassed the girls in several categories of activity: facial grimacing, low level motor activity, and being awake—these at statistically significant levels. Less dramatically, they also exceeded the girl babies on all other categories scored: low level vocal activity, high level vocal activity, and high level motor activity (Phillips et al. 1978). This study is interesting since the investigators were convinced in advance that they would find no differences. Thus, if there had been investigator bias in reporting or interpreting their findings, it would have been in the opposite direction from what they found.

Admittedly the bearing of these findings on aggression is only indirect. If we assume greater activity is correlated with greater aggression, the findings would support the elsewhere reported sex difference on that score.

Some psychoanalytic views, while accepting or assuming that there is a biological substrate for such sex differences, place greater emphasis on developmental processes which operate differentially for males than for females, inducing or encouraging greater aggressiveness in males. One recent example is this: Burness Moore argues:

> The differentiation of the libidinal and aggressive drives from the undifferentiated instinctual energies, stimulated by frustration, aids in the process of separation-individuation, provided means of aggressive discharge are available by which separation can be actively achieved by the child himself. But cultural influences, in addition to possible biological ones, tend to modify the expression of aggression in girls and women. (Moore, in Blum 1977:319)

Other psychoanalytic work in the area of separation-individuation indicates mothers are more likely to encourage active and earlier separation and individuation in boy babies than in girl babies, and to expect more aggressive activity in doing this from boys than from girls. Since this appears to be a universal differentiation, it is probable that the mothers are responding to a biological given and accentuating it further by differential interactive relationship with the child. The generating of aggressive feelings is also likely to follow different paths in girls than in boys: the kinds of diappointments and frustrations and narcissistic injuries in relation to the mother and later the father are bound to be different in the two sexes, as discussed earlier regarding pre-oedipal and oedipal libidinal and object-relations developments. For example, as discussed earlier in this chapter, girls in infancy and early childhood suffer more narcissistic injury than boys and more of a feeling of powerlessness and problematic helpless rage against the mother. Such experiences would encourage resort to techniques of deceptiveness and evasion in many situations where a boy might use physical aggression. (Behavioristically oriented studies find, in our society, that girls lie more and boys fight more. This may well be a universal difference.) Deceit and evasion are the resources of the "underdog," of minorities, whether of race, gender, or sexual orientation. (See discussion of narcissism above.)

Environmentally-minded scholars prefer to place all sex differences in aggression in the context of culturally derived socialization processes. They point out that cultures differ in the range and scope they allow for aggression in males and in females, and in the degree and kind of difference between the sexes they expect on this. However, a look at the anthropological literature shows that while some cultures allow females greater aggression release than ours does, by and large most support the kind of difference ours does: males being allowed greater play, and being expected to be more aggressive (and usually acting that way). Some make stronger sex differentiation than we do.

Margaret Mead's environmentalist work of the 1930s, specifically *Sex and Temperament in Three Primitive Societies* (1935) is frequently cited by feminists and feminist-minded social scientists to support the idea that a culture could get both sexes to be alike in being very aggressive (like the Mundugumor), or in being very unaggressive (the Arapesh tribe), or could train for a sex difference in a direction the reverse of ours, females more aggressive than males (Tchambuli). Therefore, all differences in aggressiveness are the product of differential socialization and are not innate or based on biological differences between the sexes. Advocates of this position ignore Mead's later and more reasoned work (1949), where she argues that biologically there are different basic ground plans in the two sexes that strongly limit the range of possible variation in enculturation processes, so that the two sexes experience what looks like the same kind of socialization (e.g., the Mundugumor encouraging aggressiveness in both male and female children) in quite different ways. Mead emphasizes that it is bound to be fundamentally different growing up in a girl's body than in a boy's.

Cross-culturally, we find that most cultures impose greater restrictions on overt expression of aggression in females than in males, and channelize the females' aggressions verbally, the males more physically. These are surely cultural impositions. But if they were only that, one would expect more variation from one culture to another. This suggests that all these cultures are responding to something fundamental in the human beings involved, some fundamental difference between the sexes. This difference may well be a combination of biologically based differences and differences in developmental processes in the psychosexual development. Most commonly, cultural norms tend to intensify differences that (evidently) already exist on a biological and developmental basis: some could, of course, de-emphasize such differences and give scope for female aggression expression just about equal to males'. (It could be similar in quantity, but still be different qualitatively, being imbedded in different developmental processes, e.g., in reference to identification with crucial parental figures, and the boy's typical need to disidentify with the mother.)

Currently, in our society, feminists want to de-differentiate the two genders in permissible forms of aggression expression. For example, they want girls to participate in rough aggressive body-contact sports like football, hockey, or boxing, not only with other girls, but also on co-ed team with boys. In a recent case in Ohio, a girl, who was a good football player but was not allowed to play on the otherwise all-male football team, took the case to court and won; the court ordered the high school to put the girl on the team if she qualified in competence as well as the boy members of the team.

Feminists score this as a victory. Others find this problematical, or scandalous. Some women athletes and coaches of girls' teams, who were interviewed about this case, were not enthusiastic. They felt that girls, *on average, were* different from boys, in physical strength and stamina; therefore a girl competing with boys in as rough a game as football is automatically going to be at a disadvantage. The girl who is exceptionally strong, agile, and athletically capable compared to other girls will compare poorly when pitted against males who are correspondingly high on a scale of athletic ability for boys.

Two other important psychological elements are involved in this kind of case: males' feelings about aggressive sports as marks of their masculinity, and the body contact nature of this sport, which introduces anxiety-provoking ambiguities in a cross-sex situation. Sports as validation of masculinity become attenuated if the same team admits women as well as men. (There is a parallel with the physical hardships, hazing, tests of "manly" endurance, etc. used in male puberty initiation ceremonies in tribal societies, as well as analogues in the military in complex societies. See Endleman 1967, ch. 4, for analysis.) On the other matter, body contact is allowable among males in this society in only limited ways and contexts, including in only a very limited way to express affection or tenderness—otherwise it is suspect as a mark of homosexuality—its allowable contexts being the expression of *aggression* or mock aggression. Body contact sports are the epitome of such a formation. You tackle the player of the other team aggressively, not erotically. If that player is female, however, what happens? The signals get mixed up. Body contact with a female is supposed to be erotic. How then do you tackle a woman, without its either having sexual overtones, or being an unmanly, unchivalrous attack? Men are not supposed to hit women. If they do, it is condemned as taking unfair advantage of the man's physical superiority (leaving aside the fact that that may be more theoretical than actual in a particular case).

Such all-male formations in primitive or modern societies need, of course, to be looked at as manifestations of enormous castration anxiety on the part of the males, or rather as a complex transformation and resolution of such anxiety, with great sublimation involved in the ritualization, whether that takes a religious (initiation ceremony), or athletic, or military guise. Feminists abhor all such gender restrictions, and call them sexist. By that argument it is ''sexist'' to recognize that young males on the brink of adulthood have a different set of psychological and psychosexual problems, dilemmas and difficulties from those of young adult females.

CHAPTER TEN

Implications of Sociological and Psychodynamic Objections: Vanguard Movement Mythologies

PSYCHOLOGICAL DIFFERENCES BETWEEN THE SEXES: DIFFERENT EQUALS INFERIOR?

Frequently arguments between feminists and others on psychological differences between the sexes tend to assume that all of the differences asserted on the basis of psychoanalytic inquiry mark the woman as inferior to and lesser than the man, as though the misogyny or at least condescension evident in some of Freud's writings on women were the total picture. In fact many of the differences claimed in the psychoanalytic account would certainly, from certain value positions, place women in a higher category than men: women are seen as more attuned to complex subjective states, more intuitive, more emotionally empathic, more attuned both to their own feelings and those of others, and as having a richer fantasy life.

There seems to be little disagreement that for our society of this time, at least, these differences do prevail. They may well be universal. Nothing that I know of in cross-culture accounts suggests that there is not a comparable difference between the sexes in other societies that have been studied. Some relativists or environmental determinists would prefer to see these differences, which they acknowledge exist, as the product of some features of this particular social structure or culture.

COMBINED SOCIOLOGICAL AND
PSYCHODYNAMIC APPROACHES:

Chodorow's Work

Nancy Chodorow, who is as intelligently informed and understanding of psychoanalysis as any sociologist I know of, sees these differences and connects them insightfully with her object-relations analysis of gender differences in infant and child care (1978). She nevertheless attributes as the crucial causal factor a social-structural feature: namely, the social structuring of parenting in this society, which makes mothering almost exclusively the task of women, to the exclusion of men. Such a familial structure, she argues, is a socio-cultural artifact, therefore changeable. True, she acknowledges, it would not be easy to change, since it it supported by unconscious intrapsychic dynamics of both females and males, such that in the next generation daughters who have been mothered only by mothers will have the relational qualities and the motivation to be mothers themselves, at least the predominant mothering agents if not the exclusive ones; and sons will not, and both will support and perpetuate this gender division of domestic labor. The psychological qualities just mentioned on which women outrank men—greater subjectivity, empathy, attunement to complex emotional states, richer fantasy life—are all qualities that make a person a "good mother" as that phrase is used in psychoanalysis.

There is no doubt that *some* men do have such qualities, on a par with most women, and superior to some women, and such men make excellent parents for young children—and also that such qualities distinguish men who are creative artists in whatever field (often phrased as their being attuned to the "feminine" side of their nature that most men repress)—but by and large and on average, women are more likely to excel in such qualities compared to men. Chodorow's analysis does an excellent job of showing the complex intrapsychic and social processes by which such gender difference comes about.

One conclusion one can draw from the above analysis of personality and psychosexual-developmental differences between females and males would be that the social structuring of gender role differentiation is closely associated with these differences, supports their continuation, and is supported by them. Since a great deal of the personality development involved has to do with unconscious processes, dynamically multiply-determined in the infancy and childhood development of the individual, one could conclude that associated gender-role differentiation would be difficult, if not impossible to change.

One central part of the gender-role differentiation has to do with *who* carries out the crucial infant and child care, whether it be the mother or the father or both, or neither, but rather communally designated caring agents: another crucial question is which sex is the caring agent, female or male, or do both so participate?

As discussed earlier, no societies so far have men as the sole or primary caretakers of infants and young children. Women bear the babies and take care of them, often with a lot of supportive help from other women. Some feminists challenge the inevitability of this arrangement. We can now take up Nancy Chodorow's handling of these questions in more detail: why is it women who mother, and not men? Chodorow (1978) dismisses as an inadequate answer here the biological-programming views of authors of socio-biological or anthropological-evolutionary persuasions. She also rejects as unsatisfactory the role-training answer given by many feminist-minded sociologists and social psychologists. The biological explanations she finds unpersuasive, since many hormonally less than normally "female" women nevertheless do enthusiastically mother children, while many biologically normal women do not, or do so only reluctantly; also many *men* happily mother children.

Role-training theories are inadequate, in Chodorow's view, because they focus only on conscious levels of training and learning, missing the crucial inner dynamics of unconscious forces, and also emphasizing primarily learning that goes on in the latency period, to the neglect of the crucial preoedipal and oedipal years. We have to look, rather, at the whole psycho-developmental process and see where it proceeds differently in boys and girls, and how both the motivation and the relational qualities for mothering develop in this process in girls, and not (or much less so) in boys. Much of what she comes up with we have been discussing in the preceding pages. The result is that girls become beings with psychological characteristics leading to mothering, and boys become something different. Girls become less differentiated, less separate from their internal and external maternal objects, more blurry in boundary-lines between self and outside world, or specific objects, tuned to pre-verbal kinds of empathic communication, more subjective, empathic, emotionally expressive, etc., as analyzed above. Boys by contrast become more differentiated, more separate, more distant from the world of complex emotion, less intuitive, more oriented to "external reality," using superego mechanisms emphasizing obsessional kinds of defenses like isolation of affect, compartmentalization, rigidity, intellectualization, with manifestations in concern for principle rather than personal loyalties, etc. Thus the pattern gets repeated in succeeding generations. So long, that is, as mothering is done exclusively (or at least predominantly) by *women* and not at all (or only to a limited, secondary extent) by men.

One might conceivably trace this so-far universally present result—women mother, men do not—to biologically based differences between the sexes. Or one might trace it to psychosexual-developmental imperatives that differ in the two cases. Or to the intrapsychic processes. Or to the differential object-relations in the two sexes. Chodorow, however, sees none of those as the crucial causative factor. Rather she adduces it to the social-structural factor of the social organization of parenting: because women mother and men do not, the family structure leads to certain kinds of mothering processes, with definable effects that differ significantly in the ways described for the girl, than for the boy.

But Chodorow's sociological determinism at this point does not follow implacably from her analysis. In fact, the commendable complexity and subtlety of the analysis that fills most of her book is more compatible with an interpretation that is *multiply*-determined in formulation: There are biological differences between the sexes—which Chodorow plays down, but does not deny exist—which have to be accorded a role as necessary though not sufficient conditions. Variable social structures and cultural norms may minimize or exaggerate these differences. (Ours at present are in process of minimizing them to some considerable extent.) The psychosexual-developmental processes, their associated object-relational processes as these operate intrapsychically, as analyzed above in chapter 9 and in Chodorow's work, certainly constitute crucial elements. Both feed into and are fed by the gender-role structuring of parenting. All of these forces are interdependent and interdetermined. That at least would be my formulation. This is neither biologically reductionist, nor intrapsychically reductionist nor sociologically reductionist: we need all in the picture. Together they reinforce gender role differentiation and psychological differences between the sexes.

The social-structural feature of asymmetrical parenting, however, Chodorow argues, is a human invention, and therefore changeable. It may be *difficult* to change, for its intrapsychic roots are strong and largely unconscious, as Chodorow recognizes, but not impossible. Then, as a feminist, Chodorow proceeds from "can" to "should": it *should* be changed, so that men and women carry on equally the baby and child care. If that were done, the psycho-sexual object-relational developmental processes of both sexes would change, in what Chodorow (and presumably other feminists) would regard as desirable directions. Men would develop the "positive" qualities now prevalent in women, and vice versa.

Dinnerstein

Dorothy Dinnerstein, in her provocative book *The Mermaid and the Minotaur: Sexual Arrangements and Human Malaise* (1977), carries a similar argument to much greater extremes. She too sees the asymmetrical structure of parenting as the central cause of the problem. But the problem she depicts is even more ominous and threatening. She sees both women and men as having been maimed in crucial—but different—ways by the fact of being mothered by women. Women become childish in certain ways, men childish in others, and each adopts and perpetuates unhealthy myths about the other (and themselves) and each contributes to exacerbations, in our society, of the "universal neurosis of mankind" (a concept taken from Norman O. Brown) such that we are hurtling toward technological self-destruction by a collective madness which can only be "cured" or averted in the next generation by making the mothering process the work of both sexes equally.

But then—? The Feminist Nonsequitur

The understanding both of these scholars show of how deeply and complexly these patterns are rooted in the whole intrapsychic developmental processes of growing up contradicts the feminist upbeat. Chodorow spends most of her book showing how neither biological predisposition alone, nor superficial and conscious gender-role-learning, accounts for the substantial personality differences between the sexes, especially as these are connected with the psychological requirements of mothering young infants. By contrast, she shows that both the libidinal and the object-relational aspects of baby girls being mothered by female (therefore same-sexed) mothers and only later encountering the father, and baby boys being mothered by female (therefore opposite-sexed) mothers, and only later encountering the father, produce the deeply, unconsciously rooted differences between them that lead to their taking on the same kinds of roles and procedures as mothers and fathers of the next generation. The implication of all this is to demonstrate how enormously resistant to change these patterns are likely to be.

Then, in the last chapter, Chodorow (evidently redeeming her feminist credentials) ends up on a feminist nonsequitur: since the gender roles in parenting are a societal and ideological product, they can be changed, and they should be. Both mothers and fathers should care for and rear infants and young children:

> Fathers are supposed to help children to individuate and break their dependence on their mothers. But this dependence on her and this primary identification, would not be created in the first place if men took primary parenting responsibilities. (Chodorow, p. 218)

However, children would then (with fathers doing the mothering as well as the mothers) develop such primary dependency on the person(s) providing the primary care, and then would need someone *else* to provide the means of individuation, a role now usually played by the facther. Who might that somebody else be, if the father is not distinguishable as a separate and very different parent to the child?

From another angle, critics may demur from Chodorow the feminist's recommendation of fathers co-participating in the parenting of infants and young children by asking this question: If men generally are as deficient in psychological characteristics requisite for "good mothering"—empathy, intuitiveness, etc.—as Chodorow's analysis claims they are, why would we *want* them doing the "mothering"? And would not fathers, if they were equally engaged in baby and child care along with mothers, still be experienced differentially by the children, on the basis both of their anatomical sex and of their psychological characteristics in line with their gender distinction? For example, are not Arapesh fathers (Mead 1949) for all their fond "maternalism" toward their children, still experienced as distinctively "masculine" by the children, as therefore objects of emulative identification by boys; and of proto-oedipal and later oedipal attachment by girls?

By implication in Chodorow's analysis—and more so in Dinnerstein's—the asymmetrical system of parenting produces dilemmas for both female and male children. But what they do not emphasize is that it also provides for *complementary* needs, and in effect produces a very complex, finely tuned, subtle *psychological* division of labor. This psychological bifurcation goes considerably beyond the more obvious economic, political, and social division of labor between the sexes. But then, in calling for a radical de-differentiation of child-caring and child-rearing functions, merging men and women in these tasks, Chodorow, in effect, and Dinnerstein, explicitly, are proposing the abolition of the psychological division of labor, and the de-differentiation of genders and gender boundaries.

The question that needs to be raised, then, is: in the degree of gender-role de-differentiation that is being proposed, would not gender identity for both sexes become less definite and less secure? If neither parent is perceived by the child as distinctly "other," and specifically as "other" in ways tied in with gender role assignment, and as either definitely a potential sexual object, or definintely *not* such an object, where would the child find closely connected adult persons to fulfill these functions? Why must we assume (with Chodorow, with Dinnerstein, with many other feminists) that *no* differentiation is somehow preferable to *some* differentiation (in whatever form)? And why must differentiation necessarily imply inequality, dominance, superior-inferior relationships, and the like?

Chodorow herself (quite correctly, I think) faults Freud and many of his early followers for seeing the female sexual apparatus primarily as *not*-male, as deficient in male genitals, and therefore as inferior, rather than recognizing it as *different* and having its own distinct and positively valuable reproductive and sexual functions. Clearly "different" here does not have to imply "inferior." It is patriarchal bias, as Chodorow and other feminists point out, to assume that the differences of the female must necessarily imply inferiority.

But the call for de-differentiation of the sexes in parenting seems to make the same kind of unwarranted assumption: that differentiation can be effected and enacted only by *social inequality*. But, in fact, the whole spirit of Chodorow's assiduous and perceptive inquiry should push us to ask what are the *positive, enhancing* functions of differentiation, as well as the negative, conflict-producing and dilemma-creating consequences of such differentiation that are so central to her attention. (See earlier in this section for reference to Cynthia Nelson and Virginia Olesen's critique of Western feminist conceptions of equality along similar lines.)

VANGUARD NORMS, THE FEMINIST MOVEMENT, AND REACTIVE AND MITIGATING MYTHOLOGIES

There is an enormous amount of confusion and disagreement among people in modern society, not only between men and women, but also among men and among women, as to just what the norms should be on the respective roles of women and men. Every imaginable position, ranging from the "traditional" or "patriarchal" at one end, to extremes of the "vanguard" or "feminist" at the other, and anything in between, mixing elements of both, can find vocal proponents in the present scene. With very little consensus on what the norms should be, we have something close to what Durkheim called *anomie*, a situation of normlessness or normative chaos. In that kind of situation there is necessarily a great deal of insecurity and tension. And anxiety and difficulty in adaptation. It is difficult to know exactly what to adapt to. Such a state of affairs evokes a variety of irrational and nonrational responses. This relatively anomic situation is lamented and deplored by proponents of order and security and stability in society. It can also be welcomed and applauded by proponents of social change, as the kind of situation that gets people to question established beliefs and practices and gives people greater freedom of choice, hence the possibility of "liberation."

Some of the irrational and non-rational forms of response to this relatively anomic situation will take collective form, as some kind of social movement. Some of the varieties of modern feminism should be counted as such. Such movements propound a rhetoric which is an amalgam of fairly rational and realistic assessments (in this case, for example, discriminations faced by women in the economy and polity) along with a melange of irrational and non-rational beliefs, which I call reactive and mitigating mythologies: ideological beliefs of a political, social, or religious nature—or some mixture of two or three of these—that serve a variety of functions for the believers, and that involve some basic *illusion* in the sense used by Freud. This means not only that the beliefs are false to external reality, in fact not even necessarily that; they could simply be unverifiable in any naturalistic or scientific way. But that is not essentially what distinguishes such beliefs. Rather they are beliefs that are psychologically needed and wanted by the believers, serving some important intrapsychic functions for them. To the believer these ideas carry the aura of the sacred and the taboo (two sides of the same thing). In *The Future of an Illusion* (1927) Freud saw "illusions" as beliefs that gratified a wish for the believer, most likely an unconscious wish. Built on this unconscious intrapsychic base, such beliefs tend to be extremely resistant to rational counter-argument or naturalistic reality-testing. They are motivated versions, usually distortions, of reality loaded with affective as well as cognitive significance for the believers. It is the collective versions of such beliefs that we are interested in especially here, for these are supported by the consensual validation of the community of co-believers, reinforcing the self-evident quality of the ideas portrayed.

The mythologies are reactive, or they are mitigating, or both. "Reactive mythology" means that such beliefs are reactions against other, some-times opposite, beliefs that have been prevalent in the immediate past on the part of the majority population, or some part of it, that the protesters see as an "establishment" that must be attacked, or an oppressor elite that has to be overthrown. So in the area of race relations, for example, the dominant powers' mythology of racial superiority by the top race is countered in the counter-mythology or reactive-mythology of the protes-ters, which may take the form of "black is beautiful," or "our race were the original human beings," or something of that kind. In this case, we are encountering such ideas as that women are not only the equal of men in any dimension under consideration, but probably better. Another such ideologically motivated mythology would be the notion that there are no real differences between the sexes, other than those so-called environ-mentally produced differences that are claimed to be solely the products of socialization and the perpetuation of a male-dominance system.

"Mitigating mythology" means a set of beliefs that mitigate feelings of suffering, oppression, malaise, or other negative state experienced by the believer before attaching himself to the cause. Examples would in-clude the belief in a heavenly hereafter where injustices and inequities of "this" world will be eliminated or reversed. Even the identification of the sources of one's suffering or malaise in something or some force or structure outside of oneself, externalizing the difficulties that may have in reality some intrapsychic origin, may function as part of a mitigating mythology. In the feminist movement, this is one of the functions of beliefs that male dominance and sundry difficulties women may have in work or careers are the effect of a deliberate male conspiracy against women.

Such a mythology provides some sense of certainty and definiteness in a world profuse with conflicting opinions, versions of reality, confu-sion, inconsistency, and doubt, all of which promote or increase anxiety. A dogmatic embracing of a set of beliefs provides surcease from such anxiety. Since elements of the beliefs may well conflict with other "knowledge" the person has about the world, and be subject to skeptical or contradicting responses from others in the immediate surround, the beliefs must be buttressed by further dogmatism, and unrelenting antag-onism toward non-believers, who are "pagans" or "infidels," or worse, "renegades" (formerly co-believers who have "deserted" the cause) or "traitors."

In dealing with the surrounding world in terms of such "true belief," the adherents, claiming their movement is for the "liberation" of people who have been variously enslaved or oppressed, meet the alleged intolerance of their alleged oppressors by a counter-intolerance of their own. So we find, in the women's movement, at least in some of its more extreme proponents or versions, an intense intolerance of men, or of all those men they can label "male chauvinists," and intolerance of any women who do not support their ideology all the way. For example, any woman who decides for herself that she wants to devote the next fifteen to twenty years of her life to raising her children whom she loves, and providing a comfortable and nurturing home for her husband as well, and not to go out into the labor market during that time, gets attacked with invective from the "liberationists" of the women's movement. She is somehow betraying the cause. That is the kind of intolerance I am referring to. It is hard to be persuaded that people practicing that kind of ideological cant are really "liberating" anyone, except perhaps liberating themselves to indulge their fantasies at the expense of other people. While claiming to be more "humanizing" or "humanistic" than others, they tend to be as anti-libertarian in practice as any of the alleged "oppressors" they are fighting against. They are intent on others being "free"—their way.

From major pronouncements of significant feminist spokeswomen, we can construct a schematic synoptic statement of the major articles of faith of the contemporary Western feminist creed. The following is distilled from commonalities among a variety of recent feminist thinkers (though inevitably not all of them share all of these beliefs), such as Betty Friedan, *The Feminine Mystique*, 1963; Shulamith Firestone, *The Dialectic of Sex*, 1970; Germaine Greer, *The Female Eunuch*, 1971; Vivian Gornick and Barbara Moran 1971; Kate Mil'et 1970; Robin Morgan, 1970; and others already dealt with in this section. See also Juliet Mitchell 1974 for a critical answer to other feminists' attacks on Freud and psychoanalysis within a framework that still shares most feminist values.

The articles of faith can be summarized as follows: Women are and have been oppressed: underdogs, victims, passive recipients of others' actions, less than full human beings, second-class citizens, niggers, etc. They are subject to unfair discrimination solely on the basis of their sex, have enforced upon them sundry disabilities and restrictions that are not applied to males; taught and encouraged to think of themselves as defective, incomplete, childlike, unreliable, and anything but self-reliant autonomous human beings. As the only species where the female can be raped, she is constantly subject to rape, whether in obvious direct forms, or less obvious indirect forms: in fact, all male sexual use of women is rape, and this is the history of human civilization (Brownmiller).

As an oppressed minority, women have much in common with other oppressed minorities: Blacks, Hispanics, Asians, American Indians, other racial or ethnic minorities, homosexuals, the handicapped, the retarded, political prisoners, persecuted political dissidents, all persons carrying out victimless offenses, etc. Men continue this oppression and justify it on the basis of their propaganda that women are biologically different and inferior; men actively conspire to deprive women of their rights, to discriminate against them in the economic and political worlds. Men keep women enslaved to domestic tasks which they do not want to do themselves, keeping the women out of the spheres of influence and power, and out of really meaningful work.

Further, the dogmas include these ideas: There are no differences between the sexes that coud not be changed by changing the socio-cultural arrangements that keep women in subservence. Women do not need to be chained to child care; infants and children can be taken care of by public or other nurseries, so that women who have the abilities to make a career for themselves in some demanding field can do their challenging work and at the same time have their children taken care of by such nurseries and other child-care institutions. Modern women of ability can have it all, marriage, children, career, and have it all simultaneously.

There are other versions, with such variations as these: Women should not have babies at all (Shulamith Firestone), it is too messy and nasty a business and enslaves a woman to an archaic biological function. The world is too overpopulated anyway. Women should expect to be plea-sured sexually by whatever men they, if only momentarily, fancy, and never let any man treat her as sexual property. In fact better still, she should learn to dispense with men entirely for sexual satisfaction, getting her pleasure from masturbation or relations with other women. She should develop and use all her potentialities to be active, assertive, aggressive, initiatory, materially productive, creative, and the rest, on a par with any male. She should regard all males as oppressors, or at the least as potential oppressors, and treat them as the enemy. If possible she should try to reverse the past order of dominance: women should dominate over men.

Significantly these battle cries of "oppression" and fight for "libera-tion" are coming from a segment of the female population of the world that is in reality the most privileged in terms of material comforts, luxuries, opportunities, education, options, career possibilities, of any group of women in history; who are the least patriarchically dominated women in the world; who are the least factually "enslaved" of any in the world. This is not to deny that in the Western world women are still unequal to men sociologically in many aspects of economic and political life. If the expectation is of complete equality, meaning *identity* of position, education, opportunity, employment, etc., and total de-differentiation of the gender division of labor, then yes, the reality does fall short of such demands. But if the comparison is made with either earlier periods of Western history, even the recent past, or with the situation of women in more traditional societies (which includes practically all the rest of the contemporary world) or with supposedly egalitarian "experiments" under the name of Communism in the Soviet Union and its satellites, or Communist China, or in the name of "democratic socialism" in the Israeli kibbutz, modern Western women above the working-class level—which is the level of most of the support and advocacy-articulation of the feminist movement—have, in fact, the greatest level of individual freedom, range of choices, material affluence, and the like. And they are the heirs and beneficiaries of all of the movements of modernization and enhanced personal freedom made in the Western industrial world in the past 200 years. (Typically, revolutionaries come from the ranks of the relatively privileged, not of the most downtrodden.)

The twin foci of these transformations are equality and liberty—often, significantly enough, in conflict with each other. One could expect that the demand for equality would sooner or later be taken up by the female sex, and that this would start with those women who are best off economically and the most advantaged educationally, putting them in tune with the most "advanced" ideas, in opposition to traditional restraints and restrictions. From this vantage point, anything that indicated or smacked of some kind of categorical inequality without regard to individual merits proves increasingly intolerable.

Freud and psychoanalysis have been a major part of this whole transformation of values and actual gender conditions (a fact rarely acknowledged by feminists). For whatever the defects and culturally induced blinkers in Freud's personal views of women (as discussed in the preceding chapter), psychoanalysis has been one of the major intellectual forces for combating tyrannies, crucially, in this case, the tyrannies deep within ourselves. Further, without the Freudian opening up of the previously taboo topic of sexuality, most of the late twentieth-century moves for the liberation of sexuality would be inconceivable, and the feminist movement is signally the beneficiary of these changes. And note too that psychoanalysis as a profession from its very beginning made no discriminations against women, and has all along had an impressive proportion of female practitioners (so much for the charge of male chauvinism against psychoanalysis!).

Ideas and movements have consequences, many of them unexpected and many in directions different from or opposed to what the thinkers and actors intended.

Improvements in material and social conditions of women have not made them more satisfied with their lot in life, but less. The demand for and partial fulfillment of personal liberty makes people more aware or more acutely aware of still existing constraints upon personal freedom which may not have even been noticed before, being so much part of the fabric of everyday life. As Durkheim showed, "progress" brings malaise. And we cannot "go home again" to some imaginary traditional golden past. Changes in the past century or so have been going on not simply at so fast a pace, or so uniformly accelerating a pace, but rather simultaneously at so many different paces in different spheres of life, for different categories of people, that many are constantly put off balance, feel adrift, unsure of just what to cling to. Many feel at sea between an unacceptable past and an uncertain future. *Individual* satisfactions are presupposed (rather than collective ones) in the Western pursuit of personal liberties, and this is a major theme not only in current women's movements but in the myriad other movements for improvement—enhancing "human potential," "finding oneself," having a better and more "successful" sex life, marriage, career, etc.—for the key person—me.

In many current popular novels, films, TV shows, the heroine breaks out of the "enslavement" of marriage and children to head out on her own, to parts unknown, goals unclear, to "find herself" and "fulfill her potentialities." (In the past *men* deserting wife and children claimed a masculine birthright of such personal freedom.) Disapprovers see these phenomena as narcissistic self-indulgence. They are now frequent enough and sufficiently ideologized as a positive move by the rhetoric of both (some branches of) the women's movement and those other movements of personal potential to warrant serious consideration as a collective (if not communal) phenomenon.

A related version appears in that part of the women's movement rhetoric I have just called a mythology, that is, the notion that a woman can "have it all," and "have it all *at the same time*"—the "all" being children, marriage, and career, as well as a stimulating social-cultural life with attractive others. The image is of the "super-woman" much touted currently in the media, especially the women's media, who juggles an extremely complicated schedule of peripatetic work in a "creative" career field, attention to her children, her husband, her household, complex elaborate entertaining, and somehow not only does it all, but does it all well, enjoys life enormously, has a vibrant active sex life with husband and lovers, and does it all "successfully."

That figure is, of course, a figment of imagination. No one could possibly be doing all of these things all at the same time. Any woman who tries it discovers there are constraints, limits, conflicts, contradictions. And these latter are not the product of some sexist plot by men to keep women down. That such a "superwoman" figure is touted as an ideal at all reflects a kind of narcissistic self-indulgence on the part of the formulators. Where the motto of early infancy is "All I want is all there is and then some, and all of it right now!" this version of the women's movements adds, "and all at the same time!" (Needless to add, this persuasion is not limited to the women's movement; it is shared by all those instant-gratification cults and pseudo-therapies that pepper the current cultural landscape. This part of liberation rhetoric qualifies as "mythology" in being a motivated set of illusions that fly in the face of discernible reality, and express the wish magically to make those intractable realities disappear by sheer effort of assertion and will.)

Does this sound like revival of Freudian put-down of women as infantile and unrealistic? Since this is an arena of so much embattlement, let me clarify: I do not mean all women are like this and no men; only that this part of the women's movement expresses such a feeling (rejected, incidentally, by many other feminists). Where this demand is voiced, the psychodynamic roots are probably, in a specifically feminine version, connected with the kind of bond the infant female has had with her mother, as analyzed earlier in this section, and that is different—in degree—in this way from that of the boy. In consequence, as adults, males are more likely to categorize, intellectualize, compartmentalize, and therefore recognize more readily a schedule conflict telling you you can't simultaneously be closing that important business deal and taking little Jerry to the dentist or tending to little Nancy sick at home with the flu.

A related part of mythology in the women's movement is the denial that there are very real demands and difficulties involved in taking care of infants and young children, and attending to the psychological needs of older children too. For the latter, modern families have already delegated much of that function to outside agencies, namely schools, camps, children's activity organizations, and the like, but even there, the dilemmas posed by vacation times, or by unscheduled school closings, e.g., by a teachers' strike, indicate how fragile this delegation is, and how much responsibility is still left in the hands of some parent or parent-surrogate, in contemporary non-communist societies. For younger children and even more so for infants, there is still the basic question, common to all societies: who takes care of the children? To dismiss this question casually, or with an offhanded, "others will do it," reflects failure to deal with realistic difficulties and, in many cases, individualistic self-indulgence, for which no doubt many people of both sexes are finding warrant in current me-first personal-fulfillment rhetorics and ideologies in contemporary society.

Much of the rhetoric of the women's movement is clearly *ideological*, in the worst sense of that term. One mark of ideological thinking is its tendency toward dogmatism. It flattens out and oversimplifies the world, leaving no room for the uncertainty, ambiguity, and many-sidedness of life. Feminists' impatience with the ambiguity and complexity of either psychoanalytic or sociological formulations, and their great need to reduce everything to male plots, "sexism," "male chauvinism," "oppression," and similar slogans, constitute this kind of ideological thinking. Ideological thinking also involves categorizing people, situations, and events, in all-or-nothing, either-or kinds of ways, rigid dichotomizing of with-us-versus-against-us varieties. The world lines up as either loyal supporters—who must agree with every line of the movement or the cause—or as enemies, or worse, renegades and traitors. In ideological thinking, "we" are always pure, right, correct, good, beneficent, etc., and "they" dirty, impure, wrong, incorrect, malevolent, conspiratorial, evil, oppressive, and the rest. Conversion to the ideology of the cause leads the believer to rewrite her own personal history in line with the ideology and the theme of present redemption from a past fallen state. Paranoid thinking comes into full flower, the more intellectual seeing ever more intricate and recondite "plots" by the enemies at every turn, or in remote historical or anthropological phenomena, and slogans like "sexist" and "chauvinist" replace any real thinking.

The dividing up of the world into the good and evil forces is reminiscent of the early infantile mechanisms of splitting of the inner object of the mother into entirely separate completely good and completely bad inner images, such as those reflected in the fairy tales of the good fairy godmother and the wicked stepmother-queen. It may be reassuring (momentarily) to have the world neatly divided up into the all-good on one side and the all-bad on the other, but clearly this is fantasy, not reality. More serious in implication, that kind of thinking, feeling, and action in adults not only distorts the real world, but can lead to seriously mala-

daptive reactions in response to that world. Such reactions may be collectivized into a movement and thus be given a consensual validation
that reassures the individual members that they are on the right track,
and doing the right thing at the right time—but not for long. We do have
to live in the real world.

In response to this depiction of feminism as ideological, feminists may
hurl *tu quoque* at psychoanalysis: "Isn't psychoanalysis also an ideology?
Isn't this whole discussion of 'mythologies' in the feminist movement
ideological also? Doesn't psychoanalysis put people into boxes determined by the middle-European value system of Freud's Vienna of the
turn of the twentieth century? Are not psychoanalysts constantly trying
to get people to conform to the *status quo?*"

The answer is: certainly psychoanalysts in their practice have a system
of values, and would be misleading if they claimed to be entirely value-
free. However, that value system is not the same as ideology in the sense
of defense of capitalism, or of communism, or of any particular "liberation" movement. Rather the paramount value is self-knoledge, at the
greatest depths possible, and with willingness to deal with the consequences of that self-knowledge, however uncomfortable or disturbing.
That involves precisely facing and dealing with complexity and ambiguity
and the many-sidedness of psychic and social events rather than their
evasion or denial or oversimplification. In the value system of psychoanalysis, the important distinction is not between conformity and rebellion, but rather whether a particular line of action serves adaptive or
regressive functions in the psychic economy of the individual. From this
vantage point, conforming behavior may be adaptive, or it may be regressive, for the person involved. And so may rebellious action, including
action aimed toward revolutionary ends. It is a canard to claim that
psychoanalysts only want to get their patients to conform to the prevailing
norms of their culture and time.

We also need to distinguish "adaptation" (as just used) from "adjustment." In this context, "adjustment" would mean conforming to and
going along with the existing culture and its norms, whatever they are,
and however they relate to real human needs. If Rosalyn Yalow had
bowed to the prejudices of the time of her youth that a woman could not
be a physicist, that would be "adjusting," but it would not have been
"adaptive" behavior for *her*. Fighting to have her career as a physicist
was adaptive, a rational way of dealing with difficulties in the real external
world in assertion of her own personal autonomy and intellectual talent.
Where psychoanalysts place a higher positive value on adaptation, they

do not mean by that that the person should adjust and conform to the immediately surrounding society no matter what. (See part 5 for a much more detailed and intensive discussion of this whole thorny area: the relationship between deviance or nonconformity in the sociological sense to psychopathology as psychoanalytically conceived.) Given a complex multifaceted world in modern societies, with myriad conflicts and contradictions in values among different groups and in different situations, the adaptive capacities of individuals are taxed to an extraordinary degree, and a simple-minded one-dimensional demand for strict conformity and adjustment on one side, or for its opposite, reflex nonconformity and rebellion on the other, are neither adequate to the demands of living in this society. Here psychoanalysis, far from being the enemy, is one of the surest allies in a realistic confrontation with the world.

Women's movement beliefs include a mixture of fairly rational assessments of the real situation of women in the world, alongside quite irrational beliefs (belied by scientific evidence) and nonrational articles of faith, neither substantiated nor refuted by empirical evidence. In the first category we find documentation of the disparities faced by women in training, employment, etc., and recognition that females are socialized so as to be relatively weaker in self-confidence and self-esteem than male peers. In the second category we find denial of any real differences between the sexes, and denial of the constraints and difficulties that ensue when trying to combine labor-force participation with having and rearing children, and denial of the very real difficulties involved in raising children. In the non-rational category we find such value judgments as that it is better to have no gender differentiation than to have some.

One can be against any kind of discrimination against women (as I am) in legal, political, and economic matters, favor equal pay for equal work, and women having the opportunity to pursue any careers for which they have inclination and ability, without accepting feminist ideas to the effect that all women *should* be working in the marketplace labor force and should also get special dispensation when at such work to accommodate their childbearing and child-rearing function, and without accepting the feminist idea that women should constitute half the work force in all occupations, and the associated notion that any situation, such as a university faculty in engineering, in which women constitute less than 50 percent of the staff constitutes *prima facie* evidence of discrimination. Similarly, one can be in favor of fair and equitable employment practices in relation to women that recognize differences in needs, talents, and situations, without going along with the feminist tendency (as with other kinds of ideologues) to convert permissions into obligations: e.g., not only *may* the little girl be allowed to play with trucks along with her brother, but she *should* do so, and *should* be encouraged to do so. An alternative value system (which I would espouse) places a positive emphasis on diversity, variety, and options, including the option *not* to be "liberated" by ideologists.

Part 3

SUMMARY AND CONCLUSION

Sociological analysis of the changing *norms* for gender differences in modern society shows little consensus, much confusion, and something like a state of anomie. As a heuristic device we postulate two poles around which current variations are tending, a "traditional" set of gender role norms, and a challenging set coming mostly from the feminist movement, the "vanguard" norms. Actual positions taken by real persons in modern societies may include any of a variety of combinations of these two. The "traditional" or "patriarchal" norms expect males to be strong, aggressive, assertive, competitive, objective, emotion-denying, self-disciplined, controlled, calculating, instrumental, object-related (rather than person-related), connected with mathematics, hard science and technology. Females by these norms are to be weak, dependent, submissive, intuitive, cooperative, nurturant, non-rational and irrational, emotionally attuned and labile, expressive, unreliable, less disciplined, person-oriented, attuned to nurturant and humanistic pursuits. The male was to be psychologically invested in work as a major part of life, status-conferring and intrinsic to masculine identity. The female was not to have that kind of relationship to work, and not to connect work intrinsically with her feminine identity.

By contrast, the "vanguard" norms now emerging would reduce or eliminate nearly all of these normative gender differences, and expect the female to equal the male in any of these attributes or interests defined by traditionalists as "masculine," to seek work in any field without regard to prior gender definitions of that field, to make work as central to life as any man does, to find ways to combine, if she wishes, marriage, childbearing and child-rearing with career work. She is to be assertive in any sphere, including sex, where her own satisfaction becomes at least as important as that of her man. These vanguard norms involve less of a change for the man (thus producing asymmetries) and men are less committed to them than women, producing an arena of normative conflict and potential anomie on all the questions the feminists have raised.

We postulated severe limitations on and difficulties about these vanguard norms, in the feasibility of their fulfillment, on both sociological and psychoanalytic grounds. Sociologically there seem to be limits beyond which de-differentiation of gender roles could go in any highly complex modern society. The dilemmas raised by the extreme helplessness and vulnerability of the human neonate, young infant, and young child, dictate some kind of social organization of infant and child care, which would be endangered by the kind and degree of de-differentiation the vanguard norms propose. Bluntly, "someone has to take care of babies and children." Cross-cultural data, on tribal as well as various modern societies like the USSR, China, and the Israeli kibbutz, suggest the great difficulty, if not impossibility, of the de-differentiation the vanguard norms are proposing.

On psychoanalytic grounds, consideration of the psychosexual-developmental differences between females and males also challenges the feasibility of the vanguard norms. Feminism's war against psychoanalysis is considered, on the questions of the Freudian view of female psychosexual development, the role of penis envy, differences in aggressiveness and its channeling, the female superego, and feminine masochism, passivity, narcissism, and differential reality orientation. We showed how present-day "mainstream" or "classical" psychoanalysis considers Freud wrong in his theory of the "originally masculine" nature of the growing female child, and on the centrality (though not the existence) of penis envy in female psychosexual development. Anthropological data indicating envy by each sex of the other, fills out (but does not refute) the penis envy picture.

Object-relations psychoanalysis, as one major branch in inheritance of the "classical" psychoanalytic position, portrays a complex subtle process of differential female compared to male psychosexual and object-relational early development, bifurcating into different directions from earliest infancy on the basis of the girl's having a same-sex mothering person and the boy one of opposite sex. Very distinct difficulties and dilemmas in the separation-individuation process occur in the two different sexes, with fateful consequences for all later development. Females remain much more closely connected to the intimate pre-verbal, phatically communicative infant-mother bond, and its emphasis on empathy, intuition, and incomplete reality-orientation. Oedipal involvements are distinctively different for the two sexes, based both on the difference of the sex of the mother, and on the distinctive pre-oedipal involvements of the boy and the girl baby in relation first to the mother, then to the father. We considered the "culturalist psychoanalysts" in their modifications of classical psychoanalytic theory on these matters, and the classicals' (to my mind persuasive) counter-refutation. These substantial developmental differences between the sexes, the basic features of which are probably universal, in turn create the conditions for the psychological reproduction, in each generation, of the gender division of parenting labor, by which it is *women* who mother babies, and not men. Girls develop the requisite capacities and motivations, and boys do so much less. In contrast to Chodorow's view, I see the possibility of fundamental change in that gender division as very slight. I also disagree with feminists' value judgment of the *desirability* of such change.

Sex differences in aggression are well documented in a variety of disciplines' works. We find good reason for believing there is a biological substratum for greater aggressiveness in males than in females; our evolutionary reconstruction provides an explanation for this. These differences, however, are overlaid by heavy socio-cultural influences, which can either accentuate or minimize biologically given differences, but are most unlikely to be able to eliminate them entirely. Differential developmental processes in libidinal and object-relational terms also predispose to differential patterns of both the genesis and channeling of aggression between the sexes. Feminist positions are insufficiently cognizant of how deeply and complexly rooted these sex differences are, and how, therefore, strongly resistant to change.

Lastly, we began an analysis of the vanguard or feminist movement as an ideological struggle, employing typical reactive and mitigating mythologies, similar in process to other protest, reform, or "revolutionary" movements. The ideological quality there typically flattens out and oversimplifies the real world of both psyche and society, categorizes the world into cartoon demon and hero images, peopling the world with doctrinaire loyalists and enemies, renegades and traitors, maintaining an intolerance as great as any of the alleged "oppressors," using slogans of "sexism," "chauvinism," and the like in place of thought. We pointed to the contrast between the realistically advantaged, even privileged, position, of women who are most vociferous in the feminist cause—compared to others of contemporary society, to any of the past, to any in other, either traditional or modern societies—and their cries of "oppression" and "enslavement," and elements of narcissistic self-indulgence in the demand to not only "have it all," but also "have it *all at once*," in denial of realistic difficulties and constraints in life, not the product of sexist plots. We also placed the dilemmas of the vanguard norms in the context of the whole trend toward modernization and liberalization of life and of life chances that has been proceeding apace in the modern industrialized world for at least the past two centuries, creating a multiplicity of consequences often in conflict, and world-views that emphasize greater, rather than lesser, dissatisfaction with the exigencies of life.

That discussion presages the analysis to be undertaken later (Part 5) on the connection of psychic health with either conformity or rebellion (or both), the intricate interplay between psychopathology and psychic health on one side and deviance and conformity on the other.

4

Homosexuality: Gay Liberation Confronts Psychoanalysis and the Social Sciences

. . . a homosexual radical factor rooted in human nature is inherent in the nature of all males, not just those who are inverse (exclusively homosexual) but also the vast majority of men who are not.
T. Vanggaard, *Phallos*, 1972:24

The secret of homosexuality is that it is almost always a deeply hostile relationship, masked as eroticism or love, in which the homosexual acts out his hatred of the powerful father-figure, societal or real, who has driven him out of the competition for the mother and all women.
G. Legman, *Rationale of the Dirty Joke*, 2d Series, 1975:24

"There's a new minority group that will soon be clamoring for its rights: Eskimo lesbians."
Anon. 1980

CHAPTER ELEVEN

Homophile Movement Protests

Homosexuality has become a focus of conflict and struggle in modern society. A growing homophile protest movement—styling itself "gay liberation"—has been challenging prevailing social, legal, and religious codes and opinions, and in the process posing a confrontation to many aspects of contemporary social and behavioral science and psychoanalysis. Social scientists, psychoanalysts, and psychotherapists of many persuasions have entered the lists on one side or another of various confrontation struggles.

Homosexuality is a topic on which psychoanalysis, other kinds of psychology, many varieties of sociology, and cultural anthropology have all had something to say, some of it either supportive or contradicting positions taken by one or another version of the "gay liberation" movement. Rarely have the contributions of sociology, anthropology, and psychoanalysis been brought together in a coherent manner, with one clear-cut integrating theoretical position. The usual problem of interdisciplinary boundaries and disciplinary specialization which hinders common communication among these different fields has hindered the development of a unitary view.

In this part, I shall attempt a move toward such a formulation. The challenges thrown down by the homophile protest movement can serve as a useful point of departure for the formulation of such an integrating viewpoint.

HOMOSEXUAL GRIEVANCES

The grievances of homosexuals against the dominant society are many and real. Their activist spokesmen complain: "To the law we are criminals; to the clerics, we are wicked and sinful; to the doctors we are sick; to frightened parents we are potential seducers of their children; to educational conservatives we are corrupters of the young; to conventionals we are weird," and so on.

Gays are subject to blackmail and extortion. Without recourse, to violent beatings by gangs of "macho" thugs. To police harassment on matters unrelated to sex. To various kinds of criminal depradations by others, from which gays expect little or no protection from the police, or are afraid to try to get. To less than honorable discharge from the military services, even if they have given heroic performances in the line of duty. To discrimination in employment or promotion. To difficulties in finding housing on a par with heterosexuals. To tensions in public accommodations. And generally to the slings and arrows of stigma in all its guises. To constant uncertainty about how they will be treated or reacted to if they are open to others about their sexual preference. To fear of exposure affecting careers and families. To all manner of psychological suffering attendant upon real or expected or feared negative reactions from non-homosexuals, to their form of loving and of deriving basic satisfactions that others regard as the birthright of all. To estrangement, loneliness, isolation, depression, suicidal thoughts or attempts stemming, as they see it at least, from the desperateness of being a persecuted "outsider" in the society in which one lives and wants to live. To repeated assaults on one's dignity as a human being. If secret about one's preference, to repeated exposure to anti-homosexual prejudices and actions of others toward the openly homosexual, putting one in the bind of impulse to object and protest, countered by terror at the prospect of harmful self-disclosure. For the secret deviants, to the endless strains and difficulties of living in two or more worlds, to the pain of rarely being able to "be one's own true self." For those with this preference as *one* part of their sexual life and yearning, alongside a differently accented orientation to the opposite sex as well, the pains of living with ambiguity, uncertainty, anxiety, and the struggle between the absolutist polar labels, "gay" and "straight," supported both by the conventional ("straight") world and by the deviant minority subculture of the gays, with neither of these feeling like really fitting or comfortable attire.

True, not all persons with a completely or partially homosexual erotic orientation suffer all of these indignities and oppressions all of the time. Nor are all members of the surrounding putatively heterosexual society uniformly hostile and derogatory and oppressive toward all persons of homosexual orientation all of the time, in all circumstances. (See last part of this section for assessment of proportions.) But every one of the indignities, injustices, oppressions, discriminations, and psychological assaults does occur, and everyone of homosexual orientation does run the risk of at least several of these, some of the time, and knows, if he or she is at all in contact with others of homosexual persuasion, of countless incidents of any of these kinds that others have been subjected to, and of countless instances of the kinds of psychological torment described.

Also, contrary to widely prevalent stereotypes, homosexuals are to be found in all kinds of occupations, at all class levels, in all kinds of physiques and appearances; they rarely molest students or pupils, do not make passes at coworker cops or firemen, do not infect the military, rarely proselytize.

Not surprisingly, many homosexuals, or at least their more outspoken members, are seeing themselves now as an oppressed minority group. And the more politicized among them are fighting back. The context is the ongoing struggle of various subgroups or categories of people within modern society, who are and perceive themselves to be unjustly treated, collectively to protest against these conditions and actively strive to change the social structures and cultural norms as well as the actual actions of others and themselves, to bring about a juster society, one in which they will be "liberated" from their chains and restrictions. First racial and then ethnic minorities, then women as a minority group, now add the homosexuals. They have now become a central part of ongoing political struggles. Not surprisingly, in such struggles, a central part is the battle of ideas: of how one defines the social and personal world, in this case of how one sees sexuality and its variety of expressions, of how one defines the fitting and the unfitting, the "correct" and the "incorrect" in behavior, feelings, attitudes, and patterns of thought. Politicalization of such ideas always leads to extremities of formulation, to sloganizing in place of thought, to the emotionalizing of vocabulary in its impressment in service for political ends, to the removal of propositions from the realm of scientific testing and rational argument, into that of political advocacy and passion.

This struggle of ideas now brings into the act the social and behavioral sciences, the psychic healing arts, and their associated scientific disciplines, particularly psychoanalysis and associated or derivative therapies and psychological theory disciplines. All of these become in one way or another relevant in the homophile liberation struggle, in some cases in the role of villains and enemies (psychoanalysis and psychiatry, for example) or in the role of friendly supporters (much contemporary sociology, some of social psychology), though many of the former consider themselves sympathetic and supportive, and many of the latter at least skeptical of overreacting claims by the purported "liberationists." Still others in any of these fields consider themselves as having a higher commitment to understanding and compassionate empathy than to the furthering of specific political causes. And while none of these fields is free of central value positions, and all share certain basis libertarian tendencies, most do not see their own field of endeavor as crucially and centrally an *ideological* one, which political action institutions or movements such as the one here in question do, in a significant manner.

This whole political context needs a more extensive discussion. (See "The Politicalization of Homosexuality," in chapter 14.) Here let us look at specific challenges presented by the homophile movement and its supporters in the social sciences and psychoanalysis and see what kind of reasoned and integrative analysis we can make of the questions raised from the combined viewpoints of psychoanalysis, sociology, and anthropology.

Homophile movement spokesmen and their supporters among social and behavioral scientists and therapists have attempted to challenge views of homosexuality as abnormal in any of the several meanings that term may have. They have particularly challenged the view of homosexuality as sickness, which they see being presented by psychoanalysis and allied professionals. They assert that negative reactions toward homosexuality that prevail in our society now are peculiar to this society and this era, arguing that cross-cultural and trans-historical evidence shows homosexuality as "normal" behavior and socially accepted in many other societies both primitive and advanced. They assert that homosexuals should be properly considered either as simply people following an alternative "life-style" or as a minority group subject to unjustified discrimination and persecution. They assert that psychoanalytic studies of etiology are either irrelevant or pernicious (by implying that homosexuality is *ipso facto* sick), and that efforts to "cure" in the sense of changing the individual's sexual preference from homosexual to heterosexual are invasions of a person's autonomy and freedom to choose.

I shall take these assertions as the starting point for my discussion: in what sense is homosexuality an "abnormality"? Is the equation of homosexuality with psychological sickness justified? Do cross-cultural and trans-historical studies in fact show homosexuality to be normal and acceptable sexual practice in other societies? And how shall we understand psychodynamically and sociologically both the prevalent anti-homosexual bias in society and the "gay liberation" movement's responses to it?

HOMOSEXUALITY AS "ABNORMAL"

Homosexuality has been perceived as abnormal from a number of viewpoints. In versions of the Judaeo-Christian religious tradition, as well as in other religious views, it is regarded as a violation of supernaturally derived moral codes, that is, as sin. In the laws of most of the United States and many other modern nations specific homosexual acts are crimes prosecutable by the law. It is regarded as "deviant" in opposition to commonly held social mores in many modern societies. Some view it as opposed to evolutionary dictates requiring heterosexuality as necessary for the survival of the species. Some simply see it as a statistical anomaly: it is practiced by only a small minority of the population. Still another view sees it as abnormal in the sense of opposed to standards of psychological health, that is, as "sick." Homophile protesters have challenged each of these views, singly or in combination.

On the matter of homosexuality as a sin, social scientists and psychoanalysts have typically left this question to theologians and other religious specialists and advocates. Clearly it is possible to construe some version of Christianity or of Judaism as finding some honorable and acceptable place for homosexuality within its canon. Historically, however, these religious traditions have been strongly anti-sexual generally, and particularly hostile to what they regard as "unnatural abominations." To the charge of "unnatural" one could reply that anything that appears in nature cannot be counted as "unnatural," and thus dispose of that whole question semantically. It is a terminology of little use or value in either social science or psychoanalysis.

Homosexuality as a crime is the negative evaluation of homosexuality derived from the Judaeo-Christian religious tradition translated into the laws of various countries and states. These are clearly cases of religious mores relating to emotionally held views of the perniciousness of "unnatural" sexual acts, without any foundation in demonstrable damage to other persons—at least in the case of consensual adult homosexual acts—or to society in general. Van den Haag has succinctly summarized the arguments for not considering homosexuality as any danger to society or other persons (Van den Haag 1963). Most social scientists would agree with this position, and psychoanalysts have generally either not disagreed with it or have simply not addressed themselves to this question in their discussions of homosexuality. Most would probably privately agree that there is no justification for the law, in a modern, supposedly enlightened age, proscribing private consensual homosexual acts and sanctioning them with the possibility of severe penalties, in some cases amounting to as much as thirty years in prison. On this issue, the quarrel that gay liberation supporters have is not with either social sciences or psychoanalysis, but rather with those upholders of restrictive laws against homosexuality. A necessary caveat would apply to the constraining of homosexual acts by force against unwilling persons, or the seduction of minors; these, it would be agreed, are properly enforceable by law, as would be heterosexual rape or any other imposition of sexual acts by force, or other imposition of sexuality on minors.

To the charge that homosexuality is "unnatural," homophile movement supporters respond that it occurs in nature and therefore cannot be counted as "unnatural." It occurs not only in human beings but in many other, infra-human mammals as well, under certain circumstances. Behavioral scientists responding to this piece of gay liberation rhetoric would have to point out that the rare instances that have been reported of other mammals, where one individual attempts to make sexual contact with another conspecific of the same sex, cannot accurately be called "homosexual," since to the best of our knowledge it lacks the elements that make human sexuality, in whatever version, distinctive and distinctively human. To wit: in human sexuality, there is not only action in the service of gratification of biologically given drives, but also a whole psychology of meanings and fantasy attached to sexuality in any and all of its forms of expression. If the homophile supporters mean to imply that we should take the stance of "nothing human is alien to me," then certainly most social scientists and psychoanalysts would concur in the sense that our goal should be empathetic understanding of any and all forms of human activity. As already indicated, the words "natural" and "unnatural," as used by either supporters or antagonists of homosexuality, are of little or no use or value in social-scientific or psychoanalytic discussion.

Homosexuality is also seen as "abnormal" in the sense of "deviant" behavior. This is a common rubric in sociological discussions of homosexual behavior: it is "deviant" in the sense and to the extent that the behavior in question violates strongly held mores of the population in which this occurs. Sociologists using this kind of approach insist that in this terminology they are not implying agreement with the negative value judgment placed upon this behavior by the majority population of that society, but only objectively *reporting* that this is how the people in the surrounding society do regard the behavior. Such sociological approaches to deviance imply or explicitly state that their viewpoint is relativistic; what is regarded by the people in the society as "deviant" in one case, i.e., one society or sub-society, may not be so regarded by the people of another society or sub-society. The very definition by prevailing or dominant portions of the society, of some behavior or some types of persons as "deviant" in itself becomes a significant part of social reality, with real consequences for both the stigmatized individuals and those doing the stigmatizing, and for the interactional processes between them.

We shall take up later (chapter 17) the complex question of the possible interrelationship between "deviance" in this sociological sense, and "psychopathology" in the senses in which it is used in psychoanalysis and clinical psychology. For the moment we shall postpone any extended discussion of this as it applies to homosexuality until we have taken up the problem of psychopathology.

Gay spokesmen object to the terminology of "deviance" almost as much as to that of "sin," "crime," and "unnaturalness." They see social scientists' usage of that term as implying agreement with the value judgment made by anti-homosexuals. They thus see sociologists as going along with popular prejudices to the effect that homosexuality is wrong, immoral, unnatural, against the interests of society, and the like. Sociologists answer that that is not what they mean. And, in fact, most sociologists dealing with this topic, as with most other topics of "deviance," tend to imply (if not state) a good deal of sympathy with and empathy with the objects of the deviance label, and in some cases go out of their way to try to look at the world "through the eyes of" the deviants themselves, as an exercise in the sociological imagination.

Politicized gay activists, however, are not satisfied with that. The term "deviant" is itself a kind of red flag, inciting counter-assertion that homosexuality is only an alternative "life-style," as "natural" and "good" as any other. They challenge sociologists to specify: deviant according to whom? The sociologist replies, deviant according to whoever considers homosexuality to be deviant, which is probably most of the people in present-day modern society. For such persons, homosexuality involves going against some of the norms of society.

Homophile spokesmen reply to this: (a) those holding such views may not be the majority of people in society; (b) even if they are a majority, they are not the whole society; (c) there are many varying views of homosexuality held by people in modern society; (d) the views are changing, and the proportion holding negative views, compared to those positive or indifferent or laissez-faire, is probably changing too; therefore, (e) homosexuality need not be presumed to continue to be regarded, indefinitely into the future, as deviance worthy of disapproval or contempt.

Articulators of this homophile movement position would also point out that though sociologists and other social scientists may *mean* to use the term "deviant" in a non-pejorative objective manner, this is not necessarily how such terminology is interpreted by non-social-scientific readers, who will be likely to read into such discussion their own negative value judgments. Sociologists would reply that that problem exists in all consumption of social scientific work by lay audiences. The sociologist has to tell the truth of what is going on in society as he sees it, as lucidly as possible, and cannot be held responsible for how lay citizens or people with political axes to grind may use or misinterpret the sociologist's writings. Sociologists of "deviance" are not particularly willing to drop the use of such a theoretically useful concept as "deviance" just because some of the persons whose behavior may be categorized by that label find the label insulting.

One could suggest the use of a term such as "variation," in place of "deviation," with the idea that this would be more neutral and objective. But such a practice is likely to be futile, for whatever terminology is used, in an arena so charged with affectively loaded controversy as this, itself becomes transformed into value-loaded significance. This has already happened to the term "deviance," which was intended to be free of the value loadings of such laymen's terms as "immoral," "unnatural," "sinful," and "criminal." The history of the implications of the term "sick" is also instructive in this regard. In an earlier period, viewing certain kinds of behavior as manifestations of "sickness," therefore calling for "treatment," was intended as a humane, benign revision, away from the derogatory implications of viewing the persons involved as "evil," "corrupt," "criminal," and the like. By now, the term "sick" has itself become a standard form of vituperation. And it figures significantly in the controversies about homosexuality, as we shall discuss shortly.

Still another usage of the term "abnormality" is statistical. Statistically normal would be what most people in a society are doing. How big a majority is necessary for one to consider something statistically normal is a matter of opinion. But in any case, by whatever means we may have at present to count the number of people carrying on homosexual behavior as their main sexual preference, they are surely in a minority in this society at the present time. Whether they have ever been in any society something more than a minority is another question which we shall consider at some length later.

Gay supporters would argue that even in reference to this society in this age, the size of that "minority" is likely to be much larger than the average lay observer tends to believe. They would point out that it makes a difference whether you are talking about persons who are labeled as "homosexuals," or who so see themselves, or about persons whose exclusive sexual interest is with the same sex, or whether you're talking about homosexual activity, that is any sexual activity involving genital contact with another member of one's own sex. They point [lovingly] to the Kinsey figure (Kinsey et al. 1948) of 37 percent of all the white males interviewed in America at that time reporting having had at least one sexual contact with another male leading to orgasm at some point or other during their lives. (Needless to say, that figure is grossly misleading. It includes all cases where there has been but one or but a very small number of such contacts, usually during adolescent experimentation, followed by an otherwise almost exclusively heterosexual history, as well as any and all degrees of homosexual participation, up to and including exclusive adult homosexuality, anything from Kinsey's 0 rating to his rating of 6.)

Homophile supporters will also point out that the statistical minority status is also problematical in yet another way: the average non-homosexual citizen is likely to be unaware of how many and which of the people he knows in his occupational and other less than intimate worlds are in fact secret homosexuals, and therefore likely grossly to exaggerate the majority status of heterosexuality. Obviously it is difficult if not impossible to answer this statement or test its accuracy, short of some (unlikely) research strategy that would induce *all* secret gays to reveal themselves, at least to the researcher. True, some sociological studies, such as the recent one by Bell and Weinberg (1978)—have tapped some of the secret homosexual population, but even so assiduous researchers as these will not claim that they can estimate how many such individuals there are in the United States, or what proportion of either the total population, or of the gay population, secret homosexuals represent.

Even if we limited the counting to "predominantly" or "exclusively" homosexual in both fantasy and practice, we still have no way of estimating with any assurance the number of "homosexuals" in the population, or their percentage of the total population. Current guesses run in the vicinity of 4 to 5 percent, though as typically occurs with embattled minorities, gay activists are more likely to estimate 10 percent or more. At the extreme, homosexual ideologues may claim (in private at least) that "really, if you scratch, you'll discover that *everyone* is really gay, or would like to be." Such assertions would have to be considered bits of politically motivated mystification.

A more problematical basis for imputing "abnormality" to homosexuality would be one referring to evolutionary imperatives. In earlier chapters I have discussed probable lines of evolution of the human species, and pointed out the development of strong sexual dimorphism, both physically and psychologically, as a significant feature of the evolution of this species. This would entail an evolutionary premium upon heterosexual drive and motivation as necessary for reproduction and thus species survival.

But this is in a context of the evolution of a very complex human sexuality, that is, in contrast with that of infra-human mammals, constant, lifelong, imperious, and extremely extravagant in relation to minimal reproductive necessities. It is also a sexuality that is potentially polymorphous (as it is more overtly in infancy and may continue to be, in potentiality, through all phases of life) and highly variable and variegated in its possible form of expression and gratification.

We may assume that the species had become "programmed" in evolution toward a *predominance* of adult heterosexual feeling and motivation and action. In any particular breeding population, if any significant proportion of the population so strongly preferred homosexual to heterosexual activity as to reduce the latter to an extremely small proportion, there would be a real danger of the population of that particular group dying out. But we have no good reason to believe that the species has been programmed to rule out completely alternatives to heterosexual union as possible forms of sexual gratification, for all people some of the time, for some people all of the time, and for some people some of the time.

Human sexuality has never been limited to the ends of reproduction. In fact, the whole thrust of psychoanalysis in its understanding of sexuality has been to emphasize how extravagantly varied in its forms and functions human sexuality is, and how luxuriant in forms of pleasure entirely outside the reproductive process. That is the meaning of the polymorphousness of human sexuality.

However, classical psychoanalysts may respond to that statement by pointing out that the polymorphousness that Freud was referring to was that of *infantile* sexuality, and that Freud was certainly not implying by that discovery that such a degree of polymorphousness in overt expression in adult sexuality could be considered normal.

Gay movement supporters would point out that it is typical for people with anti-homosexual bias to claim that if we let everyone do this (carry on homosexual activity) the population would die out, the family would disintegrate, and sundry other dire catastrophic consequences would ensue. Of course, it would have to be answered, if everyone engaged only in homosexual intercourse, yes the population would die out. Since we don't know of any historical or tribal societies where this was the case, and since considering the strong inborn tendency toward heterosexuality and the evident unlikelihood that most people would abandon heterosexuality entirely in any modern society, the whole argument takes on a rather theoretical cast.

A more realistic formulation might be this: in evolutionary terms, how *much* variation from heterosexual supremacy can a society allow or even encourage without threatening its reproductive survival? 20 percent? 40 percent? 50 percent? Again, the answer will have to be in the form of guesses. "Some, but not too much," might be the appropriate, though obviously evasive, answer.[1]

In "variation from heterosexual supremacy" just above, I am referring primarily to *exclusive* homosexuality, since only in this version of homosexual practice would reproduction by that individual be precluded. As a matter of fact, not even there, since it is possible for an exclusively homosexual male to donate his semen to "sperm banks" for artificial fertilization of a female. However, many persons often defined as "bisexual" because they have some intercourse with partners of both sexes may also be limiting reproduction somewhat if their heterosexual contacts are only a small proportion of their total coital activity. It is the impression of many psychoanalysts that most of the people referred to or calling themselves "bisexual" are probably *predominantly* homosexual in behavior and fantasy combined, or at least in fantasy preference. Psychoanalysts would, of course, find a purely behavioral criterion a very poor indicator of what the person is all about.

Still other answers have been given to the evolutionary argument against the "normality" of homosexuality. One is to point out that in the modern world population enhancement or even maintenance is not usually the problem. On the contrary, *over*population is more commonly the problem. Some homophile supporters have even argued that modern society should welcome a greater prevalence of homosexuality as one means of population control. Other gay spokesmen, however, use an argument that nullifies that one. They say that prevalent homosexual activity does not necessarily reduce reproduction, since many homosexual males do in fact father offspring, and that probably an even greater proportion of homosexual females have in fact borne children, usually in heterosexual marriages, and in these, often in a period prior to their taking up a predominantly or exclusively homosexual life.

We do not have any hard figures on how many such cases there are, or what proportion of the total of fathers, or of mothers, of any particular generation they represent, nor of what proportion they represent of the predominantly homosexual population of their generation. (The latter is impossible to estimate, since so far no one has figured out how to get a representative sample of the total homosexual population. See later discussion of Bell and Weinberg's significant work on this question.) Gay activist supporters or ideologues are likely to question whether it is really necessary to assume that evolution means predominance of heterosexuality in the sexual motivations of human beings, or whether one might as well argue that that is only one among a number of possibilities. This questioning ties in with gays' objections to psychoanalytic views of homosexuality as some version of sickness.

CHAPTER TWELVE

Psychoanalytic Views on Homosexuality

HOMOSEXUALITY AS "SICKNESS"?

The last and the most controversial, formulation of homosexuality as "abnormality" is that of psychopathology, or "sickness," in laymen's terms. Here the gay movement has pointed out an identified enemy, namely psychoanalysts, who, they claim, have done the worst harm in vilifying and derogating gays as "sick," when in fact there is no intrinsic connection between homosexual preference and psychological sickness or impairment. In fact, if we look closely, we find a great variety of opinions concerning the possible psychopathology of homosexuality among the various kinds of "experts" in treating people with psychopathological disorders.

These experts include not only psychoanalysts, who vary among themselves in that some are psychiatrists (necessarily with M.D.'s), some are psychologists (with Ph.D.'s, usually in clinical psychology), some are psychiatric social workers with additional psychoanalytic training, and a number are professionals from a variety of other fields who have gotten some version of psychoanalytic training and carry on a practice they identify as psychoanalysis. Some of these are sociologists and anthropologists by prior or additional professional affiliation. Many are individuals who have come out of other fields of endeavor such as law or political science or theater or any of the arts. All these "psychoanalysts" also differ among themselves on many issues relating to psychopathology, to psychoanalytic theory, and to clinical treatment modalities. In addition to psychoanalysts there are psychiatrists who do not identify themselves specifically as psychoanalysts, though some have had some psychoanalytic training.

Then there are other clinical psychologists who are not psychoanalytic in orientation or in treatment modalities. There are still other psychologists who are in some kind of clinical practice, without necessarily having clinical psychology degrees. And there are still other clinical practitioners whose background training was in social work, and who have not had specific psychoanalytic training, except for some minimal exposure to psychoanalytic ideas in the context of social work training. There are also psychiatric nurses who have had psychoanalytic training and carry on a clinical practice in a private or institutional setting. And still others of these who have not had psychoanalytic training and who have a clinical practice treating patients with psychological difficulties.

Alongside all of these varied forms of psychotherapeutic practice within something like a mainstream of such practice with some professional credentials, there is also that whole fringe of therapeutic practitioners who are in effect at the wild margins of the psychotherapy world, often attracting a large clientele at least for the period in which their kind of "therapy" is trendy and popular. These include EST, Dianetics, bio-feedback, orgone therapy, scientology, various versions of encounter and human-potential-enhancement therapies, and the like. (These are likely to escape the vitriol of gay anger in that they do not usually ally themselves with psychoanalytic views on homosexuality, or on anything else, generally.)

Within the range of practitioners who *are*, broadly speaking, psychoanalytic in orientation, can we detect some general trend on the question whether homosexuality is in itself a form of psychopathology, or indicative of some form of psychic illness? The answer is no. There are many different views.

PSYCHOANALYTIC VIEWS: CLASSICAL AND OTHER

Classical

First, what could be called a "classical" psychoanalytic view as represented at the extreme by such writers as Socarides (1968, 1978), and less extreme form by Bieber et al. (1962), by Stoller (1975), by Wiedeman (1974), and many others represented in the publications of the International Psychoanalytic Association (*International Journal of Psychoanalysis*) and those of the American Psychoanalytic Association (*Journal of the American Psychoanalytic Association*) among others.

An outline of such a "conservative" or "classical" psychoanalytic position of today would run as follows: homosexuality is a deviation of sexual object choice, which can be considered a pathology on this point alone. It may or may not be associated with other aspects of pathology in personality formation. It may be associated with neurosis, with psychosis, or with borderline formation, or with character disorder. It may be strongly associated with extreme narcissism, but in many cases it is not. The word "pathology" is applicable where it is the exclusive or strongly preferential sexual object choice, i.e., where the person *must* have a sexual partner of the same sex, or such partner is strongly preferred to one of the opposite sex. It is also possible—though we think rare—that the gender of object choice may be the only way in which this individual varies from what psychoanalysis regards as optimal psychological functioning, from optimal psychic health in the psychoanalytic sense of that term.

It would then be possible that such an individual is in fact well adjusted in his various social roles in society and may in some instances even be very adaptive, creative, or innovative in his approach to the world. He could also have a highly rewarding, mutually emotionally satisfying and supportive long-term relationship with a same-sex partner that is at least as stable as most good heterosexual marriages. (Psychoanalysts of this persuasion believe, however, that such instances are rare.) But it is also possible that the person with homosexual preference may have associated difficulties in other spheres of social adjustment and may have maladaptations of various kinds which may or may not be connected with the specific deviation of sexual object choice.

Though there is no total consensus on this, there is also a widespread view among classical psychoanalysts that homosexuality should not in itself be considered a clinical entity. Stoller has epitomized that view as follows:

> . . . homosexuality is not a diagnosis: 1) there is only a sexual preference . . . not a uniform constellation of signs and symptoms; 2) different people with this sexual preference have different psychodynamics underlying their sexual behavior; and 3) quite different life experiences can cause these dynamics and this behavior. There *is* homosexual behavior; it is varied. People with all sorts of personality types prefer homosexuality as their sexual practice; people without overt neurotic symptomatology, schizophrenics, obsessive-compulsives, alcoholics, people with other perversions—almost every category in the nomenclature. But there is no such thing as homosexuality. (Stoller 1975:199)

An essential point in these psychoanalytic views is not to take the homosexual object choice as the sole or central focus of attention in the individual concerned. One's sexuality is never isolated from other aspects of one's life or one's psychological functioning. It is always embedded in some form of total character structure, and any aspect of sexual preference or proclivity—of which the gender of the sexual partner, if any, is only one among a number of potentially significant elements—needs to be examined for how it functions in the total constellation of the personality. If a major factor in the production of the homosexual object choice is an enormous degree of castration anxiety in the male, then there are bound to be various other consequences, defenses, transformations, and associated constellations following from the same and associated dynamic factors. The kinds of functions overt homosexual action may have are also multiple and varied and not uniform from one person to another, or even within the same person at different times and in different circumstances. The essential point is that one's homosexuality needs to be examined as part of a total personality configuration.

It is certainly possible, as many revisionist psychoanalysts have argued—influenced evidently by libertarian ethos and the rhetorics of gay liberation and its sociological supporters—that the associated disturbances, in lowered self-esteem, guilt, torment, self-recriminations, that many homosexuals experience may derive (in part, at least) from reactions to societal stigma of homosexuality as sin, crime, or deviation, and not necessarily be intrinsically related to the homosexual preference *per se*. In that sense some of these reactions may be seen as secondary manifestations, not derivable from homosexual illness as such. The classically oriented psychoanalyst would be more skeptical of such a formulation, seeking out how such reactions are related to the primary sources of pathological functioning in this individual's dynamics, which might well be very closely connected with the wellsprings of his homosexual preference.

Clearly, sociologists and social psychologists of a non-psychoanalytic or anti-psychoanalytic persuasion who see all psychological difficulties homosexuals may experience as entirely a product of societal victimization are in conflict with what psychoanalysts have learned in clinical studies about the dynamics of individuals who have a homosexual preference, whether or not it is to be considered a clinical entity. How one uses one's situation of finding oneself a member of a stigmatized minority in society is also a question of inter-individual psychological variation. And the psychic uses to which such victimization (if it exists) may be put are part of an overall character formation of the individual. And both psychoanalytic and non-psychoanalytic (e.g., sociological) studies have revealed individuals who have a homosexual preference who do not *feel* particularly stigmatized by surrounding society on this account, and who experience relatively little negative self-evaluation on this account. True, these may well be a minority, just as well-integrated and psychologically well-functioning homosexuals may be a minority in the gay world. (See later discussion of Bell and Weinberg on this)

The assumption of classical psychoanalytic views that homosexual preference is per se a deviation from the "normal" heterosexual path of psychosexual development, and in that sense could be considered a pathology, is grounded in what has been identified as Freud's evolutionary framework, called by one critic an evolutionary value system. (See Roy Schafer 1974.) Schafer faults Freud for an arbitrary value position on this matter, rooted in the assumption that evolution requires a predominance of heterosexuality. Within the classic psychoanalytic tradition one can reply to Schafer as follows: True, Freud, like all of us engaged in trying to understand human behavior and diversity and to remedy psychic ills, does have some value positions, some explicit, some implicit; but on this point he is trying to make some factual substantive generalizations about human beings. The value implications of these generalizations may be diverse and mutually contradictory. Nature does not always operate in line with the value positions of human beings or of any particular human beings. Freud would appear to be on firm ground when he argues that, for better or worse, we have evolved as a species and we could not have done so without some deeply imbedded mechanisms insuring that, *usually*, there is strong motivation for heterosexual union which has the consequence of assuring reproduction. Of course, that does not exclude the possibility of some part of the population not following that plan, but it does say that not following has to be regarded as a deviation, however prevalent in some populations.

Homophile protesters react to such statements by posing the question: is not the pathway to heterosexuality just as much in need of explanation as that toward homosexuality? Why should only this variation be studied? The classical psychoanalyst's response to that is: of course, what responsible psychoanalyst ever said otherwise? Certainly the pathways toward heterosexual development need to be studied, and in fact have been intensively studied by psychoanalytic researchers through the whole development of psychoanalysis from Freud onward. And it is also full of all kinds of difficulties, pitfalls, and vicissitudes besides or alongside those involved in the development of the homosexual preference.

We earlier discussed some of these vicissitudes as they relate to the differences between female and male psychosexual development. Here that needs to be expanded to include the possible byways leading in the direction of homosexual preference in each sex. These are not simple matters, but we do know something of them from many decades of psychoanalytic work, and that is the deepest and most sophisticated kind of research there has been on these matters. Nor are all aspects of vicissitudes and their partial or substantial resolution all a clear-cut matter of pathology or absence of pathology. We shall take up etiological questions later in this chapter. For the moment, to answer the gay-lib protagonists: *all* psychosexual-developmental patterns and adult sequaelae need to be examined and analyzed in detail, not only those that are dramatically at variance with what is ordinarily assumed to be the normal heterosexual pattern.

To resume our summary of how psychoanalytic observers have formulated the presence or quality of "pathology" in homosexuality: there are many varied positions. Within or close to the "classical" psychoanalytic framework, psychoanalytic writers have variously linked homosexual object choice with pathological narcissism, that is severe disorders in the formation of the self. Some link it with difficulties in dominance-submission relationship. Some with competitive love-hate relationships in the male in connection with other males. Some see it linked to a need to defy authority or to court danger in a masochistic self-punishment syndrome. It may be connected to the construction of a "negative identity" (Erikson 1959), where being distinctive in this deviant way is felt as preferable to nothingness. It may also be associated with grave difficulties in maintaining impulse control, leading in some cases to a kind of pan-sexual polymorphousness frequently mistaken for sheer exuberance. (For some of these many formulations, see, among recent writers: Bergler 1951, 1956; Hatterer 1971; Ovesey 1969; various papers in Marmor 1965)

Interpersonal Revisionists

Revisionists of the "interpersonal" persuasion, that is followers of Harry Stack Sullivan, tend to de-emphasize libido and early psychosexual-developmental stages (at least in their specifically libidinal aspects), Oedipus complex, and the like, and to pay at least formal obeisance to the idea of cultural influences and the associated position of cultural relativism. (For an early and influential paper in the Sullivanian revisionist tradition, Thompson, 1947.) They are less likely than those in the "classical" (or "Freudian") tradition of psychoanalysis to regard homosexual object choice preference as per se indicative of a pathological process.

They are also likely to argue that the whole question has to be reformulated in such terms as these: how does this individual live his life? what is the nature of his important interpersonal relations with others around him? What functions and purposes—some of these well hidden—do his specific sexual activities and fantasies serve, and why? (These are not total qualitative differences from the "Freudians," and are in some cases only minor differences in emphasis. In terms of developmental phases, psychoanalysts of this persuasion are more likely to de-emphasize the more specifically sexual aspects of the early "psychosexual" developmental phases and their significance for later, and specifically sexual, development. It is more likely that it is among these kinds of psychoanalysts that the gay liberation rhetoric has had more influence on their thinking about sexual variations, and some have been influenced to join with the homophile supporters all the way in denying that there is necessarily any pathology whatever in the homosexual object choice.)

These are differences in shadings, rather than in fundamental propositions. As we shall see in the later section on etiological questions, both revisionists of a "culturalist" variety (influenced evidently primarily by Sullivan, Horney, and Fromm) and more "classical" or "Freudian" psychoanalysts joined in the collaborative project whose results are reported in the major work by Bieber and his associates (Bieber et al. 1962). And the differences in infra-psychoanalytic theoretical orientation did not influence the etiological findings of this study, which remains the most comprehensive to date on male homosexuality seen from the psychoanalytic depth dimension.

Psychoanalytic Replies to Homophile Objections

Homophile supporters, offended (even enraged) by psychoanalytic linkages of homosexuality with psychic illness, like to point out that after all many heterosexuals are psychologically sick, so why pick on the homosexuals? This is evidently another piece of political rhetoric. For just because many heterosexuals are, indeed, psychologically sick or impaired, does not mean that homosexuals are not. Any more than the existence of womb envy in males invalidates the existence of penis envy in females, as discussed in the preceding section. But the irrationality of such logic is but another indication of how deeply imbedded in irrationally based anxieties this whole topic is, both for gays and anti-gays. It suggests how precarious is the attainment of a productive and gratifying heterosexuality in a great many people.

Psychoanalytic probing of any kind is deeply resented by many in the gay-liberation movement, as it is by many other persons of pronounced political or other polemical interests in this society, as well as by many in the general lay public at large. In the case of the homophiles and their supporters—which would include many sociologists and sociologically-minded social psychologists—the opposition to psychoanalytic probing, besides sharing in the general anti-intellectualism and anti-intraceptiveness of political activists of many persuasions, takes the form of strong opposition to any kind of treatment for emotional difficulties of any kind, on the ground that such treatment by psychoanalytic therapists implies a judgment of pathology, and such a judgment specifically of the homosexual preference. (Ironically, even a study attempting to be empathically supportive of gays, such as that of Bell and Weinberg, uses as one "indicator" of psychological adjustment problems the fact that the subject had at any time consulted a professional psychological counselor of some kind. See discussion in following chapter. The irony here is that it is possible that some of the more deeply imbedded pathological versions of homosexuality may lead the individual to *refuse* even to consider psychotherapy; so that it is highly doubtful at the least whether going to a therapist is any better indicator of psychic disturbance than is not going.)

One psychoanalytic observer (Mitchell 1978) even suggests that psychoanalysts need to get it across to the lay public that exploration into the unconscious dynamics of one's behavior need *not* imply psychopathology; that psychoanalysts should stop scaring off potential supporters by letting the public continue in this implied linkage. He specifically applies this to how we as psychoanalysts should present ourselves in reference to homosexuality. (To my mind, this is a rather futile suggestion since it assumes a rationalistic psychological process in both supporters and opponents of gays, which is belied by the actual behavior of both.)

Some activists claim that some gays who could benefit from psychological counseling or therapy in relation to *other* difficulties in their lives, which they do not see as in any way connected with their homosexuality, are dissuaded from going into any kind of therapy because of what they expect from psychoanalysts, psychiatrists, or other therapists: that is, that the probing itself implies they are pathological, and that the therapist starts with the assumption that their homosexuality *is* the sickness, and will therefore try to change them.

Psychoanalysts will reply that there are myriad forms of resistance to treatment, some strong enough to prevent the individual from seeking therapeutic help in the first place, others coming into play during the process of the treatment, and, in fact, constantly throughout the treatment. Psychoanalysis proper is distinctive from less depth-oriented therapies precisely in the constant attention it pays precisely to this process of resistance, the exploration of its meaning, the usefulness of that exploration to an understanding of the subject's whole personality pattern, etc. Second, we would answer that not all the object of probing is into matters of pathology (though, necessarily, in the context of treatment, some of it is), but rather into the total pattern of the individual's life in all its dimensions, both functional and dysfunctional, both ego-syntonic and ego-dystonic, and so on. Freud showed us how the exploration of the pathological can illuminate the non-pathological or "normal." He also showed how these understandings can be applied to all aspects of human life, far beyond the consulting room. (See, for an obvious example, his *Psychopathology of Everyday Life,* Freud 1901.)

Homosexuals opposed to having the "sick" label applied to them are understandably correspondingly averse to any effort to "cure" them by psychoanalytic or any other form of therapeutic treatment, if "cure" means to change their sexual preference from homosexual to heterosexual. In the Bell and Weinberg study (1978), homosexuals who had gone for some kind of therapeutic help overwhelmingly claimed both that it was not their homosexuality which led them to seek such help, but "other problems," and also that they went with no wish or intention to change their sexual orientation. But some gay activists have claimed that they and other gays they know have had bitter experiences with psychoanalysts or other kinds of therapists trying to "cure" them, which they did not want.

Psychoanalysts of anything at all like a classical orientation would answer that charge by pointing out that today it would be most unlikely for any responsible trained psychoanalyst to try to change a confirmed homosexual in that way if the patient did not strongly want to change. The clinical record on this, from countless individual case histories as well as from the more systematic research such as the Bieber group's, indicate that even where there is a strong conscious motivation on the part of the subject it is difficult enough, even with prolonged and deep psychoanalysis, to effect such a change. (The Bieber group reports a 27 percent change rate—but that includes even moderate and less than complete degrees of movement toward heterosexuality—in the 106 male homosexual patients studied, and they specify a number of very difficult-to-match conditions under which such change is likely or possible. Even at that, this figure is regarded as exceptionally high by many other psychoanalytic observers who have worked with motivated homosexual patients. (See Wiedeman's overview essay, 1974; also Sagarin 1973.)

If there is little or no desire to change over toward heterosexuality at all, it would be almost totally futile for the therapist to attempt to bring about such a change. It would also violate the basic psychoanalytic ethic of respecting the autonomy of the patient's wishes. It is possible that in some individuals who are deeply conflicted about their sexual orientation, but who have attempted to deal with that conflict by exaggerating the exclusiveness of their homosexuality, coming into psychoanalytic therapy will be experienced as a threat to their precariously maintained "solution." In such cases, if the analyst does not obviously side with the patient's maintaining his exclusively homosexual preference, the patient in anxiety may react to this as though the analyst were trying to "force" him to change, to be "cured."

However, there are also psychoanalysts and other therapists, the analyst being more likely of some kind of revisionist persuasion, who would choose *not* to keep such a conflict alive and active in the patient, but would support the resolution of the conflict along the lines of maintaining the predominantly homosexual orientation. That kind of analyst might instead work on intensifying the patient's social awareness of how much of his suffering about his homosexuality is derived from what such a therapist, in line with gay activist rhetoric, construes as arbitrary and stigmatizing social standards. That kind of therapy would concentrate on reducing the ego-alien qualities that patient experiences in reference to his homosexuality. It would help him discover that being homosexual does not mean being depraved, weird, antisocial, or any of the other negative stereotypes associated with homosexuality in this society. Gay activists, who are dissatisfied with other aspects of their lives but not with their homosexuality *per se*, could probably accept that kind of therapy.

By contrast, classically oriented psychoanalysts would not consider it psychoanalytic at all actively to support (as distinct from simply not actively challenging or combating) the homosexual orientation. Classically oriented psychoanalysts would also argue that that kind of "therapy" is not necessarily in the humane spirit of psychoanalysis, which is to maximize the patient's autonomy (not necessarily his comfort). According to this perspective, autonomy is best fostered by opening up the possibility of the subject's perceiving and having actually psychologically available to himself a range of choices, not blocked off by irrational taboos deriving from deep unconscious defenses.

This is not always, perhaps not usually, the maximally most comfortable position for the patient to be in, and inevitably runs the risk of arousing perhaps unmanageable levels of anxiety in the process of confronting the possibility of change. Each analyst would, of course, in such a situation have to gauge as accurately as possible the strength of the patient's ego resources for dealing with such anxiety, and the analyst would be professionally bound to ensure, as much as this is possible, that the patient does not get into so extreme an anxiety situation that self-destructive reactions, such as life-endangering acting out, become a probability.

Homophile supporters point out that there are a growing number of "gay therapists," that is, therapists for homosexuals, many of whom are homosexual themselves, to whom gays in distress can turn for therapeutic help, and who emphasize the positive values of the gay "life style" and support a positive self-image in one's homosexuality. C. A. Tripp (1975) appears to exemplify this trend.

Classically oriented psychoanalysts respond to this trend by pointing out that such "therapy" amounts in effect, if not explicitly, to apologetics and advocacy for the gay political movement, and is thus only remotely connected with what psychoanalysts mean by therapy. Some such "patients" can no doubt get some at least short-term therapeutic effects from participating in a social movement that contributes to decreasing self-hatred and self-contempt—at least on the surface—by challenging or overthrowing previously held negative self-images the participants have maintained.

It should be clear, however, that this is a socio-political movement. Individual psychotherapy is something else again, especially if it is psychoanalysis, aimed not at furthering a social cause, but at enhancing individual intrapsychic understanding and ability to experience more deeply and to direct one's life and deal with one's psychological conflicts. By contrast, a social movement such as gay liberation tends to sweep such intrapsychic individual conflicts under the rug. In effect proclaiming "gay is good"—parallel to "black is beautiful"—amounts to an effort to change reality by word magic, to exorcise, by such word magic, the demonology about homosexuality that is prevalent in the society. Such magical endeavors are likely to have the effect of closing off the confrontation with internal psychic conflict, by forcing a resolution of it in a particular direction of action.

This means narrowing the range of choices potentially open to the individual. That does not accord with psychoanalytic ideas of fostering psychic health in the individual. In some young adults, who are still struggling to define their sexuality, their sexual and gender identity, and who have been "trying on" homosexuality, as it were, as one possibility, the drive of the movement activists and their associated "therapists" to get the individual positively to embrace his homosexual self and solidify his homosexuality, is not in fact the liberating force its proponents claim, but in many cases the reverse, another form of tyranny. For one can be tyrannized into a nonconformity position, as well as into a conforming one—especially where there are so many obvious "secondary gains" to be accrued from such a resolution—the exhilarating feeling of solidarity with an "oppressed" but now militant minority, the thrill of battle against "evil," even the very danger of confrontation in the external world (so much more palatable than confrontation with one's own much more mysterious inner demons).

But, one may ask, what is all this discussion about whether homosexuality is a sickness, or how so, when in fact a few years ago the American Psychiatric Association voted to *remove* homosexuality from its official list of categories of psychopathology given in their influential *Diagnostic and Statistical Manual of Mental Disorders*? (See Hite 1974a and b). To answer, let us be clear about what the American Psychiatric Association did. In December 1973, the trustees of the American Psychiatric Association changed the listing of homosexuality in the *Diagnostic and Statistical Manual* to "Sexual Orientation Disturbance," and that category was to apply not to homosexuality per se, but only to those homosexuals who are "distressed by their homosexual orientation." Those who are not so distressed would not come under any psychiatric diagnostic category. The change in nomenclature was approved by a 58 percent majority of the voting members of the American Psychiatric Association.

This action has been hailed as an important victory by homophile activist groups and their supporters in many fields, including sociology. That approval evidently confirms the view (held by many psychoanalysts, who opposed that change) that the change was a political move, and really had nothing to do with scientific understanding. To consider that a syndrome is to be considered psychopathological *only* if the person is experiencing subjective distress will have to be counted as an utterly absurd and untenable criterion to use in psychodiagnostics. Many people with character disorders or with other kinds of perversions experience little or no psychological distress about their symptoms. But that does not mean that no psychopathological process is going on in these individuals. In any case, you cannot hope to settle a *scientific* dispute by democratic voting.

Stoller's strictures against using "homosexuality" as a diagnostic category are of an entirely different kind. And as he himself says, such strictures could apply to practically every category we use in the currently used nomenclature of psychopathology. For example, diagnosticians would be as hard pressed to defend a diagnosis of "narcissistic disorder," and differentiate it from "borderline syndrome" in ways agreeable to most other clinicians. To follow Stoller's logic strictly, we would have to throw out the whole system of nomenclature we now have—in effect the entire DSM and not just the category of homosexuality—and start all over. He thinks, and correctly I would say, that such a procedure would be too drastic, and more destructive than helpful to our putting our understanding of psychopathology in some kind of order. In effect, a defective system of nomenclature is better than none.

But to imagine you are improving it by taking a *political* action like that taken on homosexuality is really inane. It was obviously done to placate a segment of the public that has recently become a vocal "oppressed minority." One can have justified sympathy with people who are unjustly discriminated against by the laws, in employment, in housing, and in many other ways, on the basis of irrational fears, backed by no demonstration that such persons harm others or society in general. But it is muddle-headed to mix up that socio-political sentiment with one's understanding of a clinical phenomenon. Just because gays are offended by the previous categorizing in DSM is no scientific justification for the change. If obsessionals were to take offense about being so included under "mental disorders," or if schizophrenics were so, would we then erase these from our lists also?

A side point is that the American *Psychiatric* Association should not be confused with the American *Psychoanalytic* Association. There is some overlap, but these are not the same people. All medical psychoanalysts are psychiatrists, but not all of them belong to the American Psychiatric Association, many because they disagree with non-psychoanalytic psychiatrists on many points of understanding of psychodynamics and on many aspects of treatment procedure. Many members of the American Psychiatric Association, as psychiatrists, are not psychoanalysts, and may be only minimally trained in psychoanalysis, and many in fact are openly hostile to psychoanalytic formulations. Some, for example, favor biological explanations of schizophrenia. Many favor chemical rather than psychological treatment of many psychological disorders, particularly but not exclusively the psychoses.

The lay public, including presumably many in the gay activist movement, do not adequately differentiate among these practitioners. In addition, there are the varieties of other psychotherapeutic practitioners we have already mentioned. That whole bazaar of the therapy world is itself a phenomenon worthy of sociological, or better still, psychoanalytic-sociological analysis, which would take us too far afield at this point.

WHAT "CAUSES" HOMOSEXUAL PREFERENCE? PSYCHOANALYTIC VIEWS

Homophile supporters are fond of saying no one really knows the causes of homosexuality, and since the experts disagree so much, why bother? Who cares? It's irrelevant to questions of living one's life here and now, in the midst of a hostile, or at least partly hostile, society. Not only do gay activists fault psychoanalysts for having what they, the activists, regard as a false picture of causes (the Bieber study is a major target), or fault psychoanalysis for bothering to find out the etiology at all, but they are also supported by certain brands of sociologist in this viewpoint. That sociological view was most strongly formulated in a by now much-quoted article by William Simon and John Gagnon, called "Homosexuality: The Formulation of a Sociological Perspective" (1967).

There they attack psychoanalysts and any other clinicians for being concerned with etiology at all, claiming that that concern is not only irrelevant but, as the gay activists echo, pernicious, in that it implies a prejudgement of pathology and the necessity for "cure." Not content with saying—which would be legitimate enough—that sociologists simply have a *different* set of questions to ask, they attempt to rule out of legitimate discourse a whole set of concerns that have occupied psychoanalysis for many years. In this process they evidently indicate a know-nothing and anti-intellectual bias, one that is parroted by other sociologists who are sympathetic with the gay activist movement as well as, obviously, by gay politicoes themselves. Here again political sympathies distort scientific understanding. Needless to say, I disagree profoundly with their view, and deplore the influence it has had in sociological analyses of this and other kinds of deviance.

In fact, of course, it is not at all true that we do not know what causes homosexuality. We have a great deal of knowledge from psychoanalytic case studies of how, in particular cases, the turn toward the homosexual preference came about in the life of the particular individual. Surely there may be a variety of different kinds of life history configurations that lead up to this kind of sexual orientation, as Stoller has summarized, but that variety is probably not infinite, and we do know in some detail some particular configurations that seem to be fairly common. One can exaggerate—as the gay spokesmen like to do—the degree and kind of difference in emphasis made by different researchers, even all within the same general psychoanalytic fold. From another perspective, we can say that the differences are more of detail than of basic orientation. It is not inconsistent with a theory of etiology to arrive at a proposition that says different versions or configurations, all of which have in common only the same-sex preference, have been reached, probably, by different developmental routes. We are in no worse a situation theoretically and intellectually on this set of problems than we are on other aspects of psychopathological phenomena. Skepticism and open-mindedness are called for, since many questions are still unanswered, but the nihilism that proclaims that "no one knows the causes and no one ever will" is no answer. It is rather a resignation in defeat. And in many cases it is a politically motivated position, even if sincerely believed, for members of a movement that wants to work on a social rather than a psychological level.

Within psychoanalysis, prevailing etiological theories all go back to Freud, and all diverge from him in one particular or another. These theories have in common certain basic presuppositions, which come from Freud: there is a bisexual psychological potential in all human being. Besides being basically anatomically male or female, each individual is *psychologically* both masculine and feminine in varying proportions. The balance derives from the interpersonal experiences the individual has had with the crucial persons of infancy and early childhood, usually primarily the mother.

The psychosexual orientation of the individual is a product of experience and learning imposed upon whatever constitutionally given features the infant has at birth or that emerge during maturation. The patterns an individual develops are his motivated and chosen ways of handling the problems, difficulties, and vicissitudes, and particularly the internal conflicts he experiences. We say this with the understanding that this motivation and this choosing are to a very large extent unconscious. We also assume that developments and events are not accidental but determined, and as such understandable. We also do not believe an individual is *only* a pawn of social forces. Rather, there is an internal dynamic to his life and his actions, including his sexual ones, that connects with and interacts with what sociologists call social forces in a variety of ways, but which does have an internal, that is, an intrapsychic, dimension. With that background of commonality of assumptions, we can look at some of the variations.

Since so much nonsense has been distortedly attributed to Freud, particularly by anti-Freudian political activists (today represented especially by the women's liberation and the gay liberation movements), it is worthwhile to clarify what Freud himself actually said on the question of homosexuality, not to reverently cite gospel, but as a baseline for the further more contemporary discussions, and to clear the air of many current misunderstandings.

Freud saw homosexuality, like all perversions (a term he used in a clinical, not a moralistically derogatory sense), as the result of disturbances in the infantile and early childhood psychosexual developmental pattern. He thought there could be, in some individuals, some constitutionally derived predisposing factors, such as an exceptionally high degree of constitutional bisexuality or some constitutionally determined exceptional capacity for pleasurable erotic sensation in certain nongenital parts of the body such as the mouth or the anus. But the crucial force he saw at work was psychic *conflict*.

For the boy the crucial fear is that his sexual love for his mother will lead to punishment by the father, in the form of his father cutting off his most prized body part, his penis. That would make him the same as a girl, i.e., inferior, bodily and psychologically, because of his castration. One kind of terrified response to this conflict would take the form of giving up the mother and by extension all females and submitting oneself in passive abasement to the powerful father. Doing this would involve emphasizing whatever degree of femininity the boy has already developed by identification with the mother. It could also involve reacting to the terror of the Oedipus conflict by regressing to earlier modes of libidinal satisfaction, involving the mouth or the anus particularly, or both. All of this unconscious process later gets translated, after puberty, into the overt homosexual activity which rescues the boy from the danger of the revived Oedipus situation and provides sexual gratification with orgastic release.

For the girl, the perversion would result, according to Freud, from her inability to come to terms with her already "castrated" state. She denies her lack of a penis by emphasizing her clitoris. She hangs on to the original libidinal attachment to her mother, which is a homosexual attachment by its nature. She does not take the next step of shifting this attachment to the father, and therefore does not enter the oedipal conflict at all. She does not therefore seek—as she would in the normal path of development—restitution for her lack of a penis by an attachment to the father who is expected to give her his penis in love, and a symbolic recreation of it in the form of a baby.

Freud recognized that the oedipal situation is always likely to involve not only the triangle of son-mother-father or daughter-mother-father in the classic sense. In that kind of oedipal triangle: son desires mother, is blocked by father as rival, gives up the sexual wish toward mother, acknowledging father's power, moves to consolidate identification with father as masculine person. Conversely, the girl toward her father in rivalry with the mother. Each of these Freud called the "positive Oedipus complex."

But alongside that, there is another constellation: for the boy, love for the father, desire to possess him sexually, rivalry with the mother, both of these wishes in turn repressed. This Freud called the "negative Oedipus complex." It involves the boy already in a homosexual relationship to his father. Conversely, the girl may be involved in a negative Oedipal triangle, with mother as the sex object and father the intruder rival, and mother the potential punishing agent.

This triangle could take precedence over the positive Oedipus and never be resolved, with the result of homosexuality, representing essentially a continuation of the infantile relationship to the mother. In all of these theorizings, Freud had some awareness that experiences before the oedipal period can have important predisposing effects, or provide points of regression where the child experiences unbearable internal conflict in the oedipal phase.

Later theorists have placed a great deal more emphasis on the pre-oedipal periods. For one thing, they have found bases to reject Freud's conception that the boy is stimulated in a heterosexual direction from the moment of birth, with mother as the primary sexual object. They emphasize instead that at that stage mother is less a sexual object than someone with whom the baby has a blissful symbiosis, a feeling of oneness with her. To the extent that the male baby is experiencing that, he must then be experiencing himself in a feminine mode. Then, in order to develop his masculinity and hence his movement toward heterosexuality, he must, during the separation-individuation phase, move much more actively away from this early symbiosis with the mother, and more actively differentiate himself from her. This is a painful process, which of course also has its great rewards in ego development and the development of a sense of selfhood. It is much more crucial for the boy than for the girl, since his masculinity and his maleness requires a much more drastic separation and differentiation from the mother. He must move away from identifying with her.

For the girl, the separation-individuation need not be as intense, and in many respects her achievement of primary femininity is much less problematical, since she is of the same sex as the mother. Relatively non-neurotic mothers typically deal differently with boy babies than with girl babies in these matters. They will typically and spontaneously push their sons to more distinctive separation and individuation than they will their daughters. They will also most likely be handling the boy baby differently from the girl baby, in response to their feelings of the difference between the boy's body and the mother's. This has led some authors to think that some degree of homosexuality, possibly including at least some overt genital contact, is more likely to be within the range of normality for women, more so than for men.

The greater incidence of female situational homosexuality in prisons, compared to males, would fit such a hypothesis.

Female Homosexuality: Some Current Psychoanalytic Views

Probably reflecting androcentric bias in this society, and possibly also the feeling that females are less important generally, there has been much less study and research on female homosexuality than on male. This is true for psychoanalytic work, as well as for sociological and other kinds of research. (See Kenyon 1974 for overview of various kinds of studies, mostly non-psychoanalytic, to that date; for sociological and social-psychological studies, see later in this section.) Notably we are lacking in systematic psychoanalytic studies that are both extensive (many cases, with good heterosexual control groups) and intensive (in depth, based on intensive psychoanalysis) that deal with family constellation backgrounds, comparable to the Bieber group study of homosexual men.

But from the studies that have been done, and the theorizing from clinical material, there is by now a clear recognition that female homosexuality represents a very distinct psychodynamic constellation, deriving from different etiological sources, from male homosexuality.

Within the psychoanalytic vein, studies after Freud have all emphasized pre-oedipal developmental issues, and object-relations questions in addition to libidinal ones. Essential to these studies is the noting that this feminine phenomenon is definitely rooted in *female* psychosexual and object-relational developmental processes, which are of necessity very different from those of the male (as analyzed in the preceding part).

In this process, the early infantile relation to the *mother* is clearly crucial. One essential point refers to something we touched on earlier. In adult heterosexual coitus the male can symbolically re-experience "primary love" (fusion, etc.) with the mother; the female cannot, the male partner cannot do that for her. In homosexuality, the woman can do so. Yearning for this kind of replay of symbiotic infantile fusion with the mother is thus one important psychodynamic element in female homosexuality. This "mother" may be the mother who was actually experienced in a blissful symbiosis that later, painfully, had to be renounced; or it may be the fusion-mother the girl never did have or had only incompletely. Now as an adult she still strives yearningly to capture that kind of experience.

In the overt sexual behavior, of whatever kind, in lesbian encounter, either partner may experience herself as infant to the other's mother, or vice versa, or alternately, or simultaneously, both. (The normally heterosexual lactating mother nursing her infant usually has a regressive experience, involving projective identification with the infant, recreating the mother-infant blissful exchange.) In mouth-breast sexual lesbian contact, these elements are obviously in the forefront. But also, other body parts and other kinds of sexual behavior may additionally be infused with feelings and gratifications from this oral-libidinal and symbiotic-object-relational mode.

Ruth-Jean Eisenbud (1969, 1977), basing her analysis on the life histories of lesbian women patients (hers and others reported in the psychoanalytic literature), sees the influence of early symbiotic anxiety, individuation difficulties, problems with oral aggressiveness and fixation and associated guilt, as well as phallic-oedipal stage difficulties.

Individuation from the mother may be made particularly difficult if the mother is psychotic or otherwise severely disturbed and does not permit the baby girl to individuate, or in some cases forces the baby into too early individuation by rejection, or in some cases by circumstantial separation (e.g., mother hospitalized by unrelated illness, the departure experienced by the girl as rejection). Symbiosis may thus become a frightening and threatening experience, leading the girl to turn to negative identifications: "I do not want to be that woman, or what that woman wants me to be."

Double-binds are frequent in these histories, Eisenbud finds (1977). The girl, having established definite feminine gender identity (normal by the age of about 18 months), then finds herself forbidden the active aspects of the feminine role, e.g., she is not allowed into the kitchen, which is mother's domain. Or the mother may double-bind her by making contradictory demands, e.g., that she be "feminine," and at the same time supportive and strong for the overdependent mother, implicitly taking the father's place. Or she may face the demand to be masculine in the sense of replacing the boy child the mother never had, or had and lost. Or she may expect the girl to be (narcissistically) the mother's own male self, or to be the male mother wants to depend on. Or the girl may be expected to be both feminine and at the same time active, independent, self-reliant, and supportive to her mother. The mother may show expectation of "masculine" activity and independence, and then punish the girl for any display of that, and/or for lack of sufficient dependency on the mother (Eisenbud 1977). One mother screamed in fury at her daughter, "Get out of here!" and then, when the girl tried to leave the house, yelled, "Don't you dare go out that door!"

In some cases the girl's emerging femininity meets brutal treatment by father or brother, or overwhelming experience of sexual arousal by seductiveness or seduction by father, stepfather, brother, or other male kin, leading to inhibition of heterosexual feelings—being feminine has now become forbidden and dangerous.

In the separation-individuation phase (Mahler 1968), if the girl baby cannot leave mother momentarily and reapproach mother securely convinced of the mother's object-constancy, she turns to father, still in a pre-oedipal, not an oedipal, way. His response to this can influence future development: if he shows her rejection, abandonment, or mistreatment, she may turn back again to the mother, this time eroticizing the need for the mother's body, now sought in an active, "masculine," reverse-oedipal manner. Variations on the usual processes involved in penis envy may also feed into the homosexual object choice: the fantasy is either of being a woman with a penis, who penetrates another woman, or of being a women who is loved by another woman who does have a penis, or both, alternately or simultaneously. This phallic phase constellation does not operate independently; it is usually fused and interpenetrated with oral phase elements, following the classic equations of mouth and vagina, and of nipple and penis. The homosexual partner may represent the mother's breast which needs to be reciprocally both penetrated and incorporated as in the early oral/symbiotic phase of infantile development.

Negative identification with the mother may also be derived from the girl's perception of the mother as defective, incomplete, submissive, a victim, as one in a masochistic position toward the dominant male, the father. This may be followed then by closeness to and identification with the father, then oedipal conflict, resolved by reversal of the oedipal position: "If I may not *have* my father, I will *be* my father" (Eisenbud 1977).

Unresolved or pathologically resolved pre-oedipal and oedipal problems are re-aroused in adolescence, now replayed in relation to new objects derivative from the mother and father and other objects of infancy; peers of both sexes, admired and idealized female teachers, authoritarian or erotically titillating male teachers or counselors. Entrance into homo-sexual encounter or continuing relationship at this phase may give the girl with the kind of childhood history we have described the feeling of release from all the double-binding injustices of her earlier relations, and propel her into the joy of adult sexual gratification for the first time, leading to the "Aha!" feeling, "This is *it!*" providing as well the secondary gain of social defiance and deviant counter-culture support. (On the latter, we note that one of the lesbian women telling her life story in the touching and sensitive TV documentary *Word Is Out*, on Public Television in late 1978, when asked how she expects to feel when/if public attitudes toward homosexuality become so open-minded and accepting that the need to stay "in the closet" will disappear, answered with an ironic chuckle: "You know, I think I'll be a little sad. It would end the whole lovely Little Orphan Annie secret society kind of thing we have had.")

Culturalist psychoanalysts adduce still other meanings and functions in female homosexuality. Clara Thompson (1947) cites a variety of mean-ings it may have in different individuals, either alternatively or in various combinations: fear of the opposite sex, fear of adult responsibility, need to defy authority, need to cope with or deny competition with the same sex, flight from reality into body stimulation, self- or other-destruction. Some of these, Eisenbud notes (1977) would more likely be secondary gains, others more primary etiological sources.

Of course, similar antecedents may lead in other cases to heterosexual, or to bisexual, orientation. The range of contingency factors is very large, and the expectation of predictive precision based on certain few ante-cedent cues is unrealistic in any aspect of psychoanalytic work.

Life-History Precursors:
Male Homosexuals

While psychoanalysts recognize that there are possibly a number of different early-life-history constellations leading to this sexual preference, more large-scale and more systematic studies (i.e., studies going beyond essentially anecdotal case histories) do indicate some general patterns. The largest and most comprehensive investigation of this kind is still that of Irving Bieber and his colleagues reported in *Homosexuality: A Psy-choanalytic Study of Male Homosexuals* (Bieber et al. 1962). This study compiled extremely detailed clinical and life-history data about 106 male homosexuals who were in intensive psychoanalytic treatment, compared with 100 male heterosexuals matched for education, socio-economic background, and other factors.

They found that certain kinds of family constellations were significantly more likely in the case of boys who later became homosexual, than in those of the heterosexual control group. The distinguishing constellation was not just a certain kind of mother, but the combination of that kind of mother with a certain kind of father, thus involving the growing boy in a pathological triangular situation, from which the later emerging homosexual orientation becomes the escape and attempted "solution."

The mother is what the Bieber group call "close-binding-intimate" (CBI). She has an intense relationship to this son and induces and encourages an intense dependency of the son on her. She is extremely possessive, dominating, and overprotective. She is seductive toward the boy, and then proceeds to block his development of heterosexual interest. She has intense psychological rapport with the boy. She interferes with his engaging in any kind of physical activities that might foster his masculine identification, emphasizing the dangerousness of active physical sports and the like.

The father in this constellation fits one of two predominant types. In one case he is detached and hostile. In the other he is detached and dominating. In either form, he tends unconsciously to collude with the mother's seduction of the son. Being detached and unavailable, he fails to protect the boy from the destructive activity of the mother. He spends little time with the son, making a poor presentation of a male model for identification for the boy. In some cases he may be dominated by the mother himself. Usually this is a bad marriage which is nevertheless continued, making the son the interactional focus of the interacting pathologies of the two parents. Where there are two or more sons in the family, one particular son may be "chosen" as this focal point, for any one of a number of possible reasons. Once so "chosen," he becomes the focus of the father's hostility and of the mother's excessive emotional attachment. The father may also react with hostility to any show of masculine assertiveness by the son.

For the son, the father's reactions confirm the son's unconscious recognition of the sexual rivalry situation. With a bad marriage between the father and the mother, the mother is attempting to use the relationship to the son to give her satisfactions missing in the relationship with her husband. Mostly unconsciously, of course. Her own heterosexuality may be badly impaired, and she may have a largely unconscious massive hatred of men in general. She puts the son into a double bind: she is sexually stimulating and romantically seductive toward him, and at the same time imposes all kinds of anti-sexual prohibitions upon him—anti-*heterosexual*, that is. She is simultaneously seductive and puritanical.

So in the later development of the homosexual orientation, the boy may be carrying out reparative maneuvers in a kind of desperate effort magically to regain his heterosexuality. For example, by magical incorporation of maleness in the person and the body of the powerful male partner. Heterosexual strivings are dangerous for the classical oedipal reasons: fear of attack from the father, combined with desperate need for his love, which is not forthcoming. Lacking a chance to develop relatively normal masculine interests and thus moving toward heterosexual identification with the father—identifications which could counteract or at least mitigate the destructive effects of the mother's dominating seductiveness—the boy finds himself required to repress heterosexual strivings to avoid competition with the father, as well as avoid offending the puritanical mother. Such a son also tends to lack the support of a preadolescent and adolescent male peer group, from which he withdraws or invites rejection by his fearfulness, overestimation of physical dangers, and the like, and thus another possible mitigating or counteracting force is missing.

Bieber and his colleagues are, of course, not saying that this is the kind of family background of all male homosexuals. But they do say that this constellation was significantly more frequent in the homosexual men than in the heterosexual ones—by statistical analysis. They also indicate that it was not the only constellation in the homosexual cases either, but something closely approximating it appears in about 70 to 80 percent of the (homosexual) cases. Some of the mothers did show a different pattern: eight (of the 106) were hostile, minimizing and rejecting but not detached. Nine were controlling, dominating and highly egocentric; four were hostile and detached. These together constituted 21 of the 106, or just under 20 percent.

One can cite many cases of heterosexual men who have had mothers that fit one or another of these types. How then can the Bieber group say that such mothers are predictive of homosexuality in the son? The answer is that many of the heterosexual men in analysis in the Bieber study did in fact have mothers like the CBI or one of the other types where the son became homosexual. But where she was a CBI, her influence was mitigated by a father of a type different from those in the homosexual cases. In other cases there were other mitigating factors.

These heterosexual men did in fact also show "problems about homosexuality," though they were not overtly homosexual. The problems were manifested in some cases by difficulties with female sexual partners. These would appear to be men in whom the potentiality of a homosexual adaptation is fairly high, counteracted by some degree of success in heterosexual relations and a strong feeling for the social unacceptability of homosexuality and fear of social rejection and ostracism if he were to turn to overt homosexuality. (Since these individuals were analysed in the 1950s or earlier, in a period when anti-homosexual sentiment was evidently stronger in America than it is today, it is conceivable that counterparts of such men today might be more likely to turn to a more overt homosexual orientation. Movement people would encourage that, along with their drive to get secret gays "out of the closet" and openly proclaiming their homosexuality as a positive way of life.)

This study has been much discussed, praised, and attacked from both outside and inside psychoanalytic circles. Some detractors have claimed that since the analysts were all "Freudians," of course they found what would confirm Freudian theoretical expectations. Psychoanalysts will answer: first, all observations have to be interpreted in order to make any sense, and any interpretation requires a theoretical perspective, preferably explicitly held; but second, and more important, not all the participating analysts (those contributing detailed case histories) were "Freudians" in the classical sense. Thirty percent in fact defined themselves as "culturalists," who distinguish themselves from Freudians by disbelieving in the universality and inevitability of the Oedipus complex.

Despite these differences in theoretical orientation both groups of analysts answered detailed factual questions about their patients in a large and complex questionnaire about their homosexual and heterosexual patients in much the same way, providing information about each patient on these topics: their psychosexual development; their object relations; the nature of the parents and the patient's relationship with each of them; social background factors—socioeconomic, ethnic, etc.—and sexual activities and fantasies. Since there were no statistically significant differences between the responses of the Freudians and those of the culturalists on these items, the authors concluded that differences of theoretical orientation did not bias the results. I can add, too, that since the culturalists (essentially followers of Sullivan, Horney, and Fromm) generally tended to play down the relevance of sexual factors, their concordance with the Freudians in the main lines of the findings is that much more impressive. Therefore it does not seem justifiable to claim that these investigators were predisposed to find what they did and therefore found it.

Another major objection to this study, and one most often voiced by gay activists and their supporters, is that the results cannot possibly be generalizable to the male homosexual population as a whole, since the sample is obviously biased by including only patients in psychoanalytic therapy. I shall take up this matter in more detail later in this chapter. It may not be entirely unrepresentative, though. In reference to family backgrounds, for example, a sociological study by Westwood (1960) using only a non-patient population found patterns substantially like those in the Bieber cases.

From within psychoanalysis itself come other kinds of negative or amending commentary. I have already mentioned the now widely accepted opinion that "homosexuality" cannot properly be considered a distinct clinical entity. Other psychoanalytic work—mostly in the form of case histories—has indicated other kinds of background familial constellation in the histories of males who became homosexual as adults. True, these studies have not been as extensive (in number of cases) nor as systematic (e.g., in controlled comparisons with otherwise similar heterosexuals) as the Bieber study. But they do indicate that we need not assume that all, or necessarily most, male homosexuals have had the kind of familial history the Bieber group describes.

The son may, for example, be caught in a negative oedipal situation, with father, not mother, the primary sexual object in the late-phallic stage, with mother as the rivalrous obstacle. The boy then, from puberty onwards, sets out to find the ever-unattainable father in a succession of male lovers. Or the boy may be heavily identified from the phallic stage onward with a father who is reverse-oedipally loved, and both are united in a misogynistic rejection of the mother. And then the homosocial world of the latency period—strongly institutionalized in this culture anyway— carries over easily into homosexual activity with peers, in turn continuing as overt homosexuality at puberty and thereafter. There are still other possible familial constellations out of which the homosexual adaptation may arise.

VARIATIONS IN DYNAMICS

Any of these configurations, it needs to be acknowledged, may also in other cases eventuate in a predominantly heterosexual adaptation. The dynamics may also vary, possibly fitting the kinds delineated in the Bieber cases, but also possibly following other lines. There are many possibilities.

As already suggested above, various psychoanalysts have adduced different—though not always incompatible—sets of dynamics underlying or associated with this kind of sexual orientation. It may come from phobic fear of the opposite sex: for the male, castration fear so immense that he must be constantly reassured that his partner has the prized male genital. Dominance-submission problems may be intensely involved, often related to the intense inter-individual competitiveness in males that is institutionalized in this society. Need to dominate may be expressed in taking the insertor role. Need to submit in taking the insertee role. The "insertor" type may also like performing sodomy on a female partner, some such sodomizers, who impartially take either females or young males, may not even consider themselves homosexual. The background history is likely to reveal childhood power battles with father, or mother, or both.

Homosexual activity may also represent flight from adult responsibility. (One male homosexual patient consistently referred to all the males he had ever had contact with, of whatever age, as "boys.") The childhood background for that could be extreme narcissistic indulgence by an adoring mother. Defiance of authority may be part of a masochistic quest for punishment along lines similar to those Freud described in his depiction of the "criminal from a sense of guilt" (Freud 1916). There are many varieties. It may represent flight from reality into tremendous preoccupation with body stimulation, with a same-sex partner helping one avoid the excruciating anxiety of having to deal with someone experienced as profoundly "other."

Where homosexuality is socially invested with heavy taboo, as in our culture, homosexual activity may represent for the individual acts of self-destructiveness, often combined with destructiveness toward the partner. (Thompson 1947; Wiedeman 1974; Ovesey 1969; and Hatterer 1971, among many others, have explored these variations.) Stoller discusses homosexuality as a perversion as "the erotic form of hatred" (Stoller 1975). It may also mark the assumption of a "negative identity" (Erikson 1950). Some of these functions may represent secondary gains, rather than the primary motivational dynamic involved, as discussed in reference to female homosexuals above.

The homosexual behavior may also, in some cases, serve as a crucial defense against psychic fragmentation, the danger of which arises from the overwhelming unconscious anxiety experienced by a male over the possibility of engulfment by the female, a recreation of the pre-oedipal mother. In cases like this, cessation of homosexual activity may precipitate fragmentation of the ego, and descent into something close to a psychotic state. (See Socarides 1968, in reference to what he calls "pre-oedipal type male homosexuality.")

These variations do not nullify or contradict the patterns indicated in the Bieber study; they only indicate additional variations in underlying dynamics, any of which may coexist along with those described in the Bieber work. Non-psychoanalysts, thinking that any phenomenon must be either one thing or another, tend to have difficulty with such a profusion of alternative or interacting dynamic patterns. But psychoanalytic study requires a high degree of intellectual tolerance for ambiguity and a suspension of rigidly mechanistic either-or thinking in reference to internal psychological patterns. Indeed, not only in dreams, but in unconscious functioning generally and its interaction with conscious functioning, any action or feeling may signify one thing and simultaneously its opposite or something rather different.

Summary: Relationship of Homosexuality
to Psychopathology

One may summarize psychoanalytic views about the relationship of homosexuality to psychopathology as follows: there are likely to be pathogenic processes involved in the formation of the homosexual object choice; however, it is possible that the later development of this object choice may be relatively "encapsulated," and thus not associated with other psychopathological features in the personality. This is probably not likely to be a very common outcome. What is actually found in cases coming under intensive psychoanalytic scrutiny are various other kinds of psychological difficulty or disorder. Although we cannot say with assurance that the homosexuality is itself a clinical entity, it is commonly associated with disorders of a neurotic character disorder, or psychotic variety, or with disorders of impulse control, of addiction, or of narcissism, or a borderline character organization, and it may be with any of a large number of possible versions or varieties of any of these. The impact of external stigma, or the subjective expectation of that, may have a strong influence in the particular external behavioral symptomatology associated with this form of sexual expression. And interpersonal relations of many kinds, not only those involved in sexual partnerships, may be difficult, strained, abrasive, full of dominance-submission struggles, and frequently hatred disguised as "love."

None of these are inevitable, and certainly it is possible—though we don't as yet know in detail just how—that surrounding social circumstances, including changing climates of opinion regarding sexual variations, can influence behavior and underlying feelings regarding one's sexual preference, and certainly are likely to influence the degree of consciously felt distress, guilt, self-recrimination, and the like experienced by the individual who has this kind of sexual preference. One element here is the degree of stereotyping of the homosexual role coming from the stigmatizing hostile surrounding society, and also, now more significantly than in the past, from the homophile protest movement itself, which in many respects shares with straight antagonists the tendency to box people into either/or gay-or-straight roles and identities.

CHAPTER THIRTEEN

Sociological and Anthropological Studies

CHALLENGES TO PSYCHOANALYTIC VIEWS

Homophile activists and their supporters tend to deny that there is any intrinsic implication of illness in the homosexual preference. At the extreme they make it a point of ideological dogma that homosexuality is *never* a sickness, and that any psychological distress homosexuals may feel is entirely a product of oppression by a hostile surrounding society. This latter is obviously not a defensible statement of fact, judging by the psychoanalytic and related researches. Still gay activists have assiduously sought support for their contention that gay is not sick from studies by other kinds of professionals outside the psychoanalytic framework.

Hooker's Studies

Thus, when Evelyn Hooker, in 1957, began publishing aspects of her various studies comparing average non-patient homosexuals with comparison heterosexuals, gay supporters were delighted. (See Hooker 1957, 1965, 1967.) Her 1957 paper reported on her study of 30 male homosexuals who were not in therapeutic treatment and who were "reasonably well adjusted" in her view, and compared them with a sample of 30 heterosexual men, matched for age, education, and IQ with the homosexual subjects. She gave each of them a battery of psychological tests, including the Rorschach, the TAT, and the MATS, and also got a good deal of life history information from each of them. She then got several of her clinical psychology colleagues to analyze these test materials "blind"—i.e., without knowing which tests were from homosexuals, which from heterosexuals. Her dramatic finding was that the clinicians were unable to distinguish from the test materials which subjects were homosexual and which were not. She also found that there were no significant differences between the two groups of subjects on any features indicating positive or negative mental health. In other words, this sample of homosexuals exhibited no more indications of maladjustment or psychopathology than the comparison group of heterosexuals. She concluded from this that "homosexuality as a clinical entity does not exist. Its forms are as varied as those of heterosexuality. Homosexuality may be a deviation in sexual pattern which is in the normal range, psychologically" (Hooker 1957:30).

Psychoanalytic observers would respond: not necessarily so. Her conclusions do not necessarily follow from her findings. The findings show only that this collection of homosexual men show no more indication of psychopathology than the comparison group of heterosexuals. They do not show that the homosexuals are free of all indications of psychic disturbance. It is impossible to say from her data that any significant number of homosexuals, let alone most of them, are not psychologically disturbed by any clinical criteria. She can only say that some are not, according to the criteria tapped by these particular psychological tests. More importantly, one has to have reservations about the "sample" she selected. (It is not, of course, a sample in the technical sense, since there is no means to select a representative subgroup from a universe that is unknown in the nature of the case.) She *chose* thirty homosexual men she thought "were reasonably well adjusted," and got them through the Mattachine Society, which she refers to as "an organization which has as its stated purpose the development of a homosexual ethic in order to better integrate the homosexual in society" (Hooker 1957:19). As Sagarin has pointed out (1969, 1973), this homosexual protest organization cannot be presumed to represent any cross-section of the homosexual population. Sagarin estimates that all the homophile organizations combined probably comprise only about one in 200 self-identified homosexuals.

Also, as joiners, Mattachine Society members can be assumed to be different from nonjoining deviants (again, Sagarin's estimate), and particularly from the secret ones. It is probable also that if the men were selected *by* the Mattachine Society from among their own members, they were an even more "select" group, showcases of particularly well-adjusted and psychologically well-integrated individuals, much more so than the average homosexual. So, in effect, we seem to have here a selection of particularly healthy individuals from among the homosexual population. Then the researcher can parade her results and say, "See? Homosexuals are just as healthy as anybody!" It seems made to order for the political pleading of gay organizations: While gay activists denigrate the Bieber study for having a "sample" that must be biased and unrepresentative of homosexuals as a whole (so it is claimed) because these are all patients in therapy, a different and almost opposite bias is obviously present in Hooker's kind of study. In Hooker's study, comparing a group probably representing the psychologically "best-adjusted" homosexuals with a group of average heterosexuals, it's not so surprising that the researcher did not find any marked differences between the two groups.

It is evident that her findings do *not* demonstrate that "homosexuality as a clinical entity does not exist." As we have already seen, there are *other* grounds, in much more clinically probing psychoanalytic work (see above) for claiming that homosexuality should not be considered one distinct clinical entity, but that is not the same as saying that no homosexuals are psychologically disturbed or impaired.

Other Non-Psychoanalytic Studies

There have been a number of other studies in a non-psychoanalytic vein that bear on the question of whether gay is necessarily sick. In the background review of relevant literature on this topic for their much more comprehensive research on it, Bell and Weinberg (1978), in work to be reviewed in more detail shortly, refer to several studies in various genres (other than psychoanalytic case studies). These studies are diverse in methods and strategies, using, variously, questionnaires, interview questions, personality inventories, sometimes projective tests. They are also diverse in their personality theory underpinnings, in some cases evidently having no explicit theory at all.

Bell and Weinberg's review of these studies shows diverse and often contradictory findings: some of these investigators find no psychological differences between homosexuals and heterosexuals (as in the Hooker study), while others find substantial differences in one or other of a variety of psychological indicators, ranging from commonsensical categories like "happiness" to indicators of complex clinical syndromes like "paranoia." For example, Weinberg and Williams (1974, 1975) found in male homosexuals, compared to heterosexuals, less "happiness," but not less self-acceptance and not more psychosomatic symptoms, and Friedberg (1975) found male homosexual respondents more "paranoid" than heterosexual counterparts. In other studies, no differences between homosexuals and heterosexuals were found in self-acceptance (Chang and Block 1960, for males; Freedman 1967, for females). Saghir and Robins (1973) found no difference between gay and straight men on depression, anxiety, or psychosomatic symptoms. In summary, these studies reveal that "the experts disagree."

THE BELL AND WEINBERG STUDY

The largest scale recent study that bears on this question, however, is the work of Alan Bell and Martin Weinberg (1978) entitled, deliberately, *Homosexualities* (plural): *A Study of Diversity among Men and Women*. This appears to be the most comprehensively extensive study of homosexuality yet made, and has been hailed on its publication as the "new Kinsey report." In its method and scope it goes well beyond the earlier Kinsey efforts, for it tries to examine homosexual men and women in all aspects of their lives, not merely in terms of the classic Kinsey questions about who does what to whom, sexually, how often, using what body parts, with which and how many different partners, and the like. This one goes into a wide range of the individual's personal social life, legal and other difficulties occasioned by his or her sexual orientation, relationships with family of origin, siblings, heterosexual marriage (if any), offspring (if any), and so on through the range. It also attempts a fairly extensive assessment of "psychological adjustment" by a number of devices. Bell and Weinberg at least partly attempt to answer the call by sociologists of this kind of "deviance" to move beyond a focus specifically on one's sex life to the whole pattern of the individual's life in reference to work, religion, politics, and any other social relationships. So in "depth interviews," in some cases several hours in length, their homosexual respondents were asked about all aspects of their lives. Questions dealt with the degree to which the individual was open about his homosexuality, and to whom.

The questions that particularly concern us here are those intended to tap the individual's "psychological adjustment." Each respondent was asked about his physical health, specific physical symptoms (presumed to be psychosomatic, like headaches, minor aches and pains, fatigue, etc.); his "happiness"; how frequently he felt "on top of the world" (exuberance); how much he worried and about what; how well he accepted himself, and specifically his homosexuality; how often he felt lonely; felt depressed; was suspicious and distrustful toward others (presumably indicators of "paranoia"); how often and how seriously he ever thought about suicide, and how often had actually made a serious suicidal attempt; and whether he ever sought professional psychological help, and if so, the details, how intensive, how long it lasted, how frequent the sessions, and with what results, in the eyes of the respondent.

This study is the nearest thing we have had yet to answer the alleged unrepresentativeness of samples made in other studies. Unlike the Bieber study, it is not limited to patients in therapy. And unlike the Hooker studies, it is not limited to specially chosen "showcase" individuals selected by one of the homophile protest organizations. The designers of this research aimed—and evidently succeeded—at getting as broad a representation of the whole range of types of persons with a homosexual orientation as one could ask for.

Considering that a large but unknown number of homosexuals are secret about it and that it is therefore impossible to know with any preciseness the "universe" from which any sample is to be drawn, it is impossible to say about any selection of respondents that they constitute a representative sample of all homosexuals in this society at this time. But what these researchers did was the next best thing. They got a substantially large number of cases, drawn from as broad a range of sources and backgrounds as possible. And knowing from previous studies something of the range of homosexuals, e.g., in reference to degree of participation in the gay subculture, they made it a point to recruit potential subjects from as broad a variety of sources as possible. They recruited subjects through contacts in the gay subculture of bars, baths, clubs, and informal social groups, through advertisements in homosexual publications, and the like. They also made a particular effort to reach and recruit secret homosexuals (the hardest part of the recruitment process) and, judging by their results, they succeeded in getting a fair number of such to participate in the study. Thus, their "sample" covers a broad range of occupations and educational levels and various degrees of participation in the homosexual subculture. They recruited a volunteer sample of about 5,000 homosexual men and women from the San Francisco Bay area and from these selected 979 homosexual men and women for intensive interviewing. They then selected a "control group" of 477 heterosexuals, selected to match the demographic characteristics of the homosexual sample.

The authors thus are able to claim that their "sample" includes representation of all of the varieties of homosexuals one is likely to find in this society.

The mode of the study is straightforwardly empirical with no theoretical pretensions. Besides the aim of simply "getting the facts," the authors

have a not particularly hidden agenda of supporting homophile supporters in proclaiming: (a) homosexuals are not all alike; they are as
different and diverse among themselves as anyone else in the society;
and more important, (b) it is untrue that all homosexuals are psychologically sick.

On their central point of the diversity of homosexuals, they found that
they could classify the homosexuals into five main categories, identified
by finding particular clusters of attributes: whether or not the person had
a quasi-marital relationship; the range of sexual partners; degree of self-
comfort in his or her homosexuality; degree and kind of homosexual
emotional attachments; and extensity of homosexual contacts. A substantial proportion of the homosexuals—far from all, however—could
be classified into one or another of the following five types:

1. *Close-Coupled.* Living in a quasi-marriage arrangement; showing
self-acceptance, contentment, and a high level of sexual fidelity, in a
relationship strong in emotional commitment, and long-standing, with
a high level of domestic sharing.

2. *Open-Coupled.* Co-habit as sexual partners, but have a lot of
outside sexual activity as well; less emotionally attached or mutually
dependent.

3. *Functionals.* Sexually very active, free-wheeling, comparable to
the heterosexual "swinging single"; feel positively about their homosexuality; have no regrets; report exuberance and sexual satisfaction.

4. *Dysfunctionals.* These are also very active sexually, but report
regrets about being homosexual: have "sexual problems," i.e., difficulties in their sexual activities and their sexual relationships.

5. *Asexuals.* By this curious choice of terminology, the authors do
not mean completely abstinent sexually, but rather *relatively* much
less active sexually than the other types; also less exclusively homosexual; more secretive about and more unhappy about their homosexuality.

Bell and Weinberg compared the male homosexual sample as a whole
with the male heterosexual sample as a whole on matters of psychological
adjustment. They also compared the different subgroups of homosexuals
with each other, and with the total heterosexual sample. They then made
the same comparisons for the female homosexuals. Taking the males and
females separately, here is what they found:

Males

All homosexual males compared with all heterosexual males: the
homosexuals scored higher than the heterosexuals on self-report of "ex-

uberance." They were undistinguishable from the heterosexuals in self-report of general physical health. They were *slightly* less likely than the heterosexuals to report themselves as usually feeling "pretty happy" or "very happy"; and slightly more likely to indicate feelings indicating paranoid trends (feeling suspicion or distrust toward others). Compared to the heterosexuals, the homosexuals scored *lower* on self-acceptance; had more psychosomatic symptoms; were more frequently lonely; worried more; were more frequently depressed; and they scored *significantly* different from the straights on these aspects: greater amount of tension; greater likelihood of having at some time considered suicide, and *much* greater likelihood of ever having actually made a suicidal attempt; they were also more likely to have at some time sought professional counseling or psychological help. (Suicidal thoughts, according to the respondents, were not over the issue of homosexuality; nor was homosexuality as such the reason respondent sought professional help.)

The composite picture, then, is that the homosexual men, compared to the heterosexuals, saw themselves as just as (physically) healthy, almost as happy overall, and more exuberant; reported themselves as being less self-accepting, more susceptible to psychosomatic symptoms, more lonely, more worrisome, more depressed, more tense, more paranoid, more suicidal, and more likely to have sought professional psychological counseling of some kind (Bell and Weinberg, pp. 198–208).

These overall comparisons, however, according to Bell and Weinberg, are less indicative then comparisons among the five subgroups of the homosexuals, and between each of these subgroups and the heterosexual sample as a whole. In these comparisons, they found the following:

The *Close-Coupled* were similar to the heterosexuals in general health, psychosomatic symptoms, self-acceptance, degree of loneliness, depression, tension, and paranois. They reported a *higher* level of current feeling of happiness and greater exuberance than the heterosexual sample. However, they did report worrying more and were more likely to have had suicidal ideas or attempts and to seek professional help. This type thus comes across as the least distinguishable from the heterosexuals on these measures of psychological adjustment, and, in comparison with the other homosexual types, the best adjusted on these measures.

The *Open-Coupled* homosexual males compared to the heterosexual males as follows: more exuberant; not significantly different in general health, in happiness, loneliness, or paranoia; but did have more psychosomatic complaints, lower self-acceptance, more worries, more depression, more tension, more suicidal ideas or attempts, and more psychotherapy-seeking.

The *Functionals* were also more exuberant than the heterosexuals; no different in physical health, happiness, psychosomatic symptoms, worries, depression, or paranoia; but they were more lonely, more tense, more suicidal, and more therapy-seeking than the heterosexual males.

The *Dysfunctionals* were similar to the heterosexuals only in general health and in exuberance; on all the other measures, they showed themselves psychologically worse adjusted; in psychosomatic symptoms, happiness, self-acceptance, greater loneliness, greater worries, more depression, tension, and paranois, more suicidal and more therapy-seeking.

The homosexual subgroup called the *Asexuals* compared to the heterosexuals worst of all; the only factor on which they did not differ, adversely, was exuberance; otherwise they had worse general physical health (the only homosexual subgroup that did), more psychosomatic symptoms, lower happiness, lower self-acceptance, more loneliness, more worries, more depression, tension, and paranoid trends, more suicidal thoughts and attempts, and greater likelihood to have sought professional psychological help. (Reconstructed from pp. 198–206, Bell and Weinberg, and from a careful reading of the relevant tables, 21.2–21.27.)

From this array of findings, the authors choose to emphasize that the overall difference between the homosexual males and the heterosexuals (indicating that the former do indeed show more psychological adjustment problems) is "accounted for" primarily by the adverse scores of mainly two subtypes of homosexuals, the Dysfunctionals and the Asexuals; while the Open-Coupled are in only slightly more adverse position than the heterosexuals, and the Functionals and the Close-Coupled are practically indistinguishable from the heterosexual sample, and in fact the Close-Coupled seem to be in an even better state of psychological well-being (by some measures, at least) than the heterosexuals. Emphasizing the upbeat, they make the following summary conclusion: "It would appear that homosexual adults who have come to terms with their homosexuality, who do not regret their sexual orientation, and who can function effectively sexually and socially, are no more distressed psychologically, than are heterosexual men and women" (Bell and Weinberg 1978:216).

It is evident from these findings, however, that people who do fit all these qualifications constitute only a small minority of the homosexual sample. Those in the Close-Coupled situation come closest to all these criteria, and they are only 14 percent of the homosexual males who could be classified into one of the five types. *Some* of the Functionals could also qualify.

By contrast, though these authors earnestly hope to demonstrate that the idea of the homosexual male as an anguished, disturbed, tortured individual is a myth (perpetrated mainly by psychoanalysis, it seems), they cannot avoid honestly reporting that by their psychological measures the homosexuals studied do show, in general, more psychological "adjustment problems" than the heterosexuals in general, and that at least two of the homosexual subtypes are markedly worse off psychologically than the heterosexual sample. The authors underline that these types are less well adjusted than the other homosexual types. Still, they admit that if one were to look for examples of homosexuals who fit the image of the disturbed lonely type much portrayed in the clinical literature, they could surely be found among the dysfunctionals and asexuals in this study. Together these constitute over 40 percent of the males who were type-classified. Many of the homosexual males in Open-Couples also approximated these characteristics (my calculation, from the Bell and Weinberg figures).

One could argue, of course, about whether the cup is half full or half empty. These authors emphasize the half full. But if one focused on the half empty, one would also note that on none of the twelve topics relating to "psychological adjustment"—except exuberance—were the homosexual men better off than the heterosexuals; and on only one topic in addition to that—"happiness"—was any one of the five sub-types, the Close-Coupled, better off than the heterosexuals; and even this "best-adjusted" type were still worse off than the straights on three of these topics.

Females

For the female homosexuals the picture is somewhat different. Compared to the heterosexual control sample, they were not significantly different in general health, in psychosomatic symptoms, in exuberance, in feelings of loneliness, in worry, depression, tension, paranoia, or overt suicidal attempts. However, they did report a lower estimate of current happiness, less self-acceptance, more thoughts about suicide, and greater likelihood to have sought professional help for emotional problems. Among the different sub-types, the Close-Coupled were indistinguishable from the heterosexuals on all aspects except feelings of loneliness, where they reported lower feelings of that kind. The Open-Coupled were somewhat similar, being indistinguishable from the heterosexuals on all aspects except for lower self-acceptance, more paranoid feelings, and greater therapy-seeking. The Functionals were similar to the Close-Coupled: they had no significant differences from the heterosexuals on any of the topics, except that they were *more* exuberant. The Dysfunctionals had lower psychological adjustment scores on many aspects compared to the other homosexual subgroups; and compared to the heterosexuals, they were lower in happiness, exuberance, and self-acceptance, and higher in therapy-seeking. The Asexuals also showed less psychological adjustment than the heterosexuals on these criteria: loneliness, tension, paranoid trends, and therapy-seeking. The Dysfunctionals, the Asexuals, and, to a lesser extent, the Open-Coupled were the homosexual subtypes that primarily accounted for the lower degree of psychological adjustment evidenced by the homosexual women compared to the heterosexual control group.

These findings do not support the view that homosexual women are intrinsically less psychologically well-adjusted than heterosexual women, though they do, for these samples at least, report lower levels of happiness feeling, lower self-acceptance, greater suicidal ideation, and tendency to seek professional help for emotional problems. Otherwise the homosexual women are practically indistinguishable from their heterosexual peers. Particularly, of the subtypes of homosexual women, those in closed couples and those dubbed "functionals" (i.e., happy and self-accepting in their homosexuality and sexually active) score as well as the heterosexuals generally on any of the measures of psychological well-being, and better on some. Those in open-coupled arrangements are slightly less well off, being less self-accepting, more paranoid, and more therapy-seeking. The Dysfunctionals and the Asexuals show more disturbance than the heterosexuals, but in different dimensions in each case. These two types represent the main concentration of homosexual women showing more psychological disturbance than their heterosexual sisters, and in this respect are similar to the two subtypes of the homosexual men who showed the greatest amount of adverse comparison with the heterosexuals. The degree of such differences overall is much greater for the men and also for those subtypes.

Promiscuity

What about promiscuity? Homosexuals—males at least—are reputed to be much more promiscuous than heterosexuals. What did Bell and Weinberg find?

This: Homosexual males are far more likely than heterosexuals to have a large number of sexual partners. Nearly half the white male homosexuals and a third of the black ones said they had at least five hundred different partners during their sexual careers. And 28 percent of the white male homosexuals and 19 percent of the black ones reported having had over a thousand. (The authors acknowledge that there could have been some exaggeration or boasting in these self-reports in some cases, but even allowing for some exaggeration, the numbers are impressively high.) Also, more than half of the male homosexuals said they had more than twenty different partners in the year preceding the interview. In fact, more than a quarter of the white homosexual males and about a third of the black reported having more than fifty different partners in the past year alone.

This extensity of sexual contact varied among the five homosexual types: Close-Coupled were unlikely to have many—or in some cases any—other sexual partners at the time they were in this relationship. Also, the Asexuals were less likely to have many different sexual partners. But the high number of sexual partners was characteristic for the Open-Coupled, the Functionals, and the Dysfunctionals.

Thus it becomes evident that in only one of the five categories of male homosexuals is there anything at all resembling a monogamous pairing with a fair degree of sexual fidelity. That is in the category Bell and Weinberg call Close-Coupled. This category constitutes only about 14 percent of the total of the male homosexuals who could be classified into one of the five types. Even in the other kind of couple situation, the Open-Coupled, they show a great deal of sexual activity outside of the regular sexual partnership. The Functionals and the Dysfunctionals would appear to be as promiscuous as possible. The Asexuals are not as sexually active, nor as promiscuous, but neither are they involved in anything like an ongoing partnership.

Thus the Bell and Weinberg findings confirm what has been reported in more casual observations, or what can be deduced from the psychoanalytic case literature: that, generally, male homosexuals are engaged in a large number, sometimes an extremely large number, of sexual contacts with many different partners. Most of these would evidently have to be primarily for sexual release. By their very number, such contacts could not possibly involve much in the way of intimacy, or sharing, or really personal emotional relationship. This certainly does not suggest optimal psychic health, by whatever criterion one might choose. (Interestingly, Bell and Weinberg do not include these findings in their section of "psychological adjustment.")

Similarly, we can note their finding, reported elsewhere in their presentation, that two-fifths of the homosexual males had "cruised" at least once or twice a week over the past year, meaning going out specifically to look for a sexual partner pickup in bars, baths, and other public places. This would certainly suggest confirmation, at least for these homosexuals, of the prevalent image of the male homosexual as constantly preoccupied with sex, and constantly on the go to get sexual satisfaction; and by implication rarely feeling sexually fulfilled with any one partner over any extended period of time. (The Close-Coupled would constitute an exception here.)

On the question of promiscuity, there are notable differences between the male and the female homosexuals. The lesbians are very unlikely to report having had any more than ten different same-sex partners in their lifetime. Fifty-eight percent of the white lesbians and 54 percent of the black report fewer than ten different gay partners. And about a quarter of each report fewer than five. Practically none report more than 50 (as compared to a male figure in the hundreds, up to 1,000 or more). Similarly, the vast majority of the gay women report that none of their sexual partners were strangers to them before the sexual contact (whereas this was practically never the case for the gay males). Similarly, most of the gay women reported affection for their sexual partners (most of the men said this of about half or less, or none, of their sexual contacts), that with few of their sexual partners had they had sex only once (most of the men said this about more than half of their partners), and most of the lesbians said about none of their sexual partners that they never saw them socially again.

In summary, gay women are much less, in fact hardly at all, engaged in impersonal sex with homosexual partners, devoid of other social, affectional, or personal relationship. Most of the gay men are or have been so with most of their large number of sexual partners. The same applies to the findings about number of sexual partners in the past year; the modal figure for the female homosexuals is one to two (for the males it is 20 to 50). For number of homosexual partners ever, the modal figures are for females: 5 to 9; males: 250 to 499!

Other Differences Between Male and Female Homosexuals

There are similar differences between the female and the male homosexuals on related matters. For example, in reference to cruising, 83 percent of the lesbians report never cruising at all in the past year (whereas 85 percent of the gay males report cruising some of the time, around two-thirds of them at least a few times a month. Also, practically none of the lesbians ever cruise in public places like the street, beaches, parks, and movie theaters, and there is simply no institution at all comparable to the male gay baths for the females.

Correspondingly, far more of the classifiable lesbians than of homosexual men are in close-coupled arrangements (38 percent compared to 14 percent) and correspondingly far fewer in the Dysfunctional category (8 percent compared to 18 percent for the males).

All in all, the Bell and Weinberg findings confirm what is stated or implied in other research: female homosexuals are more like female heterosexuals, particularly in low likelihood of or interest in separating sex from intimacy, than they are like male homosexuals. This is probably related to the fact that though the lesbians score somewhat worse in some details of psychological adjustment than the straight women, the amount of such discrepancy is much less than is true for the homosexual men in comparison with the heterosexual men.

The gay women are by and large more at home with their homosexuality than their male counterparts, feel less regret, have fewer social difficulties in relation to it, and are far more capable of combining sex with intimacy with their partners, and of maintaining a cohabitation partnership longer and more effectively.

This is probably connected with, though not necessarily entirely explained by, such factors as the following: Social stigma against the lesbian is far less severe than against the male homosexuals. Many states that have laws against specific male homosexual practices do not have corresponding laws against lesbian acts, and enforcement of any kind of legal constraint is likely to be close to or at zero. Female homosexuality is not generally regarded as totally incompatible with the societally defined primary female function of motherhood. There is little if any social stigma or suspiciousness attached to two adult females living together; whereas for males past college age this is highly suspect. Dynamically, one can hypothesize that since women are felt by men to be already castrated, they matter less generally, therefore their private sexual lives are less consequential (unless openly challenging the male's patriarchal dominance), whereas the male homosexual is a dangerous reminder to non-homosexual males that the male could *become* "castrated," and therefore is much more of a psychological threat.

These differences are also reflected in the vastly lesser attention that has been accorded to female homosexuality than to male homosexuality by psychoanalysts and by behavioral and social scientists of all kinds. (A woman colleague reminds me that in much of this manuscript the discussion about "homosexuality" is actually about *male* homosexuality;

often in the literature this is assumed so often as to go without any formal acknowledgement.)

Female homosexuality, studied in other contexts, shows itself quite differently from male. Studying homosexual behavior in prisons, sociologists have found that a considerably larger proportion of female prisoners, including many imprisoned for rather short terms, take to homosexual practices than is true for corresponding males. (This is in reference to prisoners whose prior or outside sex life is mainly or entirely heterosexual.) (See Ward and Kassebaum 1965, Giallombardo 1974.) They also found that female homosexual pairing most commonly played out a scenario of mother-infant bond and was much more likely to involve strong personal attachment compared to the relatively more anonymous homosexuality of imprisoned males. The females are also less oriented in that situation to playing power games, than the males.

Difficulties in the Bell
and Weinberg Study

To return to the Bell and Weinberg study: It is impressive that here, in a study whose authors evidently ardently wish to challenge stereotypes of homosexuals as unstable, unhappy, disturbed, promiscuous individuals, constantly on the hunt, in fact, the homosexual sample as whole shows more such characteristics than the comparison heterosexuals. This is more particularly true of the gay men than of the gay women. For the men, it is particularly true of two of the five subtypes, who show predominant feelings of negative self-worth, non-self-acceptance, unhappiness about their sexual orientation, more depression and suicidal thoughts and/or attempts, and enough recognition of psychological disturbance to seek professional help. Also, the male homosexuals generally were much more likely than the heterosexuals to have had a vast number of different sexual partners, and this was especially true of three of the five subtypes.

Thus Bell and Weinberg's factual findings, honestly enough presented to enable others to use them independently of these authors' interpretations, frequently contradict the authors' summaries, and particularly their obvious ideological intention to challenge prevalent conceptions about homosexuals that they see as unwarranted stereotypes.

Bell and Weinberg's device of dividing up the homosexual respondents (where possible) into five types, and comparing these types among themselves, is certainly useful in underlining their theme of the great diversity in the lives of homosexuals. But when they then compare each of the homosexual subtypes with the *total* heterosexual sample and come out with the finding that in only two of these types, or in some cases three, do the homosexuals show up as noticeably less well-adjusted psychologically than the heterosexuals, the procedure is obviously tendentious. Since the very criteria that classify someone as Dysfunctional or Asexual include such features as dissatisfaction or regret about one's homosexuality, lower self-acceptance, and the like, wherever comparisons are being made between each of the different homosexual subtypes and the total heterosexual sample, it is likely that the differences are going to be concentrated in these particular types.

But it is equally obvious that the heterosexual sample as a whole is not the relevant point of comparison. In fact, the only relevant comparisons involving the heterosexuals that these authors did make with their data are those between all the homosexual males and all the heterosexual males; then the same for the females; or between all black male homosexuals and all black male heterosexuals, and then the same for whites, then for the females of each race separately. And on practically all of these comparisons (more so for the males than the females, and more for the blacks than the whites) the homosexuals do score more adversely on many of the psychological adjustment variables. This in spite of the authors' ideological assertions to the contrary. To qualify statements of these differences by saying that it came out this way because of the low scores of only certain types of homosexuals is to obscure rather than to clarify.

If the comparisons of each of the five homosexual subtypes respectively and a relevant heterosexual sample are to make any sense, there would have to be comparable types of heterosexuals. One could posit five somewhat parallel types of heterosexuals: 1) Close-Coupled, i.e., happily married, at home with and satisfied with their heterosexuality and with their mates; not given to adulterous affairs; with a lot of close intimate emotional contact with one's spouse; 2) Open-Coupled: married (or in a functionally equivalent relationship) but not so happily; frequently engaged in adulterous affairs; some tensions with the partner, and some difficulties with the sexual aspect of marriage; 3) "Swingers": either single or divorced, and sexually very active with a lot of different partners; exuberantly in pursuit of sexual pleasures; or technically married but not much involved emotionally or sexually with the spouse; corresponding to the Functional homosexuals; 4) Dysfunctionals: single or divorced or in bad marriages; with a lot of difficulties in heterosexual relations; ill at ease with sex; experiencing a lot of guilt (perhaps unconscious) about sex; 5) Asexuals: people whose sexual contacts, when they have them, are heterosexual, but who are relatively inactive sexually; if married, have infrequent and not very satisfying sexual contact with spouse; if unmarried or divorced, are relatively isolated, rather unhappy individuals, who are "turned off" from sex rather generally.

If this kind of classification had been made, would the Close-Coupled homosexuals still come out just as well off psychologically as their heterosexual counterparts of the happily married? Would the self-professedly exuberant homosexual promiscuous Functionals still compare well, psychologically, with swinging single heterosexual counterparts? We cannot answer these questions directly from Bell and Weinberg's data as presented here, but we can estimate, as follows. Since the homosexual Close-Coupled are the "best-adjusted" of the five homosexual types, and since we could assume that the happily married heterosexuals are the psychologically best-adjusted of the heterosexuals, and since the close-coupled are similar to the *average* of all of the heterosexuals, and since it is reasonable to assume that the close-coupled (happily married) heterosexuals are better adjusted than the average of the heterosexuals, then it would follow that *probably* the close-coupled homosexuals score more adversely on psychological adjustment factors here than do their happily married heterosexual counterparts. Similarly, if the (homosexual) Functionals score close to the heterosexual *average*, and the heterosexual Swingers score *better* than the heterosexual average, then it is likely the homosexual Functionals are worse off psychologically than the heterosexual Functionals ("swingers"). We don't know precisely to what degree, and on what aspects more so, since Bell and Weinberg did not make specifically these comparisons, but the direction is likely to be as just stated.

Thus a good deal of the comparison work done in this book—other than that for all the homosexuals as compared with all the heterosexuals—is somewhat specious. And it is so, evidently, in the service of gay advocacy. To dismiss the extent to which these data do in fact demonstrate homosexuals as psychologically more disturbed than relevant comparison groups of heterosexuals, in the service of homophile protest ideology, is to serve neither truth nor justice, and certainly not compassionate understanding. That *some* homosexuals, under certain conditions, can be as psychologically well off as most heterosexuals, and live fulfilling productive lives, sometimes at a superior level of functioning, certainly has to be recognized as amply documented by this study. But they are still a small minority of the homosexual population studied here.

Otherwise the homosexuals—and more particularly two of the subtypes, and somewhat so for a third as well—do tend more to confirm than to refute prevalent images that these authors wish to dismiss as "stereotypes": psychologically troubled, often deeply so; the males tending toward promiscuity and, concomitantly, difficulty in establishing stable, lasting, close sexual-emotional relationships; very much preoccupied with sex and with getting new sexual satisfactions.

Though the data here obviously lack any of the kind of psychoanalytic "depth" that clinicians look for, and that are the baselines for the kinds of generalizations about homosexuals that have come out of the psychoanalytic literature, still this work is to be noted particularly for the fact that it has the best and largest sample of the total homosexual population of any of the studies of homosexuality that have been done so far: that it avoids the probable unrepresentativeness of studies like the Bieber group's that concentrate on therapy patients, or of studies like Hooker's, which is biased in the direction of gay protest activists and the psychologically best integrated of those at that.

What then are the implications of the findings of this large, in many ways thorough, and important study, for the questions we have been raising about the psychological characteristics associated with homosexuality? Clearly they indicate that it is not valid to consider all homosexuals as intrinsically psychologically sick by that very fact, or inevitably by association with that fact. Even in the culturally hostile environment of this anti-sexual and particularly anti-homosexual society, some homosexuals do live lives with little or no evident psychopathology. Many others are somewhat psychologically disturbed, and some are seriously so. Their proportions and the types and seriousness of such disturbance seem to be greater than for comparable heterosexual groups, though not uniformly so, and not uniformly over a range of types of psychological problems.

They also differ as between men and women, the male homosexuals showing more adverse comparisons with the heterosexual comparison groups than do the female homosexuals. The findings also strikingly document the immense variety of male homosexuals and of female homosexuals. They are vastly diverse among themselves. This diversity coheres with the psychoanalytic statement that homosexuality cannot be considered a single discrete clinical entity. (That does not mean it is not associated with psychopathology, but rather it may or may not be; it is more likely to be than not, but where it is, it can be any of a great variety of types of psychic disturbance, and have a great variety of types of connections with other psychic disturbance symptoms.)

GAY "MARRIAGES"

One of the basic questions relating to the psychological well-being of homosexuals compared to heterosexuals has to do with the quality and durability of mating arrangements. As already noted, far more female homosexuals than males are found in the Bell–Weinberg study to be settled in some kind of enduring co-habitation mating arrangement (38 percent of the females, as compared with only 14 percent of the males). Correspondingly, promiscuous, relatively impersonal sexual encounters are more the rule than otherwise for the males, and not particularly prevalent for the female. So the problem of forming and sustaining enduring love relationships seems to be more particularly a male problem for the gay population.

When heterosexual commentators note the fragility and short-livedness of gay "marriages," some homophile supporters counter by asserting that what the straights don't realize is that a different set of norms applies in gay matings than in straight marriages, and therefore the gay "marriages" should not be faulted according to heterosexual norms. There is, however, sociological research which questions whether there is really a different set of norms applying in this quasi-subculture of the gay world, or rather simply no normative consensus. For example, an illuminating sociological paper by Joseph Harry (1977) points out that there is a great variety of cohabitation mating relationships among gay males. Harry claims that none of these types is able to claim any particular structural or cultural support, either from other gays or from the dominant society. Harry continues:

> Opportunities for infidelity are widely available, and given the heterogeneity of opinion among gays on the desirability of fidelity, strong cultural support for fidelity seems lacking. Thus, marital career and life-style seem to be largely sub-institutional questions of what the given individuals within a specific relationship decide to do.

He notes that gay couples (male) who did *not* taboo outside sexual encounters, i.e., infidelity, had better chances for survival over a longer period than those where they pledged and expected fidelity. "Attempts to construct the gay relationship after the heterosexual (marriage) model seem to end in early divorce" (Harry 1977:340). (Note that Harry uses the terms "marriage" and "divorce" for a relationship and its rupture that is without legal foundation; he means, of course, that the relationship is somewhat analogous to a marriage in the heterosexual world, and the breakup of a fairly enduring cohabitation mating is somewhat *like* a divorce.) Thus he focuses on lack of institutionalization of either the mating or the mode of the breakup in the homosexual world, the lack of norms agreed to by homosexuals themselves, let alone any accorded by the dominant majority of society. Generally, of course, this is part of the broader picture of the lack of structural or cultural support from society at large for any kind of enduring homosexual relationship. As noted earlier, the hostility to male-male coupling, particularly in the form of cohabitation, seems to be greater than that given to female-female couplings. Some gay "marriage ceremonies" have in fact been performed, either by maverick clerics or by lay practitioners functioning in such a role, but they have no legal status, and have only questionable religious sanction (as yet). Heterosexual radicals, who are questioning the whole (heterosexual) marriage institution altogether, may be puzzled by the wishes of those gays who want to be legally married in the first place. In the minds of such heterosexual "liberationists," gays should be happy with their freedom from such entanglements. They forget, of course, that they—heterosexuals—have the freedom to choose to marry or not to marry; homosexuals do not have such options.

We find a lack of social structural supports i.e., there is no established social structure for a "married couple" for homosexuals, or any related structures, such as definite in-law realtionships, (a young woman puzzled about how to refer to her gay brother's lover; her "brother-in-law"? "sister-in-law" or what?); and the lack of cultural supports (i.e., a set of definite norms that define who does what, who has responsibility for what, etc., in such a relationship) such as exist in abundance for heterosexual marriage. Given those lacks, it is even surprising that any homosexual "marriages" survive for any length of time at all, and it is illuminating that Harry's study finds they are more likely to do so if the partners agree to allow some extra-marital sexual playing around, as long as it is relatively unserious, on both sides. Homophile supporters argue in response to that that if only the surrounding society were enlightened enough to institutionalize legal homosexual marriages, there would be a lot less infidelity in these relationships, and a lot less promiscuity generally among homosexuals (males, that is), as well as a lot more personal happiness, self-acceptance, and self-esteem.

However, that argument so far seems to be largely rhetoric. By contrast, thoughtful scholars who have done first-hand research on this sound a much more pessimistic note. Harry concludes his study as follows:

Although Hoffman (1968:176–77) has argued that a good measure of the social disorganization characteristic of the gay marital relationships [the reference is evidently more to male than female versions—R.E.] would disappear if the dominant heterosexual society became less hostile towards homosexuality, we are less sanguine. Hoffman and other observers of the gay community (Simon and Gagnon 1967) seem to believe that gay males would be better off if they were able to follow the heterosexual model of faithful and enduring monogamy, but we noted [in this research] that this pattern seems to be the least successful marital career pattern [in male homosexual marriages]. Attempts to construct the gay relationship after the heterosexual model seem to end in early divorce. . . . However, the alternative model of agreed-on infidelity may also be undesirable because it seems to be a simple extension of the sexual marketplace mentality into the marital relationship. An even greater glorification of the pleasures of impersonal sex seems to be the last thing the gay culture needs. Accordingly, we reach the tentative, if somewhat bleak, conclusion, that the gay marital relationship will become a more rewarding affair for its participants only when the fidelity version of that relationship acquires substantially greater structural, cultural, and socialization supports. (Harry 1977:340)

However, looked at from a psychoanalytic perspective we would have to say this: no doubt there are some such sociological bases for the difficulties in maintaining stable, enduring relationships, even in the presumably fairly "happily married" "close-coupled" people. But psychologically, we would have to relate this to the difficulties homosexuals generally, more than most heterosexuals, experience in maintaining close personal emotional ties with others. A central part of the difficulty in combining intimacy with sex in these relationships, as we see from our clinical studies, remains the fact that for many, if not most, the homosexual activity constitutes at least in part an expression of aggression and hatred—at unconscious levels, mostly, of course. At best, there is great love-hate ambivalence, which certainly bodes ill for the endurance of any sexual relationship, whether homosexual or heterosexual. This may be masked in a variety of ways in the allegedly more stable and happy "close-coupled" pairs of individuals, in a kind of encapsulation of the underlying sexual pathology. Extra-marital affairs may be a partial safety valve for the difficulties in the couple relationship, which may explain why Harry found those "marriages" more durable than those which attempt complete "fidelity." Similarly, the large amount of promiscuous sexual behavior (in the males) has to be understood psychodynamically. Such interpretation is impossible to carry on reliably from the way Bell and Weinberg organized and presented their interview data, but we can suggest interpretations based on the clinical cases with which we are familiar in psychoanalytic work. One possible function of much of the promiscuous sexual activity is to counteract depression, which seems even by Bell and Weinberg's rather superficial indicators to be widespread in the homosexual sample, at least in three of their five types. (We have no way to tell from their here presented tabulated data whether the same individuals who are most promiscuous also report the most in the way of indicators of depression. We would hypothesize that there would be such a correlation.)

Difficulties in combining sex with intimacy are *generally* greater for males than for females, for reasons explored in the preceding section, whether within the heterosexual or the homosexual mode. This is true in our society, and probably in most others. Similarly, the promiscuity of homosexual males can be compared to the macho heterosexual male pattern of prowling for as many sexual "conquests" as possible. Again, we find gay men more like straight men than like gay women; gay women more like straight women than like gay men.

CROSS-CULTURAL EVIDENCE

Homophile movement people and their social-scientific and other supporters frequently claim that the conditions of hostility toward homosexuality are peculiar to our society (or perhaps Western society generally) at this point in history. Sometimes an accessory argument is made; to wit, that though it is true that some homosexuals experience psychological disturbance or distress, this is caused entirely by the hostile environment of a homoerotophobic society; correspondingly, if the fear of and hostility toward homosexuality were to decline, or better still disappear, homosexuals would experience much less psychological distress, or none at all, or at least none other than might appear in the rest of the population, and could live happy lives in simply another variant of "normal" sexual functioning.

We shall first take up the argument that cross-culturally one can find many cultures, even a majority, that lack our particular puritanical hostility toward homosexuality. Therefore, in that sense, it is our culture that is abnormal, rather than these sex-preference variants, within it.

Tribal Societies

Looking first at the anthropological evidence from tribal and folk societies, we raise two related questions: what evidence is there of the amount and prevalence of homosexual behavior in each sex, in these societies? Second, what do we find in the way of normative attitudes toward homosexual behavior, including (where they exist) the possibility of institutionalization of distinct homosexual roles for men, or for women, or both.

There is by now a fairly substantial amount of anthropological information, and some analysis, on these topics. It is, however, quite uneven in quality and quantity, and in many cases the fact that there is no mention of either homosexual behavior or of attitudes toward it in an ethnographic monograph may only indicate that the ethnographer did not look for it, did not ask questions about it, or simply has not reported whatever bits of information he did obtain. From what information is available, we can piece together a picture that goes roughly as follows: The patterns are very varied. Some form of homosexual activity by males, or by females, or by both has been reported in a large number of tribal societies, and it is possible it also occurs (possibly more secretly) in others where it is not reported specifically by the anthropologist(s) concerned.

Some years ago the anthropologist Clellan Ford and the psychologist Frank Beach (1953), in a much-cited work, *Patterns of Sexual Behavior*, tried to tally the available information on this from the over 300 societies tabulated in the Human Relations Area Files at Yale. They found information on this topic in only 76 of those societies. They reported that in "28 [of those societies] homosexual activities on the part of adults are reported to be totally absent, rare, or carried on only in secrecy . . . [and that] this form of sexual expression is condemned in these societies . . . [but] in 49 of [those 76] societies homosexual activities of one sort or another are considered normal and socially acceptable for certain members of the community" (Ford and Beach 1953:129, 130).

Not surprisingly, that part of Ford and Beach's work has been much cited by homophile apologists. It appears that in 64 percent of the known societies homosexuality is normal and approved behavior. By that kind of counting, our society, with its emotional antihomosexual feelings and behavior, would appear abnormal and aberrant—the culture being abnormal, rather than the homosexuals.

However, a closer look at available data and a questioning of Ford and Beach's mode of presenting theirs suggest that that picture needs a lot of modification and qualification. In the first place, Ford and Beach do not at all distinguish between the existence and prevalence of certain behavior on one side, and the normative attitudes toward it on the other. Further, there are data available on many more societies, which modify their picture.

Take as a starting point their own crude categories: on one side, homosexuality is both absent or rare and strongly condemned; on the other it has some degree of prevalence at least for some categories of people, and is accepted, at least for some people in some circumstances. Then a perusal of some of the available anthropological literature reveals at least 10 additional societal cases in their category of "absent/rare/disapproved," and eight additional societal cases in their category of "present, allowable." In the former case: Ford and Beach list 28 societies.[1] One can add to that list of "absent, rare, disapproved" the ten following: the Bala of the Congo (Merriam 1971); the Arapesh and the Mundugumor of New Guinea (Mead 1935, 1949); the Andaman Islanders and the Dobuans of Melanesia (Opler 1965; Fortune 1932); the (Mescalero) Apache Indians (Boyer 1964); the Ute Indians (Opler 1965); in Polynesia, the Mangaians (Marshall 1971) and the Marquesans (Suggs 1966); also (at least for adults) the Cubeo Indians of South America (Goldman 1963). That brings that count to 38 societies (out of 95 about which information is available) or 40 percent.

One the other side—societies in which it is present in some form, for some part of the population, with some degree of prevalence, and approved or permitted—Ford and Beach listed 49 societies.[2] To those 49 should be added at least eight others: Sioux Indians (Erikson 1939, 1950; MacGregor 1946); other Plains Indian tribes; Mohave Indians (Devereux 1937, 1961); the Otoro of Africa (LeVine 1961); the Tchambuli of New Guinea (Mead 1935, 1949); the Malekula of Melanesia (Layard 1942); the Marind-Anim (Mead 1949); and the Nambutji of Australia (Róheim 1945). This would bring the figure on that side to 57, or about 60 percent of the societies thus tabulated.

Thus a search for further societal cases indicates slightly more cases are found to add to the "rare and disapproved" list than to add to the "present and permitted" list. However, in all the cases we really have to look much more closely than these crude categories. Some societies could not be reasonably classified at all by these categories. Such a case is that of the Sedang-Moi of IndoChina, studied by Devereux (1967, and elsewhere). This is a case where certain kinds of homosexual activity (specifically sodomy among the young men in the men's clubhouse) are widespread, and also kept secret as much as possible (from the women) and disapproved of by the people in the society generally (Devereux 1967:309–10). The secrecy indicates the practice is disapproved.

Another case of questionable classification (though I have just listed it in the "rare-absent" category) is that of the Cubeo Indians of the Northwest Amazon area (Goldman 1963). Rare or absent and disapproved applies to adult homosexual activity; however, there is widespread adolescent mutual masturbation between boys, and between girls. The context is extremely restrictive norms against premarital heterosexual·

activity (rare for tribal societies). Persistent adult homosexuality, however, is very rare (See Opler 1965).

Next we need to note that disapproval is not necessarily associated with rarity or absence of homosexual practice, nor is permissiveness or toleration necessarily associated with a high degree of prevalence. For example, in the Sedang-Moi sodomy is prevalent among the young men and disapproved of by the people of the society generally. On the other side, toleration may be extended to a small number of homosexual deviants occupying a particular institutionalized role, while the practice is not at all widespread in the society generally. This is true for many of the tribes that have a role such as that of the berdache, to be discussed presently.

It is probable that actual homosexual practices, by males and/or by females, may be considerably more widespread than would be revealed by a less than thorough investigation. This would apply especially in any society where it is strongly disapproved, and therefore more likely to be practiced in secret. One anthropologist (Marshall 1971) reports that homosexual practices are entirely absent in the Polynesian tribe (the Mangaians) he studied, and asserts this on the basis of having explicitly investigated this topic. In a few other cases it is reported with confidence by the investigator that it is extremely rare. Boyer (1964) reports about the Apaches, as of 1960, that his investigation revealed only two known cases of overt male homosexuality, and none for females, and that the practice is severely tabooed. Most informants deny that it occurs at all in their tribe. Marvin Opler reports similarly, on the basis of explicit questioning on this for the Ute Indians (Opler 1965).

In those societies classifiable as having homosexuality "present and permitted," there are great variations in prevalence. First, what has been reported shows much greater likelihood of prevalence for males than for females. Second, where there is some prevalence, three patterns are most likely: 1) a small minority take on an institutionalized homosexual role, such as the berdache; 2) homosexual practices are prevalent and tolerated at a particular stage of the life cycle, usually adolescence, but not in mature adulthood; 3) prevalent or even nearly universal for all males, with a specified role in adolescence and a different role in mature adulthood, namely "passive" earlier, "active" later. (To my knowledge there are no parallel cases of near-universal practice for females.) There are no reported societies where *exclusive* homosexuality is widely prevalent, much less universal, in the society. In all of the cases in the third category just mentioned, exclusive homosexuality in the adult male is either extremely rare or is non-existent.

We have no reliable estimates of *degree* of prevalence for these cases. It is unlikely that exclusive homosexuality actually occurs in any tribal societies with any greater degree of frequency than it does as estimated by the Kinsey researches for our society as of the later 1940s (about 4 percent of males, probably less for females) (Kinsey et al. 1948, 1953). Players of the institutionalized role are unlikely to be more than a very small minority. In a few tribes adolescent homosexual practices may be near-universal for males; then expected to be abandoned in mature adulthood.

Normative reactions to homosexual practices vary a great deal among tribal societies. At one extreme is complete and extreme disapproval of any homosexual acts for either sex. At the opposite extreme is toleration for homosexual practices either for certain (few) individuals in an insti-tutionalized role, or for all individuals of one sex (more likely males) at one particular stage in the life cycle, in a certain form of activity; or expectation of homosexual practice as part of male initiation ceremonies; or toleration of casual female homosexual practice as incidental and of no importance, usually alongside heterosexuality. In *no* society, how-ever, do we find unqualified approval for exclusive homosexuality. (This generalization nullifies the Ford and Beach claim that homosexuality is considered "normal and accepted" in some societies.)

There are complex interrelationships between actual appearance of certain homosexual practices, and normative opinions about such prac-tices, in different societies. Some societies listed by Ford and Beach as among those where it is rare or absent and strongly disapproved may, in fact, have rather mixed reactions to it. For example, the Manus of New Guinea. In Margaret Mead's report on them (1930) we find the following:

> Homosexuality occurs in both sexes, but rarely. Natives recognize, and take only a laughing count of it, if it occurs between unmarried boys, sometimes exploited publicly in the boys' houses. Sodomy is the only form. . . . Homo-sexual relations between women are rare. . . . Boys away from home, on plantation work, are likely to turn to homosexuality. (Mead 1930:102; Mentor ed., 1953:120)

In the relatively disapproving category we find societies like the Mar-quesan Islanders of Polynesia. From the discussion of this tribe by Linton in Kardiner and Linton (1939) one gets the impression that homosexuality is a permissible variant there. Yet Robert Suggs, in a more recent and more thoroughly probing study of that tribe, found that the Marquesans condone homosexual acts in only two situations: in early adolescence, for boys, when they sometimes have difficulty finding age-mate female sexual partners (the latter being more physically and socially mature); and second, where an adult man is in a situation where he has no access to women and a young boy is taken as a substitute. Otherwise, homosexual behavior is strongly disapproved, particularly between two adult males. There is a strongly stigmatized label, *mahu*, for any male who has more than fleeting sexual contact with other males. There is a very small number of such men, and a still smaller number of male homosexual transvestites who do feminine domestic chores (Suggs 1966, 1971). Suggs indicates (1971) that some female homosexuality occurs, but had no data on frequency.

This can also be considered as belonging in the category of relatively tolerant in reference to certain life-cycle stages (adolescence) and under certain conditions.

In some societies there is a certain toleration toward homosexual practices which take the form of the institutionalization of a particular role for the exclusively or nearly exclusively homosexual: the existence of such a socially recognized man-woman or woman-man role is often pointed out by homophile apologists as evidence that homosexuality can be simply a "normal" variant. In fact, a closer look at how such a sex-role reversal functions in societies having this practice, reveals something quite different.

In some tribes this role is one only for a man taking on feminine dress and occupations, in some for both a man functioning as a woman and for a woman functioning as a man. I know of no instances where there is such a role for females but not for males. The males only situation appears to be more common. Such a male carries out a rather comprehensive sex-role reversal and is socially, often ritually, recognized as such. Sexually this man usually is homosexual and may become the "wife" of another male, playing the recipient, thus the "feminine" role in anal coitus with the partner. The "husband" in these cases is considered to be heterosexual and may have other, female, wives, in addition to the transvestite "wife."

In the Americas in the early days of European exploration, French explorers dubbed such "men-women" *berdaches* (a corruption of a Persian word taken over into Arabic, meaning male prostitute or kept boy, sometimes slave); the word has become part of the anthropological language to refer to such homosexual transvestite males. (In some cases it is uncertain if the male was, in fact, homosexual, or merely adopted the feminine gender role out of felt inadequacy for meeting masculine standards of bravery in a warrior society.) Some tribes have a corresponding female transvestite role, such as a woman taking another (usually heterosexual) female for a "wife." (The "wife" is not usually considered homosexual.) Such institutionalized roles may be highly developed for both sexes as in the Mohave (Devereux 1937 and elsewhere). In some cases it is only for the male.

In some cases this role is associated with shamanism. This is prevalent among the Siberian tribes (from whom we got the term shaman), such as the Chuckchee. The shaman is recognized as peculiar and psychologically unbalanced (as well as valuable to the tribe), and the "abnormality" may or may not be focused on his/her homosexuality (Bogaras 1904–09; Ducey 1976).

In some societies, it is reported that the role is *not* accompanied by homosexual practice. For example, the Bala tribe of the Congo (Merriam 1971), where male incumbents of this role deny that they have homosexual relations with other men (they are accused of it) and are heterosexually married to women. The female counterpart is not even transvestite, only avoids women's work, and is definitely not homosexual. Comparable cross-gender identity roles for both males and females who are definitely not homosexual are reported for the Mangaians of Polynesia (Marshall 1971).

The normative attitude toward the homosexual transvestite in the institutionalized berdache-like role is far from acceptance of this as simply some casual "normal" variant, and certainly not outright approval. The attitude is more complex. True, they are more accepting toward such homosexuals than most people in our society are toward gays in our midst. Still, they evidence feelings of discomfort and incongruity, often expressed by sniggering embarrassment and ridicule behind the transvestite's back. For the Mohave Devereux notes: "When ridiculing a transvestite, the Mohave refer to a transvestite's anatomical sex; otherwise . . . to his adopted sex" (Devereux 1961:517, fn.). The discrepancy indicates the dual attitude. Note also there *is* ridicule and people's awareness of the incongruity. Another instance for the Mohave: if a woman has been abducted from her husband by another man, it was customary for the aggrieved husband to paint his face black like a warrior on the warpath and, armed, set out to take revenge on the culprit. Devereux mentions "One man, married to a passive male homosexual who deserted him, actually attempted this [i.e., the warpaint, etc.] just to give the tribe's reactions are far from unambivalent acceptance of such "marriages" as "normal."

Teasing and ridicule accorded the "husband" of such a transvestite male (who, however, is not considered homosexual) also indicates that the tribe's reactions are far from unambivalent acceptance of such "marriages" as "normal."

The potential candidate for the berdache role, identified by interpretation of a significant dream around puberty, may in fact fear and resist such role assignment, even going so far as to choose suicide rather than adopt the role (Lowie 1924). Some Chuckchee men "fear being supernaturally changed into transvestite-shamans even though the procedure might enhance their social standing" (Ford and Beach 1953:131, drawing on Bogaras 1907). Why such dread if the status is so good, or the role so "normal"? Similarly, the transvestite male "wife" in the Lango tribe of Uganda is believed to be "impotent" and "supernaturally afflicted" (Ford and Beach 1953:131). "Afflicted" does not suggest positive "normality."

Devereux sees the institutionalization of the transvestite role in cases like the Mohave as a *marginal* implementation of impulses which are both ego-dystonic and culture-dystonic, constituting in effect a kind of ex post facto sanctioning of the inevitable. A key word in that phrase is "marginal": the role adopted is not part of the central institutionalizations of the society.

The Mohave also took a very negative view of exclusive homosexuality in any individual other than the occupant of the institutionalized role. To call any non-transvestite grown person a homosexual was a fiercely resented insult. This is a tribe with a very free-for-all kind of heterosexual activity and much juvenile sexual experimentation, which could include homosexual contacts that were dismissed as juvenile fun or naughtiness rather than as harbingers of adult homosexuality.

The future male homosexual transvestite, however, was something else again. He was usually "different" and "strange" from early childhood, giving signs of cross-sex gender identification usually before the age of ten. The condition was thought to be inborn and unfortunate, but because inborn, the individual could not help it, nor be blamed. The boy was then put through the *alyha* initiation ceremony. If he did dance to the sacred transvestite-initiation ceremony songs performed by a special ceremonial singer, he confirmed the supernaturally destined designation. If he did not dance, he was not an *alyha*, and the family was *relieved*. Typically the family was not proud to have an *alyha* in the family. Like everyone else, they considered transvestites at least somewhat crazy. All this in spite of the institutionalization (and in that sense social acceptance) of the role. All still respond to the incongruity of an anatomical male being a "woman," and for the female being a "man." The response is discomfort but a certain compassionate acceptance; it was supernaturally ordained. This spares the incumbent much of the torment, guilt, self-contempt, and the like that plague many homosexuals in our society. But to claim they regard homosexuality as "normal and acceptable" is a distortion. And only the transvestite is tolerated in exclusive homosexuality.

The spouse of such a transvestite was not labeled a "homosexual," but was subjected to ridicule. Such a person was not usually exclusively homosexual. Devereux refers to men who married a transvestite "as persons who (evidently) had bisexual tendencies, did not go through any formal initiation, and were not designated by any special name" (Devereux 1937). Such a marriage might be a temporary practical and domestic convenience, or a temporary retreat from the demands of heterosexuality, and neither this nor a few homosexual acts in a prevalently heterosexual history got a man a homosexual label. Such a marriage might coexist with heterosexual marriage(s) where, as in Mohave and many other tribes, polygyny is permitted. It produced no crisis of heterosexual identity for the man involved.

The transvestite, by contrast, went through a comprehensive sex role reversal. The male dressed and acted like a woman, learned feminine skills (often outdoing women at them); simulated menstruation, pregnancy, and childbirth (then reporting the baby born dead); took the "feminine" role in sodomy; observed all the proper feminine taboos (Devereux 1937, for the Mohave; this was similar for the berdache in many other Amerindian tribes).

The berdache type of institution thus provides one type of partial acceptance of homosexuality for a small minority of designated individuals. It did not indicate that homosexual practices were widespread, and certainly not that they were accepted as "normal." Partners of transvestites were subject to some ridicule, but were not considered "homosexual" (on the basis of otherwise predominantly heterosexual history), and any non-transvestite exclusive homosexual was strongly condemned. It was a compassionate and humane, but not unambivalent, way of handling deviance and incongruity.

Another type of partial tolerance and acceptance is found in those societies where all or most of the males during adolescence engage in homosexual relations, then later marry, heterosexually, while continuing to have homosexual relations as well. The most likely pattern in these cases is that adolescents play the recipient part in sodomy with an older male partner; later in their lives, these males switch to the insertor role with younger male partners. In these cases, adult male homosexual acts are rare or unknown and may be strongly condemned, and usually any *exclusive* homosexuality in the male is *strongly* disapproved.

Societies having such a pattern include the Siwans of Libya (Cline 1936), the Marind-Anim (Mead 1949), the Koraki of New Guinea (Ford and Beach 1953), the Aranda and the Nambuti of Australia (Strehlow 1915, Róheim 1945 and elsewhere). Siwa mature males take each other's adolescent sons as lovers. Later the boys are expected to marry, heterosexually, and also take a younger male as a homosexual partner. Exclusive homosexuality is, however, evidently rare and is condemned.

In the Keraki of New Guinea, bachelors universally practice sodomy. In the puberty rites each boy is initiated into anal intercourse by the older males. After his first year of playing the recipient role, he spends the rest of his bachelorhood sodomizing the newly initiated. "Though fully sanctioned by the males, these initiatory practices are supposed to be kept secret from the women" (Ford and Beach 1953:132). The secrecy suggests a recognition that the sodomy expresses hostility toward women. (Secrecy from women is typical in male puberty ceremonies. In some tribes, aboriginally, a woman could be executed for even accidentally witnessing part of such male ceremonies. Such secrecy has been interpreted by Bettelheim (1954) as indicating unconscious recognition that the ceremonies "don't work," i.e., fail in their symbolic goal of proving men just as good as women in creating new life (see Endleman 1967, ch. 4). Such secrecy and implied guilt and hostility belie the notion (dear to homophile ideologists) that such practices show homosexuality as part of a "normal," "psychologically healthy" pattern.

Some other tribes have been reported as having a pattern of partial acceptance, involving tolerance of homosexual relations between non-adult unmarried male peers, and between grown men and prepubescent boys (age seven to eleven), but definite disapproval and deviance labeling to any other male homosexual acts, particularly between two adult males. Davenport (1965) reports this pattern for a Melanesian tribe. There, exclusive adult male homosexuality is considered unthinkable. This is in a context where the norms are puritanically restrictive against heterosexual relations before or outside of marriage. And again we note here, as elsewhere, exclusive homosexuality is condemned. Most of the males were bisexual in practice (in the pattern indicated), some exclusively heterosexual after marriage, and none (at least by their own admission) exclusively homosexual. Nearly all claimed to prefer heterosexual to homosexual coitus.

In another case, the Cubeo, Opler (1965) reports adolescent homosexual activity and other occasional homosexual experimentation not being negatively sanctioned, for males. However, persistent or exclusive homosexuality was absent and definitely condemned.

What about female homosexuality in tribal societies? As usual, and as for other societies, our information for the females is much more sparse than for the males. Reports of female homosexuality are far less frequent than for male. This may reflect the predominance of male anthropologists (earlier), but we have had many competent women anthropologists in the field for at least two generations now. Ford and Beach noted that in other societies, as in ours, female homosexuality is typically accorded less attention than male. Ford and Beach were able to locate only 17 societies with such information. We can add two others to their list: the Tchambuli as reported by Mead (1935, 1949) and the Mohave. Some of these 19 tribes have institutionalized transvestite-homosexual roles for women as well as men (e.g., the Mohave, see above). The Tchambuli women have homosexual play while masked for ceremonials on festive occasions. On other ceremonial occasions, where older males wear "male" masks and younger males wear "female" masks, women pay court to young men; Mead notes the double-entendre: women courting males disguised as females.

That homosexual practices may be associated with difficulties in heterosexual relationships is indicated by the Dahomeans of West Africa and the Haitians. The Dahomeans believe common homosexual practices of the women cause frigidity in (heterosexual) marriage. The Haitians reverse this: a woman frigid with her husband seeks another woman (Ford and Beach 1953:133).

Females playing an institutionalized transvestite role, as in the Mohave, evoke a mixture of partial acceptance along with tension, fear, discomfort, and anxiety.

Thus, the cross-cultural data available both on the existence and prevalence of homosexual practices, and on normative attitudes toward homosexuality in tribal societies, offers only partial support for some aspects of gay liberation rhetoric, and none on other aspects. The data do indicate that some forms of homosexual behavior between men or between women do appear in many other socieites, and we cannot say with confidence that they are entirely absent in any. Thus, there is support for the proposition that homosexual behavior, and certainly homosexual emotional response, is part of the basic pan-human potentiality of human beings.

The extent of such practices can vary enormously from one society to another, from zero or near zero in some, to other cases where it may involve close to or actually 100 percent of the population (at least of males) of a particular age category. Exclusive homosexuality is rarer in tribal than in complex societies (Gebhard 1971:215). Normatively there is also great variation; but universally we can say that nowhere is exclusive homosexuality in either sex given unqualified approval or regarded as normatively on a par (in that sense "normal") with heterosexuality. It may be given a specialized exemption for a small minority in an institutionalized role, such as the berdache, which may be available for a few men, or a few men and a few women, in the society, but even there it is regarded with mixed feelings, including at least embarrassment, incongruity, or ridicule, and often fear, anxiety, and some hostility. In a few societies, homosexual practices may be allowed alongside of heterosexual, or in a life stage preliminary to the assumption of full adult heterosexuality, and then only in certain age-status combinations, while condemned if the primary or exclusive practice of a mature adult. Such allowances typically permit an equation of immature males with females as the objects of "active" practice by "masculine" adult males. Female homosexuality is either rarer in practice or simply accorded less notice or attention.

Complex Societies

What about cross-cultural evidence from more complex societies? Gay rights supporters are fond of pointing to other highly civilized societies where, they allege, homosexuality was normal and universal or at least prevalent, showing up our culture as puritanically restrictive and bigoted, with again the argument that therefore it is our culture, not the homosexuals, that should be regarded as pathological. Ancient Athens of Plato's time is the favorite case. Plato extolled an army consisting of numbers of paired lovers. And the sexual bond between mature male lover and young boy or adolescent was, it is said, ennobling, educational, and fostering of manly virtue. How does a psychoanalytic social science deal with these allegations?

Such practices did indeed exist, and they are indeed celebrated in Plato, reflecting the views of Socrates and his circle of elite intellectuals and their followers. Such homosexuality, however, was probably limited to only the highest class of men. It also was rarely exclusive homosexuality, all of the adult men being expected to marry and have an active heterosexual life. According to Vanggaard (1972) it was not associated with effeminacy or a style one can find in exclusive or near-exclusive homosexuals in modern society. It was always a relationship between a mature man and a young boy or youth, never between age-mates, and certainly not between two adult men. Permissiveness toward male homosexual relations also never extended to exclusive homosexuality. The value, even honor, accorded the man-boy relations by Socrates and his circle was, according to many commentators, definitely limited to that small coterie of the leisured elite who had time and freedom to pursue philosophical discourse and sophisticated sexual pursuits.

This was evidently a minority viewpoint. Karlen (1971;36ff.) suggests this positive view was certainly not shared by the populace at large. He contends that a more reliable guide to general opinion toward male homosexuality in Athens at the time should be sought in the plays of Aristophanes, who wrote for a mass audience. "His withering satire of pederasts, effeminates, and secret homosexuals probably represents common Greek opinion far more than Plato's *Symposium* does. . . . *Lysistrata* hardly suggests homosexuality or even bisexuality was universal in Athens" (Karlen, p. 36). Elsewhere, also in Greek literature, we find prevalent mockery and denunciation of homosexuality. To society at large, Karlen maintains, it was considered a deviation. Also, mistrust and hostility between the sexes, with downgrading of women, is an important part of the *background* of male homosexuality (not necessarily its explanation) in ancient Greece, as in many other societies. "To the bisexual Greek [man], women and boys were both 'the ones who are fucked,' submissive non-males.

Many non-Western societies have similar attitudes, and behavior patterns, and one finds this in slightly diluted form in much of the Mediterranean world today. A man can have boys as well as women without his masculinity being questioned by himself or others, as long as he takes the dominant role. . . . Such a sexual-dominance pattern [shows] psychic sadism, and can hardly be called a sign of untrammeled naturalness or psychosexual health" (Karlen, p. 34). The rationale that, as practiced by mature men with boys or young men, it was a civilizing force has been questioned by some more skeptical commentators as a cover for predominantly sensual objectives.

But, the gay apologists argue, there were other complex societies besides ancient Athens where homosexuality was associated with great cultural achievements. For example, the European Renaissance. Many of its greatest artists and thinkers were allegedly homosexual or bisexual: Leonardo da Vinci, Michelangelo, Aretino, Cellini, and many others. And for the England of Elizabeth I, both of its greatest dramatists, Shakespeare and Marlowe, have been claimed for this camp. And if so, gay rhetoric argues, how can one still argue homosexuality is inevitably a pathology?

These are understandable homosexual apologetics, a comfort for homosexuals agonizing under latter-day societal stigma. The factual evidence for all these allegations, however, is questionable. Karlen (1971) is again a reasonable guide, having rather thoroughly tracked down the evidence for each of these allegations. He finds the evidence scanty, or at least equivocal, for all of them. Leonardo and Michelangelo, he concludes, were mostly sexually inactive. Only one important Italian painter of the Renaissance was surely homosexual, Giovanni Bazzi, popularly known as "Sodoma" (Karlen, p. 109). Aretino was preferentially heterosexual, though he did pursue boys on occasion. Cellini was *accused* by enemies of homosexuality, and denied it. Karlen finds no evidence for it. The accusation also indicates that the *norms* for the place and period were definitely anti-homosexual. Shakespeare? A consideration of the by now vast literature on this topic led Karlen to conclude: "not proven." The internal evidence of the plays shows dominant heterosexual preoccupation, and "direct references to homosexuality [therein] shows pitying scorn . . . also it is far from certain that the sonnets [allegedly addressed to a young *man*] are autobiographical" (Karlen, p. 119).

Similarly, A. L. Rowse (1963), one of the foremost present-day scholars of Elizabethan England, concludes that the whole corpus of evidence clearly indicates that Shakespeare was *not* homosexual, that he had a strong intense love of and appreciation of women. Rowse also concludes that the claim that the love sonnets were in fact addressed to a young *man* is erroneous; rather Shakespeare had an entirely platonic liking and admiration for his young male noble patron (a relationship not uncommon in that culture), but no sexual interest in him. Rowse claims that those alleging Shakespeare's homosexuality are ignorant of the relevant scholarship, or they, like Oscar Wilde, have a vested interest in claiming Shakespeare for their own. Karlen similarly decimates the case for Marlowe's "homosexuality."

Karlen summarizes his consideration of the Renaissance as follows:

> The ideal of the bisexual creative man of the Renaissance collapses even more foolishly than that of the happily homoerotic philosopher of ancient Greece. In France and England, as in Italy, the number of homosexuals among artists and intellectuals was, if anything, smaller than one would expect at that level of society; the inclusion of borderline or doubtful cases hardly changes the picture. Though we have no idea of the exact number or percentage of deviants, homosexuality was not an extreme rarity, and

permissiveness, experimentation, and possibly sexual kinks were increasingly common among the noble and wealthy, in cities and courts, from the later Middle Ages through the Renaissance. What needs understanding is not homosexuality among creative men of the time, but its relative absence, and the insistence during the past century on reversing the balance of historical evidence. To the law, the church, and society at large, homosexuality remained a ghastly breach of the social order—as did heterosexual sodomy. (Karlen, p. 120)

The import of Karlen's discussion leads in two partially contradictory directions. One, he contradicts gay polemic statements alleging the association of homosexuality with great artists and writers. Two, at the same time, he acknowledges that in courtly circles (with which great artists tended to be associated) homosexuality or bisexuality was not entirely uncommon (its exact prevalence undeterminable) and was regarded with an openness and tolerance quite different from the prevailing views of the law, the church, and the public at large. The situation would be comparable to the dilemmas that would face some historian of the future in assessing the prevalence of and attitudes toward homosexuality in late twentieth-century America, if he had available only statements of the Gay Activists Alliance, or only those of Anita Bryant and her supporters.

And just as gay apologists like to count creative giants like Shakespeare and Leonardo as part of their company, so do they revel in pointing out the whole roster of recent and contemporary writers, artists, playwrights, who are or were homosexual or bisexual, citing, among others, Oscar Wilde, André Gide, Verlaine, Auden, Whitman, Maugham, Virginia Woolf, Tennessee Williams, Edward Albee, Jean Genet, Truman Capote. While verifiable, these lists in themselves do not tell us anything. Considerably longer and equally impressive lists can be drawn up of writers, artists, etc., who were or are heterosexual.[3]

But what we would need to know is what percentage of the total homosexual population such creative geniuses or major talents constitute, and correspondingly for the heterosexuals, what percentage of the total heterosexual population do they constitute. No doubt for every Genet or Capote there are thousands of gay busboys, street hustlers, stevedores, office clerks, Bloomingdale's salesmen, and so on, through the whole roster of occupations. But since we have no way of knowing with any assurance what the total adult homosexual population is (and unless it became entirely safe for everyone who is to be open about it, which is unlikely, probably we will never know), it's impossible to make the computations, even if we could find agreement among scorers on whom to include among the "creative geniuses," and could reliably say which ones are homosexual.

It has sometimes been argued that the special marginality of homosexuals in modern society may give them special sensitivity and insight into the human condition, as suggested by Benjamin De Mott in the first issue of *New American Review* (1967). This argument would work on the analogy of the highly disproportionate number of intellectuals and creative writers, artists, and scientists among the Jews, who have also been marginal in most modern societies. But one would have to wonder whether marginality is the key element here. In the case of the Jews, there have been a number of other crucial prerequisite conditions, such as millenia-long traditions of literacy, reverence for book learning, religious ideology of "chosenness," peculiar occupational distribution in the diaspora, etc., etc. Chinese in *their* diaspora, also a marginal trading people, do not have a similar record. Nor do most other ethnic or racial groups who have been victimized or marginalized in some way. Nor do such marginal categories as criminals, prostitutes, drug addicts, or the psychotically pathological. Probably the sexual preference of homosexuals, as well as in some instances particular qualities in the *style* of the gay subculture (e.g., "camp"), affect the *content* of a creative genius's work—much as a creative genius who has had a bout with schizophrenia can use that in the *content* of her poetry—but in neither case does this demonstrate that either homosexuality or psychosis is intrinsically connected with creative genius.

The need of the gay movement to make such connections itself needs to be analyzed sociologically and dynamically, as part of the ideological mythologies of the movement.

Probably, historically, both the prevalence of homosexual or bisexual practice and normative responses toward it have waxed and waned and shifted from one period or place to another. Reactions have rarely included positive acceptance (a "live-and-let-live" tolerance, at most, in more sophisticated circles) and frequently it was ferocious denunciation, with extreme legal penalties, even to the extent of capital punishment. Moralists, religious spokesmen, and the law have been more commonly strongly negative than otherwise, and their legacies are still with us in prevailing legal, religious, and social responses toward homosexuality. Incidence seems to have been larger in courts and sophisticated circles in cities, but that could be an impression produced by the fact that more has been written about these parts of society. Moralists have periodically inveighed against this "vice" having been brought into their presumably previously pure populace by vice-ridden foreign invaders or influences, the Normans infecting the Anglo-Saxons, etc., in typical xenophobic fashion.

For historical periods, we have nothing at all resembling reliable evidence. As Karlen comments: "For at least three thousand years Westerners have been claiming that there is more sex and more homosexuality than in the past. Obviously most of them have been wrong" (Karlen 1971:453). Even for our own society the evidence is fragmentary, the nearest thing to a scientifically based estimate being the results of the Kinsey studies of the late 1940s and early 1950s, showing a (white) male figure of about 4 percent exclusively homosexual and a corresponding female figure of at or less than 1 percent (Kinsey et al. 1948, 1953). We can only guess for historical societies, but it seems unlikely that it was any less rare in fifteenth-century Florence or Elizabethan England. And for homosexual experience alongside of heterosexual in the same individual, we have no good reason for believing it was any more or less prevalent in those contexts than in San Francisco or London or Paris or Rome today.

Summary of the Cross-cultural and Trans-historical Evidence

To round out the cross-cultural and trans-historical survey: the findings give us good reason to believe that overt homosexual behavior is a pan-human potentiality for persons of both sexes. Whether it will, in fact, be expressed overtly will probably depend on a whole complex of sociological and psychological factors, the full details of which we are not yet in a position to delineate completely. For more complex societies, it does seem to be associated with greater urbanism and greater leisure. But that would not account for its appearance, with some frequency, in tribal societies that are not at all urban and not particularly leisured.

For complex civilizations, some observers see it associated with a stage past the peak of that civilization, a stage of incipient or evident decay. (This may only reflect moralistic bias: "if this horrible activity is going on, civilization must be falling apart.") Some observers associate male homosexuality with high levels of militarism, as in ancient Rome and modern Germany, or as an alternative in warrior tribes like the Plains Indians, but other militaristic societies were not famous (or notorious) for this, and many non-militaristic societies are. Prevalence varies from a rarely reported zero, to very high figures (reaching toward 100 percent) for a life-stage-specific homosexuality within a broader life pattern of heterosexuality—and that only for the males, without, to my knowledge, comparable institutions for females that apply to the whole population of that sex.

Similarly normative responses vary greatly. But nowhere do we find exclusive homosexuality, in either sex, given unambiguous approval or even acceptance, except for a very small minority in a sacredly sanctioned institutionalized role, and even there it is reacted to with a mixture of embarrassment, anxiety, fear, and tolerance. The Keraki and the Siwa are unusual in their acceptance of nearly universal adolescent and later man-boy homosexuality, within the usual male heterosexual career, and have no corresponding relations for females. We know a lot less generally about female homosexuality which, however, as far as we know, seems generally to be less severely stigmatized than male, probably on the basis of the widespread belief that females do not count as much anyhow, and as already castrated beings, cannot be further castrated by homosexual behavior; and that such activity on their part is not intrinsically antagonistic to their reproductive and maternal roles, nor to their sexual availability to males.

There are considerable variations on the matter of whether or not there is a distinct homosexual role, for men, or for women, or for both. Where there is, for men, it may be the institutionalized one or refer only to *exclusive* homosexuality. In many societies, the adult male who fucks boys or youths *as well as* women does not have his masculinity impugned. This is evidently true in much of the Mediterranean world as well as in such Far Eastern countries as Japan and Korea, where unsystematic reports refer to much recreational sex between adult men and boys or youths, alongside of an extensive heterosexual life. Whether there is as much *exclusive* male homosexuality in those countries as in the present-day United States we have no way of knowing. But considering the greater leniency of both law and custom toward such occasional non-exclusive contacts, one would expect not. It would appear that *probably* the greater association of homosexual practice with psychopathology in the United States and other parts of the West, and greater likelihood here of polarization and either-or thinking—that is, both straights and gays insisting that you must be entirely one or the other—would make exclusive homosexuality, in males at least, more prevalent here. That is speculation, of course.

There have been ample records, too, in countless modern societies of much *situational* homosexual behavior of males in all-male groups isolated from females, as in the prisons mentioned before, as well as in the military, in one-sex boarding schools (England the notorious case), as well as in certain occupations that isolate groups of men for extended periods from women, e.g., in logging camps, isolated mining locations, cowboys in the "Wild West," etc. Freud long ago recognized this kind of homosexual behavior as a distinct variety, not to be confused with homosexual behavior by choice where the alternative is available. (True, some participants may be acting from deeper dynamic impulsions, and some may have sought the all-male-group situation to facilitate such possibilities. Rates and persistence of such behavior are, however, matters of speculation. We know of no systematic data. There is some on prisons, however.)

We know practically nothing of the psychodynamics or the developmental etiology of homosexual configurations in other societies; for historical ones we can only guess where some adequate biographical data are available (which is rare, in any case), and for tribal ones, next to nothing, since psychoanalytically qualified anthropologists (rare also) have not as yet given us analyses in detail of homosexual members of tribal societies, nor systematic comparisons of them with heterosexual compatriots. Given certain pan-human universals of infancy and relations of the infant and child to crucial adults of both sexes, as well as what we know can be universally applied to psychodynamic developmental questions about all human beings in all societies, it does seem unlikely that the processes leading to the development of this deviation would be significantly different in other societies than we know them to be in our own society. This we believe would be true even though the processes of deviance-definition and responses to it could be significantly different in different socio-cultural settings, as, for example, where the husband of the berdache is not considered homosexual.

CHAPTER FOURTEEN

Homosexuality As a Political Issue

THE POLITICALIZATION OF HOMOSEXUALITY

Whenever social scientists or psychoanalysts demonstrate the untenability of particular arguments in gay political polemic the response from many gay politicos is that we are being reactionary and supporting the legal, religious, and social oppression of homosexuals, that we are favoring their deprivation of basic civic rights in jobs, housing, and public accommodations. This accusation has frequently been sufficiently powerful in provoking (evidently) guilt reactions in social and psychological scientists to the point where they tailor their statements on homosexuality to avoid offending that minority. Such "enlightenment" temporizing is, of course, pernicious to truth and ultimately to justice.

Homosexuals by now have entered the mainstream of minority group political-social struggles that have characterized the later part of the twentieth century in America, in other Western countries, and in many other parts of the world. These struggles call out for sociological and psychodynamic analyses, and that is the task of psychoanalytic sociology. Efforts to tell the truth clearly and unabashedly will inevitably offend some listeners or readers (as the reception of Freud's naturalistic explorations into the psychic underworld of sex clearly demonstrated). To be deterred by others' taking such offense would disable us from ever understanding anything clearly and well.

One can support, as most social scientists and psychoanalysts do, homosexuals' being accorded equal treatment before the law, in economic life, in housing, in public accommodations, and the rest, without endorsing every piece of homosexual apologetics.

Homosexuals do suffer many injustices and discriminations in modern society solely on the basis of their sexual orientation, as earlier discussed, in employment, in dealings with the police, in housing, in the church, in the military, in exposure to blackmail and extortion, and the rest. They do have grounds for seeing themselves as another oppressed minority group. And the militants among them are fighting back.

There is no question but that there is strong anti-homosexual bias in this society. Just how strong it is, how variable by different categories of people, how it is translated into actual action against homosexuals or indifference to their rights, are matters of debate, and we do not have recent hard data to document. Backlash movements like Anita Bryant's and others attempt to overthrow gay rights bills that have already passed in some localities or to thwart their passage in others. ("Liberal" New York City has a council that has fought off such a bill many times in the past decade.) How much the civil-rights gains that homosexuals *have* made in the past decade of "gay-liberation" political struggle have, in fact, provoked the "backlash" of conservative anti-homosexual action, is hard to gauge.

Teachers still get fired if they publicly proclaim themselves and fight for gay rights. Many partially sympathetic non-gays say, okay, we realize there already are many gay teachers, and we won't object as long as they are quiet about it; but asking us to go ahead and knowingly hire a publicly self-proclaiming homosexual, that's too much. A heterosexual, calling in on the audience call-in portion of a public television program on the problems of gays "coming out" in their work situations, said he did not *want* to know about his co-workers' private sex life. He evidently did not want to be burdened with gays making public proclamations of their homosexuality at his workplace. The gays on the program said gays should not be forced to be secret about their homosexuality just to satisfy the sensibilities of that kind of straight colleague (WNET Channel 13, New York, October 10, 1978, program called *Gays at Work*).

The ambiguity of the current situation is also demonstrated by the fact that even in that part of the population usually more "liberal" on most social issues—supporters of civil liberties, of opportunities for racial/ethnic minorities and women, and the like—what they say in public may be quite different from views they express in more private situations. For example, a neither concealing nor self-proclaiming homosexual college dean is vilified as a "fag" behind his back by "liberal" faculty members. On another campus, sophisticated cosmopolitan faculty, ACLU supporters, would privately attack a factional antagonist on the (irrelevant) ground of his homosexuality. Situations like this can be multiplied indefinitely. Homosexuals "in the closet" overhear comments like these repeatedly. If it occurs at their place of work, most are hesitant to say anything about it, let alone to "come out" and declare themselves, fearing (probably justifiably) to lose their jobs, or at least damage their chances for fair treatment at work.

Some sociological studies have attempted to get more systematic data on public attitudes toward homosexuals. Simmons (1965) asked 180 respondents to name "deviants"; homosexuals were the most frequently mentioned. Terms applied to homosexuals were "sexually abnormal," "perverted," "mentally ill," "maladjusted," and "effiminate" (in rank order). These do not suggest positive acceptance. A CBS poll, in 1966, found a third of the public considered homosexuality detrimental to society, and ranked homosexuality third on a list of sex-related "social threats" (Drum, 1967). Public response to a Harris poll in 1965: 82 percent of the males and 58 percent of the females ranked homosexuals third (behind communists and atheists) as "most harmful to the nation" (Washington Post, 1965). In 1969, 63 percent on another Harris poll said homosexuals were harmful to American life (Time, 1969). In the CBS poll, less than 20 percent favored legalizing private consensual homosexual acts. Majorities both formulated the "badness" of homosexuality mainly as "sickness" and supported its being punished by the law. By contrast, however, Hacker (1971) claimed that other studies as well as her own informal interviewing showed rather more acceptance. She cites a study by Kitsuse (1962), which found that in a group of 700 undergraduates, a "live and let live" feeling toward homosexuals was fairly common, and even negative reactions were fairly mild and far from homogeneous. The combination of this set of variable findings suggests a situation of some degree of normative complexity. The variability and unpredictability itself may make the situation even more tense for the homosexual torn between wishes to reveal and the need to conceal (Hacker 1971:84).

It is possible, of course, that all of these findings are somewhat out of date. Still, when one looks at backlash reactions evident in recent years, we can doubt it. We can also consider that the underlying dynamics of anti-homosexual feeling are unlikely to have changed substantially, since they operate intrapsychically and are not fully dependent on particular social-structural conditions.

There is reason to believe anti-homosexual feelings are concentrated more on male homosexuality than on female homosexuality. It is also probable that among the heterosexuals males have more such feelings than females, as suggested by the Harris poll finding of 82 percent of the males, and only 58 percent of the females ranking homosexuals harmful (see above). (There is also the otherwise curious fact that while some men are sexually aroused by the fact or fantasy of two women making love to each other, women are not titillated by a parallel male homosexual scene. Also porno films aimed at a presumably heterosexual audience may include two women in sexual acts, but never two men.)

The dynamics we posit are these: female-female sex does not preclude women functioning as lovers of men, or at least passive sexual objects of men, as wives, as childbearers, and child rearers. Male indifference to the female, or antagonism to her (implied in much male homosexuality), is by contrast, perceived as more of a threat to reproductive continuity of the group. Margaret Mead writes, "The worry that boys will not grow up to be men is much more widespread than that girls will not grow up to be women" (Mead 1949:123). The male has to actively *do* something to function in heterosexual intercourse. His sense of sexual identity and adequacy is probably more fragile than is the female's. Therefore, the very presence of males who demonstrate what can be considered a voluntarily castrated state is threatening to other males. They arouse strong castration anxiety. Then, you are likely to have incidents where gangs of "tough" young males beat up "fags" with baseball bats.

It is doubtful any amount of rationally enlightened improvement in conscious public support for gay "civil rights" will change substantially the basic problem of castration anxiety that is central to anti-homosexual biases. If even in tribes with an institutionalized homosexual role, there is still touchiness and anxiety in reaction to it, we cannot easily expect a widespread, open, "live-and-let-live" attitude toward homosexuals in a society like ours with no institutionalized role. Correspondingly, lack of structural and cultural support for gay "marriages" will probably continue to make such relationships fragile and unstable and encourage the continuation of prevalent promiscuity. All of this more for the males than the females, for reasons already discussed.

Anxiety-ridden imagery about homosexuality portrays it as something like a contagious disease. It is assumed that impressionable young adults will "catch it" if exposed to homosexual "role models." Alternatively, or along with such imagery, is the imagery of seduction: it will appear so seductively attractive to otherwise heading-for-heterosexuality youth that they will turn that way. Some deep inner vulnerability to this will lead weak youth to be magically entranced in that corrupt direction. The imagery has similarities to notions of "dope fiends" (who can hook your kids on drugs) and "sex fiends," or pied-piper type hippies luring your children into antinomian chaos. (Interestingly, closeted gays, who lead culturally very conventional lives, find the more "freaky" types marching in "gay liberation" demonstrations offensive, and off-putting, much as bourgeois blacks are embarrassed by "niggers.")

Challenges to well- and painfully learned gender categories are also unsettling, producing anxiety, with one response being aggression, directed at the conveniently labeled outgroup. And just as any creativity that draws on the individual's capacity to empathize with many kinds of others, including those of the opposite sex, can be unsettling to those with more limited gender-role repertoire, so it can be even more unsettling if explicitly linked with homosexual propensities. There is the danger in those hidden recesses of oneself that might be unleashed by the mere presence of sexually ambiguous others in one's midst. And if these dangerous sexually ambiguous beings are in positions of trust in relation to one's children (like teachers in the schools or religious clergy), then the anxiety and hence the reactive hatred may become intense.

Similarly, policemen fear an openly gay fellow officer as a source of intolerable sexual tension in the close male-to-male contact of partnership in a squad car and a disturbing element in the macho buddiness of the locker room. Here, as in many areas now, the message is: okay, we know there are gays in our work, but keep quiet about it, so we don't have to face it. Similarly, the military is unlikely to move toward Plato's conception. And if even supposedly sophisticated, culturally advanced intellectuals engage in fag-baiting in private conversation, what does one expect of more "ordinary" folk at far less "liberal" points in the political spectrum? Gay liberation efforts to convince more homosexuals to "come out of the closet" may well be ill-advised, in the sense that such acts may intensify anxieties of the anti-homosexual straights and contribute to backlash.

The fears of the anti-homosexuals are, of course, largely irrational, but sexuality is hardly a topic to induce purely rational responses from anyone. In this respect, the homophile movement's fondness for referring to their sexual preference as a "life-style," is either foolish or disingenuous or both. For this is not parallel to a taste for health foods, or dyeing one's hair, or yoga, or snowmobiling, any of which is easily accommodatable in the mosaic of a culturally pluralistic society. To anti-homosexuals this is a sin that should be treated by law as a crime, an unacceptable violation of emotionally held *mores*, an affront to public decency, and the like. To the deeply anti-homosexual, the taboos being broken by people who do this are deeply sacred, and the sexual preference does not appear as simply a casual variation. (In any case use of the term "life-style" is further misleading in suggesting that the sexual preference is the prime defining characteristic of the person, and everything else about one's pattern of living, where it is open to choice at all, flows from that fact, an implication many homosexuals reject. The implication is also, interestingly, parallel to the assumption of anti-gay heterosexuals that a person's homosexuality is *the* defining statement about that person. Gays here mimic the stereotyping of their oppressors. Identification with the aggressor is prominent here.)

Gay liberation rhetoric, in response, contains a mélange of reasonable propositions and counter-mythology. Among the reasonable statements are the following: Homosexuals are found in all walks of life, at all class levels, in all kinds of occupations—stevedores and football players as well as limp-wristed florists and decorators. Similarly, homosexual males are not all soft epicenes. Gay males come in the whole spectrum of body types and appearance, as do lesbians. Only a small minority fit the stereotype of the effeminate male or the masculinized female. Cases of homosexual teachers molesting a student are extremely rare and nowhere in the league with the number of cases of heterosexual male teachers molesting or propositioning a female student. Gay cops or firemen do not go around making passes at their straight work-colleagues, and certainly are unlikely to try to "convert" any unwilling other party. Gays generally do not proselytize; persons not already inclined are unlikely converts in any case.

GAY LIBERATION MYTHOLOGIES

Alongside such more reasonable and documentable statements, gay-liberationist rhetoric also includes a host of ideological mythologies, parallel in many ways to the mythologies of the anti-homosexual world. Many of these statements are distortions or partial distortions, others entirely non-demonstrable. One is the notion of homosexuality as simply some incidental normal variant of sexuality, worthy of no more note than hair color or taste in food. Another is the allegation that it has nothing to do with psychic sickness in any way, discussed at length earlier. A variation on this is that if some homosexuals are troubled, depressed, or otherwise psychologically disturbed, it is entirely the product of oppression by a hostile society.[1]

Correspondingly, liberation rhetoric alleges, efforts to "cure" are not only futile and pointless, but also probably pernicious attacks on the

individual's autonomy to choose his own sexual style and are thus instruments of social control over stigmatized deviants, rather than the
"helping" measures they claim to be. Gays should not even be encouraged in any wish they may have to change in the heterosexual direction,
but rather should be persuaded of the truth that the problem is society's,
not their personal "sickness." Psychoanalytic probing into the "causes"
of a person's homosexuality is irrelevant and unimportant.

One version of this argument is that no one can ever find out what
"causes" homosexuality; it is mysterious and can be different for different
persons; the question is unanswerable, but in any case the wrong question; the problem is society, not you. Another version on this is simply
that one was born that way. (A statement flatly disproved by all psychoanalytic studies. This one lets the individual completely off the hook,
re personal responsibility and any possible guilt. However, many, while
believing this, feel guilty about their homosexuality just the same.) The
"born that way" argument is similar to the belief of the tribalists that the
future berdache was supernaturally predestined to be that way: there is
no personal choice involved, therefore no responsibility. This avoids a
lot of self-recrimination and self-hatred, feelings common in American
and other modern society homosexuals.

Gays are just as good, the rhetoric says, just as moral, as productive,
as virtuous, kind, loving, etc., as anyone else. In fact homosexuals number in their ranks many of the greatest creative geniuses of all time.
Homosexuals have a finer sensitivity to cultural aspects of life, and are
more sensitive generally to social and cultural nuances (and absurdities)
because of living their lives (often secretly) in a hostile society. Thus,
homosexuals are not only just as good as straights, but even better in
many ways. "Gay is good" is shouted in public demonstrations. (The
need to do so reveals how hard it is to convince the shouters, as well
as anyone else, of this "truth." No one has to shout "straight is good"
in the streets.)

It is not the gays but the hostile straights who have a "pathology"—
named "homophobia." Homosexuality is a "life style" deserving of space
in a pluralistic society alongside any other. Also, there are thousands,
even millions, more of gays than the straight public imagines; gays are
everywhere, if one only knew how to recognize them. A related notion
is that unconsciously at least, below the surface, everyone is really homosexual (a politically self-serving distortion of the psychoanalytic idea of
latency, whose only valid meaning in this context is "potentiality.")
Alternatively, one believes that the whole world is classifiable into only
these two categories: gay and straight. One is definitively either one or

the other. "Coming out" signals one's finally recognizing one's "true" nature, concealed up till now beneath societally enforced charades of heterosexuality. (One then retrospectively rewrites one's whole biography to accord with this conversion illumination.)

This tactic also mimics hostile straights' reactions to gays: rigid dichotomizing and stereotyping, categorizing, you're either with us or against us, etc. It also implies the denial that one could be some complex combination of homosexual and heterosexual. "There's no such thing as a true bisexual," say many heterosexuals and so do many homosexuals as part of movement ideology. Such gays can be as nastily hostile toward anyone who "plays it both ways" as any exclusive heterosexual.

Such ideological perspectives are supported, at least in part, by many social scientists (e.g., Simon and Gagnon 1967, and Gagnon and Simon 1967) and by some psychiatrists and psychotherapists (e.g., Martin Hoffman's *The Gay World*, 1968; George Weinberg, *Society and the Healthy Homosexual*, 1972; and the psychotherapist C. A. Tripp, in *The Homosexual Matrix*, 1975). In gay activist writings they are represented by, among others, Franklin Kameny (1971).

Other elements of the mythology include the assertion that it is our culture that is sick, as evidenced by the (alleged) fact that many other cultures accept homosexuality as "normal." In turn, society can be induced (or forced) to change its anti-homosexual biases by demonstrations of how ordinary and "normal" its homosexual members actually are, their occupational and cultural diversity, etc.; the whole topic can be de-mystified; therefore it is up to secret homosexuals publicly to declare themselves. "If you are not with us, you are against us." Much of the rhetoric has obviously been derived or borrowed from the rhetoric of the Black civil rights movement, particularly in its more activist versions, and from the new-left radicalism of the 1960s, out of which many of the gay activists (as of the women's liberation activists) have emerged. Some combine all three, as in the Radicalesbians.

Gay movement mythologies—there are many variations, of course—constitute "reactive and mitigating mythologies," as discussed earlier in reference to the parallel phenomenon in the women's movement. They are reactive in the sense of reacting against stigmatizing and otherwise negative views of the minority group that prevail in the dominant society. They are reactive also in (often unconsciously) imitating the ideational-emotional style of the mythologies of their "enemies" in the dominant society: stereotyping, over-generalizing, ingroup-outgroup dichotomizing, and also anti-intellectualism and anti-intraceptive modes; intolerance of ambiguity and complexity, hostility toward the multifaceted quality of intrapsychic life and toward any effort to probe it, hostility toward recognition of complexity in society as well, and generally an authoritarian penchant for telling other people what is good for them. Just as extremists in the women's movement wish to liberate women, and people generally, *their* way, so do the counterparts in the gay movement wish to dictate to all gays how they should liberate themselves, e.g., by coming out of the closet, regardless of cost.

Another instance of the authoritarianism sometimes demonstrated by movement ideologues and protesters is in their frequently anti-civil-libertarian way of dealing with people, groups, or organizations whose viewpoint the gay militants oppose. At the time of this writing (August 1979), gay militants are not only verbally protesting against, but physically trying to stop, the filming in New York of a movie to be called "Cruising," which the gay activists claim is anti-homosexual and likely to incite violence against homosexuals. Many self-professed liberals are supporting the gays' efforts in this instance. It seems not to matter to the protesters that the filmmakers' freedom of public communication is to be curtailed in a manner not dissimilar to the way state agencies curtail freedom of speech in totalitarian regimes. This from gay militants who are avid that *their* right to present their viewpoint (by speech, by nonviolent demonstrations) be affirmed and protected, which by and large it is, in modern Western democratic societies. One does not have to support the sentiments presented in the film (whatever they are) to affirm the filmmakers' rights to present their views, just as one affirms the rights of the gays to say what they have to say.

Similarly, one does not have to agree with anti-gays like Anita Bryant (which I do not) to deplore the authoritarianism of gays' methods of preventing her. The tendency of professedly libertarian protest organizations toward totalitarianism is repeatedly demonstrated in recent history; but contemporary protesters, like those of the new left activists of the 1960s, never learn such lessons. Another feature of such authoritarianism is the way of dealing with young adults, particularly males, who are still wavering and uncertain about their sexual preference direction: the message is something like this: "if you're in doubt, you're gay; don't fight it; accept it; enjoy it; be proud of it; cast aside all doubts; any contrary feelings you may have are products of anti-gay propaganda; ignore them; suppress them; etc." This kind of message is being increasingly purveyed not only by gay ideologists, but also by counselors and self-styled therapists coming from the gay movement or its supporters, and by others, including many heterosexual "therapists," presumably well-meaning but misguided in their "libertarian" zeal. This is a version of liberal or counter-culture authoritarianism, just as anti-humane as counselors or therapists insisting that such a conflicted young person should be making every effort to be as nearly exclusively heterosexual as possible. (It is also likely to turn many such conflicted young people away from genuine therapy.)

Such mythologies are also "mitigating." They give to members of a self-defined "oppressed minority" some mitigation of the suffering derived from stigma and the self-devaluation that goes with it. The very existence of an identifiable collectivity to which one can feel oneself belonging mitigates the pain of stigmatized individuals who might otherwise feel agonizingly alone and isolated in their spoiled identity. And they are mitigating in providing counter statements against prevailing negative stereotypes and ideologies of the majority.

One important and not so obvious element in homophile mythology is the reification of the concept of "a homosexual," i.e., the idea of "being homosexual" (as distinct from being a person who sometimes or often has sexual responses to persons of his own sex, or who performs homosexual acts). Sagarin argues there is no such thing as a homosexual: the concept is a reification, an artificially created entity. What exists are people with same-sex erotic desires or activity. The desires are feeling, the acts are doing, but neither is being. People are entrapped in a false consciousness of identifying themselves as "being homosexuals." They "discover" what they "are," learn this identity, become involved in it, get boxed into their own biographies (Sagarin 1973:10). Of course, the straight world constructs this reification; gays willingly go along with it. The movement intensifies it, with its either-or, we-they thinking, despite the diversity in the sexual histories in most people who think of themselves as "homosexual."

However, ambiguity arouses anxiety. People troubled by this ambiguity in themselves "solve" it by embracing the reification, suppressing the "other" side of themselves. Social support, both in negative reactions from straight majority and positive ones from activist gay minority, buttresses these trends. Barry Dank documents this process in his study of "coming out" (1971), even while implicitly accepting the reification in presenting it. "Labeling theory" sociologists (Lemert 1951, 1967; Becker 1963, 1964; and others) emphasize how the "deviant person" is a social construction, a product of labeling by representatives of "society" (teachers, police, judges, psychiatrists, nurses, social workers, etc.) and the person himself.

The implication is that the labels are arbitrary and therefore mutable. Though the precise content and lexicon of such labels may change over time, or vary from one society to another, it is difficult to see how any society is likely to function without some such labels, some such reifications. The Mohave *alyha* is just as much boxed in to the reification of that concept—often against part of his conscious, let alone unconscious, motivation—as is the confirmed homosexual of our society. But there is no such category for the "husband" of the *alyha*, who though subject to some ridicule, is not stigmatized as "homosexual" in the way a corresponding male would be in our society. Similarly, the Marquesan male, who has the usual adolescent peer homosexual pairing or adult-male-to-young-boy sexual activity, is not countered by any label of "homosexual," while there *is* such a label, *mahu*, reserved for adult males who have persistent sexual contact with other adult males. As discussed earlier, in chapter 13, different societies cut the pie differently on this matter. While many do not use *our* labeling system, they all have *some* labeling, some reification, for some persons engaging in homosexual acts in designated contexts.

A comparison with racial categories is interesting. In the United States anyone with any identifiable black African ancestry is Negro or Black. By contrast, in Brazil, anyone with any identifiable European white ancestry is "white." In both cases, regardless of actual overt skin color. Both societies have some racial categories. South Africa reserves the term "coloured" for people of mixed black and white ancestry.

Our cross-cultural and trans-historical survey (see above) revealed no societies entirely casual about all forms of homosexual activity or lacking in categories referring to homosexual action or feeling. This suggests that it is unlikely that any society could de-reify homosexuality entirely, as distinct from marginally changing the categories. One could postulate that a society needs to have some such reification of forms of sexual behavior, with one classification dealing with sex of preferred object. At the individual level we see the need for relief from ambiguity, conflict, and uncertainty which can be provided by self-labeling in this way. Therapists are familiar with the patient being unsettled, leading to acting out, in phases of the therapy where previously consolidated self-conceptions are challenged by the results of explorations into the unconscious motivations. "Maybe I'm not really a committed homosexual after all," can be as upsetting as a predominantly heterosexual's discovery of (previously) unconscious homosexual longing for his father. Not surprisingly, many committed and "adjusted" homosexuals declare themselves totally mentally healthy. Related ideas are presented in Mary McIntosh's thoughtful paper, "The Homosexual Role" (1968) (which is, however, marred by distorted presentation of psychoanalytic and psychiatric conceptions and inaccurate anthropological material).

A major aspect of reactive and mitigating mythological elements in the gay liberation rhetoric is the formulation of homosexuals as a minority group, often explicitly in opposition to their treatment as "deviants." This formulation has some sociological justification. Sagarin pointedly includes homosexuality among *The Other Minorities* (1971), a collection of papers about various collectivities other than racial and ethnic minorities. Kameny, in that volume (1971), utilizes Louis Wirth's conceptualization of a minority group (Wirth 1945) and sees homosexuals as fitting in 1) having a minority characteristic; 2) facing prejudice and discrimination on that basis; 3) stereotyping; 4) development of a minority group consciousness. Hacker, in the same volume (1971), refines these conceptualizations: a "minority group" is a collectivity that is subjected to differential treatment, which the so-treated group regards as illegitimate; the treatment, therefore, in the eyes of the minority members constitutes discrimination.

At the same time, majority members may regard the differential treatment as justified, therefore not "discrimination." This happens where there is a conflict of values. (Hacker here borrows from Myrdal's treatment of the "race problem" in America as a value-conflict problem. See Myrdal 1944.) In a minority group situation, "persons with some socially defined characteristic . . . are denied full participation in certain social roles for which these attributes are deemed irrelevant" (Hacker 1971:65). Irrelevant by whose values? "Only when there is some cleavage of values can we speak of minority group status, because obviously if everyone agreed on the criteria for entrance into a social status, there would be equal consensus on when exclusion was warranted or when it represented discrimination" (Hacker 1971:65–66). By this analysis, homosexuals do qualify as a minority. Cleavage of values is evident in controversies over whether it is justifiable to exclude homosexuals from grade or high school teaching, or whether that constitutes "discrimination."

The classic minority group (racial or ethnic) has members who are discriminated against on the basis of a characteristic or cluster that is involuntary and immutable; dark skin in Blacks, ethnic affiliation by birth, and the like. Homophile apologists claim this is true of homosexuality: it is either genetically determined, or produced very early in life by irreversible childhood experiences. (Psychoanalytic studies refute both of these versions; it is definitely not inborn, nor is it necessarily irreversible. See Bieber et al., Socarides, etc.). Gay liberationists need to believe

it is immutable; otherwise it is much more difficult to argue "discrimination." Hacker, while doubting the immutability, does point out the
irrelevance of homosexuality for the performance of practically all non-
sexual social roles. The stigmatized characteristic need not be immutable;
it need only be irrelevant. To Hacker, it obviously is; hence it is discrimination. And like racial and ethnic minorities, homosexuals *are* subjected to stigmatizing stereotypes.

If a minority group consciousness be considered a prerequisite characteristic for a collectivity to be counted as a minority group, do homosexuals qualify? What recent data do we have that bear on this question?
Some of those found in the Bell and Weinberg study (1978), (see preceding chapter) provide some clues, for America, at least. In their sample,
for example, only a little over 20 percent of the homosexuals interviewed
belonged to any homophile organization. (Bell and Weinberg, deduced
from table 19.11, p. 414; 24 percent of white males, 13 percent of black
males, 21 percent of white females, but only 8 percent of black females,
belonged.) This suggests much of the rhetoric of the gay movement represents only a minority of the homosexual population.

Other questions Bell and Weinberg asked have bearing on how stigmatized or discriminated against the individual feels on the basis of his/
her homosexuality. For example, about a quarter of the males and slightly
less of the females (26 percent and 23 percent—more for whites than for
blacks in each case) felt "some regret" or "a great deal of regret" over
their homosexuality, and of those, a bit under half mentioned "societal
rejection" as one reason for such regret (*ibid.*, deduced from table 12,
p. 357). About a fourth of the males (more for whites than for blacks) but
only 14 percent of the females felt their homosexuality has been harmful
to their work career (but 12 percent of the males and 6 percent of the
females felt it has been *helpful* in terms of improved contacts, etc.),
more for black males than whites (*ibid.*, table 14.3). When cruising, 23
percent of the males worried about being caught by the police (only 4
percent of the females did), more so for whites than blacks; and 11
percent of the males (again, more so for white), but 16 percent of the
females (far more for the blacks) worried about their homosexuality being
publicly exposed (deduced from table 6).

Being homosexual made the individual have less confidence in the
present political system in this country in about a fifth of the males (much
more so for whites than blacks), but in only 8 percent of the females.
Practically none said this made them have *more* confidence (1 percent of
white males; none at all of the others) (computed from table 16.6). Well
over a fourth of the males had been arrested or picked up by the police

at least once in reference to homosexuality (30 percent of the white, but only 12 percent of the blacks; averaging 27 percent); only 4 percent of the females had had such an experience. Being *booked* on some charge relating to homosexuality brought the figure to only 22 percent of the males; only 2 percent of the females (more white males than black) (tables 20.3, 20.5). And 14 percent of the males (more whites again), but less than 1 percent of the females, were actually convicted on a homosexual charge. Many of the males (over a third) had at some time or other been robbed or rolled in the context of a homosexual pickup (again far more for the whites: whites 38 percent; blacks 21 percent; males overall, 35 percent). Very few of the females (4 percent), but more for blacks, had such an experience.

Female homosexuals were more subjected to threats of exposure of their homosexuality by someone seeking to get something from the re-spondent than were males: 21 percent of the females, 15 percent of the males. The nature of the threat tended to be different: for the females it was more likely to come from the partner, to keep from breaking up the relationship; for the males it was more commonly for money or material goods (tables 20.10, 20.11). Subjection to extortion by police or someone posing as police turned out to be quite rare (contrary to some statements in gay polemics): none of the female homosexuals had ever experienced this; and only 6 percent of the males; interestingly, again, fewer of the blacks (table 20.8).

Thus, it appears from these data that only a relatively small proportion of the homosexual population sampled in that study shows much of the kind of minority group consciousness reflected in membership in a hom-ophile organization. About a fourth (of males, but fewer of females) felt their careers were adversely affected—while about half that number ac-tually felt their careers helped by their homosexuality. Only about a quarter hold regrets about their homosexuality, and of those only around half mentioned societal reaction as the reason for regret. None felt any more confidence in the existing political system because of their hom-osexuality, but only about a fifth of the males (far fewer of the females) felt *less* confidence because of this. The vast majority show themselves indifferent to most political issues, although self-professed liberals out-weigh conservatives among them, but more still are basically indifferent. They certainly do not come across as a particularly activist collection of people, on any issues, including homosexual ones. (And this was in San Francisco in 1970, a scene and time of much political activism generally, and strong stirrings of the gay movement in particular.)

Thus, only minorities of this sampled population show any strong sense of victimization on the basis of their homosexuality, or feel their work careers have been damaged by their sexual preference (while a few even felt *helped* by being gay); only a minority of them had had brushes with the law on this account (though the homosexual males had had more police encounters generally, not necessarily about sexual matters, than their heterosexual peers—possibly a reflection of police harassment; we don't know from the data here). Similarly, small percentages indicate regret over their homosexuality, and of those only about half mention societal negative reaction as the reason for their regret.

From these data, this does not appear, then, to be a population of people seriously at loggerheads with the society around them. However, the data on their "psychological adjustment" reviewed earlier suggest difficulties: greater loneliness, more depression, more paranoid feelings, and more suicidalism than in matched heterosexual groups.

Most of these gays do have some connection with what sociologists have called the homosexual subculture—or better, subculture*s*—but it varies a great deal in degree and kind of involvement. These subcultures are ethnographically described again in an appendix to the Bell and Weinberg study (1978), and have been previously explored by Leznoff and Wesley (1956), Simon and Gagnon (1967), Evelyn Hooker (1967), Martin Hoffman (1968), Cory (1951), Schofield (1965), Weinberg and Williams (1974), and many others, including several papers in the Gagnon and Simon (1967) collection.

Hacker summarized the functions of such a community for individual homosexuals as providing 1) social support for a positive self-image; 2) shared norms and practices, overcoming anomie; 3) sexual marketplace; 4) other, nonsexual gratifications (friendship, recreation, etc.); 5) sense of identity; 6) enjoyment of camp behavior; 7) agency of social control against impulsive "acting out"; 8) upward mobility opportunity structure; 9) reduction of anxiety and conflicts, relieving tensions of concealment, enabling more productive performance outside the (homosexual) community; 10) social services to meet individual problems and crimes (Hacker 1971:86–87).

It is evident homosexuals *can* be described as a minority group: they are pejoratively defined and discriminated against on the basis of an irrelevant characteristic; resent this discrimination; and have some sense of group identification and distinctive subculture in reaction to it. The degree of minority group consciousness and individual involvement in the minority group as such does, however, vary quite widely with, apparently, only a fraction of the homosexual population feeling at all strongly the stigma, the discrimination, and the victimization that the militant activists in the homophile movement claim is the common lot of oppression for all homosexuals.

Some supporters of the homophile movement, such as Evelyn Hooker, link certain psychological characteristics found in many homosexuals specifically to "victimization," on the model of such traits in other victimized minorities, such as blacks. Such traits would include hypersensitivity to rejection or stigma, hyper-acute awareness of the characteristics given pejorative definition by the majority society (as blacks focus on skin color, gays focus on their sexuality); paranoid suspiciousness toward outgroups; uncertain self-esteem; uncertainty whether the majority may in fact be right in its negative assessment of one's group, therefore of oneself (in that, some degree of identification with the aggressor); difficulty in steering a path, in dealing with the dominant majority, between obsequious self-abasement and rebellious defiance; and ingroup-outgroup dichotomizing parallel to that of the majority group. Hooker and other such observers claim that all such characteristics are entirely attributable to victimization, in a polemical attack on illness conceptions of homosexuality. Typically anti-psychoanalytic, such thinkers deny that such features could stem from intrapsychic processes. My response to this is obviously to disagree: there is no intrinsic contradiction between emphasizing the interpersonal and intergroup processes those authors deal with under the concept of "victimization" and dealing with the intrapsychic dynamics that we have explored earlier.

Homosexuals also *differ* from other kinds of minority groups, as Hacker also points out. Someone born as a black or a Jew in this society grows up in a context of supportive kin sharing this minority status, thus deriving crucial aspects of positive identity. The future homosexual, by contrast, lacks such familial and socialization supports, grows up in an atmosphere highlighting his individual "strangeness," furthering isolation. He also lacks the supportive ties that racial or ethnic minority group members have, extending through the whole range of one's social and cultural life. The homosexual has in common with other homosexuals, at the extreme, only the sexual preference, lacking supportive structures relating to class or cultural position in society. This is a very limited basis for a movement. Another difference is the lack, for gays, of anticipatory socialization in childhood for this minority group status and role.

Another sociological angle on the homophile movement and the homosexual minority community is to discuss these in the context of the concepts of "dominant" and "subterranean" cultural traditions in modern society. Many of the distinctions drawn, stereotypically, between heterosexuals and homosexuals (for males) correspond rather closely to those between the dominant and the subterranean: Heterosexual males are supposed to be rational, logical, tough, tough-minded, strong, decisive, aggressive, anti-emotional, instrumental, well-organized, and technologically, mathematically, and hard-science minded. Correspondingly, the opposite characteristics in a male are thought to indicate deficient masculinity and the suspicion of homosexuality: softness, estheticism, artistic talent or interest, tender-mindedness, expressiveness, openness to the inner psychological world. In this respect, some part of the gay liberation movement is allied with the feminist movement in challenging such stereotypes and aiming to "liberate" men from the constrictions of the "dominant" modes of masculinity. And as the subterranean traditions were epitomized in the 1960s by the hippie movement, a partial successor of the 1970s and beyond appears to be the gay movement, now constituting one of the major foci of cleavage in modern society. (See Burroughs's *Naked Lunch*, 1959, for a surrealistic fictional treatment of this theme: he sees a near future in which gay versus straight has become the main political conflict in the modern world.) Sociologists' interest in homosexuality today is a lot like their interest in the hippies in the 1960s: fascination with a deviant group; sympathy with the "oppressed"; some identification with them; rebelliousness toward felt authoritarianism of dominant majorities; and shared antinomian views and expressiveness, all play a part. With the collapse of the radical and hippie movements of the 1960s, women's rights and gay rights have moved to center stage as the salient issues of the day.

At the same time, part of the (*male*) gay movement shows identification with the aggressor by assuming postures, costuming, etc., closely approximating dominant style "masculinity": tough aggressive stands, a macho appearance, interest in cowboy styles, moustaches and other marks of the "hip," presumably heterosexual, male. Some of this, in the rhetoric of gay activists, is calculated to convince the majority world that gays are just like everyone else. (For reasons already discussed, I doubt this is likely to alter appreciably the anti-homosexual bias prevalent in the dominant society.)

Summary and Conclusion

In part 4, I have tried to bring together psychoanalytic, sociological, and anthropological views, along with those of the gay activist movement. These obviously conflict among themselves at many points, and at many others the different viewpoints talk more or less past each other, because the spokesmen are raising different kinds of theoretical or practical questions. Thus, many sociologists make a point of *not* dealing with etiology, which they declare an irrelevant question for an understanding of the social dynamics of the homosexual role and its players and the subcultures of this variant collectivity—a judgment I obviously do not share, since I believe that from both theoretical and practical perspectives etiology must be understood to get the whole picture clear. Similarly, psychoanalysts have sometimes been inadequately attentive to the social processes involved in the acquisition and perpetuation of a homosexual identity, which are crucial aspects, along with the intrapsychic forces, of how the person lives his life in relation to his sexuality and to the surrounding society and its relevant parts. We have noted that an attempt to understand etiology in the context of the historical genesis of homosexual orientations in the individual's infancy, childhood, and adolescence is not necessarily unequivocally tied to a conception of any homosexual activity as indicative of psychopathology; nor unequivocally tied to attempts to "cure" in the sense of changing a person from a predominantly homosexual to a predominantly or exclusively heterosexual pattern. This aspect has been a major bone of contention between, on one side, psychoanalysts and other therapists who focus on psychopathological features here, and those on the "other side," which includes most sociologists who have dealt with homosexuality, some anthropologists, some psychologists, and, of course, representatives of the homophile movement, who have been vigorous in asserting—without ever proving, to my mind—that homosexual persons are simply not psychologically sick.

The brief review of psychoanalytic and related viewpoints and researches on this question reveals that careful students of this matter find a great range and variety of likely linkages between overt homosexual behavior and various other aspects of psychological functioning. Basically, there seems to have emerged some consensus that homosexuality *per se* cannot properly be considered a clinical entity. At the same time it can be associated with almost any of the whole range of recognized psychopathological conditions or processes, in one form or another, as well as be associated with a personality configuration that is highly well integrated and functioning well in essential aspects of life, although it is questionable whether this latter category—the psychologically very healthy homosexual—could in fact include more than a very small proportion of the population of people who have homosexual responses and activity. Since there is an evolutionarily derived predisposition toward heterosexuality as a requirement for this species' reproduction system, serious departures away from an at least predominantly heterosexual orientation must be considered a problematical variation. This is not to say that species survival requires that *all* human beings be heterosexually oriented, only that departures from this need to be limited to no more than a minority of the population. This is also not to say that heterosexuality needs no explanation, but it does mean to say that the need for an explanation of homosexuality is of a different order. This is reflected transculturally in the universal disapproval of exclusive homosexuality in all cultures about which we have information, even though many of them are variably permissive or tolerant toward some forms of homosexuality in some persons and/or in some circumstances, usually not excluding heterosexual relations as well. True, a few societies have institutionalized a role for an exclusive homosexual as a berdache, but only for a very small and specially (supernaturally) chosen minority.

We have found that there is good reason to believe that overt homosexuality is a pan-human *potentiality*, but that does not mean that it is in fact likely to be expressed; and that we know something of the dynamics, intrapsychically, that are likely to increase the probability that it will be so, at least in some societies. For Western societies at least, its etiology in the male is particularly associated with a particular kind of familial constellation of a close-binding-intimate mother and distant and/or hostile father, as one major precursor—though other constellations are also possible and do appear. Pre-oedipal difficulties are most likely to precede the major critical period, that of the Oedipus complex, which is here not resolved in the manner that ordinarily leads to predominant heterosexuality. The abandonment of incestuous aims spreads to taboo on the entire opposite sex, and abandonment of parricidal correlates of the incestuous wish leads to pathological patterns of sexual submission to or domination over other males, attempts at magical incorporation of their superior masculinity, symbolic reenactments of aggression against the father, and/or a host of other erotic or erotic-aggressive disguises for the never attained relationship with the father. Extreme castration anxiety is a significant determinant. This is true of homosexuality itself, as it is also true of intense anti-homosexual fears, biases, and hatreds existing in the heterosexuals of the society.

We are postulating that there would have to be psychopathological processes involved in the adoption of exclusive homosexuality certainly, and probably also in any pattern in which overt homosexual relations are more than an incidental feature of a person's sexual history. But just as certain kinds of pathological etiology can eventuate in some kind of stabilized character structure in some persons who are devoid, ordinarily, of any intense neurotic suffering, so we can also postulate that certain kinds of pathological etiology leading toward exclusive or preferential homosexuality can also lead to a stabilized character in which overt homosexuality is only one feature in a structure that includes a good deal of ego strength and some relative degree of stability, along with a sense of reasonably high well-being, comparable to that found in relatively non-neurotic heterosexuals.

In these kinds of cases it would appear somewhat far-fetched to regard such individuals as psychologically "sick," and on that point, and for these individuals, we can concede some validity to the viewpoints of non-psychoanalysts, sociologists, and gay rights spokesmen. However, it needs to be emphasized that such well-integrated and "well-adjusted" homosexuals, some of them functioning at very high levels of productivity or creativity or civic contribution, appear, by all presently available evidence, to be only a very small minority of homosexuals in modern society. (The pretensions that large numbers of great creative figures of the past were homosexual or bisexual, we have seen, are frequently misrepresentations or misunderstandings of available evidence, adduced in the interests of homosexual apologetics.)

From all the available studies, which include researches not only clinically by psychoanalysts on patient populations (claimed by gay ideologists, without evidence, to be an unrepresentative sample), but also by a variety of other means by sociologists and social psychologists, it would appear that the vast majority of homosexuals, perhaps more so for the males than for the females, in Western societies, suffer from a variety and various degrees of psychological impairments, to an extent greater than comparison non-homosexual populations. They are more likely than comparison heterosexuals to lead promiscuous unstable personal-sexual lives, to have great difficulty establishing and maintaining close intimacy relationships, to be plagued by self-doubts and self-contempt, to regard the world around them as hostile or unsupportive, to be narcissistically self-involved or to feel depressed and sometimes suicidal, or to show any combination of these features. These certainly do not indicate a state of optimal psychic health, or anything even near it.

Gay ideologists and many of their sociological and behavioral science supporters claim, when grudgingly recognizing any of these findings, that any such psychic distress can be attributed entirely to the effects of societal hostility and stigmatization, and cannot represent real underlying intrapsychic disturbance. This I maintain is an untenable interpretation of the evidence, and a misunderstanding of the relationship between social and intrapsychic forces in producing patterns of human behavior. Those holding such views are likely to take a correspondingly hostile attitude toward therapy, which they misconstrue as oppressive pressure toward "cure," depriving many who might potentially be helped of much-needed surcease from associated symptoms.

The cross-cultural and trans-historical evidence indicates, as already stated, a great variety of levels of incidence of homosexual behavior, in a number of different contexts, more for males than for females (so far as we know), but rarely any more than a very small minority exhibit exclusive homosexuality. The incidence of some kind of homosexual behavior can vary from zero to close to 100 percent of the males, and in the cases with higher incidence is always associated with a predominantly heterosexual life pattern, and usually limited to particular life cycle stages and contexts. We know practically nothing of the psychodynamic patterns of etiology and development of these patterns of homosexual behavior in other societies. In a few cases we can make informed guesses, as in the case of Greece of Socrates's time, where it was associated with the low status of women and pervasive misogyny. Given the pan-human universality of parenting with adults of two sexes being involved, and the universality of basic psychological mechanisms of defense and adaptation, which have been found in all cultures we know of on these points, it seems unlikely that the mechanisms leading to the development of a prevalently homosexual orientation in the individual's sexual life would be significantly different from those we find in modern societies where they have been intensively studied by psychoanalytic methods. This is a hypothesis, to be sure, still to be tested by reliable evidence.

In normative responses to homosexual behavior, we find considerable variety, but *nowhere* do we find that a pattern that is exclusively or predominantly homosexual, in an individual, is given unambiguous approval, or considered "normal" or "natural" on a par with heterosexuality. In the vast majority of cultures it is definitely condemned; in others it is socially encapsulated in an institutionalized role for a very small minority of persons, given some kind of sacred warrant, and considered a kind of affliction by forces over which the incumbent has no control, and the incumbent is therefore excused of blame or responsibility. All recognize it as a departure from the statistically and culturally normal of the society. The normative response toward incidental or context-limited accessory homosexual activity within a predominantly heterosexual pattern is, however, more variable from one society to another, ranging from a fair degree of acceptance or tolerance to considerable disapproval, as in our own society in recent times.

A major point of variation among societies revolves around the question of whether or not there is a definite "homosexual role." Where there is, as in our society, and evidently in Western societies since around the end of the seventeenth century, there is a tendency to get everyone categorized as either fitting that role or not, i.e., as *being* definitely homosexual or being definitely heterosexual, with the implication that there is no in between. As discussed, this is a reification which greatly oversimplifies and falsifies the realities of people's sexual responses and behavior, and does tend to "box people in" to roles which fit only one aspect of their total sexuality.

Correspondingly, where there is a definite homosexual role, there develop distinctive deviant-subcultural institutions surrounding it, further consolidating the deviant identity for those who embrace them. These in turn may allay, or intensify, or stabilize into social patterns, psychological patterns, including some quite pathological ones, that derive from familial-etiological origins, psychological mechanisms of adaptation and defense in relation to these, as well as from efforts to deal with current adult social situations and strains, including the prevailing stigma and its institutional expressions, as well as those strains deriving from the deviant subculture itself. Many of these patterns have close analogies to patterns displayed by minority group persons of racial or ethnic category, though there are also important differences between homosexuals as a minority group and racial/ethnic minorities. Most importantly, the lack of anticipatory socialization in a familial and kinship context that provides positive self-esteem counterparts to the negative status, in loving supportive kin and generational continuity.

The labeling perspective toward deviance propounded by much recent sociology provides important insights into processes of interaction between stigmatized persons and surrounding society. At the same time its insistence that deviance is entirely (or at least essentially) a social creation seriously distorts the reality of interplay between intrapsychic and social mechanisms, and, at its extreme, paints the false picture of human beings as entirely the pawns of social pressures and without an intrapsychic history and capacity for self-determination of their own. It includes a correlative assumption of a radical cultural relativism—from which one could conclude that any imaginable human behavior or psychological mode could be counted as "normal" in some society, or that any widely prevalent pattern—e.g., heterosexuality—could be counted as deviant in some societies. Such an assumption is belied by the fact of a distinctly finite—large but still finite—range of possibilities in human societies, particularly in reference to the primary drives of sex and aggression, and to possible cultural arrangements for reproduction and infant care and socialization. These latter involve the finite number of possibilities for kinship and family, and the universality of primary incest taboos, and of some (though varied) forms of secondary incest taboos, in all human societies.

There are clearly problems of social justice involved in the ways persons defined as homosexuals are treated in modern society, and most social and behavioral scientists have shown a definite value concern to remedy such injustice as pejorative treatment of a segment of the population on the basis of an irrelevant characteristic. Sharing such a libertarian concern need not, however, blind us in our clinical judgments of psychopathology where it exists, nor in our social-scientific recognition of the tendentious distortions of reality propagated by politically motivated "liberators." It is an ironic historical circumstance that consideration of homosexuality as sickness or indicative of sickness, earlier a libertarian advance over moralistic condemnation of it as moral corruption, or sin, or legal condemnation of it as a felony offense, now comes to be seen, or used, as itself a mode of condemnation. Thus "sick" has come to replace "evil," "immoral," or "sinful" in the modern lexicon of opprobrium. This should not, however, lead us to abandon legitimate assessments of psychopathology. The quest for truth and understanding and the effort to tell honestly what we see and understand have never been guarantees of popular approval or political acclaim. In fact, they have at their extreme usually produced disapproval, condemnation, and controversy. Tailoring scientific findings to political causes is a sure path to distortion.

Both the prevalence and forms of anti-homosexual bias, prejudice, and discrimination in modern societies and the forms of reactive protest against this on the part of the homophile movement cry out for a combination of psychoanalytic and sociological analysis. We have made the beginnings of such analysis. For prevalently heterosexual males, for example, the universality of some degree of castration anxiety in the process of infantile and childhood psychosexual development is certainly pivotal as a component in reactions to other males who are perceived as castrated and as having willingly put themselves into the passive submissive "feminine" position. Evidently there is a good deal of variation in the intensity and forms of this reaction which are worthy of close study.

The protest against this by the homophile movement and its supporters, including many behavioral and social scientists as well as some varieties of therapist, itself indicates reactive and mitigating mythologies, responsive to and partly mirroring the mythologies of the anti-homosexuals. The polarization that is emerging can be examined sociologically along lines of similar polarizations in other political and social movements. The counter-mythologies of the gay rights movement reveal dynamics of stigmatized minorities asserting a contended positive image, denial of psychological disturbance and other politically self-serving distortions, as well as parallels to their antagonists' modes of dichotomizing into we–they polarities, stereotyping overgeneralization, xenophobic ethnocentrism, vilification of motives of all who disagree, attempts at authoritarian control and pressure to conform over backsliding or erring members of one's own group, and the rest of the typical modes of protest political-social movements.

These processes are clearly not in the interests of truth, and only minimally, if at all, in the interests of justice, tending as they do to the substitution of in-group minority-group tyranny for tyrannies deriving from the dominant society. Social scientists and therapists of civil-libertarian political persuasions are all too easily seduced by these sympathies into support for propositions and stances that contradict their scientific or clinical judgment. They need to learn that support for repeal of legal disabilities of a harmless sexual minority and for legal and social guarantees of fair treatment need not require assent to views without scientific foundation, or that are clearly contradicted by scientific evidence.

We also need to sustain a hard-headed realization that the conflicts involved are not readily soluble, that the "problem" will not go away, that homosexuality will neither disappear nor eventually find a broad spectrum of acceptance—much less universal approval as simply an innocuous variant. Plus ça change.

5

Deviation, Psychopathology, and "Normality"

A woman comes to a psychiatrist. "I'm happily married. I love my husband and children. I own an advertising agency which I've built up over the years. I get along fine with my employees and associates. I don't have an ulcer. I enjoy my work. I never advertise a product I don't like or respect. We have no internal political battles in my firm. Nobody is knifing others in the back."

PSYCHIATRIST: "So what is your problem?"

PATIENT: "Why can't I be like everyone else?"

Mental health can be precisely defined as a limiting concept. But the class so defined, however useful it may be in psychoanalytic theory, is found to have no actual members."

—R. E. Money-Kyrle. Introduction to Melanie Klein et al., eds.,
New Directions in Psychoanalysis

CHAPTER FIFTEEN

Conceptions of Normality

In the earlier chapters we have repeatedly come up against the problem of what is "normality" and what is "abnormality." What are the criteria for assessing some behavior or personality pattern psychopathology? Is deviation from social norms to be equated with psychopathology? Can one be deviant in psychologically healthy ways, and conformist in psychologically pathological ones? Does our evolutionary heritage provide any warrant for constructing pan-human universal criteria for psychic health and illness? We found psychoanalysts and sociologists differing on standards of "normality," and psychoanalysts differing among themselves, and sociologists differing among themselves. Modern anthropology brings in cultural relativism suggesting each culture has its own standards and could only with injustice be evaluated according to the standards of some other culture. We then traced some probable reconstructions of the evolution of the human species, which may provide some kinds of guidelines for understanding of the universal human potentiality for psychic disturbance. For example, irrationality might be—if only partially—defined as failure to assess accurately a present reality—and one of the present (and endless) realities is the dimorphism of the sexes and the need, for species survival, of heterosexual reproduction. Therefore, it is possible to argue that to consider any person as human first and only secondarily as male or female is a defective appreciation of human reality, and therefore irrational. Similarly, to consider primary incest taboos as dispensable in some hypothetical future "utopian" society is also to be counted an irrational fantasy. Also, to consider variations from a predominantly heterosexual motivation in one's pattern of sexuality as merely incidental and of no consequence, societally variable and therefore changeable without significant cost, may also be counted as implying an inaccurate perception of the human reality of the evolutionary requirement of heterosexuality, and in that sense irrational. We have also touched on the tendency of many scholars, social scientists mainly, to imply that any behavior or pattern that is *prevalent* is therefore to be counted as "normal" in the sense of "natural"—i.e., that it occurs in nature. (Technically speaking, of course, if it occurs in nature, even as a rare minority pattern, it would have to then be considered "natural." This would, of course, make the concept practically meaningless for any social scientific analysis.)

The frequency with which this problem of defining "normality" keeps coming up in social scientific and psychological work, and repeatedly fails to get resolved to the satisfaction of any broad professional public suggests the intractable nature of the dilemmas involved, and perhaps also the anxieties that the problem arouses. Some of the "solutions" some thinkers provide to the problem are so oversimplified that they raise more questions than they answer.

One version of these is to define normality entirely in statistical terms; whatever pattern of personality prevails in a particular society, that is "normal." Or whatever psychological mechanisms are commonly used by the majority, these are "normal." The problem with this kind of definition is that whatever behavior is prevalent, or personality pattern is prevalent, may or may not conform to the culturally institutionalized norms of that particular society, and we have no way of knowing whether it does or not without specific research on this point that does not beg the question in advance by presupposing that the statistically prevalent "normal" in that sense is also the "normative" in the sense of complying with culturally patterned norms of right and wrong, correct or incorrect, etc., of that particular society. Another and even more important difficulty with the statistical view of normality is that there is no guarantee whatever that the prevalence, commonness, or even universality of a particular behavior pattern in a particular society is any indication that it is psychologically *healthy* or not psychologically pathological, by some kind of clinical standard. This question is obvious in reference to Kinsey's studies, which imply that statistically average or prevalent signifies any behavior as psychologically "normal," or at least that it could not be psychologically "abnormal" or unhealthy if it in fact appears to a majority of the people of a particular society, or even in a substantial minority of the people. His figure of 37 percent of American males having had at some time or other in their lives at least *one* overt homosexual genital-contact experience leading to orgasm has been repeatedly cited by homosexual apologists and sundry social scientists and psychological practitioners as indicating that something so widespread could not possibly be psychologically "sick." We can leave aside for the moment the obvious point we made in the last section, that the figure is almost meaningless in that it includes persons for whom such an experience was a single instance or one of a very few such instances in his whole sexual life, therefore a very minor and incidental part of the totality, along with all others ranging from some, to much, to predominant, to totally exclusive, homosexuality. Even if the figure referred to the proportion of men who had a substantial amount of homosexual activity, there would still be no way of telling from the statistical evidence whether and how the pattern was psychologically unhealthy or not. And even if nearly 100 percent of the Keraki males, or the Siwah males, as discussed in the preceding section, have experience of anal intercourse with other males in childhood or adolescence in either role, in adulthood only with younger males and only in the insertor role, that still does not tell us the psychodynamic pattern of this activity, and the statistical "normality" of this activity is no warrant of its psychological "normality" in terms of standards of health, or minimally, of absence of serious psychopathology. Similarly, it may have been statistically normal for the Puritans of colonial Salem to believe in and persecute witches. But there is good ground for believing that this statistical "normality" included a serious psychopathological distortion of reality and psychopathological mechanisms for dealing with inner conflict in these devout citizens.

STATISTICAL, CULTURAL, AND TRANSCULTURAL VIEWS

We can take off from the distinction made in my 1967 book, *Personality and Social Life* (pp. 576–98). There I differentiate three significantly different ways in which scholars of various persuasions have conceptualized "normality" and "abnormality." These are the *statistical*, the *cultural*, and the *transcultural* conceptions of normality. By the *statistical*, whatever is prevalent, or average, or appears in the majority is "normal," and whatever is atypical, rare, or appears only in small minorities is "abnormal." In the second, the *cultural*, or culturally-relativistic conception of normality, "normal" equals conforming to the prevailing norms, the standards of should and ought, of right and wrong, just or unjust, etc., that operate in a particular society. These standards tell people how they are expected to act, to think, and to feel, and indicate what general configuration of personality or character is considered right, or preferable, or to be honored, in that society, at that historical time. Correspondingly, "abnormal" in that perspective means nonconforming, failing to live up to standards or expectations, being delinquent or criminal, being oddball or weird in some unapproved expressive manner, dissenting from prevailing orthodoxies in political, religious, or social beliefs, or simply feeling "out of tune" with prevailing expectations, finding in them no resonance with one's own deeper sense of self, feeling "maladjusted" in the world in which one lives.

The third type of conception of "normality" can be called *transcultural* in that it attempts to transcend the limitations and dilemmas of the culturally relativistic view of normality, by positing standards for psychic health or illness which would apply to any human beings in any society at any time in the history of the species. This view emphasizes the universalities of human experience—as opposed to their cross-cultural divergences—and the postulated universalities of requirements for adequate psychological functioning. In this view psychoanalysis provides the deepest and most searching exploration of the processes of psychological growth and mechanisms of defense against universally occurring inner conflict and modes of adaptation that apply to all human beings, in whatever culture. As there is no time in the unconscious, so there are no cross-cultural variations, fundamentally, in the unconscious. In our dreams, all humanity is one. And no wonder. In evolution, we are one species, all with the same evolutionary history. The problems we face are universal. These are the problems of human infancy, of dealing with the dimorphism of the sexes, with basic pan-human sexual drives and their vicissitudes, of dealing with parents and siblings and offspring and their symbolic extensions, of coming to terms with both sex and aggression and their interrelations, of finding a path between isolation and total immersion in a mass of others. These are universal, pan-human problems, and the range of possible "solutions" for them, while broad, is by no means infinite. And we are well along in being able to characterize the configurations of such modes, and to evaluate them in terms of lesser or greater degrees of pathology. It is probably true that the "psychologically ideally healthy" person has never existed, any more than the ideally *totally* analyzed individual coming out of psychoanalysis has ever existed. Probably neither could ever exist. Still, that does not mean that we cannot distinguish different *degrees* of psychopathology, as well as different varieties of it. It does not mean that we are unable to recognize an individual who is in a state of *remission* from a more florid psychopathological state without insight and hence without "cure"—one in whom the underlying conflicts have not been really resolved, but only covered over by some culturally approved form of adjustment which at least relieves the extremes of feeling alienated from one's social world, but where these conflicts may at any future time again erupt into more manifest behavioral indicators of the underlying pathology. It does not mean that we are not able to differentiate such an individual both from one who does not have the same kind of underlying unconscious conflict in the first place, and from one who deals with a similar unconscious conflict in a more adaptive and less pathogenic manner; or from one with a similar area of conflict and similar prior pathological symptoms, who in treatment arrives at an adequate confrontation with the unconscious sources, develops insight, and adequately "works through" the difficulty in the transference and in changed behavior in the outside world, arriving at a degree of "cure" from the psychopathology. While it is true that psychoanalysis has been more adequate at recognizing and understanding forms of psychopathology than it has been in formulating positive standards of psychic health, let alone creating people who fit those standards, this does not mean that it is irrelevant or futile to attempt the formulation of positive standards. Much less does it mean that we have to fall back on cultural relativism and say simply that each culture has its own standards, which may differ profoundly from those of others.

The value of the distinction among the statistical, the cultural, and the transcultural viewpoints on normality lies in noting that classifying any behavior, or personality pattern, as "normal" by one of these standards does not necessarily predict that it will be so classified by either of the other two. The same for classifying as "abnormal." The statistically abnormal may be healthy by a transcultural standard and deviant by a cultural standard. The culturally conforming may be statistically normal and also represent a serious character disorder by transcultural mental health standards, in this case one with cultural validation and reinforcement that resists modification or change in any of its elements, particularly because of its warrant of cultural approval. Extreme consumerism in our society may well be an example of this. At least it may be one symptom in a configuration of socially stylized character disorder. The Nazis drew upon statistically prevalent psychological trends of authoritarian submission and authoritarian aggression, and made them "culturally normal" for conforming Nazi Germans. In transcultural terms these trends were however, distinctly psychopathological.

Ruth Benedict propounded, in *Patterns of Culture* in 1934, a vision of the world that presents cultural relativism as in effect the basic ideology of modern anthropology, urging as doctrine of liberal enlightenment our refraining from making value judgments upon exotic tribal cultures with cultural standards very different from our own, and urging us to look at each such culture in terms of its own standards, not ours, shunning the fatal anthropological sin of ethnocentrism. Still, when she came to discuss, within that framework, some aspects of the modern world, she was confronted with the phenomenon, then coming to its full flower, of German Nazism. To follow the logic of the position she had so eloquently developed, she would have had to grant to that society, that culture, the same dignity and value she accords to each of the tribal cultures, and regard it as good and implicitly healthy on its own terms. She could not quite bring herself to do this, liberal anti-fascist as she was, along with most other social scientists of the time. But cultural relativism could give her no handle on formulating a way of describing and analyzing such a society as psychologically abnormal, as well as being morally repulsive, and not only by culture- and time-bound standards of a democratic Western society of the 1930s. A similar non-judgmentalism, in line with cultural relativism, appears in the attitude of many more recent anthropologists in regard to Communism whether in the Soviet Union, or in China, or in any of the Soviet satellite regimes of Eastern Europe, in Cuba, or—pronouncedly by American anthropologists during the 1960s and since—in Vietnam.[1] (With an inconsistency from which scholars are not always spared, many of these same anthropologists have had no hesitation in abandoning cultural relativism and value neutrality in reference to their own society, the United States, or at least toward its government, which they have frequently roundly condemned for its "imperialism" and sundry other social and moral sins.)

EIGHT POSSIBLE COMBINATIONS

To be rigorous about it, with each of the three conceptualizations having two polar positions of "normal" and "abnormal"—to omit as unwieldy all the possibilities in between—there are eight possible combinations.

1. A person or a personality pattern or a piece of behavior could be totally normal statistically, also culturally, also transculturally (e.g., being motivated for and actually living out a pattern of heterosexual mating in a culturally approved form of marriage).

2. At the opposite extreme, a pattern could be totally abnormal in all three ways: statistically, culturally, and transculturally (e.g., persistently and overtly violating primary incest taboos as an adult). The other six variations follow.

3. Statistically and culturally normal, but transculturally abnormal, as in the case of devout Nazi aggressors just mentioned. Patterns of authoritarian aggression combined with authoritarian submission were, according to many observers, statistically prevalent in the German population of the immediate pre-Hitler and the Hitler period. They thus constituted a statistical normality. The Nazis encouraged and required such psychological trends in the populace, assuring authoritarian submission to the regime and the party, and irrational expression of authoritarian aggression against outgroups like the Jews, as well as any other alleged internal or external enemies of Germany. They were thus culturally normal. The dynamics of these processes have been presented in many works (e.g., Fromm 1941; Devereux 1956; Adorno et al. 1950, LaBarre 1954; Cohn 1961) and we can hardly doubt that serious psychopathological processes are at work. To claim that they were normal because statistically prevalent, or because culturally required and in tune with the demands of a given regime, is to betray a serious limitation of vision.

4. Statistically normal, culturally abnormal, and transculturally normal. This is an unlikely combination, though possible; hypothetically it would apply to a situation where most or a majority of people were asserting positive adaptive capacities indicating mental health, against or in defiance of some prevailing cultural standards. This might occur where a population previously strong in psychological health have been overrun and conquered by an alien people who impose anti-humane restrictive norms upon the captive population, against which the subject people covertly (or perhaps even overtly) rebel. In this example, however, the "culturally abnormal" may apply in reference to norms imposed by the conquerors, while the rebellious behavior may be culturally approved and supported by standards persisting in the conquered group. Thus, from that perspective, that is, the subculture of the conquered people, the pattern may then in fact be regarded as normal culturally, as well as statistically and transculturally.

Another example could be the prevalence of people living together without marriage and producing children in such "consensual unions" in Caribbean cultures. While there is toleration for these unions, the normative evaluations of the participants themselves, as well as others, put them in a normatively inferior category compared to legitimate marriages, i.e., unions sanctioned by legal and religious ceremony. (Incidentally, as William Goode points out, these situations do not falsify Malinowski's "principle of legitimacy," i.e., that in all societies there are norms specifying that the child should have a legitimate father, i.e., a man married to the mother by the ceremonial standards of that society. See Malinowski 1930 and Goode 1960.) Thus the cohabitation pattern is statistically normal, and the motivations of the participants probably transculturally normal in the sense that there is no obvious indication that doing this indicates psychopathology, but the pattern is culturally abnormal, i.e., "deviant," even though not *severely* disapproved.

5. The next possible combination is statistically normal, while both culturally and transculturally abnormal. Thus, for example, some deviant form of sexual expression, disapproved by the cultural norms of that society, may be sufficiently widespread as to be statistically normal or almost so; and at the same time it may constitute an expression of a pathological mode of dealing with inner conflicts, and thus be a departure from transcultural normality or optimal mental health. It can be widespread, and not be validated by prevailing cultural norms, or even by the norms of some distinctive subgroup developing its own subculture. This is not to say that all culturally disapproved forms of sexual expression are necessarily psychopathological, whether or not they are behaviorally prevalent in a society. Whether they are or not has to be determined by a careful examination of the total psychodynamic constellation in which they occur, and how necessary such a form of expression is to the individual's maintaining some kind of (usually neurotic) equilibrium, which is not synonymous with psychological health.

6. A sixth possible combination is statistically abnormal, culturally normal, and transculturally normal. This is another unlikely combination. A psychologically healthy as well as culturally approved pattern is rather unlikely to be statistically rare in a particular population. It *could* possibly be, if the reference is to some extreme ideal standard of almost utopian quality, the psychologically ideally healthy personality, which a particular culture may also extol and hold forth as its ideal, but which practically no one in fact approximates in reality, thus making the pattern statistically rare. Just as there is "good-enough mothering" (Winnicott 1965), we can also postulate a more modest conception of "good-enough psychological functioning" that falls short of the utopian ideal of psychological patterns totally devoid of any pathological elements. About such a person we could say that he falls short of *never* using any neurotic defenses against inner conflict; of *never* showing inadequate resolution of the Oedipus complex; of *never* showing any difficulty in maintenance of a strong and consistent sexual identity; of *never* losing his balance and falling into temporary depression; of *never* having any moments of delusional perceptions of the world around him, and so on. But for this person, none of these indicators of pathology are a consistent, persistent,

or predominating part of his personality functioning. This could be an example of "reasonably healthy" or "good enough" functioning. Such an individual would not quite fulfill a utopian conception of mental health, or a culturally supported ideal of that kind if it existed in a particular society or subsociety. (To some extent, such an ideal is implied, in some psychoanalytically sophisticated circles within modern society.) And the rarity of complete fulfillment of such an ideal would qualify it as being statistically abnormal.

Where conceptions of "good enough" healthy psychological functioning, derived from some version of psychoanalytic thinking, are explicitly or implicitly supported by cultural ideals, we find the cultural prescriptions providing societal support for certain processes of the formation of the individual's ego-ideal. Basically the ego-ideal enables the individual to comply with the society's *rational* demands (as distinguished from superego which is the intrapsychic agency for the support of irrational societal demands—see Devereux 1956). Positive and reasonably rational adaptation to cultural demands that are themselves not pathological nor exceptionally irrational would amount to a kind of ego-syntonic conformity and be experienced as being at home in the social and cultural world in which one lives. (I say "not exceptionally irrational," because to a certain extent and in certain degrees, all cultural prescriptions have some quality of irrationality, a theme that has to be developed further.) In such a fortunate conjunction of transcultural and cultural norms, it is most unlikely that behavior fitting both criteria would be statistically rare or abnormal in that sense.

7. Another possible combination would be statistically abnormal, culturally normal, and transculturally abnormal. Certain kinds of "saints" or "heroes" might fit into this kind of constellation. They fulfill to an extraordinary degree certain cultural ideals, such as the spirit of brotherhood, selflessness, and the like. They are certainly statistically rare, there being very few such individuals in reality in any age. While the cultural norms extol such persons and their actions in the world, they might, nevertheless, be quite pathological in terms of a transcultural standard of mental health. Most of the Christian saints, for example, would probably qualify for a judgment of psychological abnormality. The saintliness of total abstention from sex—especially if after a libertine earlier life, as in the case of Augustine—would suggest a psychologically abnormal degree of reaction against normal sexual desires. Correspondingly, the "hero" who exhibits acts of superhuman physical courage may be enacting a profound death wish. Or he may, like the compulsive gambler, be taking risks as an attempt at magical solution of unconscious

conflicts (see Bergler 1943). Or he may be enacting self-punishment to relieve the guilt brought about by unconscious "criminal" fantasies. Interestingly, while following prevailing cultural norms, the populace at large shows admiration for any such saints and heroes—though often not until long after they are dead—they may also show, while the hero is in their midst, quite mixed reactions. The person of superhuman qualities typically makes mere ordinary people feel uncomfortable, reminding them of their imperfections in relation to the ideal norms of the society. Perhaps the negative side of such reactions indicates some at least subliminal awareness by the audience of the potentially psychopathological substratum underlying such saintly or heroic behavior. Sometimes this may be expressed overtly: "he may be a hero, but he's nuts!" or "She's a saint, all right, but she's crazy!"

8. The last combination would be statistically abnormal, culturally abnormal, and transculturally normal or healthy. An example would be a rare but psychologically healthy and adaptive rebellion against anti-humane and destructively repressive cultural norms. Psychologically healthy dissidents against totalitarian regimes such as Nazi Germany or Communist Russia, in statistically rare acts of rebellion against state-imposed cultural norms, would fit this pattern. Again, it would require an empirical clinical analysis to determine if the action is in fact coming from psychologically healthy and adaptive motivations, or rather from pathological self-destructive impulses. That cannot be gauged only from the nature of the acts themselves. But ill-timed revolt that grossly miscalculates available knowledge of reality in such a way as to escalate risks to the point of the near certainty of failure and self-destruction would certainly suggest some neurotic elements in the motivation, to say the least. Also the rebellious orientation may include elements of counter-ideology and counter-mythology that are so grossly at odds with some outside objective view of "reality" (if such be possible) as to indicate irrational needs for illusion, along the lines of the reactive and mitigating mythologies such as those of the feminist and gay-rights movements of current times. Analogies are found in many if not most movements of revolt against perceived oppression. (See Endleman 1970a, 1970b, 1972, 1975b, on such elements in the 1960s student revolts.) Revolt against oppressive authority can very well be mature, healthy, and adaptive. It can also be infantile, maladaptive, regressive, and pathological. We need to examine the particular case in both cultural and psychodynamic detail to decide which it is , or in what degrees it combines elements of both. Reactions of professional observers—social scientists, psychologists, psychoanalysts, etc.—to the student revolts of the late 1960s tended to get

polarized both in moral evaluations of the rebels—mainly approving or mainly disapproving (predominantly the former)—and in psychological evaluations of the rebels' "health" or "illness." (For examples of professionals perceiving the rebels as admirably healthy, see Keniston 1968, Hampden-Turner 1970, Liebert 1971, Flacks 1967. For professionals taking a contrary view see Feuer 1969; Endleman 1970a, 1970b; and, partially, Hendin 1971, 1975). Such extreme divergences of evaluation on the psychic health dimension suggest the enormous difficulty of making such evaluations on the basis of evidence far short of that required in the clinical situation. It also indicates how such evaluations are influenced, regardless of the values of objectivity maintained by the professionals in these fields, by one or more forms of ideological conviction deriving from extra-professional sources. They also suggest that different populations are being described (see below).

Consideration of such cases also points to the complexity of evaluating whether any pattern—of behavior, of psychic mechanism, or of total personality configuration—is normal or abnormal according to the cultural standard of normality, since there can very well be a plurality of such standards operating simultaneously in any particular society at any given, time—and that is certainly the case for any modern advanced technological society of today.

Again, the case of the student rebels of the 1960s provides a good example. Several different and conflicting kinds of culturally derived standards were operative in that situation. There were the standards of the substantial minority, later to become a majority, of the American population that was opposed to the Vietnam war. Within that population, there was a variety of cultural standards in reference to allowable forms of dissent or rebellion against constituted authority. There were variable standards of personal expressiveness and variable standards on the priority of personal autonomy over conformity to established authority. Thus, in a number of different and related subcultures within the larger American culture (to concentrate only on the American case), there was some degree of cultural approval for the rebellions, so that we cannot say that the phenomenon was entirely culturally abnormal, nor that it was entirely culturally normal. But the important point is that their evaluation as culturally approved or culturally disapproved is not necessarily correlated with clinical judgments of the psychological health or sickness of the actions or the participants.

Cultural or culturally relativistic standards of normality are the most prevalent in society generally and in major parts of the social-scientific and psychological professional world. They are influenced by the ideological pressure of anthropological cultural relativism that has been enormously influential on the modern consciousness, most explicitly among social scientists, and some psychologists and psychoanalysts, who perceive of themselves as in the vanguard of "advanced" "enlightened" thought in modern society. Such a standard implies an "adjustment" criterion of psychological health, equating adjustment to existing cultural norms with optimal psychological functioning. True, in some parts of this public, as just discussed, the culture to which one is expected to be adjusted is the subculture of the educationally sophisticated, for whom autonomy outranks submission to authority as a primary value, "liberated" personal expressiveness outranks conforming to older religious and secular moral norms repressive of many aspects of spontaneity, and innovationism outranks traditionalism as a central perspective on the world. In this subculture, some orientations considered deviant by a more traditional majority are counted as appropriate, approved, and tantamount to demonstrations of psychic health. This can be as strongly a conformist subculture as any other, or as the traditional majority, differing from others only in the *content* of the behavior prescribed or proscribed, rather than in the fact and mode of the conformity pressure itself. Again, its mode of conformity and the psychological motivations underlying it may be healthy or sick, adaptive or regressive, resolving conflicts or perpetuating them, from a transcultural mental-health perspective, and there is no necessary correlation between conformity and health, or deviance and sickness, or the reverse.

Elaine Morgan, in *The Descent of Woman* (1972), a work much admired and cited by some feminists, demonstrates a much more skeptical approach toward changing sexual norms than do many of her admirers. She makes a case for believing that we in modern culture have not really become more liberated in our attitudes toward sex and various other matters. She writes:

> Guilt and anxiety are not being dispersed, only attached to different situations. There is less shame attached to losing one's virginity too soon, and more attached to keeping it too long. It is less taboo to say "shit" and more taboo to say "nigger." There is less fear that you can be unbalanced by masturbation, a new conviction that you can be unbalanced by abstention. Less obloquy attaches to sleeping with a girl without giving her a wedding ring; but to do it without giving her an orgasm is a newly patent way of lousing up your self-esteem and peace of mind.
>
> Tolerance is not really being enlarged; it is moving its targets. The woman who cuts loose from an unpleasant husband because she cannot bear to live with him is praised, where once she was condemned. But the woman who

hangs on to a reluctant husband because she cannot bear to live without him is condemned, where once she was praised. Anyone who succumbs to alcoholism meets with less censure and more compassion than formerly ("it's an illness, really . . .") but anyone who succumbs to obesity gets short shrift ("no excuse for it these days . . . only needs a bit of will power . . . *other* people manage not to let themselves go . . ."). The total number of moral attitudes struck, the difficulty of trying to conform to them all, and the weight of social disapproval visited on those who fail, vary hardly at all. (Morgan 1972:229)

Thus the tyranny of enlightened minorities can be as great as that of benighted majorities. In both cases the normative judgments have no necessary connection with transcultural standards of psychological health. At the same time, in educationally sophisticated circles, terms such as "sick" are converted from clinical judgments to expressions of moral or social disapproval, replacing the older lexicon derived from religion and earlier conceptions of morality and ethics. This tendency compounds the confusion between "adjustment" and "psychic health," or between "maladjustment" or "deviance" and psychopathology.

Sociologists studying deviance have implied, if not stated explicitly, a culturally relativistic standard of normality. Deviance is in the eyes of the beholders, or the audience or public. It is seen in terms of norms that are potentially if not actually cross-culturally and transtemporally variable, and therefore in some sense arbitrary and changeable.

In the much cited Merton scheme ("Social Structure and Anomie," originally 1937, reprinted in Merton 1949, and in many other collections), conformity or deviance may be described in two dimensions, one as related to culturally prescribed goals of a particular society or subsociety, the other pertaining to using the institutionally prescribed means of achieving these goals. One could be totally conforming on both of these, e.g., the good American who seeks success by hard work, ability, and a crafty sensitivity to available legitimate opportunities. At the opposite extreme, one may deviate by rejecting both the goals and the legitimate means. Or one may accept and strive for the goals, e.g., success, but renounce or reject legitimate means, using instead means considered illegitimate, thus following a pattern of delinquency or crime. (This pattern itself tends to follow certain regularities, conformity to subinstitutional norms of this kind of deviant subculture.) Or one may overconform in reference to means, ritualizing "correct" behavior, at the sacrifice of reaching the supposed goals—a pattern Merton calls "ritualism."

A further pattern of partial rejection (while including partial acceptance) of both goals and means may involve attempts to transform the organized structure of the society to be better in line with ideal norms not ordinarily fulfilled—nor more than tokenly pursued—in that society, such as universalistic standards of social justice. In that pattern, commonly called "radicalism" (Merton calls it "rebellion"), there is selective rejection of some of the conventional goals, while retaining others; and similarly selective rejection of some of the legitimate means (e.g., enthusiasts may knowingly violate certain of the laws they consider unjust or inappropriate, to pursue their vision, while not condoning all forms of criminal acts) and improvising other means, which are until that point unusual or eccentric but not illegal, such as the passive resistance developed by Gandhian and other movements. All of these possibilities are further subject to many additional variations, if one considers a plurality of possible goals, as well as a plurality of possible means as all falling, in some way, within the normative structure of a particular culture. Indeed, a number of sociologists have been inspired by Merton's scheme to develop further such variations, multiplying the number of variables and subvariables, hence the even greater number of possible combinations. What is conformist within a particular context of goals-means "normality" can be deviant or nonconformist within another.

Social-psychologically, conformity is likely to be experienced as "adjustment" to the prevailing society or to the specific subsocietal segment that is the focus of one's life. Correspondingly, non-conformity will be regarded as "maladjustment." Such "adjustment" or "maladjustment" may refer not so specifically to particular items of behavioral conformity or nonconformity, but rather more diffusely to the whole pattern of the way the individual experiences and feels his life. He may feel that prevalently expected motivations, while not totally alien or abhorrent to him, are nevertheless not nearly so central or important in his life as the people all around seem to feel. So he "marches to the tune of a different drummer." Or he may be maladjusted in the sense Riesman refers to (Riesman et al. 1950) as not fitting well into the "characterological needs of his society." There are some such individuals in any society, who are neither delinquent or criminal ("innovationists" in Merton's scheme), nor totally apathetically withdrawn (Merton's "retreatists"), nor rebels or revolutionaries trying to transform the society to be better in line with their presumably superior ideals. They are *in*, but not fully *of*, the society in which they live. An "adjustment" psychology tends to assume that such individuals are also psychopathologically disturbed, which may or may not actually be the case. Sociological and other romanticists of deviance are likely to assume the opposite, that this kind of "maladjusted" individual is in fact the healthy one, and it is the surrounding society that is "sick." This *could* be the case, but the fact that the deviant and his admirers think so does not prove that it is. It *is* possible, of course, to construct, along the lines of a *trans*cultural standard of normality, criteria for evaluating a whole society, or a subsociety, as "sick" in the psychic-health sense—which we shall presently attempt. Here all that it is relevant to say is that the "maladjusted" person's sense of discomfort is not an adequate warrant for saying that it is.

A "SICK" SOCIETY?

One quality of individual psychopathology is the vicious-circle process (see Devereux 1956). There is a basic conflict, derived either from some infantile or childhood trauma never adequately dealt with, or from a series of events which together add up to a trauma, or from whatever other sources. (Different schools of psychoanalytic thinking vary on these points in ways which would take us too far afield to discuss at this point.) The basic conflict evokes in the individual primary patterns of defense. These defenses in turn create new difficulties, both interpersonally and in relation (often) to cultural norms, as well as intrapsychically. Then, further, secondary defenses need to be developed against these difficulties. And so it continues in a never-ending spiral. For example, self-imposed withdrawal from others produces negative, even hostile responses from the others, which then confirm paranoid suspicions on the part of the subject, which leads to further withdrawal and so on. The individual spends all his psychological attention on the tension experienced in relation to others, fighting back his own hostile (often murderous) impulses toward them, turning inward into further isolation. (One recalls the priceless Steinberg cartoon of a bitter-faced man cramped inside a box, saying, "All the world is no damn good!")

In analogy, we can think of a whole society, or a subsociety, as psychologically "sick" in the same sense of being caught in a vicious circle (see Devereux 1956:24). The people get involved in a basic conflict at the social or cultural level. They perceive the conflict in various less than rational ways. They seek ways out of the conflict that not only do not solve the conflict but lead them to sink ever deeper into the socio-psychic quicksand that is their own socio-cultural creation. A tribal example is that of the Tonkawa. They "clung so tenaciously to cannibalism that finally nearly all their neighbors waged a war of extermination against them" (Devereux 1956:24).

Obvious comparable examples are patterns of racial oppression of whites against blacks in the United States, in which reactions to fantasied threats produced dominative oppression or aversive social exclusion, leading to reactions against that, requiring further defensive shoring up of the oppression system, and so on indefinitely. In the process, the psychological health of persons on both sides of the color line suffers, producing further defensive or defiant-reactive counteractions. (See Kovel on *White Racism*, 1970, and the earlier work of Dollard 1937, to mention only a small part of a voluminous literature on this subject.)

Nazi Germany has frequently been cited as a society that would eminently qualify as a society that is sick (and not only that its leaders, Hitler preeminently, were clearly suffering from identifiable psychopathology.) In line with Devereux's formulation, the underlying and never-resolved conflicts of the Weimar period (of course with earlier historical roots), produced the defense mechanisms of first authoritarian and then later totalitarian control, and the quest to uproot imaginary internal enemies (Jews, Gypsies, "Communists," etc.), as well as to avoid encirclement by foreign powers, led in turn to ever more desperate and irrational counter-aggressive measures. These in turn led to the creation of even more and ever more real internal enemies, and eventually to the creation of an outside military-political alliance pledged to the destruction of Nazism. The counter-reactions in turn produced more extreme defensive-aggressive reactions by the regime. (This is, of course, a simplified picture, leaving out an enormous amount of attendant detail, but not oversimplified in that it outlines the essential pattern of the dynamics involved, and its parallel to the vicious-circle pattern in individual psychopathology.)

A comparable recent instance, not at the society-wide level, but at a crucial point in the executive branch of government, would be the Nixon presidency, not only in the Watergate scandal, but in many other aspects of his presidency. Here the basic conflicts (the many unresolved contemporary tensions of American society, including the crises of governmental legitimacy induced by the Vietnam war, the unresolved racial conflict, etc.) produced a paranoid defense in the form of construction of external enemies, inept paralegal attempts to get rid of these "enemies," etc.; the defense causes further conflicts and difficulties, leading to ever more extreme suppressions and violations, producing further reactive opposition, justifying the paranoid ideation, leading to still more self-destructive actions, getting himself and his cohorts eventually caught in the whole web of his own machinations, leading to his political self-destruction.

Along the same lines, one can perceive as a sick subsociety the followers of the radical student movement of the 1960s. They, too, particularly the leadership, got caught in a vicious circle. To the primary conflict, initially (for part of the movement at least) controversy about the American participation in the Vietnam war, which served as a plausible baseline for social protest, they reacted with the defense of a protest ever-broadening in its stated grievances and ever more ready to commit paralegal acts of defiance justified by self-conceived superior morality. This in turn created counter-actions and more definable specific external enemies. These in turn were countered by the protesters in ever more provocative gestures of defiance and "liberation." These gestures and the accompanying developing ideology created not only external enemies but also enemies internal to the movement itself, leading to intensifying concern with "heresy" from within as well as "oppression" from without, in typical paranoid spiral. The paranoid vision is "confirmed" by acts of oppression from the authorities, now more clearly polarized as the enemy, and by the doubts and hesitations—hence "heresy"—of erstwhile but more moderate supporters. Ever more extreme reactions by the rebels then alienate ever widening numbers of former supporters, leaving the remaining hard-core "revolutionaries" ever more isolated and more impelled into desperate acts of largely self-destructive terrorism (see Endleman 1970b, 1972; Feuer 1969; and others.)

1960S REBELLIONS:
COMPLEXITIES OF A CASE

The foregoing is a considerable oversimplification of the complexities of the 1960s student revolts. Elsewhere I have presented a more differentiated picture (Endleman 1970b, 1972). One way out of the oversimplified portraits of the student rebels that exaggerates either their psychic health (as in Keniston 1968; Hampden-Turner 1970) or exaggerates their psychopathology (e.g., Feuer 1969), is to differentiate among the variety of personality types who did in fact become active in these revolts. Though ultimately the number of such types could be nearly as great as the number of individuals involved—since each person is at the extreme unique and unlike all others—for heuristic purposes it is possible and useful to distinguish a small number of types that are distinctive from one another in certain broad but crucial psychodynamic and social dimensions. (Obviously, since the type is a heuristic device, of course no one individual fits the type totally in all respects; he or she can only be said to fit better into this type than into one of the others.) The types I distinguish are these three: the Apocalyptic, the Proto-Commissar, and the Humanistic-Worker. (For details, see Endleman 1970b, ch. 5.)

The Apocalyptic

The Apocalyptic correspond essentially to the type distinguished by Hendin (1971, 1975) as "revolutionaries"—as distinguished from merely "radical." These were the most extreme, and the most likely to escalate the struggle into violent all-out attacks on "the system." With the demise of the campus rebellions, these diehards gravitated to the more extreme off-campus movements moving toward terrorism, such as the Weathermen (the terroristic offshoot of the once merely "radical" SDS of the 1960s revolts). At the other extreme, the "Humanistic Workers" (of my categories) would correspond more or less closely to those rebels rather lovingly portrayed as psychologically healthier than other students by such interpreters as Keniston (1968 and elsewhere). These were much less given to irrational and nonrational extremes. The other category in my scheme is that of the Proto-Commissar, represented by students whose values emphasized power, rather than apocalypse, or than humanistic transformation.

We have had a sufficient number of personality portraits in some degree of psychodynamic probing of individuals who would fit one or another of these types to be able to make some generalizations, which in turn can help us see the collective psychosocial dynamics of a historical moment such as that of the 1960s students revolts. It is worth exploring some of this in somewhat more detail here in this context, since it can illuminate how segments or aspects of an ongoing society can be "sick," interacting with other segments of aspects that are relatively less pathological.

The Apocalyptic is a man by demons possessed. "The revolution" fills his whole being. He has a consuming drive to spectacular heroic action of catastrophic proportions. His whole life is stripped of irrelevancies or distractions. Women, enthralled by the violence they see in him, come unbidden to his bed. He uses them as objects and despises their motivation, otherwise has no feeling for them. Consumed with ideals for the good of "humanity," he has no empathy, no humane warmth, for particular human beings. They are to be manipulated for the Cause, in which he has absolute conviction. Underneath that hard surface, he is lonely and terrified of any deep commitment to any particular other human being. His demands upon the Enemy, and also upon comrades in the struggle, are totalistic and uncompromising. He is enraged by any hint of "deals" or "negotiated settlements" that any of his weaker comrades might try, or seem, to make with the Enemy. Nothing short of complete capitulation will be acceptable. Refusing that, the Enemy will unleash violence, and the Revolution is advanced. Of course there will be bloodshed. Terrorism will be the necessary next stage. Earlier the universities had some relevance in this struggle. By the early 1970s, they have become irrelevant, and the Revolution moves into the streets and into the society at large. Bloodshed will be a necessity. The Revolutionary must be prepared at all times to sacrifice anything for the Cause, including one's life. One expects that many of one's comrades will be killed, perhaps even oneself. The Apocalyptic's visions are full of blood, violence, death. Intense emotional connectedness is experienced only in relation to such apocalyptic fantasies, or anything coming close to their realization, as, for example, a particularly violent police "bust" of a campus building occupation. In terms of social categories, the Apocalyptic accepts unquestioningly his being part of a vanguard elite (necessary to make a revolution), but accepts too the strategic value of pretenses of egalitarianism in the Movement as a device for bringing in supporting troops from the masses of the student body. He concentrates on the Struggle itself. He pays little—if any—attention to drawing blueprints for the future better society (that is, presumably, to be brought about by the overthrow of the existing one). He has a feeling he will not live to see that day. A Future that could be a real world with a working social organization and culture is in fact, at deep levels, not conceivable to him. His image of his own destruction in the apocalyptic final struggle is something that could well be a self-fulfilling prophecy: his own self-destructive drives may well bring this about, if the "reactionaries" do not do it for him. The demons by which this revolutionary is consumed are his own unconscious rage, or the unconscious underpinnings of what now is a conscious rage; i.e., a rage at the emotional abandonment he has experienced by parents who have never actually emotionally responded to him as a real human being. Typically, students of this kind have had family backgrounds which fit neither the widely held notion that the radicals were the spoiled kids of affluent parents who were overpermissive and never required the child to develop self-control or self-discipline, nor the other widely portrayed notion that they were the rational libertarian children of rational libertarian and warmly humanistic parents. Studies such as Hendin's of these "revolutionaries" indicates that typically the parents were materially providing but emotionally extremely unresponsive to the child, while maintaining a facade of a pleasant cooperative family life and an illusionary conception of the child in question which bore little relationship to what the child was actually like, and particularly made no connection with the child's emotional needs. Materially sated, they were emotionally starved, and developed defenses of non-involvement or of brittle irony against this devastating experience of abandonment, a feeling that could never be acknowledged, since the reality of its having happened was never recognized, let alone confronted, by the parents themselves. These were not really "permissive" parents. They were negligent and essentially uncaring. Neglect is rationalized as enlightened, "letting the child go his own way." As a result, showing your feelings at all, or even being able to get closely in touch with them, becomes extremely taboo. One student said, "If you show your feelings, you get your legs cut off" (Hendin 1971:24). In many cases, in the families where such a student grew up, political discussions were the nearest thing to a personal exchange that took place within the family. Hendin sees this as connected with these students' use of politics to express feelings that are personal (*ibid.*, p. 26). Outside authorities—more broadly "the system"—become the displaced targets of that inner rage aroused by the parents' emotional non-existence. By the time of young adulthood, and caught up fortuitously in the "right historical moment" of the student rebellions, the student can then declare his parents—his specific parents—"irrelevant," an appropriate revenge for their having in effect treated him as irrelevant up to that time.

Participation in a political action that the actors can declare as not only meaningful but fateful for the whole society gives the Apocalyptic's life a focus and, for once, a crux of emotional meaning. He also acquires a pseudo-*Gemeinschaft* of the comrades in the struggle—though he has some inkling of how shallow that "community" is likely to be, as the Movement constantly generates factional battles and "heresies" in its ever-more paranoid enactment of persecutory and avenging fantasy. In the process, more reasonable, more rational, less hatred-consumed, more politically moderate, erstwhile supporters—such as those more like the Humanistic-Worker type, find themselves ever more dissatisfied and repelled by the increasingly evident violence, totalitarianism, and self-destructiveness of the Apocalyptic revolutionaries, and depart from the Struggle (or rechannel their political protest into more reformist measures essentially "within the system"), thus casting themselves, in the remaining revolutionaries' eyes, as having sold out, and become part of the Enemy. (Sociologically, the Movement at that stage faces the twin dangers of repression and co-optation—see Endleman 1972—repression from the authorities, especially the police, that incarnation of evil; and co-optation, i.e., recruitment of the erstwhile radicals into reformistic change systems cooperating with the more benign of the authorities of the established system. As co-optation of increasing numbers of relatively healthier and more rational radicals into reformist and liberal endeavors depopulates the "movement," its leadership becomes ever more desperate, and falls increasingly into the hands of the apocalyptics, rather than the proto-commissars.) But the apocalyptics are not only caught up in the kinds of paranoid spirals in relation to external and internal enemies that we have already described, but more than that: cataclysm is essential to their psychological being. Thus the direction toward terrorism is clear, and since the dissolution of the campus rebellions of the 1960s, we find specifically the apocalyptics reappearing in the guise of a wave of variegated terrorist groups operating in many parts of the world, and under a great variety of ideological guises.

I have referred to the Apocalyptic in the preceding paragraphs as "he." Needless to say, this type could as well be a "she." In fact, some of the most ferocious of the student revolutionaries have been women, as have many, if not quite half, of the more recent terrorists. The dynamics of the women student revolutionaries whom Hendin studied (1971, 1975) have shown a similar kind of family situation with uncaring, neglectful, emotionally absent parents, leaving the child with a great rage which has been denied recognition, let alone expression, and is therefore very susceptible to being displaced onto outside figures in the sociopolitical world. Perhaps women who gravitate into this apocalyptic political role are even more ferocious and prone to violence than the men, on the model of the overconforming marginal person who needs more desperately than the one in the established position to prove her purity. If aggression is a masculine hallmark (see chapter 9) in conventional conceptions, then the women radicals must prove themselves even more aggressive than the males. But surprisingly, some of the women student radicals of this more apocalyptic type, when confronted with the persistence of "male chauvinism" on the college barricades—"hey, we need a chick to type this up"—turned in the direction of developing radical feminist groups combining left-wing political radicalism with feminist politics. The more ferocious of these in turn have moved in the direction of terrorism, while others, fitting more closely either the Proto-Commissar or the Humanistic-Worker types, have directed their political energies in the feminist struggle in one or another version not so violently at odds with established structures. And some of these are combining the radical struggle with both feminism and gay liberation in the form of the "Radicalesbian" movement. (See previous chapter.)

The Proto-Commissar

The second type is the *Proto-Commissar*. His guiding drive is Power. His modus vivendi is the concentrated direction of his high intelligence and drive upon the strategies and tactics of the revolutionary task. Consciously, for him, the fomenting and directing of campus disruption is an instrumental strategy in the radicalization of potential troops. The "bust" is a necessary instrument in this cause. There must be no negotiated settlement, for that would slow down and subvert the processes of polarization and radicalization. The manifest issues and demands of the campus confrontation are necessary pretexts. Their being met is no goal, except as such momentary victory demonstrates the impotence of the authorities and the power of the radical Movement as a step toward the next stage. Strategically it may be more important to destroy the universities than to get concessions from them, depending on instrumental calculations of comparative short-range and long-range gains and losses. There is ostensibly rational controversy within the Movement on these points. Some see winning on current issues as counter-productive—it involves too much risk of cooptation of wavering radicals into cooperation with the university establishment. Others see it as increasing the opportunities for boring from within.

Essentially the Proto-Commissar is driven to destroy the power of the existing authorities, so that the Movement, with himself in a crucial role, will take over that power. In the Liberation brought by the Revolution, he and the small group of cohorts around him will direct the new society. His parricidal rage against all authorities is aimed at supplanting them in power. A facade of democracy will be necessary to bring the masses to the correct side, but the masses must be taught what is good for them. That, of course, is part of the task of the vanguard elite. He has seen enough of the vapidity, unreliability, and sentimentality of student followers to know that neither they nor the broad masses are capable of *directing* the making of the Revolution (though they may be necessary to carry it out). No more are they capable of running the future liberated society. They have neither the intelligence nor the single-mindedness of purpose and dedication. That is to be found only in the vanguard elite. Only they are capable of the sacrifice, devotion, and discipline needed for the struggle, which will be long and bloody. Unlike the apocalyptic, he does not especially relish the bloodiness, and will therefore not consciously throw himself into needless dangerous heroics. He regards any of his comrades, such as the Apocalyptic types, who do so, as dangerous not alone to themselves, but also to the Movement, which could be needlessly set back by terroristic adventurism. Terrorism is acceptable, however, if rationally strategic for a given short-run or long-run political goal. He regards people who have moral constraints against using it where practically necessary as sentimental, a prime defect of the bourgeoisie.

This apparently rational machiavellianism is, however, not without its irrational adjuncts. One of these is the cultivation of paranoid suspiciousness. All who are not your allies are automatically your enemies—at least potentially. They must therefore be watched closely, especially all your comrades in the struggle. Infiltration by enemy spies and agents of all kinds—from the police, the FBI, the CIA, university authorities, competing self-styled radical groups—is an ever-present danger or reality. As organization gets tighter in the escalation of revolutionary struggle, this wariness becomes ever more necessary, and increases accordingly. Ultimately there is no one you can thoroughly trust. The slightest trace of doctrinal impurity in any of your comrades must be carefully observed and scrutinized. On the campus, everyone you come in contact with must be appraised for his probable loyalties both now and in the next stage of revolutionary ferment, especially all left-liberal or seemingly radical faculty. All clear-cut enemies must be noted and marked for appropriate retribution "after the revolution." All those having ambiguous loyalties must be scrutinized to determine their future fate in the new order.

In this atmosphere, it is hard to determine where realistic appraisals leave off and fantasy takes over. The whole atmosphere of suspicion conduces to self-fulfilling prophecies. His own aggressive drives are discovered by projection in anyone and everyone in the world around him. That this "discovery" often corresponds in fact to some objectively verifiable reality in the world outside does not negate the fact of intrapsychic origins of the need to make such "discoveries." His parricidal rage finds the reciprocation (and justification) in the hostilities the authorities direct against him and his comrades. These in turn are gratifying, for they confirm his intellectual picture of the world and also validate his importance as a danger to the established order. He also harbors, below consciousness, a heavy reservoir of guilt. This is shown in the combination of expectation of harsh punishment from the authorities and the obsessive repetitive assertion of his own moral purity. (If he were so convinced of this purity, why the necessity to reassert it constantly?) The whole process of purification of himself (by concentrated dedication to the Cause, to the exclusion of all other interests) and of the whole revolutionary vanguard is also probably testimony to the underlying guilt.

Paranoid suspiciousness is also connected, in the males, with underlying anxieties about the adequacy of one's masculinity. The oedipal picture in the background here, as attested by many psycho-social familial studies of the student radicals (e.g., Keniston 1968, Flacks 1967, and others), does not show a classical authoritarian father against whom the sons rebel in the mythical Totem and Taboo manner. Rather more likely the father has been a relatively ineffectual figure, whose major sin has been failure to buffer between the son and the competent and sometimes overwhelming mother. She may not have been quite the CBI mother of the childhood of many homosexuals (see chapter 11, particularly the work of Bieber 1962), but she has tendencies in that direction, mitigated by the greater likelihood of career work in the labor force. The effect is of fairly egalitarian parents in relation to each other, and particularly a lack of patriarchal power in the father. While this produces something of the modern, "enlightened" family supposedly fostering the children's independence and autonomy, it also leaves the son without either a clear-cut powerful father against whom to rebel, and also measure himself, but also any clear-cut model of masculine identification. I think a part of my analysis of "oedipal" elements in student rebellions (1970a) applies particularly here to students who need, in effect, to *construct* powerful, hostile, even violent, authorities for their adversaries—if necessary, bringing them into being by the students' own provocations,— as an emotionally necessary process of testing their own manhood, and denying their own anxieties about their own weakness on this score. As I suggested earlier, that the sacred-taboo language of obscenity that was prominent in the 1960s campus uprisings included, quite significantly, references to homosexual acts suggests the effort magically to exorcise those demons of failed masculinity. And also significantly, this reflected throwing back at the enemy, the cops, precisely those outrageous insults of homosexual attribution that the police made against the male students. (The relationship between paranoia and unconscious homosexual feelings was long ago presented by Freud in the Schreber case—see Freud 1911—and, though needing later qualification, is still a staple of psychoanalytic interpretation.)

The sectarian fractionating that develops as the Movement intensifies indicates the casting off of negative fragments of the self. The bitterest hatreds are directed at ideological factions closest to one's own, that have split off over a minute doctrinal point. The narcissism of small differences comes into play here. The "impure" faction epitomizes a hated, split-off, unrecognized part of oneself. (Parallels abound in overtly religious sects.) At this point the movement consumes itself in fratricidal wars, as though in repentance over the (fantasied) killing of the father. The struggles within the New Left by the end of the 1960s showed this process. Thus part of Feuer's (1969) picture of irrational destructiveness seems to fit this type of radical as well: the elitist amorality, cynical manipulation of others (disguised as "liberation"), destructiveness (in the guise of rational strategy), and great intensity of (probably oedipal) guilt and parricidal rage.

The Humanistic Worker

The third type I call the *Humanistic Worker*. This one more closely approximates the Keniston type of portrait of the student radical. His main drive is not for apocalypse, nor for power, but for expressive freedom. He is opposed to authority in all its guises. (This leads him as confrontations intensify to discover that the more apocalyptic or proto-commissar types in the movement are as likely to push him and others around as are the "establishment" authorities, and at times more ruthlessly so.)

He wants to be able to pursue—now!—whatever interests him at the moment and, given the freedom to do so, will pursue it with passionate intensity, a hallmark of youth. He is impulsive, moody, frequently beset with anxiety. Life is full of contingency—a source of anxiety at times, but also of expressive exuberance. He is infuriated by routinization and bureaucratic rules that are (to him) irrational and unnecessary restrictions on people's freedom. He hungers for simple straightforward answers to the dilemmas of life, and is infuriated by professors who emphasize the complexity and many-sidedness of the world. He has a passion for what he thinks is social justice: people are being oppressed, that should be stopped; the nation is fighting an immoral and unjust war, that should be stopped; professors and administrators oppress students, that should be stopped. He is impatient to do something, sick of endless ratiocination. He is likely to be a "red-diaper baby," i.e., to have grown up in a family of liberal to radical parents stressing a high degree of freedom and "democracy" within the family. His "idealism" is not so much a reaction against overtly authoritarian parents as it is an attempt to extend into the wider world the ideals of his parents, often with a feeling that the parents themselves have fallen short of practical realization of these ideals. His idealism, however, does not extend to the fanaticism of the apocalyptic or the power-games of the proto-commissar. He is thus willing to work hard where his pragmatic sense leads him to believe in the viability of the particular action, but pulls back when encountering the authoritarianism and irrational destructiveness that leaders of the movement who approximate either of the two other types display.

This type is the most easily co-opted into idealistically tinged meliorist activity "within the system." When he participates in a major confrontation, such as occupying a campus building, he finds himself in a confusion of feelings. He is scared of the cops. But a ferocious girl from SDS makes him feel he has no balls, so he stays; besides he can't let his "comrades" down. He feels vaguely guilty much of the time. Not sure whether it is because he has acted, or because he has not acted.

The more aggressive women in the group make him uneasy. The ferocity of the "revolutionaries" makes him anxious. If the confrontation reaches the climax sought after by the more revolutionary, i.e., a police action ("bust") against the rebels, this type is momentarily convinced by this event that the whole system is brutal, rotten, oppressive, and the rest. But such conviction does not last as the rebellion fizzles out and the movement fractionates into the fratricidal wars just mentioned.

The Rebellions as an "Abnormal" Phenomenon?

Thus, a phenomenon such as the student rebellions of the late 1960s shows a good deal of internal complexity. The statistical normality of the events was relatively low, though they did become quite widespread in 1968 and 1969. The cultural normality varied according to the perspective of the observer, many considering themselves modern enlightened sophisticates finding much to approve in the feistiness and anti-authoritarianism of the rebels, the display of "autonomy," and their expressive exuberance, while these same qualities won disapproval from more traditional and more conventional people in this society. Their later turn toward more violent and more totalitarian modes of protest then alienated others including some erstwhile supporters. In psychodynamics, participants of course varied widely, but three broad types were discernible, two of them—the apocalyptic and the proto-commissars—approximating the negative picture of the rebels' psychic health portrayed by many observers, such as Feuer and Endleman, while the third approximated the allegedly more "healthy" rebel or radical as portrayed by more admiring clinicians or social scientists, such as Keniston, Liebert, and Flacks.

The first two showed different but clinically unmistakable psychological patterns that few clinicians would fail to regard as psychopathological, and Hendin clinically described the more "apocalyptic" (my term, not his) in his portrait of the "revolutionaries" (as distinct from the merely "radical"). Some of Feuer's depiction fits what I have here called the "proto-commissars," as does much of the dynamic pattern I earlier portrayed as part of an "oedipal rebellion" (Endleman 1970a). It is not the deviance per se that qualifies for assessment of psychopathology here, but rather the underlining dynamics, their irrationalities, and the vicious circle quality of the kind Devereux portrays.

The third type, whom I have dubbed "Humanistic Workers," or idealistic workers, are more questionable regarding assessment of pathology, though they were certainly not without psychological difficulties of various kinds. Their degree of flexibility, their capacity to reevaluate their participation in a social struggle that first appeared libertarian, but later disintegrated (for those most committed to it) into fratricidal rage and distinctly anti-libertarian modes, would indicate reserves of positive psychic health, not shared by the first two types.

For the apocalyptic, the vicious circle process is sufficiently extreme that they must, in response to the "failure" of the campus rebellions, move to ever more violent, ever more terroristic "revolutionary" action, ever more filled with irrational hate and rage. Proto-commissars, conversely, seek alternate arenas for their struggles for power.

CHAPTER SIXTEEN

The Sociology of Deviance and the Transcultural Alternative

APPROACHES FROM THE SOCIOLOGY OF DEVIANCE

There is a major point of discrepancy between approaches to norm-violating behavior that focus on the relationship to individual psychopathology and approaches that prevail in the sociology of deviance. As in Merton and all other sociologists following in that tradition, the sources of commonly patterned deviant behavior or deviant conduct are to be sought in strains and difficulties in the social structure—and not in intrapsychic functioning of individuals. Merton did not totally deny that psychopathological functioning might be involved in any of the kinds of manifestations of deviance he dealt with in that seminal paper—crime, withdrawal, radicalism, etc.—but rather he saw the *sociological* task as fundamentally different (as Durkheim did before him) from the psychological one. He emphasized that his categories referred to role behavior in the context of personality structure.

This is a distinction crucial to much sociological work. In reference to deviance, it involves bracketing or setting aside entirely, as outside the sociological domain, the psychological questions of possible health or sickness in the personalities involved. In some cases it sees psychological questions as totally irrelevant. In even more extreme formulation (e.g., Simon and Gagnon on homosexuality, 1967, as discussed in the previous section) it rejects psychological questions entirely. Some thinkers along these lines regard any consideration of psychological etiology as part of a process of oppression against deviants by organized authority.

To be more exact, present-day sociology features particularly approaches to deviance that go beyond the social-structural context of Merton's functionalist emphasis and concentrate on the problem of society through its established representatives designating what are to be counted as deviant acts or states and designating particular individuals as deviants. This kind of approach in sociology has come to be referred to as "labeling theory." According to this view, what constitutes deviance is entirely a matter of labeling by persons in positions of sufficient power or relevant authority to do this labeling. In this process, persons who do so become labeled, e.g., as delinquents, as alcoholics, as drug addicts, as sexual deviants, undergo a process of victimization, stigmatization, and, frequently, degradation and persecution. This position is, of course, as already said, an entirely relativistic one: what kinds of behavior or psychological stance will get one labeled as deviant, and as deviant of a particular kind, does, of course, vary from one society to another, from one period in history to another. In that sense it is arbitrary, in that the same or comparable behavior or attitude in a different society, or a different age, or even a different subsegment of the same society, would not receive the same labeling, the same stigmatization, and the life of the individual concerned would be free of the kinds of victimization visited upon him in this particular society. The exponents of this viewpoint in sociology are among the major figures of contemporary sociology, such as Howard Becker (1963, 1964), Kai Erikson (1962), and Erving Goffman (1961, 1963), Edwin Schur (1971), and many others. A representative definition of deviance from this labeling perspective is provided by Schur: He suggests the following "working definition of deviance":

> Human behavior is deviant *to the extent that* it comes to be viewed as involving *personally discreditable* departure from a group's normative expectations *and it elicits* interpersonal or collective reactions that serve to "isolate, "treat," "correct," or "punish" *individuals* engaged in such behavior. (Schur 1971:24; italics in original)

The emphases that Schur makes in this working definition are for the purposes of certain theoretical points he is concerned to make in that work, some of which do not concern us here. The essential points of such a definition for our purposes is that there must be something personally discreditable about the violation of norms that the individual commits, and that there must be a reaction to this behavior, of one or more of the kinds indicated.

In this perspective, the deviance inheres not in the nature of the way the individual is different from others, or violates social norms, but rather in the societal definition and reaction. Thus, persons who steal or cheat and are never caught are not *labeled*, while others who do so and are caught are so labeled, and it is only the latter who are sociologically in the category of criminals as far as society is concerned. Also, others may be so labeled in the basis of false accusations and incriminating "evidence," even if in fact that have not committed the acts attributed to them. It is the labeling that is crucial to the person's future path of life.

In this perspective, many sociologists feel they must take the viewpoint of the victims of such labeling, since, they say, for too long social scientists had simply accepted without question the viewpoint of the legal and other established authorities, or simply of the "common sense" of people in their society, who "knew" that illegal acts by a small number of crooks and hoodlums were "the problem." This newer viewpoint reveals that "the problem" lies elsewhere, in the very arbitrariness and frequent injustice and inhumanity in the way in which official representatives impose degraded status upon all those who can be so classified, and thus use them as the whipping boys of the rest of society. It is therefore pointless to try to study how "criminals," for example, are any different—psychologically, in class background, or whatever—from the rest of society, since the population so labeled does not represent all persons who have ever committed acts against the law, but only a very skewed sampling, including particularly persons of already low status who are especially vulnerable to such victimization in the form of labeling and stigma. And on the other side, many persons who may have in fact committed such "offenses" but were never caught are arbitrarily classified in the "normal" sample. Thus crime statistics are invariably biased to give the impression that criminal acts occur much more prevalently in the lower class. By contrast, "white collar' offenses—stock market frauds, manipulations by corporate executives, the more recent computer-system frauds, as well as all kinds of malfeasance in public office—typically are much more likely to escape detection or official attention—and, where they do not, are treated in extraordinarily lenient fashion.

Some of the advantages of the labeling approach in the sociological study of deviance are stated by Schur as follows:

> . . . its strong relativism reinforces the growing challenge to conventional thinking about problems of deviation, a challenge that has itself . . . partly

contributed to the current popularity of the labeling approach . . .
[also] by dramatizing the stigmatizing nature of negative labeling, the approach has led to somewhat greater caution in the use of negative labels
and to less glib resort to euphemistic terminology for processes that are not
less harsh or punishing . . . [also] the voluntaristic theme underlying some
labeling analyses may have served a useful purpose in causing various specialists to reassess earlier, largely unquestioned deterministic assumptions
about the causes of deviance. (Schur 1971; 171)

Obviously, then, this is an extremely culturally relativistic viewpoint.
Taken to its extreme, society seems to consist entirely of victims, oppressors, and others who get away with things. This is the kind of viewpoint that produces assertions to the effect that there are hundreds of
thousands of "political prisoners" (namely black ones) in American prisons, since blacks are so disproportionately represented in the prison
population. According to this line of thinking, they are there because
they are black and powerless, not because they have in fact committed
robberies, thefts, assaults, and homicides, the ostensible reasons for their
being arrested, arraigned, tried, convicted, and sent to prison. This is
relativism gone wild. One would suppose from such allegations that
there are no such events as acts that are intrinsically harmful to others
in society. One would find nowhere in this view any recognition of the
fact that every society we know of negatively sanctions in-group homi-
cide, various other forms of in-group aggression, incest, violations of the
exogamy rules, rape, cheating, violations of its specific property rules,
exclusive homosexuality, and most other forms of sexual "paraphilias."

We can also find, as one of the consequences of such excessive relativism, courts intended to deal with subadults who have committed
serious offenses against others or the community taking a viewpoint
which implies or even states that the juvenile offender is himself a victim
of circumstances over which he has no control, and refraining from
imposing any effective sanctions on youngsters who have in some cases
in fact committed murder, and who thus discover that they can really
"get away with murder," literally, as long as they are under a certain
age.

The Schur quotation certainly acknowledges the relativism of this approach. Where I differ from him, of course, is in my value judgments of
such relativism. Where he obviously approves of what he sees as its
"challenge to conventional thinking," I would claim not to see any
greater moral superiority in questioning conventional thinking, for the
sake of questioning, than there is in the conventional thinking itself,
especially where the "conventional thinking" involves conceptions such

as that people should enjoy safety of their persons and property, should not be subject to sexual assault or such assault upon their children, and the like.

No doubt the kind of debunking of legitimate authorities that may be supported by the labeling approach is attractive to some neophyte (and other not so novice) social scientists, whose interest in this field derives from rebelliousness and antinomianism. But that kind of appeal is hardly any warrant for the soundness of the approach. It is no more so than an appeal which stood entirely behind the most traditional values and supported "legitimate authority" all the way—through the latter kind of thinking is in fact exceedingly rare in the social sciences—at least in sociology, which seems to have attracted, in the twentieth century, an extraordinarily large proportion of people with some kind of maverick or rebel orientation toward the world, at a minimum in the direction of reforming society to make it more closely fit the "good" ideals of Western culture.

By contrast, very few supporters of the status quo, of established political order, or of the economic power system, are attracted to sociology. In clinical psychology and the branch of psychoanalysis now coming out of the medical schools, the tendency is similar, if not quite as extreme. Most such professionals, while not likely to be as political as most sociologists, are likely to be at least in the liberal range of the political spectrum, if not farther left than that, as these terms are generally, if only vaguely, understood in modern Western democratic nations.

As I have already indicated, the relativistic emphasis of this labeling approach is not only political and value-loaded—a fact which Schur and some other sociologists of this persuasion readily acknowledge—but it is so in a way that is distorting of reality and, in its implications and potential consequences, just as likely to be anti-libertarian (quite in opposition to its proponents' intentions), as are the views the labeling theory sociologists oppose and vilify. For example, it makes no distinction between totalitarian usages of official labeling, as in the Soviet Union's characterization of political dissidents as psychologically disturbed, followed by their incarceration and brainwashing in psychiatric hospitals, and the procedure by which designated psychotics are committed to psychiatric hospitals in Western democratic countries like the United States. Because other individuals, who may be no less disoriented or disturbed than those who are sent to hospitals, are not so handled, sociologists of this persuasion argue that therefore those who are sent (or commit themselves) to psychiatric hospitals are not in fact sick, and should not in any justice be so institutionalized. It is claimed that the only way they differ from others with similar psychological patterns is that somehow their behavior came to the attention of someone motivated and able to set in motion an official process labeling this individual as insane or psychotic. At the extreme, this viewpoint denies that there is any such entity as mental illness, that it is all a matter of contingencies that lead some people to be so labeled, while others, psychologically no different, escape this labeling.

This viewpoint ignores, or in extreme phrasings simply denies, the fact that there are persons not psychologically capable of handling their simplest everyday affairs, not capable of distinguishing between fantasy and reality, or subject to delusions of reference and other kinds, or so totally emotionally withdrawn that they cannot bear even minimal emotional contact with another human being. It denies there are persons so overwhelmed with feelings of hopelessness and doom that they cannot put themselves in even the simplest ways into the everyday stream of life, or who see enemies everywhere and cannot believe there exists any person in the world who has no hostile intent toward them. It ignores or denies the existence of persons who truly believe they are Napoleon or Mary Mother of God, or Joan of Arc, and can ingeniously interpret events or information coming to them to fit these beliefs. To claim, as the labeling theorists do, that the psychopathology of such individuals is entirely a matter of their being victimized by unfair negative labeling by establishment authorities (psychiatrists and psychotherapists presumably) is not only a literally fantastic distortion of the reality of these individuals' situation, but also implicitly an anti-humane denial of the right any decent society would accord them to be treated appropriately in terms of their actual psychological state.

Some labeling sociologists have taken up Erving Goffman's famous book *Asylums* (1961), particularly its chapters on mental hospital life, to support the kind of view of mental hospitalization as pure victimization just described. Goffman is, of course, not to be held accountable for what other sociologists have done with his work. Goffman himself, in that and other work, did *not* draw the conclusion that all psychosis is merely socio-political victimization, and does not deny the sufferings of the mental patient. His analysis, not being intended to deal with the intrapsychic processes of the disturbed patient, did focus rather on the social, essentially political, processes involved in getting that person into the hospital and how he is dealt with there. (At least in that state hospital at that time—late 1950s.) Other sociologists, however, have run with that material to the extreme of regarding all designated psychosis as only victimization. They write as though all of the pain and sufferings of the psychotically afflicted individual were entirely a product of stigmatization and of the process of hospitalization.

I am not denying that many often brutal or dehumanizing actions are taken toward and against psychiatric hospital patients, and that in such instances a patient's talking about these need not be in the nature of paranoid delusion. But that is not at all the same as saying there is no such thing as mental illness, or that the patients are, in fact, free of any psychopathology, and that its alleged existence is entirely a socio-politically created artifact.

Some labeling theory sociologists and other sociologists with an animus against psychiatry and psychoanalysis find warrant and support for their position in the work of a very different writer, the psychoanalyst Thomas Szasz, in works like his most influential one, *The Myth of Mental Illness* (1961). Szasz has focused primarily on psychiatry as practiced in state psychiatric hospitals and finds there—not entirely inaccurately—a *socio-political* process which serves a function of social control of persons considered troublesome in some way. He claims that psychiatric categorization ("diagnosis") bears no relationship to the actual psychological state of individuals so labeled, but rather serves the political purpose of domination over what sociologists call "deviants." He goes further to dismiss any claim psychiatrists or other therapeutic professionals may make for helping sick people as self-serving rationalizations for their actual function as agents of social control. He sees an establishment, including psychiatrists, intent on creating a class of scapegoats—the "mentally ill"—parallel to the witches of earlier centuries. This kind of message—particularly coming as it does from someone who is himself part of the psychiatric world—is welcome news to labeling sociologists intent on seeing the world as victims and oppressors, and on denying intrapsychic realities.

Hostility toward psychiatry or psychoanalysis on the part of some sociologists may find support from yet another and different quarter, namely the work of Ronald Laing (1967, and other writings), which, unlike Szasz's right-wing libertarianism, comes from a politically left-wing direction. Laing and his supporters romanticize schizophrenia as a "sane response to an insane society," as part of an indictment, along proto-Marxist lines, of "capitalist" society, where the usual psychiatric treatment of schizophrenics is seen as part of a general process of capitalistic oppression. The Laingians' romanticizing of schizophrenia does a major disservice to people actually suffering from psychological disturbance of this psychotic variety. It ignores the suffering, the private hell, of that experience, the tyranny of fantasy at a largely primary process level, the inability to have any kind of ego-integrated satisfactions or gratifications, the inability to share with others consensualized understandings and appreciations of the ongoing reality of the surrounding world. Instead, it seeks to portray all sufferings of hospitalized patients as deriving totally from the dominations and oppressions imposed on them by the institutional authorities or their even more sadistic underlings.

Thus, although of course Goffman, Szasz, and Laing are three very different thinkers, with different sociopolitical orientations, the uses of which their respective works are put by labeling theory and similarly-minded sociologists show certain affinities, such as the distorting view of the world as oppressors and victims and the aversion to dealing with intrapsychic processes of the personality.

The distortions involved in this kind of vision are not very dissimilar to those of the ideologists of the gay liberation movement. There is the same denial that sufferings experienced by the persons involved—in one case the sexual deviants called homosexual, in the other the psychological deviants called madmen—can possibly derive from internal psychological features of the individuals concerned, but must all be attributable to outside oppression. Some of the rhetoric of more extreme versions of the feminist movement has a similar quality; if some women are in fact submissive, frightened, unassertive, overly dependent, and so on, that is only because they have been pushed to become like that by men, or by socialization by equally damaged mothers and female teachers. There is a peculiar kind of environmental determinism implied in all of these views, curiously at odds with the usually unconnected ideological conviction that many of these same liberationists assert or imply, that human beings can and should be able, in their own autonomous capacities, to direct and rule their own lives.

ALTERNATIVE: A TRANSCULTURAL VIEW

If the cultural or culturally relativistic viewpoint toward normality is inadequate in the ways we have indicated, what then would constitute a workable *trans*cultural view? And why the word *trans*cultural, rather than cross-cultural?

Transcultural is used because the word cross-cultural already has an established usage that is usually associated with a relativistic viewpoint: "cross-cultural comparisons" imply that we need to take into account the *differences* among cultures, and typically imply the relativistic view that it is illegitimate to use the standards of one culture in analyzing and evaluating another. "Transcultural" is meant to be differentiated from that view, and also to indicate that the set of standards to be described by this term *transcends* cultural differences and is intended to point to pan-human *universals*. So this set of criteria makes reference to the nature of the human animal as it has emerged in evolution—once and only once—in a particular set of evolutionary-historical circumstances, and that has a peculiar combination of characteristics different from all forms of animal life, that are in large part a product of the particular evolutionary circumstances. Of these, signal importance attaches to the premature birth of the human neonate, its extreme helplessness and dependency, the prolongation of this dependency through the peculiarly human latency period, the peculiarities of human non-seasonal, precocious, lifelong, and voracious sexuality, the particular combination of strong sexual dimorphism and psychological bisexuality, infantile polymorphousness, the peculiarly human combination of dependency and omnipotence in infancy, the peculiarities of human aggressive drives, the proneness of human beings to magical thinking and magical "solutions" to problems, and the diverse psycho-social concatenations of human sexuality and its array of possible transformations.

In these characteristics, the human animal is different from other animals, and also, *all* human beings share these universal human-animal characteristics. All share the same need for sociality that is far more intense than in other animals. All share the same need and propensity for symbolism, for linguistic communication, for mythologizing the world. All show continuation throughout life, in some form, of infantile dependency, infantile fears of abandonment or attack, infantile magical approaches to the world, as well as the capacities developed later in childhood and beyond, for ego-directed, more realistic appraisals of the world, for self-direction, for autonomy, for pursuit of gratification in more socially oriented ways, for joining with others in instrumental endeavors and in expressive communion. All share the contingent nature of existence, its dangers, sorrows, and disappointments, regardless of how variably these may be presented, in detail, in different cultures, different ages. All have to deal with love and death, with the passage of time and life seasons, with work and aggression and aggression's transformations. All have to deal with the progression of the life-stages in psycho-sexual development, from infancy to early childhood to the juvenile stage to puberty to adolescence and on to adulthood, and with the oft mysterious differences between the sexes in these stages. All have to deal with the conflicts and dilemmas and difficulties—never entirely absent—of each of these stages, and find some kind of "solution" to each of these and in turn to the further problems or difficulties each such "solution" brings in later stages. All have to deal with the "vicissitudes" of the drives of sex and aggression in themselves and in the other human beings closest to them. All of these statements may sound like obvious truisms to some. But they do have to be made, since cultural relativism has generally so strongly resisted such statements about a universal "human nature." The term "human nature" itself came into very bad odor among anthropologists and others influenced by them in the twentieth century as the explorations of the exotic diversities of human cultures took center stage and as anthropologists and other social scientists felt it urgent to argue against and expose the ethnocentrism of such conceptions as the equation of profit-making with universal human nature. However, more recently anthropologists have shown more willingness to state and explore "cultural universals"—features that in some form are to be found in all cultures—and this needs to be extended, here, to the psychological realm: not only the universality of primary incest taboos to be found in all societies as a cultural institution, but also the universality of its psychological counterpart, oedipal conflict, found in some version in all societies.

For all of the basic problems that human beings must face in some form in any society in any historical age, there are relatively more "healthy" or "psychologically integrated" patterns of dealing with them, and there are relatively more "pathological" or "psychologically sick" or "psychologically inadequate" ways of dealing with them, regardless of the culture. And "healthy" need not coincide with conformity to prevailing cultural norms. And "sick" need not coincide with nonconformity or deviance. Either may, or may not, coincide in this way.

The transcultural viewpoint emphasizes that these are independent categories. We can specify what kinds of mechanisms, what kinds of patterns of stage-by-stage development, are relatively more pathological, by a set of criteria that would apply to all human beings in any society. These are the criteria for psychopathology that have been developed by psychoanalysis and allied clinical disciplines. True, they were developed in Western societies in a particular historical period. But they were developed as part of a particular set of patterns of Western culture that are the most universalistic of those to be found in this culture, and in the context of the universalistic endeavors of naturalistic science. The standards of such naturalistic science are not ethnocentrically Western, as is often claimed, since they are readily learnable and usable by any human beings in any society, and intrinsically transcend national or societal boundaries. (The disastrous consequences of trying to conduct science in a nationalistically parochial manner are well illustrated by the detour into Lysenkoism in Russian biology.)

Poorly informed commentators, who have claimed Freud's work was parochially grounded in late-nineteenth-century Vienna and therefore cannot claim a transnational and trans-historical relevance, ignore the massive evidence of applicability of basic psychoanalytic ideas to the understanding of mythologies from all around the world and all periods of history to the understanding of any of the hundreds of diverse and exotic tribal societies, as demonstrated by psychoanalytically minded anthropologists such as Devereux, Anne Parsons, Róheim, and many others. When someone on the basis of some anthropological report said to Freud that the tribal people concerned had no problems in relation to the anal stage, Freud's tart reply was" "Was, haben *die* Leute kein Anus?" ("What? Don't those people have an anus?") (In case any readers need explication: if you have an anus, and if your culture, like all others, insists on *some* kind of training for control of bowel movements, then it is impossible that there be no problems whatever that can be referred to as "problems of the anal stage.")

The psychological mechanisms of defense and adaptation that psychoanalysis has explored are universal human mechanisms. We find them being used by human beings anywhere in the world, anytime in history. Parisians and Patagonians both use projection. Russians use repression no less than Riffians do. Irishmen and Hidatsa Indians all introject. Sublimation is found in Soho and the Sudan. Regression is used by Rumanians and Rossel Islanders of Oceania. And adaptive regression in Andalusia and Assam. Rural Japanese and Caribbean Rastiferians resort to reaction-formation as much as any of the rest of us. Denial appears in Dobu, in Dakar, and in Dayton, Ohio, too. Projective identification appears in the psychic repertoire of Paraguayans and Pago-Pagoans alike. Polygynous Mbundu and polyandrous Marquesans are as susceptible to the infantile megalomanic defense as are monogamous Milanese. And Finns and Fox Indians are just as vulnerable to fixation, at whatever psychosexual stage. Hunting-gathering Ifugaon natives of the Philippines use identification as well as computer-technician Italians. And identification with the aggressor is found in Iatmul initiation ceremonies as well as in the army of Iran. Eskimos and Englishmen may all carry on extrusion of hostile introjects. And intellectualization we find in the Incas, in the Israelis, and everywhere else. Tanalans and Turks internalize. Franks and Fijiians fantasize. And symbolizing is a basic human activity everywhere from Samoa to Saskatchewan. Trobriand Islander Kula traders and Toronto stockbrokers are all capable of transformations of internal psychic stress. Isolation appears in the Aymara and in India. Displacement in Dahomey or on the Danube. Chinese or Crow may as readily compartmentalize. And undoing is done by Utes and Uruguayans. And splitting in Sparta and Split.

In short, we all live in the same kind of bodies, have the same range of psychological problems, and the same repertoire of psychic devices for dealing with them. We differ only, from one individual to another, and from one society to another, in the precise detail of the ways these are combined.

Besides the same basic mechanisms of defense and adaptation, we are all subject to certain kinds of psychic experiences that are common to all human beings. Ambivalence is universal from the Andaman Islands to Asbury Park. Anxiety knows no geography of space or time, from Alaska to Alor, from the Argonauts of ancient Greece to the astronauts of modern Moscow. Bad objects as well as good objects are internalized by babies from Boulder to Bombay. And cannibalistic fantasies are un-coverable in primitive Chuckchee as well as in sophisticated modern Canadians. Castration anxiety can be found anywhere from the Keraki to Castile. And in Tonga and Toledo (as well as everywhere else) babies latch on to transitional objects as part of the process of negotiating in-fancy. Narcissism is no less potential in the Navaho than in the natives of Nantucket. And good-enough mothering is to be found among the BaGanda and the Greeks, and in most, if not all, other peoples of the world. The oral stage has to be dealt with from Orinoco to Ottawa. Anal difficulties are potential from Afghanistan to Altoona. And the phallic stage is not limited to Phoenicia and the Philippines. Oedipal problems may arise in Easter Island and Easthampton. Latency may be a bit less latent in Lesu and other Oceanic tribes, but elsewhere it is evident from Latvia to London. Puberty is a significant life-stage to be dealt with, if not a crisis, in Ponape as well as Pennsylvania. And heterosexual mating is potentially problematical for Hopi and Hungarians as well as people of all other societies.

Thus we have baselines for comparing all human beings. And all human cultures.

What qualifies for a categorizing as psychopathology is not in the use of one or another of the basic mechanisms, but rather in the particular *pattern* of their use. Similarly, experiencing the Oedipus complex in itself does not distinguish one individual from another, or one society from another, since it is a universal human experience. How it is handled can and will vary, and there are more and there are less pathological ways of attempting some resolution of this human problem. That one has had, and in some senses still has, infantile oral cravings does not distinguish anyone from the rest of humanity. But one can have such cravings in such a way and in such a pattern as to differentiate from others in the direction of pathology. Psychopathology is not an all or nothing matter, it is always more or less. And within it, it is differentiated qualitatively in a number of ways—but not infinitely. We may all mourn the loss of someone important to us, and such mourning does not distinguish this human being from all others who have had a similar experience, nor qualify for a label of psychopathology. But melancholia, as Freud long ago showed (Freud 1917) in an analysis upon which only marginal improving qualifications have been made since that time, is distinguishable from normal mourning, and has a progressively more pathological quality, not remediable by the usual processes of working through a normal mourning experience. We find mourning in all human beings; and, in many cultures, a culturally defined and recognized pathological process that is basically what Freud called melancholia and that we today call depression. Among the Mohave Indians, as studied by Devereux (1937, 1939, 1961, 1970a) old men deserted by young wives—but never old wives deserted by young husbands—exhibit a pattern of reactions called the "heartbreak syndrome," which Devereux shows is explainable entirely within so-called Western psychodynamic conceptions as a classical mourning depression (Devereux, 1956:39).

The basic processes of psychological functioning and of development in infancy and childhood involve conflict and defense. Life without conflict is impossible. No infant can be totally and completely gratified all of the time. Nor in fact could his ego develop at all adequately if he were. Conflict is answered by defense. Some defensive systems are forward-moving in the development of the individual; others block forward development and lead in the direction of a vicious circle, where the defense causes more problems than it solves, leading in turn to the need for further defenses, causing more problems, and so on in unending spiral.

Irrationality is a major quality of psychopathology. To some extent and at least some of the time all human beings act or think irrationally, and also some aspects of every culture are irrational. Knowable or known information is ignored or denied out of emotional need. We act in contradiction to expressed or implied goals. We act in ways to defeat conscious purposes. We simultaneously believe two propositions that patently are in mutual contradiction. We use means to an end that are manifestly and knowably inadequate for the purpose, or contradictory to the purpose. We unreasonably fear something or some situation that presents no objectively verifiable danger. We invent spirits or beings that have no objective referent in the real world. We elaborate excessive details of procedure that have no demonstrable relationship to stated objectives, but help reduce anxiety. We can believe any number of objectively preposterous statements about the world. We are capable of assuming we have some omnipotent power over the world around us which is readily contradicted by such a common event as a hurricane. Or we can believe that we are provided some protection against such dangers by a purely imaginary being whose reality exists only in men's minds. And so on and on. If we concentrate only on those aspects of our thinking and acting that fit into any of these categories, we can believe along with Norman Brown (1959) that all societies participate in the common neurosis—or perhaps even psychosis—of mankind. A similar formulation appears in Weston LaBarre's book *The Human Animal* (1954) in which he argues, rather cogently (but I think with some flaws) that every culture is in effect a collective psychosis, that the only real differences between a psychosis and a culture is in the number of adherents. (LaBarre somewhat modulated this view in his later major work, *The Ghost Dance: Origins of Religion*, 1970, which recognizes that irrationalities such as those embodied in the collective illusions of a religion are not the only things operating in a culture, and that indeed—as instrumentally-minded anthropologists insist—some aspects of culture are, in fact, realistically adaptive. That is, even in the groups of a fantastic religious cult, the people of a society may still have a hold on those ego functions of reality-testing and reality-orientation that enable them to survive, subsist, manage everday affairs in the world.)

Since all human beings partake of the irrational to some degree and some of the time, where is the line between normality and psychopathology to be drawn? We can suggest an answer: it is psychopathological where irrational qualities dominate most or the whole of one's life and psychic functioning. The obsessive-compulsive is psychopathological to the extent that his obsessions and compulsions interfere with the range and particularly the spontaneity of his everyday dealings with the world, by the great elaboration of ritualization of endless details in the areas of conduct where he can safely function, with an attendant enormous constriction of action, thought, and feelings. Granted this can be channeled into culturally approved kinds of activities, as is commonly done in societies like our own, which show a high degree of culturally stylized transformation of anal derivatives. In this context, rationality in the sense of a high degree of logical coordination and regularization of units to be experienced, handled, worked over, transformed, etc., as *objects*, as is common in our own and in other advanced modern industrial societies, may very well be carried to points of irrationality, where means override rationality of ends in ways elucidated by such sociologists as Weber and Merton and others. At what point the degree of elaboration and ritualization is to be considered psychopathological is a tricky matter of evaluation, but one way of approaching it is to inquire about the degree of flexibility as against rigidity in the responses, and the ease or difficulty by which people are able to change. We also have distinctions in psychoanalysis between obsessive-compulsive *neurosis*, where the psychological style is experienced as both compulsory and as ego-*dystonic*, as contrasted with obsessive-compulsive *character* disorder or simply character style, in which the obsessive or compulsive rituals are largely ego-*syntonic* and may not even be recognized as ritualized behavior. The latter may also *not* be experienced as socially deviant or maladjusted, especially if the prevailing culture supports that style, as would be true for more puritanical elements in modern populations. In any of these cases, psychopathological patterns may or may not be socially deviant or maladjusted, depending on the particular norms operating in that society or subsociety. And needless to say, also, they may or may not be statistically abnormal as well.

Devereux, rejecting purely cultural (relativistic, adjustment-oriented) criteria of psychological normality, suggests that "the crux of mental health is not adjustment, but the capacity for constant readjustment" (Devereux 1956:41). Thus, most commonly, the shaman in an Indian tribe can be considered by this standard either a severe neurotic or a psychotic who, while functioning as a shaman, is in a state of remission, implying the possibility—more likely probability—that he will go back, under certain circumstances, to a more pathological state, such as a distinctly schizophrenic psychotic one. But he is "in remission only with reference to a particular type of social setting: his own tribe. He is adapted or adjusted to that setting, and only to that setting. He is not adaptable, and above all, not readaptable" (*ibid.*, p. 41). We can, with Devereux, compare this kind of marginally socially adjusted individual, who in fact is psychopathological though currently in remission, to persons hospitalized in a psychiatric hospital who seem rational, cooperative, and well-behaved, *in the hospital*, thus showing adjustment to the hospital subsociety, and who on release immediately "crack up" all over again. Similarly, we find individuals who have become rehabilitated from heroin addiction in such settings as Synanon, or Maher's San Francisco "Delancey House" (see Hampden-Turner 1976), but who are quite unable to function outside that setting. Admirers of Synanon (see Yablonsky

1965) or of Delancey House, or of other such nearly total institutions, are impressed with the "cures" they have (or claim to have) effected of individuals who had been both socially badly maladjusted and deviant, and psychologically very disoriented, in short pathological, and who had been resistant to both the punitive measures of prisons and the like and the permissive measures of attempt at insight therapy. This is not to derogate the "gain" represented by their becoming decent, reasonably cooperative, and socially responsive citizens of this essentially closed society—as distinguished from the chaotic self- and other-destroyers they had been. But what is significant is that such change lasts only as long as they remain within the limited and both restrictive and supportive environment of this specially designed institution. They are thus comparable to persons who have undergone a "transference cure" or "purely symptomatic relief" in some kind of psychotherapeutic encounter where lacking the development of deep insight based on assiduous working through of the underlying unconscious conflicts, they are susceptible to return to the disturbed state under particular adverse circumstances.

Similarly, there are pathologies associated with inadequate maneuvering through and resolution of the problems of the oral stage, others related to etiologies from the anal stage, still others from the phallic stage. So there is schizoid withdrawal, difficulty, or impossibility of forming close intimate bonds with any other persons. There is a range of disorders collectively called the schizophrenias, where there are gross deficits (derived, evidently, from defects in the early oral stage) in various of the more crucial functions of the ego, such as reality testing, where a line between fantasy and reality is not only not maintained, but often not even recognized as possible at all. There are disorders of affect, particularly those involving feelings of enormous abandonment or loss, often accompanied by ferocious superego functioning imposing enormous burdens of guilt and worthlessness. Here there are major failures of the ego functions of mood control. Though descent into psychotic versions of this kind of disorder, depression, may seem to be precipitated by an external event such as death of a loved one (more likely a close object both loved and hated with great intensity), there is most likely to be a substratum of potentiality for this kind of disorder existing in the structure of the personality since early childhood, specifically since the oral phase. Any of these—schizoid, schizophrenic, or depressive—are likely to show definite psychological symptoms, of a more or less florid or obtrusive quality, and any of them experienced as distinctly ego-dystonic. Another variety of disorder of oral-stage origin would be the "oral character," in which extremes of oral greediness, or more subtle derivatives of them, are experienced, but in an ego-syntonic way, and often enough, in many cultures (such as our own) in a *culture*-syntonic way, i.e., in a way where the culture generally gives approval, or at least permission, to indulge oneself in these ways (e.g., consumerism in our society).

Disorders with primarily anal stage etiology (or, in some cases, more precisely, an etiology involving regressing to the anal stage) include the obsessive-compulsive neuroses and the obsessive-compulsive character disorders already discussed. The difference is that the former involve distinct symptoms that are experienced as alien and unsettling; the latter involves a style the individual is comfortable with (ego-syntonic), often supported, as discussed, by cultural mandates. Individuals showing any of these pathologies may also show elements of difficulties deriving from oral stage problems not adequately resolved, and in some cases masked by the obsessive-compulsive defenses. The prominent defenses here are isolation of affect, intellectualization, and compartmentalization. As a character style they are to be found not only in intellectuals, librarians, bookkeepers, accountants, and sundry varieties of bureaucratic workers in our society, but in comparable occupations in many other societies and kinds of societies, such as Pueblo priests and the bearers of complex oral traditions in many tribal societies, not to mention all those who serve as guardians and perpetuators of complex religious rituals. As Freud long ago suggested, a religion is a collectivized obsessive-compulsive neurosis or character disorder, while art corresponds to hysteria and philosophy to paranoia.

Hysterical neurosis and the closely related phobic disorders have been regarded in classical psychoanalysis, since their pioneering study by Freud, as deriving from inadequately worked through struggles of the phallic phase and its attendant triangular crises in the Oedipus complex. More recent psychoanalytic work finds a good deal of oral stage substratum in cases that seem at first like classical hysterias or hysterias with phobic symptoms. And also, more recent psychoanalytic work suggests that frequently what looks like more classical neurosis of the obsessive-compulsive or hysterical variety may turn out to be a defensive facade, protecting the "sufferer" from even more severe disintegration into distinctly psychotic kinds of disorder.

There are also the disorders of superego functioning that have been called psychopathy or psychopathic personality,[1] which fit neither the neurotic nor the psychotic pattern, involving neither ego-dystonic symptoms that interfere with ordinary functions and satisfactions, nor with the failures of ego-integration or of mood equilibrium characterizing the schizophrenias or the depressions, respectively. In these cases, we find an almost complete absence of personally-experienced moral sense (accompanied often by an exhaustively detailed and accurate knowledge of *what the norms are,* for one's own society and its relevant subgroups, and frequently by considerable knowledge of just how these norms are applied, the probability of their enforcement, etc.). Ego functions of reality knowledge and reality testing are not only intact, but often superior, in a context of a higher than average intelligence. And in this type, social graces may be highly developed, to the point of ingratiating charm, and used entirely on an expedient basis, to aid oneself to succeed in whatever instrumental goals one has set for himself. Personal relationships never involve deep affective involvement of any kind, and are usually maintained for expedient instrumental purposes. The degree of malignancy of the underlying disorder may almost totally escape the attention of others dealing with such a person, especially in a society like our own, where casual, essentially impersonal, relationships with large numbers of other persons are a usual experience, and where norms of privacy can more readily keep the underlying psychic nature of individuals concealed from surrounding others.

Then there is the whole range of disorders of sexual functioning, which may or may not be accompanied by classically neurotic, or psychotic, or character disorders, or by psychopathy. One major version of these, homosexuality, we have discussed at length in the preceding section. In most psychoanalytic views, this, as well as other sexual departures, is seen as a psychopathological variation, even though it may be extremely encapsulated and not notably affect other aspects of psychological functioning.

Then there are the paranoid states, which may appear in the context of neurosis, or in one of psychosis as in schizophrenia—though neither are all schizophrenics paranoid nor all paranoids schizophrenic. Here the most notable aspect of the symptomatology appears in the cognitive functions, with ideas of reference, sometimes extreme enough to amount to delusions of either persecution or of grandeur or of both. Here one sees particularly florid, often exotic, versions of the vicious circle of psychopathology: paranoid suspiciousness toward others leads the individual to act in hostile-seclusive or hostile-aggressive ways toward others, inducing in the others hostile counter-reactions, thus confirming the suspicion that others are "out to get me," leading to further hostile actions, evoking further counteractions, etc. Some authors have referred to the "paranoid pseudo-community" in this context (see Cameron 1943). The social-interactional elements may be particularly strong in this kind of disorder, and here particularly the approaches of sociology and psychoanalysis combined may be particularly needed to sort out just how and to what extent the elaborated ideations of the paranoid are in fact reality-oriented and where they are not. Being frightened and suspicious of others on a New York subway would scarcely qualify as a paranoid response to the reality of living with the dangers of that city. The predominant defense mechanism in paranoid states is, of course, projection: not only does the paranoid attribute to others his own conscious and unconscious hostilities; he also has an exquisite sensitivity to the unconscious aggressiveness of others, which he erroneously identifies only (or mainly) to the extent of regarding it as conscious and deliberate. Since some paranoid thinking may be found in conjunction with many other configurations, there is reasonable debate on whether it is an identifiable clinical entity in itself.

Another series of syndromes has been identified, distinguishable from the classic hysterias and obsessive-compulsive disorders, as well as from schizophrenia and depression, and these are the narcissistic disorders, much attended to in recent psychoanalytic work. In any of these states, we may find elements of psychopathic orientation to the world, some characteristics similar to depressive disorders, some delusional thinking suggestive of schizophrenia, and sometimes the kind of labile affect typical of the hysterias. It is often extremely difficult to arrive at a differential diagnosis. What seems to set such individuals apart from most other neurotics, particularly symptom-neurotics, is the disturbance in the sense of the *self*. Narcissistic disturbances have been subject to a diversity of interpretations and theoretical analysis in recent psychoanalysis, much of it reaching a kind of Talmudic or Jesuitical intensity of hairsplitting refinement. (See, for the major exponents, Kohut 1971 and Kernberg 1975.)

The alleged increasing prevalence of such narcissistic disorders in contemporary America, and perhaps other Western countries too, is a significant point of controversy, since we do not have any adequate ways of knowing whether precisely this kind of psychopathological configuration *has* become more frequent in this society, or whether its apparent increase is merely an artifact of changing diagnostics, or of the changing character (socio-economically and in other social category terms) of the patient population seen by psychoanalytic therapists, with their greater numbers and diffusion in North America. Or perhaps both of these factors are at work. An observation favoring the changing-diagnostics view is that many of the "classical" hysterical cases written about by Freud and some of his earliest followers would today be seen as having many indicators of narcissistic disorder, not so observable within the framework of early psychoanalysis.[2]

There are also a series of identifiable syndromes which are termed in more recent psychoanalysis "borderline conditions," the phrase once indicating something on the edge of psychosis (presumably schizophrenic), but increasingly being considered as distinct in etiology, determining conditions, probable lines of development and, correspondingly, demanding different modes of treatment. (See Kernberg 1975 for systematic discussion.) The differentiating characteristics of this pattern from that of the narcissistic disorders take up a major part of prominent debate in the psychoanalytic journals of today. (See Kohut 1971 and Kernberg 1975 on varying interpretations of narcissistic disorders compared to borderline.) The details of these often Talmudic controversies are beyond the scope of our present discussion. Suffice for the moment to note that none of the protagonists would claim any such patients should be considered free of pathology. In all of these syndromes, as distinguishable from classical obsessional or hysterical ones, the evidence points to serious, very early disturbance in ego-functions, in the formation of the self, as well as in the handling of the basic problems of the oral and anal stage.

The foregoing is, of course, a highly simplified and schematized outline of the main kinds of psychopathology recognized in Western psychoanalytically based psychiatry. At almost every point in that discussion there are divergent opinions within psychoanalysis—not to mention other kinds of psychologies—on the nature and etiology of these syndromes, or about many of them, whether they should properly be considered a clinical entity at all. Stoller's criteria (see chapter 12, ref. to Stoller 1975), according to which he concluded homosexuality was not strictly speaking a clinical entity when applied to any of these syndromes, might very well lead some analysts to conclude that none of these, either, is strictly speaking a clinical entity. And all experience working clinically with patients demonstrates that precise diagnosis of a patient in terms of these categories can be an extraordinarily difficult and tricky problem, since the same patient, even in the initial clinical interview, may show indications pointing to hysteria, to compulsive neurosis, to oral character, to schizoid condition, to mildly psychopathic states, to schizophrenic delusional thinking, to depressive psychosis, and/or to paranoid states, in any combination.

The fact, however, that there is much divergence of opinion within the psychotherapeutic worlds, and within psychoanalysis specifically, itself, need not deter us from noting both that there are still main lines of consensus, and that there are definable psychopathological processes that signalize that persons exhibiting them are in terms of psychoanalytic standards of mental health more or less seriously disturbed in definable ways—even if different clinicians cannot agree entirely on the details—and in ways which differentiate such individuals from other persons who, in these respects, are relatively free of serious pathology and enjoy areas of at least "good-enough functioning" in most aspects of their lives. The differences lie in the greater irrationality in the disturbed (in extreme psychotic cases, almost total dominance by irrational perceptions of the world, magical thinking, and the like, by identifiable delusions, etc.) as compared to the relatively "well," their greater likelihood of involvement in a vicious circle of pathology from conflict, to primary but inadequate defense, to secondary difficulties and conflicts, to secondary defenses, etc., their greater fixity, rigidity, and incapacity to change and to adapt to new conditions and circumstances.

We can also note that the obtrusiveness or floridity of the symptom-atology of the individual is not by itself an indicator of the degree of malignancy of the underlying process. In fact Devereux suggests (1956:29) that, for the series hysteria, phobia, obsessive-compulsive neurosis, and character disorder, these show up in *decreasing* order of obtrusiveness of symptoms (and correspondingly likely to be regarded as "weird," "strange," or "deviant" in a society like our own), and correspondingly, in *increasing* order of severity of the underlying pathology. Similarly, within the schizophrenias, those apparently acting most "crazy" are probably likely to have a more favorable prognosis than those who are most pliable and controllable by the hospital staff, those who are most withdrawn and isolated into themselves.

CHAPTER SEVENTEEN

Psychopathology and Deviance

Those psychologically disturbed may or may not also be regarded as socially "deviant" in a particular society. Some forms, such as certain types of character disorder, may be so well meshed with adjustment requirements of a particular society—such as obsessive-compulsive character disorders with certain occupations in our society, as already discussed—that they are not perceived as deviant by themselves or by others within the same society, or at least within the same social milieus. Milder versions of hysterical disturbance may be highly associated with certain artistic-performing occupations, to the extent that exhibiting such characteristics may not be considered "deviant" in that context, even though the individual may be defined as "off-beat," "unpredictable," "eccentric," in relation to what are thought to be the norms of the placid majority population of nonartistic people. "Artistic temperament" may signify allowable variation, implying some recognition of psychological functioning different from the normal in some respects, as well as leeway for action, particularly impulsive action, not accorded solid citizens, and justified by the alleged spark of genius (or at least superior talent) by which the artistic have been gifted by some mysterious, perhaps supernatural, powers. Similar things can be said for milder versions of narcissism, short of extreme narcissistic disorder. (The latter would probably incapacitate a gifted individual from doing any kind of coherent artistic work in whatever genre.) Some degree of paranoid suspiciousness—usually associated with higher than average intelligence—may be a boon to anyone undertaking work involving detection, the unearthing of new evidence, discovering hidden meanings in apparently innocuous or otherwise unremarkable material, and the like, such as in the work of the detective, the archeologist, certain kinds of legal professions, sociologists given to conspiracy theories, and, of course, psychoanalysts themselves, as Freud long ago recognized. And isolation of affect may very well be a useful (if not essential) psychological technique for people to use who are working with people or situations that constantly assault one's sensibilities in one way or another, such as garbage collectors, prison guards, mental hospital attendants, and the like. In hiring a cleaning woman, one would be much better advised to find an obsessive-compulsive than a hysteric.

Still, the more seriously neurotically disturbed, all psychotics, and psychopaths when they are recognized in their role of violating the law, are all likely to be regarded as "deviant." For neurotics, this is much more likely to happen where their symptoms involve interpersonal situations where they come into significant conflict with others. (The schizoid may be seen as only a bit odd and shy and is not as likely to come to others' attention in ways disturbing to them. By contrast, a hysteric whose outbursts "cause a scene" may be the object of frequent complaints from neighbors to the police.) Sociologists of deviance who want to absolve psychotics from the label of psychopathology by noting that some very disturbed individuals never get hospitalized, and only people who are a trouble to others suffer this indignity, do have a kernel of truth which, however, they have misinterpreted in line with their ideological view. True, hospitalization is not necessarily an indicator that someone is *more* seriously disturbed than someone else who just doesn't happen to come to the attention of the relevant professionals and authorities. But it does not mean that the identified "patient" is not in fact suffering from some kind of psychopathology. And while it is true that the whole labeling process, as applied to persons seen as mentally ill enough to require psychiatric hospitalization, itself sets in train a whole series of sociological processes that are, theoretically at least, independent of the question of original psychopathology, and may produce secondary reactions that both exacerbate psychopathological processes and intensify the likelihood of being considered socially "deviant," none of that contradicts the existence of prior intrapsychic processes of a pathological order.

There is also the factor, as noted by Devereux (1940, 1956), that at least in some forms of psychotic or near-psychotic illness, there is an important element of social negativism, the individual in effect defying social expectations and the conventions of ordinary thinking, often in ways that are obviously provocative toward others, inviting some kind of sanctions. From one perspective, the reality-testing is quite defective, the individual seeming not to recognize that his actions are going to get him into a lot of trouble, at least with neighbors, if not with the law.

From another perspective, however, it is evident that the "external reality" (in this case the surrounding social world) is being perceived with great accuracy, including accurate awareness of unconscious processes in others, and is being deliberately (if only unconsciously) provoked, to serve the particular (probably largely unconscious) purposes of the sick individual. This is particularly obvious in paranoid states, but it appears in other kinds of psychopathological conditions as well, if only less obviously and more subtly. In sexual deviations such as homosexuality, the very existence of a deviant category may have an important influence in the "choice of pathology," and may be an important contribution to the maintenance of the symptom, whose negative social validation provides yet another means for the masochistically inclined individual to aggress yet again and in yet another manner against himself. As indicated in the previous chapter, however, there are, of course, many different kinds of psychological constellations within which this particular form of sexual deviation may appear, and we know enough now not to confuse the overt behavioral deviation, or even its associated fantasies, with just one particular clinical constellation.

One can be deviant *and* sick; deviant and not sick; or sick and not deviant; or neither deviant nor sick. Because labeling as deviant has certain arbitrary elements to it that may be independent of any particular intrapsychic processes of a pathological nature does not warrant the anti-intraceptive posture of most labeling theory sociologists, who deny that there can be any psychopathology whatever in any of these cases. The implications for intervention are evident: where the deviant is also sick, purely social kinds of intervention are unlikely to resolve the difficulties. For example, neither stigmatizing, nor destigmatizing homosexuality addresses itself at all to the intrapsychic problems involved in this sexual variation. Conversely, if the problem is all social, and not at all intrapsychic psychological, then psychological interventions will not properly address themselves to the difficulty. Attempting to "cure" a healthy rebel against a sick totalitarian regime will not solve problems, but only add another dimension of oppression. (The difficulty in such cases, of course, is in demonstrating that the rebel is "healthy" and the society he is rebelling against "sick." It is possible, of course, but in practicality very difficult. And most likely no "solution" will satisfy the variety of observers, commentators, and ideologues concerned with such a case.) The sick who are not deviant are not as likely to be noticed, or, if seen, not seen as particularly problematical, though in many cases, as in certain types of character disorder, the degree of their intrapsychic malignancy might be among the most severe of all.

Critics have asked, even if psychoanalytic formulations of psychic process are applicable to modern Western societies, are these modes of intrapsychic analysis really also applicable to people of other cultures, other times? The transculturalists' answer is definitely yes: we're all human and all subject to the same possibilities of going awry in certain (finitely numbered) configurations, and though we may not find identifiable hysterias or schizophrenias exactly corresponding to those we are familiar with from Western psychiatry in all other societies, or in similar proportions of the population in other societies, something like these is a potential in all of them, and it is a matter for further research to find just what forms of psychopathology do in fact occur, and in what frequencies, in different societies.

The *cross*-cultural (relativistic) critics claim, in opposition, that certain forms of Western-identified pathology do not appear at all in certain other societies—or certain types of other societies—while certain other societies have displayed other, to our mind very exotic, forms of psychic disturbance unknown among ourselves. On the former point, even *some* transculturalists like Devereux have asserted that schizophrenia is extremely rare in *totally* primitive societies (in contrast to those "primitive" societies which we know from anthropology where the very fact of their accessibility to study indicates that the people have already been at least partly acculturated to Western or other advanced society's culture) (Devereux 1961 and elsewhere).

Apparently inconsistently, however, this same psychoanalytic anthropologist has argued very cogently that shamans in tribal societies must be considered as probably psychotics in remission, or at the very least severe hysterical neurotics (Devereux 1956:27ff). From the context it is evident that the kind of psychosis Devereux has in mind is either schizophrenia (though some incidents in the shaman's work show indications of mania, too) or a form of disorder which Devereux, following earlier psychiatric conventions, refers to as hysterial psychosis, or a psychotic version of hysteria, which in his view is distinguishable from the schizophrenias. (More recent psychoanalytically oriented work has dropped the term hysterical psychosis for such disturbance and tends to count disorders of this type among the schizophrenias. Obviously, there are innumerable knotty problems of diagnostics involved in these controversies, getting into which would take us far too far afield at this juncture.)

It is possible, of course, that the shamans encountered and sufficiently well described, and in a few cases analytically interpreted, as in Devereux's work, are already in a state of sufficient acculturation to standards of some advanced society as not to qualify for what Devereux means by "truly primitive." Extreme versions of the latter are, of course, unknown to us directly, in the nature of the case; contact sufficient for high-civilization visitors or scientists to observe them automatically has destroyed the isolation of their prior primitive state.

Devereux has also asserted that he can find (after assiduous search) extremely little evidence for cases of psychopathic personality in tribal societies (his phrasing is "an almost infinitesimally small number of possible cases of so-called psychopathy"—Devereux 1956:39n).

The rarity or even complete absence of some of our particular types of psychological disorder in some other societies does not, of course, invalidate the possible universal applicability of allegedly Western ethnocentric conceptions of psychodynamic *processes*. It may only say, as Devereux does say, that different societies may have distinctive types of psychological disorder, what he calls the "ethnic psychoses." By this he means characteristic ways of becoming psychotic that typify a particular society, just as medical epidemiological studies show certain kinds of physical malady as being more typical of some societies than others, or as having an incidence significantly higher in one society than another. Thus cancer is more typical of late twentieth-century America than of other societies. Correspondingly, Devereux argues, schizophrenia and the psychopathic conditions could be considered the "ethnic psychoses" of such advanced—and we would add, internally enormously conflicted—societies as ours. And they are much rarer, or totally absent, in tribal societies, the nearer they are to their earlier, culturally primitive state, characterized by a high degree of *Gemeinschaft* with its combination of close personal support and close personal control.

On the second point: that some other societies show forms of psychological aberration that are distinctive syndromes not classifiable by Western psychodynamic concepts or nosological categories. Here we enter into the exotic realm of anthropological curiosities, such as running *amok* in Malay; the *windigo* psychosis of Northern Algonquin tribes in Canada; "Crazy-Dog-wishes-to-die" among the Crow Indians; *imu* of the Ainu of Japan; *latah* of Southeast Asia; *susto* of Indians of the South American Andes; *mal ojo* in Mexican Americans as well as in many other Latin-American communities, as well as comparable disorders in much of the Mediterranean world and its American offshoots. To these we could add culturally patterned *attaque* suffered by blocked or frustrated women in certain parts of Puerto Rico (see Kathleen Wolf 1952, represented in an adapted version in Endleman 1967:82–126); the "heartbreak syndrome" of the Mohave (Devereux 1961).

While it is impossible to get into this enormous and complicated subject in any detail here (see references in Devereux 1970a for recent treatments), we can say, following Devereux, whom we regard as our surest and most sophisticated guide in that kind of territory, that probably all of these can be shown to follow patterns entirely explainable by Western psychoanalytic concepts (at least to the same extent as any of "our" psychopathologies are explainable in that way). The Mohave "heartbreak syndrome," as already mentioned, is clearly a classical mourning depression. *Imu* and *latah* are "almost certainly hysterias." And so on (Devereux 1956:39).

In short, though none of these exotic "ethnic psychoses" is precisely like what we know as schizophrenia or depressive psychosis in Western society, nor precisely like our psychotic paranoid states, or our psychopathies, they *are* comprehensible with reference to the same basic mechanisms of defense and of adaptation that we find in Western—or for that matter in any other—society, as long as we pay attention to that fact that here too—as universally anywhere else—the influence of particular cultural patternings on the course of the psychological disorder must be recognized and understood. Thus *latah* is not the same as running *amok*, nor as a "catathymic crisis" to be found in Western society, nor is going *berserk* in the original Viking context the same as events that have been given that label in modern complex societies. But in any of these cases, the disorder is comprehensible in terms of the same psychological principles. And these principles have been most profoundly and with greatest sophistication developed by a *psychoanalytic* psychology. We need, yes, to enrich that psychology by transcultural understandings linking culture and psychic process that have been provided by the psychoanalytic—as distinguished from the merely psychological—anthropologists such as Róheim, Devereux, and LaBarre, and others.

FIVE KINDS OF PSYCHOPATHOLOGY

Building on the work of Devereux (1956, 1970) we can outline five major kinds of relationship of psychopathology to social and cultural structure and to social categories of deviance:

Ethnic psychoses
Idosyncratic psychoses
Culturally stylized psychopathological variant
Culturally stylized character disorder
Idiosyncratic neuroses and character disorders

Ethnic Psychoses

The term *ethnic psychoses* comes from Devereux (1956, 1970b). It refers to severe forms of derangement, each of which is peculiar to the particular society and culture in which it appears. The disorder in each case is of the severity and quality to be characterized as a psychosis. That is, it is a fundamental break from ordinary reality involving severe impoverishment of the ego, extreme de-differentiation, and de-individualization (Devereux 1970b:50).

It is derived from extreme idiosyncratic but statistically prevalent traumata in the early life experience of the individual, for which there are not culturally standardized defenses provided, but which are culturally recognized as following in a particular pattern, and for which the culture (in effect) prescribes certain forms of enactment of the role of the person so afflicted. In effect, individuals so afflicted are being told, "Don't go crazy, but if you do, you do it in this particular way."

The exotic maladies—*imu, latah, windigo*, etc.—belong in this category. And, Devereux supposes, we could characterize the common forms of schizophrenia and of psychopathic personality as ethnic psychoses (or at least severe disturbances) of our society. The responses to the traumata, and the experiencing of the traumata, originate in the individual or idiosyncratic portion of the unconscious (as distinguished from the "ethnic unconscious," i.e., those aspects of unconscious functioning that derive from culturally standardized aspects of repression in the individual).

Though recognized culturally, these disturbances are definitely ego-dystonic, and they are clearly socially deviant in the society in question. They are also statistically rare.

Idiosyncratic Psychoses and Other Serious Psychopathological Disturbances

These originate in the idiosyncratic rather than the ethnic part of the unconscious, and are responses to idiosyncratic traumata that are *not* statistically prevalent in that society. There are also situations for which there are no culturally stylized patterns of defense. In effect, this individual is faced with a situation where he is told, "Don't go crazy; but if you do, you're on your own; you've got to invent your own way of expressing it."

The particular symptomatology here can vary dramatically from one individual to another. Typically, in Western and Western-influenced societies, psychotic residents of psychiatric hospitals are remarkably diverse, with very few approximating the "classical" syndrome of whatever category of psychotic disorder they fit. This leads, of course, to those conditions conducive to great skepticism about the reliability of psychiatric understanding. Experts can disagree substantially about the appropriate diagnosis and therefore appropriate treatment program for a particular patient, since each case may appear, in its combination of symptoms, to be essentially unique.

Still, they all have in common severe impairment of ego-functions (in some cases, they have never developed at all) and in a certain sense, paradoxically, the combination of extreme individuality ("no other case is exactly like this") and extreme de-individualization (there is no coherent recognizable "structure" to this person, he—or she—is all in bits and pieces, scraps of many different potential personalities). These instances are not to be confused with either the ethnic psychoses, nor the following type of case, which is best exemplified by shamanism in many different (essentially tribal) societies. They are ego-dystonic, socially deviant, and statistically rare.

Culturally Stylized Psychopathological Variant

The most notable example of this type is the *shaman*, on whom by now there is a very substantial anthropological and ethnopsychiatric literature (see Devereux 1956, 1970; Ducey 1976; and references therein). Here again Devereux's formulation is most instructive: the role is institutionalized; still, the person who becomes a shaman and practices as such is socially recognized within the tribe as a disturbed person who is essentially "crazy," but in a way that is culturally useful, perhaps even essential, to the tribe.

He or she has been variously described as a "lightning conductor" of the troubles of the tribe, as the person, par excellence, that enables the members of the tribe to survive, psychologically, the strains and stresses that the technological culture of the tribe is unable to handle. This is the one who helps people to deal with the problems of existence and ultimate concerns, as distinguished from the more mundane problems of subsistence and practical protection (to the extent technologically possible for them) from dangers in the material and interpersonal and intertribal world. This is the one who helps people deal with problems of the soul, as well as, in many aspects, those of the body, though typically in tribal societies that dichotomy is not part of the familiar philosophical territory.

The shaman is distinctive from both the ethnic-psychotic and the idiosyncratic-psychotic. His difficulties originate in traumatic experiences that concern the *ethnic unconscious*, that is, those aspects of repressed material that are common to people of the tribe or society, and unconscious defenses related to these that are partially those commonly shared and partially those that have a particular individualized quality that nevertheless resonates with unconscious needs of many other people of the society.

This may produce in non-shaman onlookers or audience participants feelings of "uncanny" recognition and appreciation that enable the shaman to function professionally. His kind of "craziness" is both stylized and in a certain sense culturally institutionalized. He (or she, again, since in many societies shamans may as well be women as men) is regarded with a mixture of awe, fear, dread, anxiety, and respect, as well as often with some skepticism which leads some hardy souls to question and challenge the shaman's supernatural imprimatur.

The origins are in culturally stylized (therefore cross-culturally variable) kinds of traumata which are, however, though recognizable, not statistically prevalent in the society. The responses to such traumata are also culturally stylized to some extent. There are culturally stylized and provided defenses here, but they do not typically lead to stabilization of the personality; rather, in the typical fashion of psychopathology, they lead to further difficulties and the necessity for further, secondary defenses, etc., in a vicious cycle manner. Or they may lead to periods of apparent stability, which is in fact but a period of remission, since the underlying conflict has not been resolved.

What distinguishes this kind of variant from the purely idiosyncratic kind of psychotic, or neurotic for that matter, is that there is an institutionalized role into which one can be fitted, or fit oneself, the criteria for entrance into which include the sort of psychopathological disturbance the potential shaman experiences, which in tribal societies is typically interpreted in supernaturalistic terms. (Basically, supernatural equals the unconscious.) Thus, here the concrete details of the symptoms e.g., just how the individual "rants and raves" and with what imagery, etc., when he is "in one of his states," will be definitely patterned according to the culture. But in addition, and just as important, the psychic *mechanisms* used will be culturally patterned.

Partly the psychic experiences of the shaman can be described as ego-syntonic, partly as ego-dystonic. It can vary from one time to another.

The very affective volatility of this kind of individual is itself a mark of the shaman type. This is clearly a socially deviant type, one that is institutionalized, culturally patterned, and socially structured.

The formula here is: "If you go crazy, or act strangely, you may do so in this particular way; everyone will still see you as crazy, but also treat you with awe, respect, and fear." The message also says, "Once you have started in this direction, and shown the signs of this, you must go through with it; there is no turning back." The surrounding relatively normal people of the society thus typecast the shaman-deviant, and encourage him to melodramatic enactments of his "calling." Such encouragement resonates with his histrionic hysterical qualities.

Besides the dramatic example of the shaman, there are other examples that fit this category: the berdache (as discussed in chapter 13); in certain senses the "village idiot" of small rural communities in many parts of the world; and the local eccentric or "wild man," again more typical of small communities, who is in effect licensed to be oddball in his own particular way, and in fact is typecast in that role and not allowed to act otherwise. (Erikson's cases of young people taking on a "negative identity" (Erikson 1950) are a similar, though usually more transitory, phenomenon.) Other examples would be the *guapo* (hyper-aggressive and hyper-sexual rogue male) of certain rural Puerto Rican communities (Endleman 1967:90–92, based on the work of Kathleen Wolf 1952), as well as the "clown-idiot" role of these same communities.

Statistical rarity is essential to these types. There must be relatively few of them in any one community.

(Parenthetically: while sociological studies of deviance have illuminated some of the social processes in the interaction between the putatively normal and the designated deviant in such cases, such studies have either denied the existence of any psychopathology in the deviant, or more or less explicitly declared it irrelevant to the social interaction process. My approach, by contrast, insists that the psychodynamics—both of the "deviant" and of the onlookers—are an essential part of the total picture, the understanding of which is defective without inclusion of this element and its correct designation. We all have intrapsychic processes, and we also all do play social roles, and we all live in interaction with others, pay attention to or violate social norms, and all participate in, sometimes creatively expanding or modifying, an ongoing culture. No one part of these distinguishable processes excludes any of the others. If the stigmatizers subject the deviant to stereotyping, discrimination, or any kind of victimization—themes prevalent in the sociology of deviance—we also want to know by what intrapsychic processes they come to be acting this way, by what projections, displacements, reaction-formations, and the like, and in relation to what prior intra-psychic experiences.)

Culturally Stylized Character Disorder

Rather than being rare, the culturally stylized character disorder type may well be statistically prevalent in a particular society or subsociety. He is also different from the others in *not* being considered deviant by other people in the society. In fact, the character trends he exhibits are presumed to be normal by others, as well as by himself, in that society. "Normal" in this case means conformist or adjusted to the prevailing expectations in that society.

Correspondingly, the characteristics which would correspond to the symptoms of the neurotic are experienced as ego-syntonic, and do not arouse feelings of internal conflict or distress. The most obvious example would be, in our society, extremes of obsessive-compulsiveness dis-played by minor bureaucrats, librarians, accountants, certain types of scholars, and people in many other occupations that require a high degree of time-discipline, orderliness, punctiliousness, scrupulous attention to large quantities of detail, and the like. Here reaction-formations against anal messiness are consolidated into an entire character style which is experienced positively, and ego-syntonically, and serves—ordinarily— as a strong protection against anxiety.

Some might question whether this should really be considered a dis-order, since unlike the obsessive-compulsive neurotic who is in agonies of conflict and internal distress, and whose rituals, while allaying anxiety, are still experienced as ego-alien, the compulsive character type expe-riences his orientation as ego-syntonic and gratifying, and feels com-fortably conformist to the demands of his roles. Still, the *rigidity* of this orientation would indicate its qualifying as a disorder.

At the extreme, we find individuals so mired in the petty details of the rules and regulations that have to be obeyed or enforced in their work that they are unable to adapt to even minor changes of situation, or handle any circumstance that departs in the slightest way from the pattern they expect to encounter. As noted before, this kind of hyper-develop-ment of means-logicality may well subvert the larger goals of the orga-nization or enterprise in which this work is enmeshed.

An obvious cost of such punctiliousness, for the individual caught up in this pattern, is lack of spontaneity, isolation of affect, incapacity to "open up" emotionally, frequently enough also lack of access to one's own feelings. These characteristics can hardly be regarded as indicative of optimal psychic functioning.

This is probably the most striking kind of case of statistical normality or prevalence, combined with cultural normality in conformity to occupational and other cultural demands, along with transcultural abnormality in the form of character disorder. It must be noted that in this kind of case, however, it is a culturally stylized and supported character disorder, and such stylization and support have implications for and effects upon the total balance and equilibrium of such a personality, and are therefore not to be dismissed as irrelevant to understanding the intrapsychic processes involved.

Idiosyncratic Neuroses and Character Disorders

In contrast to culturally stylized character disorders, the idiosyncratic ones do not have particular cultural support and stylizations. This is also true for idiosyncratic neuroses. These maladies are also experienced as ego-alien, and there is a definite feeling of conflict and of suffering. In some forms the idiosyncratic neurotic or character disordered individual may be so unobtrusive as to escape much attention from the surrounding society, and therefore not be much subject to labeling and stigmatization as a deviant. This would be more likely in the case of individuals with more schizoid trends. Still, in most other cases, if the neurotic difficulty gets expressed in particular interactive contexts, it is quite likely that the idiosyncratic neurotic will also be considered a deviant in some way. In present-day modern societies, if one's neurosis comes out as one's being seen as odd or difficult or abrasive, the label "sick" that others may pin on this person definitely connotes deviance and unacceptability.

The conflicts that lead to these individualized neuroses and character disorders originate in the idiosyncratic rather than the ethnic portion of the unconscious, and the defenses used to deal with these conflicts may not have strong cultural stylization. Hence inter-individual variability, and also the neurotic's sense of isolation and aloneness in relation to others in his society. (This is distinguishable from the "differentness" of someone like the shaman, which in a sense *connects* him with others—as practitioner—rather than separating him from them.) To the extent that the neurotic or idiosyncratic character-disordered feels that his difficulties and sufferings separate him from others, and do not evoke an answering call of empathy from others, his intrapsychic troubles are compounded by interpersonal alienation. Then the feeling that the social world around is mainly a hostile and alien place tends to be confirmed by the actual reactions of others, in a vicious circle of interpersonal pathology compounding the intrapsychic pathology. The formulation of the modes of experiencing and expressing his intrapsychic conflicts may be statistically prevalent in his society, or in his specific social milieu within that society, and at the same time *not* be culturally stylized in any manner comparable to that of the culturally patterned character disorder, or of the culturally stylized pathological variant like the shaman or ber-dache. In fact, the individually suffering neurotic, particularly one whose anxieties keep him largely isolated from others, is likely to be quite unaware of how statistically prevalent his kinds of problems are, and imagine or assume that he is the only person in the world in this kind of psychic state, or at most one of a very small number. Thus, a state of what has been called "pluralistic ignorance" may prevail, in which num-bers, even large numbers, of individuals are all in a state of similar and similarly derived psychic distress without being aware of the common-ality among themselves.

The reversal of this is found in situations such as a homosexual's "coming out"—i.e., the first time he recognizes himself as being a homosexual, accompanied by recognition that there are thousands or millions of others out there just like himself—whereas in adolescence he had assumed that he was the only person in the world with these feelings and the attendant guilt, anxiety, etc. The recognition of kinship and similarity with a large collectivity of others, who share the same deeper feelings and intimate responses, may have such an intense anxiety-relieving and alienation-dissolving effect that the individual, almost in a flash, now consolidates his distinct social and psychic identity with a great rush of positive self-feeling, and an experience that all the past and recent psychic distress is suddenly, in one moment, dissolved and ended. That it takes, also, a good deal of denial (of ambivalences and inner conflict and anxiety) to accomplish such an instantaneous transformation should go without saying, and is not to be ignored in any appraisal of the state of psychic well-being of individuals in such a phase. Ideological affinities should not blind us to whatever might be the psychic costs and sequaelae to such a state of inner illumination.

The ordinary "garden-variety" neurotic, however, is largely lacking in such collective validation, nor does he find it possible to construct rationalizations proclaiming his difference from supposedly "normal" people as positive and culturally worthy. While he may be well aware that there are many others who are also impaired in some way, possibly similar, he usually tends to feel that the others cannot possibly be suffering precisely in the same way that he is. While homosexuals may constitute a "minority group" (see preceding section), it is unusual (though not unheard-of) to refer to "neurotics as a minority group." They do not generally get discriminated against on the basis of some commonly held and negatively valued characteristic, and correspondingly do not have the positive supports of a minority group subculture.

Summary

We thus have five different varieties of psychopathology as related to culture patterns and to social processes of defining deviance and conformity. They differ among themselves in the *severity* of the disorder— psychoses as compared to pathological variant (possibly or intermittently psychotic), as compared to character disorders, as compared to neuroses. They differ in the *origins* of the pathology: as coming from the ethnic portion of the unconscious, as in the case of the shaman and any other culturally stylized pathological variant, and probably as in the case of culturally stylized character disorders; or in contrast, as coming from the more idiosyncratic portion of the unconscious, as in the case of idiosyncratic psychoses, ethnic psychoses, and idiosyncratic neuroses and character disorders.

They differ also in *ego-syntonicity*. The culturally stylized character disordered is experienced as ego-syntonic; the culturally stylized psychopathological variant like the shaman experiences his pathology as partly ego-syntonic and partly ego-alien. In the other three, the ethnic psychoses, the idiosyncratic psychoses, and the idiosyncratic neuroses and character disorders, all experience their state or their symptoms as ego-alien, to greater or lesser degree. (None of these situations is an all-or-nothing case.)

They differ in the *degree* of cultural stylization of the defensive process. The shaman-type variant as well as the culturally patterned character disordered both have defensive systems that are essentially provided by the culture, and thus have validation from the surrounding social world— if only, as in the case of the shaman, in an identity that is recognized as deviant. By contrast, in the other three cases, all types of psychoses, and the idiosyncratic neuroses and character disorders, the individual has had, in effect, to improvise his own personal defensive systems, leaving him without important cultural supports.

There is room, of course, in such individually improvised defensive systems for the development of a certain idiosyncratic creativity. The kernel of truth in that observation is what has led some observers to claim that every psychotic is in effect a creative artist, a claim that itself has some bit of truth to it, but which, made without important qualification, is seriously distorting and misleading.

True, either the ethnic-psychotic or the idiosyncratic psychotic has a kind of access to primary process thinking that the rest of us approximate only in our dreams, and various types of neurotics may be closer in some ways to aspects of functioning that are unconscious, heavily repressed in more "normal" people. And also true, creative artists need and use such access. What is missing in the individualized psychopathological individual that is present in the creative artist—*when* he is functioning and really doing creative work—is the measure of ego strength and creative mastery over the warring and dissident elements in the personality, and the capacity to transform these into creative products as works of the imagination.

The different kinds of psychopathology here discussed differ also in their *relationship* to deviance and its attribution. The psychotic— whether expressing an ethnic psychosis, or an idiosyncratic one—are all clearly seen as deviant by other people in their society. Their symptoms may take forms that dramatically express deviation from prevailing cultural norms: e.g., speaking in ways considered grossly aberrant by the surrounding community; violating certain fundamental aspects of folkways—habits of personal cleanliness, restraint in revealing intimate aspects of oneself to others not in an intimate relationship, and the like. They may show distinctive "social negativism" (see Devereux 1940) in the form of financial irresponsibility, failure to take care of children, etc. In more florid paranoid forms, their interpersonal hostilities may go far beyond what is commonly expected or accepted in their cultural milieu.

The ethnic-psychotic is deviant in a more culturally standardized way (every case is a classic "textbook" case), but deviant nonetheless. However, since he is deviant in a standardized and therefore expectable way, there are standardized ways for others to respond to such an individual.

By contrast, the great idiosyncratic variety of individualized psychotic behavior and symptomatology makes such an individual's deviance more disturbing to the onlookers and interacting persons. They don't know quite what to expect; therefore their anxieties are greater than those of the onlookers to the ethnically psychotic.

Idiosyncratic neurotics and character-disordered are also likely to be considered deviant by the people around them. The extent and quality of such characterization can vary a good deal, depending on the nature of the symptoms and the way in which these are socially defined. The obtrusiveness of the symptomatology is likely to be positively correlated with the degree of deviance attributed to the individual, whereas it is likely to be negatively correlated with the severity of the underlying malignancy of the pathological process (see Devereux 1956 and 1970b).

The shamanistic-type disorders—culturally stylized psychopathological variants—are considered deviant, but because the role is institutionalized, it is deviant in a somewhat acceptable way. (It is a "right way to do wrong things.") It therefore does not arouse a uniformly negative reaction from the onlookers, who are rather more ambivalent toward the practitioner of such a role.

By contrast with all of the others, those with culturally stylized character disorders are not considered deviant at all, at least by those with whom they are connected in standardized interactive processes. The petty bureaucrat, ritualistically devoted to the letter of the rules, may be annoying, but he is "doing his job." Even here, however, there may be differences of degree. Some of the interacting role-players may be more instrumentally—and less sacredly—oriented to the rules and regulations, and regard the over-punctilious as "deviant" in the sense of "overconforming."

To repeat: the deviant is not necessarily psychopathological and the psychopathological is not necessarily deviant. There are analytically distinct categories, and coalescing them into one and the same is a serious distortion of psychosocial reality.

Being considered deviant when one is not pathological, basically, in one's personality structure, may cause a good deal of distress, which one may then try to deal with by defensive maneuvers that in turn may create some vicious-circle processes. But someone with a relatively strong ego-structure, and well-functioning conflict-free portions of the ego, is likely to be able to withstand the stresses of such deviance-attribution, if those attributes that others regard as deviant stem from healthy capacities for adaptation.

The difficulty with any such situation, of course, is the thorny question: adaptation to what? Clearly, if deviancy consists in failure or refusal to adapt to what is essentially a "sick society," then it is not difficult to attribute psychic health to such refusal, and to empathize with the "deviant's" difficulties as a matter of trouble with external relationships.

Such instances, however, are likely to be rare. More likely nonconformity may be a complex mixture of both adaptive and regressive features, involving *some* kinds of psychopathological processes. (See above, combination 8 of the possible combinations of statistical, cultural, and transcultural normality or abnormality.)

Part 5

SUMMARY AND CONCLUSION

I have tried to show how there may or may not be any connection between deviance (as defined by the standards of one's particular society or subsociety in a particular epoch in history) and suffering from some form of psychopathology. I have argued that criteria for assessment of the latter need not be culture-bound, and have argued against the prevailing influence of the culturally relativistic approach both in the social sciences of the twentieth century and in the "intelligent lay public" as well. An evolutionarily grounded anthropology of the complex human animal points the way for *trans*cultural understandings that transcend the parochial views of any particular culture or any particular historical time.

In short, I propose the revival and revitalization of the idea of the "psychic unity of mankind." Cultural relativism taken to its extreme produces biases that are not very different from forms of "racism" arguing that different peoples are fundamentally different on a biological basis— only now the point of reference is culture. If the culture of the Vietnamese is so alien that we cannot hope psychologically to understand the Vietnamese, we can be as benightedly hostile or insensitive to them as human beings as one could be by assuming (and rationalizing) that the Vietnamese are biologically so different we need not consider them as basically human.[1]

The transcultural perspective on normality and abnormality, by contrast, emphasizes the universal human repertoire of psychological mechanisms, the universal set of common human psychological experiences and situations, and the universally potential range of relatively more adaptive and relatively less adaptive (i.e., "sick") ways of dealing with repeatedly appearing situations of human stress and difficulty, both intrapsychic and interpersonal. This view is not a reductionist one, as sometimes claimed. It does not reduce complex social and cultural situations to individual psychological mechanisms or types, but rather insists that human beings are all of these: animal (biological), psychological (including intrapsychic interplay of conscious and unconscious, primary and secondary process, etc.), social (playing roles, interacting with others in both role-oriented and nonrole-oriented ways), and cultural (partaking of a pre-existing culture acquired through socialization and enculturation processes through the formative years and beyond, as well as creatively using, modifying, and, in some cases, innovating new versions of culture during one's lifetime).

One cannot be fully human without being social and cultural, and the dichotomy between these and intrapsychic influences or experiences is an analytic abstraction that as often impedes as facilitates understanding. To say that "culture influences" us is not to deny that there are intrapsychic processes within ourselves which are the *ways* in which that abstraction "culture" is (metaphorically) able to do anything at all. The same for that abstraction "society."

I dissent particularly from that version of cultural relativism that has been especially influential in recent sociology, namely, the "labeling" approach to deviance, which implicitly and often explicitly, denies that there ever is any kind of psychopathology in those forms of "deviant behavior" about which laymen or officials may apply the label "sick." I emphasize that deviance *may* involve sickness, or it *may not*, but the question of whether it does in a particular case, or type of cases, is not settled by fiat, as in labeling theorists saying it is all a matter of unjust stigmatization, but needs to be empirically examined.

To do that examination, we need the tools of both sociological and socio-cultural-anthropological analysis on one side, and of psychodynamic analysis, deriving at its best from psychoanalysis, on the other— and we need these simultaneously, interwoven, not simply placed side by side, or presented serially by competing specialists at a conference or symposium. In other words, we need a psychoanalytic social science, not only a psychoanalytically informed sociology or a sociologically informed psychoanalysis, but rather a fusion of the two.

I think I have shown how that is possible in the presentation of the evolutionary problems of human beings in part 2 above. I have attempted to demonstrate it again in the discussion of women, their psychology, their place in society and culture, and their current rebellion against older formulations. I tried it again in the discussion of homosexuality. There we need more than the intrapsychic examination by psychoanalytic work. We need more than the anthropological cross-cultural surveys. We need more than an examination by sociologists who are ideologically attuned to "liberation." We need a fusion of social-scientific and psychoanalytic frameworks that does not foreclose the question of the relationship between deviance and possible psychopathology.

We can utilize the contributions of the "labeling" approach sociologists, who have illuminated some aspects of the interaction between the putatively normal and the designated deviant. We do not need to, nor should we, go along with the tendency in much of that work to deny the existence of psychopathology in such a phenomenon as homosexuality—a viewpoint that simply takes over ideological assertions of the gay liberation movement without any foundation in independent research. Nor need we, nor should we, go along with the tendency of some labeling type sociologists to declare as totally irrelevant to our understanding, questions about psychological underpinnings of the motivation for the "deviant" conduct.

I have tried to show how, by contrast, we need to examine the psychodynamics of the surrounding persons or officials who do the labeling or stigmatizing. We need to understand why either or both of these role players or types of role players utilize elements of irrationality in their approach to the world, or specifically to this kind of deviation, and understand the defense mechanisms being employed on both sides. These elements are not mere decorative trimmings, but an essential part of understanding the interactive process. The social psychology of such process is incomplete and therefore likely to be badly distorted if it proceeds from a defective or grossly incomplete conception of human psychic processes.

Such defectiveness or incompleteness is bound to appear as long as the investigators lack, or deny the relevance of, grounding in basic human psychodynamics, for which psychoanalysis and psychoanalytically-derived psychology provides, in our view, the best available approach. Clearly psychoanalytic understanding of the whole range of human behavior and feeling is at present far from complete or adequate. But like democracy in the political realm, defective as it presently is, it is still the best we have. No other kind of psychology comes near it in being able to deal with the intrapsychic complexities of real human beings.

It is essential, though enormously difficult, to be as free of ideological bias as is humanly possible, and thus to recognize and combat the ideological biases that have come into being in the wake of the massive influence of a purportedly non-judgmental cultural relativism whose effects, however, in the real world, have been to promote the ideological messages of the alleged "liberation" of allegedly persecuted minorities, racial, ethnic, sexual, or sexpreferential, as the case may be. A thorough psychoanalytically educated social science needs to be alert to the existence, the purveying, and the underlying motivations of new, allegedly "liberating" mythologies, reactive and mitigating, in relationship to past and more established mythologies. Just as a thorough social science needs to be able to dissect, expose, and understand old ideologies, so does it need to do this with new utopias and utopian-related conceptions of "liberation."

Historical knowledge of how past revolutions have ushered in new tyrannies replacing the old ones they overthrew, along with psychodynamic understanding of the psychological bases and functions of such new mythologies, can help us understand these phenomena, and help us, in the practical world, steer a course that avoids the pitfalls of new collective illusions, and maintain skepticism without falling into nihilistic cynicism. Maintaining a skeptical sense of humor about the foibles old and new (and the "new" turn out always to be new versions of something from the old, if not today's, then yesterday's or the day before's) can be a salutary corrective. And we can attain or retain such a sense on the basis of the vast and ever impressive capacities of the at-least-good-enough-functioning adaptive egos of people who are not too neurotic, nor too devoted to their own primary processes, yet not too alien to these subterranean wellsprings within themselves.

Alongside of the earlier and pessimistically tinged sense of psychoanalysis, in Freud himself and his immediate followers, of the massive role of conflict and defense in human psychic functioning and the enormous difficulty of maintaining any kind of freedom from infantile illusion and delusion about the world, we can also range more recent emphases, still within what can be considered the classical psychoanalytic tradition, upon conflict-free areas of the ego, capacities for more or less spontaneous overcoming of at least not too severe inner psychic conflict and its more malign defensive systems. These are the capacities for creative mastery, creative humor, and creative re-adaptation to new situations in the world, all of which are both part of the more superficial and more conscious layers of the personality, and more importantly, connected with the deeper wellsprings of the unconscious that are there in us all, and reachable not only in sickness, but also in feats of adaptive good psychic health.

Far from requiring us to accept a gloomy determinism which sees our whole lives as having been preset by the age of five, as some interpretations of Freud's ideas have claimed, we can derive from our psychoanalytic explorations a good deal of support for the view that we all have the potential for continued development and transformations well beyond the childhood years, even though that potentiality is far from infinite, and even though it is indeed circumscribed by patterns set in motion in the earliest years. Here again, we can debate whether the cup is half full—capable of further growth—or half empty—limited by what has gone before.

But even if the determinism attributed to the Freudian vision, in earlier times, is not entirely supportable by clinically demonstrated facts, it is still not true that the potentialities are infinite, and certainly not true that all that needs to be done is consciously to take hold and proceed, without paying attention to intrapsychic processes of resistance and their underlying dynamic reasons. If we can see the need for a psychology that goes beyond the baselines of conflict and defense and the consequences of these, as basically earlier psychoanalysis did, this does not mean that conflict—inner conflict, of course, in this instance—and defense are irrelevant, nor that they need not be considered in dealing with social and cultural phenomena. If they are not a sufficient basis for a human psychology, they are nevertheless *necessary* to its development.

We need to avoid getting caught in any singular one-sided view. We are animal, and we are a distinctive kind of animal, too. We are infantile, and capable of great feats of mature adaptability. We are intrapsychic beings, and we are social beings too. We are rooted in instinctual drives, and creators and creatures of culture too. We are vastly various and alarmingly alike. Our cultures range in an enormous gamut of potentialities, and also all have certain basic elements in common.

And not surprisingly so. For we all arrived—or the ancestors of all of us arrived—as one species on the evolutionary scene, in the same way and by definable processes which set the nature of the human species and all its succeeding generations. Our personalities are enormously diverse, but not at all infinitely so, for we all have to draw on the same human repertoire of psychic mechanisms and deal with the same basic problems of being human beings and going through a life process with definable stages that transcend any particular cultural variabilities.

It is past time to assess and consolidate the gains in understanding that have come with the anthropological protagonists of cultural relativism, not discard them, but go on from there and recapture, with our now expanded vision, the understandings of the universalities of human existence. For this we definitely need psychoanalysis, but a psychoanalysis enriched by the work of sociological and cultural anthropological sciences; and we need a social science—sociology and anthropology and the accessory social sciences, enriched by the intrapsychic knowledge provided by psychoanalysis. Better still, we need a psychoanalytic social science, to see and understand human beings in all of their dimensions. It is not only possible, it is already coming into being.

Notes

1. The Problem and the Prospects

1. To any professional readers in whatever discipline who may be displeased, offended, or outraged that their favorite authors (or they themselves) have not been mentioned in this chapter, let me first make this disclaimer: I am not trying here to be encyclopedic or to give an exhaustive account of all the writing that in some manner make some kind of connection between psychoanalysis and the social sciences. Whole areas of work that I am aware of have been either omitted or only perfunctorily referred to in this chapter, and no doubt (since I do not profess omniscience) there are many others whose work I have the misfortune not to have read. Some related work is dealt with in later chapters. Some I don't take up at all in this book, but have dealt with in earlier work (e.g., Endleman 1967, and other writings; see bibliography).

There is a lot of work by anthropologists, and some by sociologists, under such rubrics as "personality-and-culture" or "personality-and-social-structure" to which the reader can find guidance in such anthologies as Smelser and Smelser 1963, 1970; Norbeck, Price-Williams, and McCord 1968; the old Kluckhohn and Murray collection 1948, 1954; Francis Hsu 1961; Bert Kaplan 1961; Gladwin and Sturtevant 1962; and DeVos 1976; also in such textbooks as LeVine 1973; Honigmann 1954; Barnouw 1963, rev. 1973; Wallace 1961.

2. These comments referring to "sociology" should be understood to apply to anthropology as well, with the assumption for present purposes that sociology-anthropology constitutes a unitary social-scientific field.

3. We leave aside for the time being all the knotty and often convoluted arguments and disagreements *within* psychoanalysis on a whole range of issues. For example, how shall we formulate the *nature* of these important social relationships? How shall we describe the nature of the formative influence of the early relationships in the person's life, on the subsequent developments, defenses,

and adaptations? Can we reconcile "object-relations" psychoanalysis with the psychoanalysis of drive and defense, and that of the structural model—id, ego, superego? How can we integrate recent emphases on "pre-oedipal" phases with classical psychoanalytic formulation of the crucial quality of the oedipal period?

Suffice it for the moment to note that movement of progressively further uncovering of earlier stages is entirely consonant with what Freud saw as the likely tasks and line of development of his successors. We as successors have all been standing on the shoulders of the giant Freud and of his early followers and colleagues in the creations of psychoanalysis. Some aspects of the divergent "newer" (post-1945) developments in psychoanalysis will be discussed in the context of examining different integrative efforts.

2. Obstacles to Integration

1. This classification will no doubt be considered rather oversimplified by many sociologists. Some will surely demur from classification of Marxist sociology as simply one variant of "conflict theory." Nor will all sociologists agree about Ritzer's placement of "exchange theory" in the social behaviorism category. The classification given here also overlooks large-scale comparative history works drawing on both Marx and Weber, as well as newer work in demographic and family history sociologically considered. However, such emendations could be carried on ad infinitum without furthering my present discussion. Since my purpose at this juncture is merely to point out that there are great variations within contemporary sociology, I have eschewed any attempt at exhaustive classification and discussion. Ritzer's scheme is but one handy device for encompassing these variations, or at least some of them, in a coherent limited set of categories.

2. This epistemological usage is not to be confused with another usage of the term parameter in psychoanalysis, as by Kurt Eissler (1953) where the term refers to variations from standard "classical" procedure in the clinical practice of psychoanalysis, such as allowing a breach in the anonymity of the analyst under certain conditions.

3. I would see this work as neo-Freudian in its orientation. Other observers disagree, thinking it to be grounded in more orthodox Freudian thinking. Adorno, they point out, was in many writings critical of neo-Freudian revisionism, in a style more in line with orthodox Freudian thought than with Fromm-style neo-Freudianism. However, in this work, clearly the whole concept of the authoritarian personality is an adaptation of Fromm's treatment of authoritarianism, which was itself a watering down of classical psychoanalytic conceptions of the anal-sadistic characters. However, the distinction—i.e., whether this work should be labeled Freudian or neo-Freudian—is not particularly relevant for my present purposes.

4. I think Schneider is more correct than otherwise in this judgment. Some critics may find such a charge unjustified, as applied specifically to Fromm, an

avowed socialist, and Kardiner, a left-progressive, and Horney, a not particularly political left-liberal. One would suppose that none of these would counsel un-thinking adjustment to the existing social order, especially in its politico-eco-nomic aspects. However, Schneider is correct as to the sociopolitical *potential* of neo-Freudian revisionism. He follows Marcuse's faulting of the neo-Freudians for subtracting from psychoanalysis the most revolutionary potentials of Freud's outlook. (See Marcuse 1955.) And even though many neo-Freudian therapists may personally favor a left-liberal or even socialist political persuasion, it is not at all inconsistent with their kind of relativism to deal with therapy as (in part) in effect an adjustment process.

The implicit formula here would be: true, relativism teaches us there are many different social and cultural systems, but our patients are living in *this* one and have to adjust to the "reality-principles" of this particular society. The culturally relativistic perspective favored by neo-Freudians easily lends itself to an adjust-ment viewpoint in therapy and in social counseling, in contrast to classical Freudianism which is basically *trans*cultural in implication. (See chapter 15 of this book.)

In practice, it may well be that some therapists of *either* Freudian or neo-Freudian theoretical position act in an adjustment-oriented way, while others of both persuasions encourage patients' critical sociopolitical stances. Both of these in spite of the fact that the strict psychoanalytic view of the therapy process advises the psychoanalyst to be as abstinent as possible about expressing socio-political value preferences—an ideal probably more often honored in the breach. There may be no correlation between theoretical orientation (Freudian vs. neo-Freudian) and the favoring of either adjustment to or critique of the sociopolitical order. (I know of no systematic empirical research on this question, and it would be interesting to see what such research would uncover.) Basically, there is no guarantee that either conformity to or rebellion against prevailing sociopolitical order reflects a healthy, ego-adaptive psychodynamic, or a regressive-patholog-ical one either.

It is hardly news to informed readers that psychoanalysis has both revolutionary and very conservative implicative potentialities, never fully reconciled in Freud's work or in psychoanalysis ever since. See Lichtenberg 1969; Rieff 1959, 1966; Benjamin Nelson 1954 and elsewhere; some of Dennis Wrong's essays, 1976; Norman Brown 1959; Brigid Brophy 1962; Wilhelm Reich 1933b; Marcuse 1955 and elsewhere; and Paul Ricoeur 1970, for but a beginning into that intricate topic. I certainly do not presume to deal here in anything like an adequate way with the difficulties surrounding these contradictions, though much of what follows in the remaining chapters in this work has bearing on those topics.

5. Robinson's interesting book *The Freudian Left* uses the strange notion that Róheim can be classed with Wilhelm Reich and Herbert Marcuse as being on the political "left." Róheim was far from that in his political views. True, Róheim's psychoanalysis was "radically Freudian" in the sense of holding firm to the most profoundly subversive root ideas of Freud, that had been abandoned or at least diluted to the point of irrelevance in neo-Freudian revisionism. But he never

drew from these ideas warrant for politically revolutionary attack on the prevailing socioeconomic-political order of capitalism, as both Reich and Marcuse, in their different ways, have done.

6. For a psychoanalyst who doubts that the underlying psychopathology has in fact substantially changed over the years, see Peter Giovacchini, *The Treatment of Primitive Mental States* (1979), who writes:

Basic psychopathology most likely has not changed to any great extent throughout the years. Cultural factors undoubtedly exert a strong influence, but rather than determine the degree and severity of psychopathology, they probably affect its manifestations. The patients analysts see today differ from those Freud saw mainly in the way they present themselves, that is in their basic symptomatic expression and character traits, rather than in basic structure and core difficulties. (1979:14)

Essentially, I agree with this position, but recognize it is impressionistic.

3. Integrative Work

1. No doubt many psychoanalysts will object to classifying in the same category these such different thinkers. This is a matter of emphasis. For present purposes, their similarities in emphasizing object-relations rather than instinctual drives, are more salient than their clearly evident differences.

2. There are complexities in trying to reconcile and integrate object-relations theory in psychoanalysis with Freudian libido theory. To attempt to deal with this topic in detail here would take me too far afield for present purposes. See recent works of Otto Kernberg (1975, 1976) and Peter Giovacchini (1975, 1979) for work in mainstream psychoanalysis that does attempt to synthesize these positions.

5. Language Origins and Related Developments

1. However, the Gardners' chimpanzees did have to be *taught* the gesture language initially, by *human* mentors, and did not invent it themselves. We have no way of knowing whether chimpanzees in the wilds *might* invent such a communication system on their own, going far beyond what gestural communication they already have. Given that caveat, the conservative phrasing of what we have learned from these studies is that chimpanzees have the *capacities* to learn, use— and probably, to transmit—such a gestural "language," which capacities are greater than had earlier been attributed to nonhuman primates.

Critics may also query whether the *extent* of the space-time displacement demonstrated by the chimps in their gesturing does or can go anywhere near as far as what humans show in being able to communicate *about* events, actions, etc. Can the chimps "talk" about such events *some considerable time* after they have occurred, and can they "talk" about future possible events, or conditional or hypothetical events? Can they use "if—then" linguistic constructions? So far (to the best of my knowledge) there is no evidence that they can. (That of course is not the same as saying they definitely *cannot*.) It is this kind of representational use of language that has long been claimed to be a distinctively human attribute.

2. This distinction between speech and language, or more precisely between speech-language and any other forms of language that would qualify by Hockett's seven criteria, is not at all the same as the famous distinction by De Saussure (1916) between *parole* and *langue*. DeSaussure's concepts *both* refer to speech-language, and within that general category (De Saussure's *langage*) make a different conceptual distinction: between the individual act of speaking (*parole*) and the general *system* of sound symbols used, independent of the volition of individual speakers (*langue*).

6. *Totem and Taboo* Again?

1. Michael Young's brilliant social-science fiction, a dystopian satire, *The Rise of the Meritocracy* (1958)—the origin of the term—can be read as intended, to be sure, as an *attack* on "meritocracy" in the sense of stratification by genetically determined intelligence. By a not uncommon irony, however, the term "meritocracy," coming into broader usage, has come to be used by some with an intended *positive* value leading. For example, some see it as consistent with universalistic Western values of equality of opportunity and careers open to talent. Some use the term in opposition to governmental programs such as Affirmative Action which explicitly depart from meritocratic recruitment. In its now widespread usage it comes across in such a dictionary entry as: "1. a system in which advancement is based on ability or achievement; 2a. an elite composed of talented achievers; b. leadership by such an elite." (*American Heritage Dictionary*, 1978.) Note this usage refers to *any* kind of ability, not only whatever is measured by IQ tests; and *any* kind of achievement; it also omits the question of *genetic* origin of differences in such abilities, thus evading the issue exercising present-day ideologues. Some of the latter are so incensed by the idea of *any* kind of inequality among human beings that they regard any recognition of obvious ability differences among individuals as "elitist" (a cardinal sin alongside racism and sexism) and/or, by implication, biologically determinist, also a sin. Just how large a role genetic determination does play in such differences—it is to my mind demonstrably far above zero—is, of course, a matter to be settled by scientific research, not by impassioned political demonstrations.

7. "Traditional" vs. "Vanguard" Norms
on Sex Differences

1. Some feminists, hearing this story, found nothing funny. Ideologues typically lack a sense of humor. (Dynamically, no doubt, lack of humor on this point must reflect deep psychological pressures within the individual concerned. Pos-

sibly this is a defensive hostility on the part of women who feel themselves deeply hurt by men, a hostility so pervasive nothing at all connected with the subject can be taken lightly.)

8. Difficulties with the Vanguard Norms: Sociological

1. Note that this phrasing leaves open the question of the direction of caus- ation. It can be either that women entering an occupation in great numbers makes it a low-status occupation, or that an occupation that already has lower status then has women entering it in greater numbers. In the USSR it was probably the latter; in the early days after the revolution doctors were in less demand than other types of professionals such as engineers, and in any case physicians, state employees, would, by that fact, have lower status in the Soviet Union than their counterparts, who are entrepreneurial free professionals in western capitalist countries. Then the presence of women in large numbers in an occupation in turn may help perpetuate the low status of that profession in a "vicious circle" effect.

9. Difficulties with the Vanguard Norms: Psychodynamic

1. In the classical psychoanalytic view, the early infancy girl *does* take her mother as a sexual object, following the polymorphousness of infantile sexual feelings, cathecting specifically the mother's breast, and more generally the mother's whole body. This is a *pre*-oedipal mode of taking the mother as a sexual object, not an oedipal one. It is an oral cathexis, and one involving the whole surface of the skin in body-contact eroticism, and it can have concomitants of genital excitation. Similarly, the infant boy has a libidinal cathexis of the mother that is pre-oedipal, becoming later more oedipal in the sense of specifically genital striving toward the mother as a sexual object.

2. Critics have argued that this and other psychoanalytically based accounts of personality development assume the universality of presence of the nuclear family consisting of husband and wife and offspring, or of some family form very close to it. They have then claimed that anthropological evidence on primitive societies and sociological on many variations in modern societies (e.g., Israeli kibbutz or many Caribbean lower-class communities) challenge the assumption of universal nuclear families.

My response is that something very close to the nuclear family—not necessarily with all the specific details it shows in out society at this time—is actually found in nearly all human societies. The exceptions are very rare. True, the nuclear family may in many societies be imbedded in a wider kinship organization, consisting of an extended family (three-plus generations in the same household), and it may exist alongside a unilineal descent kinship organization, which in effect crosscuts nuclear or conjugal families (e.g., the matrilineal clan consists of mothers and daughters and their brothers, and not the brothers' children, and not the husbands of any of these females: but where it exists, as in many tribal societies, there is *also* a household unit which most commonly consists of a marital pair and their offspring.)

The nuclear family may take a polygamous form—most often in that case polygynous—i.e., plural *wives*—and there each mother-plus-her-children segment may constitute a separate sub-household, making a complete nuclear family at those times the husband-father is spending with that particular wife and that set of children. This is expansion of, not the absence of, the nuclear family. Similarly for other versions of extended families.

Even in those cases where the statistically normal arrangement is of mother-plus-children with no regularly present husband-father as in lower class communities in many modern societies, this is considered—by the women themselves—as a *normatively* undesirable arrangement. Thus, while some social scientists and feminists drawing on their work would like to think of the nuclear family as culturally very variable (and therefore, by implication, dispensable or replaceable by other forms) its reality is well-nigh universal, and evolutionary reconstructions would suggest (as we do in the preceding section) that it developed very early in the formation of the human species, serving fundamental psycho-social needs. Latter-day development on the kibbutzim—see earlier, in chapter 8—would suggest the very great difficulty involved for any society dispensing entirely with the nuclear family (or a very close approximation). See also Endleman 1967, ch. 1.

3. Culturalist psychoanalysts like Clara Thompson have emphasized cultural factors in women's low self-esteem. In a patriarchal society, this argument runs, females being defined as inferior inevitably leads women to have lower self-esteem (Thompson 1942, 1964). Similar themes are presented by other Sullivanians, e.g., Natalie Shainess (1969) and Ruth Moulton (1973). These themes have been taken up by feminist critics of Freudian views, including many sociologists. For reasons developed at length in this present chapter, I do not find these arguments persuasive. At best they are partial truths. The research in the classical psychoanalytic tradition and the work of object-relations psychoanalysts make it evident that cultural pressures cannot be the whole picture. Such culturalist propositions are also defective in psychoanalytic depth, focusing as they do entirely on *conscious* ideas and self-perceptions, omitting the crucial unconscious dimension.

4. This phrase, when quoted from Freud (both by supporters and by critics), is usually taken to refer to the anatomical differences between the two sexes. In fact, the phrase appears in two different places in Freud's work, with very different referents in each case. The connection to sex differences appears in the 1924 paper, "The Dissolution of the Oedipus Complex" (Freud 1924; S.E.19:180). The relevant passage is this: "the morphological difference [between the sexes] must express itself in differences in the development of the mind. 'Anatomy is destiny' to vary a saying of Napoleon's." However, twelve years earlier, Freud had first used the phrase in a very different context, one that did not refer to the

difference between the sexes at all. Here is that passage:

"at its beginning, the sexual instinct is divided into a large number of components—or, rather, it develops from them—not all of which can be carried on into its final form: some have to be suppressed or turned to other uses before the final form results. Above all, the coprophilic elements in the instinct have proved incompatible with our aesthetic ideas . . . further, a considerable proportion of the sadistic elements belonging to the erotic instinct, have to be abandoned. . . . The fundamental processes which promote erotic excitation remain always the same. Excremental things are all too intimately and inseparably bound up with sexual things: the position of the genital organs—*inter urinas et faeces*—remains the decisive and unchangeable factor. One might say, modifying a well known saying of the great Napoleon's, "Anatomy is destiny." The genitals themselves have not undergone the development of the rest of the human form in the direction of beauty; they have retained their animal cast; and so even to-day love, too, is in essence as animal as it ever was." (Freud 1912; S.E. 11:189)

5. A thoughtful critic (Helen Hacker) has asked: do I mean here "in *any* culture"? The answer is yes. She has raised the question: just what is my position on whether the differential treatment of boys and girls, by mother, and by father, is a cultural universal based on their biological difference, or a cultural variable subject to change? My answer is that, of course, I think biologically based imperatives do operate universally, contributing to cultural universals in this sphere. And yes, differential treatment of boys and girls is culturally universal, to the best of our knowledge. We know of no human societies that do not so differentiate. Exactly *how* they differentiate, and how *much* so, is of course variable, and thus changeable—but only within certain limits.

On the question of the being-vs.-doing distinction as a feminine-vs.-masculine distinction, I know of no cultures where this kind of differentiation does not appear.

10. Implications of Sociological and Psychodynamic Objections: Vanguard Movement Mythologies

1. True, there is a complementary theme in much of the current women's movement that emphasizes communal and collective action: some women have joined women's communes; women are banding together collectively in "sisterhood" fighting various common battles, or supporting individual women fighting employment-discrimination cases, and the like; and proclaiming that (collectively) "Sisterhood is Powerful" (Morgan 1970).

11. Homophile Movement Protests

1. Dennis Wrong, far more expert than I on demographic analysis, points out, in connection with this passage, that it would be quite possible, without mere

guesswork, for a demographer to figure out how much "variation from hetero-sexual supremacy" a society could stand, assuming he had available a good estimate of its infant mortality rates. (These we do, of course, have for modern industrial societies.) Infant mortality has invariably been high in all societies before our own in this century. Demographers have tried to estimate the fertility losses from celibate priesthoods in medieval Europe and Tibet. They could use the same method in doing the same for homosexuality, Wrong argues. (Personal communication)

13. Sociological and Anthropological Studies

1. These are: Alorese, Balinese, Chiricahua, Cuna, Goajiro, Haitians, Ifugao, Klamath, Kurtatchi, Kwakiutl, Kwoma, Lakher, Lepcha, Manus, Mashallese, Mbundu, Ojibwa, Ramkokamekra, Rwala, Sanpoil, Sinkaietk, Siriono, Tikopia, Tongana, Trobrianders, Trukese, Tswana (males only), and Yaruro (Ford-Beach, p. 129n).

2. Ford and Beach's list: Aranda, Aymara, Azande, Chamorro, Chuckchee, Creek, Crow, Dahomeans, Easter Islanders, Hidatsa, Hopi, Ila, Keraki, Kiwai, Koniag, Koryak, Lango, Mandan, Maricopa, Menomini, Nama, Naskapi, Natchez, Navaho, Omaha, Oto, Palauans, Papago, Ponca, Pukapukans, Qui-nault, Reddi, Samoans, Seminole, Siwans, Tanala, Thonga, Tinguian, Tswana (females only), Tubatulabal, Tupinamba, Witoto, Wogee, Wolof, Yakut, Yuma, Yungar, Yurok, Zuni (Ford and Beach, p. 130, fn.).

3. For example, Rosenberg and Fliegel's study of New York vanguard artists suggests that few if any of these were overtly homosexual (Rosenberg and Fliegel 1965).

14. Homosexuality as a Political Issue

1. Gay liberation rhetoric may in many cases be "sincere" on this point, i.e., the speaker really believes this to be the case, and the belief may function as a rationalization in the psychological sense of that term. However, in some cases, the distortion may be a deliberate lie told in the service of a political cause. Sagarin (1969), for example, notes that Mattachine Society leaders, who privately recognize that most gays they know are psychologically disturbed, will never-theless insist on the public rhetoric denying that homosexuals are sick, to induce prospective members to join: "They don't want to be told they're sick; they hear that everywhere else," one such spokesman told Sagarin (Sagarin 1969:10). "Noble lies?"

15. Conceptions of Normality

1. Dennis Wrong comments on this passage that, though cultural relativism has indeed been used to support the non-judgmentalism here described, it need not preclude a "love the sinner, hate the sin" position, e.g., cannibalism is an

undesirable cultural pattern, but individual cannibals are not to be blamed or thought wicked because they practice it as conforming members of their culture (Wrong, personal communication). This sounds to me, though, perilously close to saying we cannot blame the "good Germans" who went along with the Nazi persecutions because they were good conforming subjects of the regime.

16. The Sociology of Deviance and the Transcultural Alternative

1. True, this term has had more currency—in the past—in criminological studies, and has been regarded as very problematic by many psychoanalysts. And true, too, it has been commonly replaced in sociological and criminological writings by the term "sociopathic." That usage suggests a behavioral rather than psychodynamic emphasis, common to much in the sociological-criminological literature. LaBarre makes a very good case for retaining the term "psychopathic personality" precisely because it does refer to an intrapsychic process, and for not using the substitute "sociopathic." (See LaBarre 1969, ch. 11.)

2. Some mainstream psychoanalysts (e.g., Giovacchini 1979) however, believe that underlying psychopathology itself has not changed substantially over the years. (See chapter 2, note 6, in this book.)

Part 5. Summary and Conclusion

1. A parallel situation, where this consequence of extreme cultural relativism appears, arises in the debates among sociologists and policy officials over the "culture of poverty" and over "cultural deficit" theories in education. Here, relativism leads to thinking about the poor as living in a world so culturally distinct from the presumably middle-class culture of the educators and social workers that we must think of the people involved almost as a distinctive variety of human species, not comprehensible by our usual middle-class standards.

The effects are not far from a kind of racism with another name. Significantly, some of the same social scientists who espouse views of this kind on poverty and "cultural deficit" may assert culturally relativistic statements on matters of deviance, which, being in line with another variant of liberal orthodoxy, are at odds with the implicit racism of their culture-of-poverty views. If these social scientists took a consistently transcultural view on both these kinds of problems, they would not find themselves in such paradoxically inconsistent positions. (This parallel was pointed out to me by Dennis Wrong, personal communication.)

Bibliography

Abraham, Karl. 1927. "Contributions to the Theory of the Anal Character." *Selected Papers*. London: Institute for Psychoanalysis and Hogarth Press.

Adler, Alfred. 1927. *Understanding Human Nature*. New York: Greenberg.

Adler, Freda. 1975. *Sisters in Crime*. New York: McGraw-Hill.

Adorno, T. W. et al. 1950. *The Authoritarian Personality*. New York: Harper.

Altmann, S. 1967. "The Structure of Primate Communication." In S. Altman, ed., *Social Communication among Primates*, pp. 325–62. Chicago: University of Chicago Press.

American Psychiatric Association. 1968. *Diagnostic and Statistical Manual of Mental Disorders*. Washington, D.C.

Balint, Alice. 1939. "Love for the Mother and Mother-Love." In Michael Balint, ed., *Primary Love and Psychoanalytic Technique*. London: Tavistock; New York: Liveright, 1965.

——1954. *The Early Years of Life: A Psychoanalytic Study*. New York: Basic Books.

Balint, Michael. 1956. "Perversions and Genitality." In *Primary Love and Psychoanalytic Technique*.

——1968. *The Basic Fault: Therapeutic Aspects of Regression*. London: Tavistock.

Balint, Michael, ed. 1965. *Primary Love and Psychoanalytic Technique*. London: Tavistock; New York: Liveright.

Bardwick, Judith M. 1971. *The Psychology of Women: A Study of Bio-Cultural Conflicts*. New York: Harper and Row.

Barglow, Peter and Margret Schaefer. 1977. "A New Female Psychology?" In Harold Blum, ed., *Female Psychology: Contemporary Psy-*

choanalytic Views, pp. 393–438. New York: International Universities Press.

Barnouw, Victor. 1963. 1973. *Culture and Personality*. Homewood, Ill.: Dorsey.

Beach, Frank A., ed. 1965. *Sex and Behavior*. New York: Wiley.

Beals, Ralph L. and Harry Hoijer. 1953, 1959, 1965. *An Introductión to Anthropology*. New York: Macmillan.

Becker, Howard S. 1963. *Outsiders: Studies in the Sociology of Deviance*. New York: Free Press.

Becker, Howard S., ed. 1964. *The Other Side: Perspectives on Deviance*. New York: Free Press.

Bell, Alan and Martin Weinberg. 1978. *Homosexualities: A Study of Diversity among Men and Women*. New York: Simon and Schuster.

Bendix, Reinhard. 1952. "Compliant Behavior and Individual Personality." *American Journal of Sociology* 58:292–303.

Benedict, Ruth. 1934a. "Anthropology and the Abnormal." *Journal of General Psychology* 10:59–82. Reprinted in Margaret Mead, ed., *An Anthropologist at Work: Writings of Ruth Benedict*. Boston: Houghton Mifflin.

——1934b. *Patterns of Culture*. Boston: Houghton Mifflin.

Bensman, Joseph and Bernard Rosenberg. 1976. *Mass, Class, and Bureaucracy: An Introduction to Sociology*. New York: Praeger.

Berger, Peter. 1963. *Invitation to Sociology*. Garden City, N.Y.: Doubleday.

Berger, Peter and Thomas Luckman. 1967. *The Social Construction of Reality*. Garden City, N.Y.: Doubleday.

Bergler, Edmund. 1943. "The Gambler: A Misunderstood Neurotic." *Journal of Criminal Psychopathology* 4:379–93.

——1951. *Counterfeit Sex*. New York: Grune and Stratton.

——1956. *Homosexuality: Disease or Way of Life?* New York: Hill and Wang.

——1957. *The Psychology of Gambling*. New York: Hill and Wang.

Bettelheim, Bruno. 1954. *Symbolic Wounds: Puberty Rites and the Envious Male*. New York: Free Press.

Bieber, Irving et al. 1962. *Homosexuality: A Psychoanalytic Study of Male Homosexuals*. New York: Basic Books.

Binion, Rudolph. 1968. *Frau Lou: Nietzsche's Wayward Disciple*. Princeton, N.J.: Princeton University Press.

——1977. *Hitler among the Germans*. New York: Elsevier.

Binswanger, Ludwig. 1963. *Being-in-the-World: Selected Papers of Ludwig Binswanger*. New York: Basic Books.

Birdwhistell, Ray. 1970. *Kinesics and Context: Essays in Body Motion and Communication*. Philadelphia: University of Pennsylvania Press.

Birnbaum, Norman. 1969. *The Crisis of Industrial Society*. New York: Oxford University Press.

——1971. *Toward a Critical Sociology*. New York: Oxford University Press.

Blos, Peter. 1962. *On Adolescence*. New York: Free Press.

Blum, Harold P., ed. 1977. *Female Psychology: Contemporary Psychoanalytic Views*. New York: International Universities Press.

Bogaras, W. 1907. *The Chuckchee*. Vol. 2, *Religion*. In *Memoirs of the American Museum of Natural History*, 1904–09, vol. 11. F. Boas, ed. New York: Stechert.

Bonaparte, Marie. 1951. *Female Sexuality*. Paris: Presses Universitaires.

Bottomore, T. B. 1965. *Elites and Society*. New York: Basic Books.

——1966. *Classes in Modern Society*. New York: Random House.

Bowlby, John. 1969. *Attachment and Loss*. Vol. 1: *Attachment*. London: Penguin.

Boyer, L. Bryce. 1964. "Psychological Problems of a Group of Apaches: Alcoholic Hallucinosis and Latent Homosexuality among Typical Men." In W. Muensterberger and S. Axelrad, eds., *The Psychoanalytic Study of Society*, vol. 3. New York: International Universities Press.

——1978. "On Aspects of the Mutual Influences of Anthropology and Psychoanalysis." *Journal of Psychological Anthropology* 1(3):265–96.

Boyer, L. Bryce and Ruth M. Boyer. 1967. "Some Influences of Acculturation and Personality Traits of the Old People of the Mescalero and Chiracahua Apache." In W. Muensterberger and S. Axelrad, eds., *The Psychoanalytic Study of Society*, 4:170–84. New York: International Universities Press.

——1972. "Effects of Acculturation on the Vicissitudes of the Aggressive Drive among the Apaches of the Mescalero Indian Reservation." In W. Muensterberger, A. Esman, and L. B. Boyer, eds., *The Psychoanalytic Study of Society*, 5:40–82. New York: International Universities Press.

——1976. "Prolonged Adolescence and Early Identification: A Cross-Cultural Study." In W. Muensterberger, A. Esman, and L. B. Boyer, eds., *The Psychoanalytic Study of Society*, 7:95–106. New Haven and London: Yale University Press.

Brierley, Marjorie. 1932. "Some Problems of Integration in Women." *International Journal of Psychoanalysis* 13:433–48.

Brophy, Brigid. 1962. *Black Ship to Hell*. New York: Harcourt, Brace, and World.

Brown, Norman O. 1959. *Life Against Death*. Middletown, Conn.: Wesleyan University Press.

Brownmiller, Susan. 1975. *Against Our Will: Men, Women and Rape*. New York: Simon and Schuster.

Brunswick, Ruth Mack. 1940. "The Pre-Oedipal Phase of Libido Development." *Psychoanalytic Quarterly* 9:293–319. Rpt. in Robert Fliess, ed., *The Psychoanalytic Reader*, pp. 231–53. New York: International Universities Press, 1969.

Burroughs, William. 1959. *Naked Lunch*. New York: Grove Press.

Bushnell, John and Donna Bushnell. 1971. "Sociocultural and Psychodynamic Correlates of Polygyny in a Highland Mexican Village." *Ethnology* 4:44–55.

——"Wealth, Work, and World-View in Native Northwest California: Sacred Significance and Psychoanalytic Symbolism." In T. Blackburn, ed., *Flowers of the Wind*. Socorro, N.M.: Ballena Press.

Cameron, Norman. 1943. "The Paranoid Pseudo-Community." *American Journal of Sociology* 49:32–39.

Chance, R. A. and A. P. Mead. 1953. "Social Behavior and Primate Evolution." *Symposia of the Society for Experimental Biology* 7:395–439. New York: Academic Press.

Chang, Judy and Jack Block. 1960. "A Study of Identification in Male Homosexuals." *Journal of Consulting Psychology* 24:307–10.

Chasseguet-Smirgel, Janine. 1964. "Feminine Guilt and the Oedipus Complex." In Chasseguet-Smirgel et al. 1970, pp. 94–134.

Chasseguet-Smirgel, Janine et al. 1970. *Female Sexuality: New Psychoanalytic Views*. Ann Arbor: University of Michigan Press.

Chodorow, Nancy. 1978. *The Reproduction of Mothering*. Berkeley: University of California Press.

Christie, Richard and Marie Jehoda, eds. 1954. *Studies in the Scope and Method of "The Authoritarian Personality."* New York: Free Press.

Cline, W. 1936. "Notes on the People of Siwah and El Garah in the Libyan Desert." *General Series in Anthropology*. Menasha, Wis.

Cohn, Norman. 1961. *The Pursuit of the Millenium*. New York: Harper.

Comfort, Alex. 1963. *Sex in Society*. London: Duckworth.

Cory, Donald Webster. 1951. *The Homosexual in America*. New York: Greenberg.

Coser, Lewis. 1956. *The Functions of Social Conflict*. New York: Free Press.

Dank, Barry M. 1971. "Coming Out in the Gay World." *Psychiatry* 34:180–97.

Davenport, William. 1965. "Sexual Patterns and their Regulation in a Society of the Southwest Pacific." In Beach 1965.

Davis, Glenn. 1977. *Childhood and History in America.* New York: Psychohistory Press.

DeMause, Lloyd. 1979. *Foundations of Psychohistory.* New York: Psychohistory Press.

DeMause, Lloyd and Henry Ebel, eds. 1977. *Jimmy Carter and American Fantasy.* New York: Psychohistory Press.

DeMause, Lloyd, ed. 1974. *The History of Childhood.* New York: Psychohistory Press.

——1975. *The New Psychohistory.* New York: Psychohistory Press.

DeMott, Benjamin. 1967. "But He's a Homosexual . . ." *New American Review* 1:166–82.

DeSaussure, Ferdinand. 1916. *Cours de Linguistique Générale.* (*Course in General Linguistics,* Wade Baskin, trans. New York: Philosophical Library, 1959.)

Deutsch, Helene. 1925. "The Psychology of Women in Relation to the Functions of Reproduction." *International Journal of Psychoanalysis* 6:405–418.

——1930. "The Significance of Masochism in the Mental Life of Women." *International Journal of Psychoanalysis* 11:48–60.

——1944, 1945. *The Psychology of Women,* Vols. 1, 2. New York: Grune and Stratton.

Devereux, George. 1937. "Institutionalized Homosexuality of the Mohave Indians." *Human Biology* 9:498–527. Rpt. In Ruitenbeek 1963a.

——1939. "Mohave Culture and Personality." *Character and Personality* 8:91–109.

——1940. "Social Negativism and Criminal Psychopathology." *Journal of Criminal Psychopathology* 1:325–38.

——1951. *Reality and Dream: The Psychotherapy of a Plains Indian.* New York: International Universities Press.

——1956. "Normal and Abnormal: The Key Problem of Psychiatric Anthropology." In J. Casagrande and T. Gladwin, eds., *Some Uses of Anthropology: Theoretical and Applied,* pp. 23–48, plus references. Washington, D.C.: Anthropological Society of Washington. (Also in much expanded version in French, in Devereux, 1970a:1–83.)

——1961. *Mohave Ethnopsychiatry: The Psychic Disturbances of an Indian Tribe.* Washington, D.C.: Smithsonian Institution Press.

——1967. *From Anxiety to Method in the Behavioral Sciences.* The Hague and Paris: Mouton.

——1970a. *Essais d'Ethnopsychiatrie Generale.* Paris: Gallimard.

——1970b. "Normal et Anormal." In Devereux 1970a:1–83.

——1976. *Dreams in Greek Tragedy: An Ethnopsychoanalytic Study.* Berkeley: University of California Press.

——1978. *Ethnopsychoanalysis: Psychoanalysis and Anthropology as Complementary Frames of Reference.* Berkeley: University of California Press.

Devore, Ivan. 1965. *Primate Behavior.* New York: Holt, Rinehart, and Winston.

DeVos, George. 1961. "Symbolic Analysis in the Cross-Cultural Study of Personality." In B. Kaplan, ed., *Studying Personality Cross-Culturally.* Evanston, Ill.: Row, Peterson.

DeVos, George, ed. 1976. *Responses to Change: Society, Culture and Personality.* New York: Van Nostrand.

DeVos, George, Hiroshi Wagatsuma, et al. 1966. *Japan's Invisible Race: Caste in Culture and Personality.* Berkeley: University of California Press.

Dinnerstein, Dorothy. 1977. *The Mermaid and the Minotaur: Sexual Arrangements and Human Malaise.* New York: Harper.

Dobzhansky, Theodore. 1962. *Mankind Evolving: The Evolution of the Human Species.* New Haven: Yale University Press.

Dollard, John. 1937. *Caste and Class in a Southern Town.* New Haven: Yale University Press. Rpt. Garden City, N.Y.: Doubleday, 1957.

Dowling, Joseph. 1977. "Millenialism and Psychology." *Journal of Psychohistory* 5:121–30.

Drum (Magazine). 1967. Report on an Opinion Research Center Poll. Reported in Weinberg and Williams 1974:19.

Ducey, Charles. 1976. "The Life History and Creative Psychopathology of the Shaman: Ethnopsychoanalytic Perspectives." In W. Muensterberger, A. Esman, and L. B. Boyer, eds., *The Psychoanalytic Study of Society,* 7:173–230. New Haven and London: Yale University Press.

Durkheim, Émile. 1895. *Rules of the Sociological Method.* New York: Free Press, 1950.

——1897. *Suicide.* New York: Free Press, 1951.

Eisenbud, Ruth-Jean. 1969. "Female Homosexuality: A Sweet Enfranchisement." In G. Goldman and D. Milman, eds., *Modern Woman,* pp. 247–68. Springfield, Ill.: C. C Thomas.

——1977. "The Psychoanalyst and Gay Liberation: A Discussion of Female Homosexuality." Paper presented to the Colloquium of the New York University Postdoctoral Program.

Eissler, K. R. 1953. "The Effect of the Structure of the Ego on Psychoanalytic Technique." *Journal of the American Psychoanalytic Association*, 1:104–43.

Endleman, Robert. 1966. "Reflections on the Human Revolution." *Psychoanalytic Review*, 53:169–88.

——1967. *Personality and Social Life*. New York: Random House.

——1970a. "Oedipal Elements in Student Rebellions." *Psychoanalytic Review*, 57:442–71.

——1970b. "The Ritual of Student Rebellions." MS.

——1972. "The Student Revolt: Afterthoughts and Prospects." *Contemporary Sociology* 1:3–10.

——1973. "Dominant vs. Subterranean Cultural Patterns in Modern Societies." MS.

——1975a. "Review of F. Weinstein and G. Platt, *Psychoanalytic Sociology*." *Contemporary Sociology*, 4(2):168–69.

——1975b. "Student Rebellion as Ritual." In H. Silverstein, ed., *Youth: Evolution and Revolution*. New York: Macmillan.

——1977a. "Familistic Social Change on the Israeli Kibbutz." *Annals of the New York Academy of Sciences* 285:605–11.

——1977b. "Female Psychosexual Development in the Light of Changing Feminine Gender Roles." Paper presented at the VI International Forum for Psychoanalysis, Berlin, West Germany.

Erikson, Erik. 1939. "Observations on Sioux Education." *Journal of Psychology* 7:101–56.

——1943. "Observations on the Yurok: Childhood and World Image." *University of California Publications in American Archaeology and Ethnology* 35:257–301.

——1945. "Childhood and Tradition in Two American Indian Tribes." In A. Freud, H. Hartmann, and E. Kris, eds., *The Psychoanalytic Study of the Child* 1:319–50. New York: International Universities Press.

——1950. *Childhood and Society*. New York: Norton.

——1958. *Young Man Luther: A Study in Psychoanalysis and History*. New York: Norton.

——1959. "Identity and the Life Cycle." *Psychological Issues* 1. New York: International Universities Press.

——1969. *Gandhi's Truth*. New York: Norton.

Erikson, Kai. 1962. "Notes on the Sociology of Deviance." *Social Problems* 9:307–14.

Fairbairn, W. R. D. 1952. *An Object Relations Theory of the Personality*. New York: Basic Books.

Farber, Leslie. 1976. *Lying, Despair, Jealousy, Envy, Sex, Suicide, Drugs and the Good Life*. New York: Basic Books.

Fenichel, Otto. 1945. *The Psychoanalytic Theory of Neurosis*. New York: Norton.

Ferenczi, Sandor. 1951. *Sex in Psychoanalysis*. New York: Basic Books.

Feuer, Lewis. 1969. *The Conflict of Generations*. New York: Basic Books.

Fine, Reuben. 1975a. *Psychoanalytic Psychology*. New York: Jason Aronson.

——1975b. "The Idea of a Psychoanalytic University." *History of Childhood Quarterly (Journal of Psychohistory)* 3:103–15.

——1977. "Psychoanalysis as a Philosophical System: The Basis for Integrating the Social Sciences." *Journal of Psychohistory* 5:1–66.

Firestone, Shulamith. 1970. *The Dialectic of Sex*. New York: Morrow.

Flacks, Richard. 1967. "The Liberated Generation: Exploration of the Roots of Student Protest." *Journal of Social Issues* 23:52–75.

Ford, Clellan S. and Frank Beach. 1953. *Patterns of Sexual Behavior*. New York: Harper.

Fortune, Reo. 1932. *Sorcerers of Dobu*. New York: Dutton.

Fraiberg, Selma. 1977. *Every Child's Birthright: In Defense of Mothering*. New York: Basic Books.

Freedman, Mark J. 1967. "Homosexuality among Women and Psychological Adjustment." Ph.D. Diss., Case Western Reserve University.

Freeman, Derek. 1967. "*Totem and Taboo*: A Reappraisal." In W. Muensterberger and S. Axelrad, eds., *The Psychoanalytic Study of Society*, 4:9–33. New York: International Universities Press.

Freud, Anna. 1937. *The Ego and the Mechanisms of Defense*. London: Hogarth.

——1961ff. *The Writings of Anna Freud*. Vols. 1–6. New York: International Universities Press.

Freud, Sigmund. (All references following are to the English language *Standard Edition of the Complete Psychological Works of Sigmund Freud*. London: Hogarth Press. Hereafter cited as *S.E.* with the volume number and year of publication of that volume.)

——1901. *The Psychopathology of Everyday Life*. *S.E.* 6, 1960.

——1905a. *Jokes and Their Relation ot the Unconscious*. *S.E.* 8, 1960.

——1905b. *Three Essays on a Theory of Sexuality*. *S.E.* 7, 1953 (with additions in editions of 1910, 1915, 1920, 1922, 1924).

——1911. "Psycho-analytic notes on an autobiographical account of a case of paranoia (dementia paranoides)." *S.E.* 12, 1958.

——1912. "On the Universal Tendency toward Debasement in the Sphere of Love." *S.E.* 11, 1957.

——1913. *Totem and Taboo*. *S.E.* 13, 1955:1–164.

——1916. "Some Character Types Met With in Psychoanalytic Work: III: Criminals from a Sense of Guilt." *S.E.* 14, 1957:332–37.

——1917. "Mourning and Melancholia." *S.E.* 14, 1957:243–60.

——1921. *Group Psychology and Analysis of the Ego*. *S.E.* 18, 1955:67–145.

——1923. "Infantile Genital Organization of the Libido." *S.E.* 19, 1961:141–48.

——1924. "The Dissolution of the Oedipus Complex." *S.E.* 19, 1961:173–82.

——1925a. *An Autobiographical Study*. *S.E.* 20, 1959:7–76.

——1925b. "On Negation." *S.E.* 19, 1961:235–42.

——1925c. "Some Physical Consequences of the Anatomical Distinction Between the Sexes." *S.E.* 19, 1961:248–60.

——1926–27. *The Question of Lay Analysis*. *S.E.* 20, 1959:179–260.

——1927. *The Future of an Illusion*. *S.E.* 21, 1961:3–58.

——1930. *Civilization and its Discontents*. *S.E.* 21, 1961:59–148.

——1931. "Female Sexuality." *S.E.* 21, 1961:223–46.

——1933a. "Femininity." In *New Introductory Lectures in Psychoanalysis*. *S.E.* 22, 1964:112–35.

——1933b. *New Introductory Lectures in Psychoanalysis*. *S.E.* 23, 1964:7–184.

——1939. *Moses and Monotheism*. *S.E.* 23, 1964:3–140.

——1940. *An Outline of Psychoanalysis*. *S.E.* 23, 1964:141–208.

Friedan, Betty. 1963. *The Feminine Mystique*. New York: Norton.

Friedberg, Ronald L. 1975. "Early Recollections of Homosexuals as Indicators of Their Life Styles." *Journal of Individual Psychology* 31:196–204.

Fromm, Erich. 1941. *Escape from Freedom*. New York: Rinehart.

——1947. *Man for Himself*. New York: Rinehart.

——1955. *The Sane Society*. New York: Holt, Rinehart and Winston.

Gagnon, John and William Simon, eds. 1967. *Sexual Deviance*. New York: Harper.

Galenson, Eleanor. 1976. Report on the American Psychoanalytic Association Panel on the Psychology of Women (at the Annual meeting of 1974). *Journal of the American Psychoanalytic Association* 24:141–60. (Includes reports on presentations of Stoller, Wolff, Kleeman, Galenson and Roiphe, Glenn, Byerly, Buxbaum, Clower, I. Bernstein, E. Kaplan, and Colonna.)

Galenson, Eleanor and Herman Roiphe. 1977. "Some Suggested Revisions Concerning Early Female Development." In Blum 1977:29–58.

Gardner, Allen and Beatrice Gardner. 1969. "Teaching Sign Language to a Chimpanzee." *Science* 165:664–72.

——1971. "Two-Way Communication with an Infant Chimpanzee." In A. Schier et al., eds., *Behavior in Non-Human Primates*. New York: Academic Press.

Garfinkel, Harold. 1967. *Studies in Ethnomethodology*. Englewood Cliffs, N.J.: Prentice-Hall.

Gebhard, Paul H. 1971. "Human Sexual Behavior: A Summary Statement." In D. Marshall and R. Suggs, eds., 1971:206–17.

Gerth, Hans and C. Wright Mills. 1953. *Character and Social Structure*. New York: Harcourt, Brace.

Giallombardo, Rose. 1974. *The Social World of Imprisoned Girls*. New York: Wiley.

Giovacchini, Peter L. 1975. *Psychoanalysis of Character Disorders*. New York: Jason Aronson.

——1979. *Treatment of Primitive Mental States*. New York: Jason Aronson.

Gladwin, Thomas and William Sturtevant (Anthropological Society of Washington), eds. 1962. *Anthropology and Human Behavior*. Washington, D.C.: Anthropological Society of Washington.

Goffman, Erving. 1959. *The Presentation of Self in Everyday Life*. Garden City, N.Y.: Doubleday.

——1961. *Asylums*. Garden City, N.Y.: Doubleday.

——1963. *Stigma*. Englewood Cliffs. N.J.: Prentice-Hall.

Goldberg, Steven. 1973. *The Inevitability of Patriarchy*. New York: Morrow.

Goldman, Irving. 1963. *The Cubeo: Indians of the Northwest Amazon*. Illinois Studies in Anthropology, No. 2. Urbana: University of Illinois Press.

Goodall, Jane. 1971. *In the Shadow of Man*. Boston: Houghton Mifflin.

Goode, William, 1960. "A Deviant Case: Illegitimacy in the Caribbean." *American Sociological Review* 25:21–30.

——1970. *World Revolution and Family Patterns*. New York: Free Press.

Gornick, Vivian and Barbara Moran, eds. *Woman in Sexist Society*. New York: New American Library.

Gough, Kathleen. 1971. "The Origin of the Family." *The Journal of Marriage and the Family* 33:760–70.

Gouldner, Alvin. 1972. *The Coming Crisis in Western Sociology*. New York: Basic Books.

Greer, Germaine, 1971. *The Female Eunuch*. London: Paladin.

Grunberger, Bela. 1970. "Outline for a Study of Narcissism in Female Sexuality." In Chasseguet-Smirgel et al. 1970:68–83.

Guntrip, Harry. 1971. *Psychoanalytic Theory, Therapy, and the Self*. New York: Basic Books.

Habermas, Jurgen. 1968. *Knowledge and Human Interests*. Jeremy Shapiro, trans. Boston: Beacon.

Hacker, Helen Mayer. 1951. "Women as a Minority Group." *Social Forces* 30:60–69.

——1971. "Homosexuals: Deviant or Minority Group?" In Sagarin 1971:65–92.

——1976. "Gender Roles from a Cross-Cultural Perspective." In Lucile Duberman, *Gender and Sex in Society*. New York: Praeger.

Hampden-Turner, Charles. 1970. *Radical Man*. Cambridge, Mass.: Schenkman.

——1976. *Sane Asylum*. San Francisco: San Francisco Book.

Hardy, A. C. 1960. "Was Man More Aquatic in the Past?" *New Scientist* 7:642–45.

Harris, Marvin. 1977. "Why Men Dominate Women." *New York Times Magazine*. Nov. 13, 1977.

Harry, Joseph. 1977. "Marriage among Gay Males: The Separation of Intimacy and Sex." In Scott McNall, ed., *The Sociological Perspective*, pp. 330–40. 4th ed. Boston: Little, Brown.

Hartmann, Heinz. 1939. *Ego Psychology and the Problem of Adaptation*. New York: International Universities Press.

——1944. "Psychoanalysis and Sociology." In S. Lorand, ed., *Psychoanalysis Today*. New York: International Universities Press. (Also rpt. in Hartmann, 1964.)

——1964. *Essays in Ego Psychology*. New York: International Universities Press.

Hartmann, Heinz, Ernst Kris, and R. M. Loewenstein. 1951. "Some Psychoanalytic Comments on "Culture and Personality." In G. Wilbur and W. Muensterberger, eds., *Psychoanalysis and Culture*. New York: International Universities Press.

——1964. "Papers in Psychoanalytic Psychology." *Psychological Issues*, No. 14. New York: International Universities Press.

Hatterer, Lawrence. 1971. *Changing Homosexuality in the Male*. New York: Dell.

Hendin, Herbert. 1964. *Suicide and Scandinavia*. New York: Grune and Stratton.

——1969. *Black Suicide*. New York: Basic Books.

——1971. "A Psychoanalyst Looks at Student Revolutionaries." *New York Times Magazine*, Jan. 17, 1971.

——1975. *The Age of Sensation*. New York: Norton.

Hewes, Gordon. 1971a. "An Explicit Formulation of the Relationship between Tool-Using, Tool-Making and the Emergence of Language." *Abstracts. American Anthropological Association.* Annual Meeting. New York: American Anthropological Association.

——1971b. *Language Origins: A Bibliography*. Boulder: University of Colorado Press.

——1973. "Primate Communication and the Gestural Origin of Language." *Current Anthropology* 14:5–12.

Hippler, Arthur. 1974. "The North Alaska Eskimos: A Culture and Personality Perspective." *American Ethnologist* 1:449–70.

——1977. "Cultural Evolution." *Journal of Psychohistory* 4:419–39.

——1978. "A Culture and Personality Perspective on the Yolngu of Northeastern Arnhem Land: Part I: Early Socialization." *Journal of Psychological Anthropology* 1:221–44.

Hippler, Arthur, L. Bryce Boyer and Ruth M. Boyer. 1975. "The Psychocultural Significance of the Alaska Athabaskan Potlatch Ceremony." In W. Muensterberger et al., eds., *The Psychoanalytic Study of Society*, 6:204–34. New York: International Universities Press.

Hite, C. 1974a. "APA Rules Homosexuality Not Necessarily a Disorder." *Psychiatric News* 9:1.

——1974b. "Members Uphold DSM-II Change." *Psychiatric News* 9:9.

Hockett, Charles. 1958. *A Course in Modern Linguistics*. New York: Macmillan.

Hockett, Charles and Robert Ascher. 1964. "The Human Revolution." *Current Anthropology* 5:135–47.

Hoebel, E. Adamson. 1966. *Anthropology*. New York: McGraw-Hill.

Hoffman, Martin. 1968. *The Gay World: Male Homosexuality and the Social Creation of Evil*. New York: Basic Books.

Homans, George. 1961. *Social Behavior: Its Elementary Forms*. New York: Harcourt, Brace and World.

Honigmann, John. 1954. *Culture and Personality*. New York: Harper.

Hooker, Evelyn. 1957. "The Adjustment of the Male Overt Homosexual." *Journal of Projective Techniques* 21:16–31.

——1965. "Male Homosexuals and Their Worlds." In Marmor 1965:83–107.

——1967. "The Homosexual Community." In Gagnon and Simon 1967:167–84.

Horkheimer, Max. 1972. *Critical Theory: Selected Essays*. Matthew M. O'Connell et al., trans. New York: Herder and Herder.

Horney, Karen. 1926. "The Flight from Womanhood: The Masculinity Complex in Women as Viewed by Men and Women." In Horney 1967; also in Strouse 1974.

——1932. "The Dread of Women." *International Journal of Psychoanalysis* 13:348–60.

——1933. "The Denial of the Vagina." *International Journal of Psychoanalysis* 14:57–70.

——1937. *The Neurotic Personality of Our Time*. New York: Norton.

——1967. *Feminine Psychology*. New York: Norton.

Hsu, Francis L. K., ed. 1961. *Psychological Anthropology*. Homewood, Ill.: Dorsey.

Inkeles, Alex. 1959. "Personality and Social Structure." In R. K. Merton, L. Broom, and L. Cottrell, eds., *Sociology Today*, pp. 249–76. New York: Basic Books.

Inkeles, Alex and Daniel Levinson. 1954. "National Character." In Gardner Lindzey, ed., *Handbook of Social Psychology*. Vol. 2. Reading, Mass.: Addison-Wesley.

Jacobson, Edith. 1964. *The Self and the Ojbect World*. New York: International Universities Press.

Jones, Ernest, 1924. "Mother-Right and the Sexual Ignorance of Savages." In Jones, *Essays in Applied Psychoanalysis* 2:145–73. New York: International Universities Press, 1964.

——1927. "The Early Development of Female Sexuality." *International Journal of Psychoanalysis* 8:459–72.

——1933. "The Phallic Phase." *International Journal of Psychoanalysis* 14:1–33.

——1935. "Early Female Sexuality." *International Journal of Psychoanalysis*. 16:263–73.

Jung, Carl G. 1902ff. *Collected Works* R. F. C. Hull, trans., H. Read et al., ed. London: Routledge and Kegan Paul; New York: Bollingen.

——1958. *Psyche and Symbol*. A Selection of the Writings of C. G. Jung. Violet de Laszlo, ed., Garden City, N.Y.: Doubleday.

———1959. *Basic Writings of C. G. Jung.* Violet de Laszlo, ed. New York: Random House.

Kagan, J. and M. Lewis. 1971. *Change and Continuity in Infancy.* New York: Wiley.

Kameny, Franklin E. 1971. "Homosexuals as a Minority Group." In Sagarin 1971:50–65.

Kaplan, Bert, ed. 1961. *Studying Personality Cross-Culturally.* Evanston, Ill.: Row, Peterson.

Kardiner, Abram. 1945. *The Psychological Frontiers of Society.* New York: Columbia University Press.

Kardiner, Abram and Ralph Linton 1939. *The Individual and His Society.* New York: Columbia University Press.

Karlen, Arno. 1971. *Sexuality and Homosexuality: A New View.* New York: Norton.

Keniston, Kenneth. 1960. *The Uncommitted.* New York: Harcourt, Brace and World.

———1968. *Young Radicals.* New York: Harcourt, Brace and World.

Kenyon, F. Edwin. 1974. "Female Homosexuality: A Review" In J. A. Loraine, ed., *Understanding Homosexuality.* New York: Elsevier.

Kernberg, Otto. 1975. *Borderline Conditions and Pathological Narcissism.* New York: Jason Aronson.

———1976. *Object Relations Theory and Clinical Psychoanalysis.* New York: Jason Aronson.

Kinsey, Alfred, W. B. Pomeroy, and Clyde E. Martin. 1948. *Sexual Behavior in the Human Male.* Philadelphia: Saunders.

Kinsey, Alfred, W. B. Pomeroy, Clyde E. Martin, and Paul Gebhard. 1953. *Sexual Behavior in the Human Female.* Philadelphia: Saunders.

Kitsuse, John I. 1962. "Societal Reaction to Deviant Behavior." *Social Problems* 9:247–56.

Kleeman, James. 1977. "Freud's Views on Early Female Sexuality in the Light of Direct Child Observation." In Blum 1977:3–28.

Klein, Melanie. 1928. "Early Stages of the Oedipus Conflict." *International Journal of Psychoanalysis* 9:167–80.

———1932. *The Psychoanalysis of Children.* London: Hogarth and Institute for Psychoanalysis.

Kluckhohn, Clyde. 1949. *Mirror for Man.* New York: McGraw-Hill.

Kluckhohn, Clyde and Henry Murray (in later edition also with David Schneider), eds. 1948, 1954. *Personality in Nature, Society and Culture.* New York: Knopf.

Kohut, Heinz. 1971. *The Analysis of the Self.* New York: International Universities Press.

——1978. *The Restoration of the Self.* New York: International Universities Press.

Komarovsky, Mirra. 1962. *Blue Collar Marriage.* New York: Random House.

——1976. *Dilemmas of Masculinity.* New York: Norton.

Kovel, Joel. 1970. *White Racism.* New York: Random House.

Krantz, G. S. 1961. "Pithecanthropine Brain Size and Its Cultural Consequences." *Man* 61:85–87.

Kris, Ernst. 1952. *Psychoanalytic Explorations in Art.* New York: International Universities Press.

Kroeber, A. L. 1948. *Anthropology.* New York: Harcourt, Brace.

Kurzweil, Edith. 1975. "The Mythology of Structuralism." *Partisan Review* 42:416–30.

——1980. *The Structuralist Age: Lévi-Strauss to Foucault.* New York: Columbia University Press.

LaBarre, Weston. 1954. *The Human Animal.* Chicago: University of Chicago Press.

——1958. "The Influence of Freud on Anthropology." *American Imago* 15:275–328.

——1964. "Commentary on the Hockett-Ascher Paper on the Human Revolution." *Current Anthropology* 5:149–50.

——1968. "Personality from a Psychoanalytic Viewpoint." In E. Norbeck, D. Price-Williams, and W. McCord, eds., *The Study of Personality: An Interdisciplinary Appraisal.* New York: Holt, Rinehart and Winston.

——1969. *They Shall Take Up Serpents.* New York: Schocken.

——1970. *The Ghost Dance: Origins of Religion.* Garden City, N.Y.: Doubleday.

——1978a. "Freudian Biology, Magic and Religion." *Journal of the American Psychoanalytic Association* 26:813–30.

——1978b. "Psychoanalysis and the Biology of Religion." *Journal of Psychological Anthropology* 1:57–64.

Laing, Ronald D. 1967. *The Politics of Experience.* New York: Random House.

Lampl-de-Groot, Jeanne. 1928. "The Evolution of the Oedipus Complex in Women." *International Journal of Psychoanalysis* 9:332ff. (Rpt. in Robert Fliess, ed., *The Psychoanalytic Reader,* 1968, pp. 207–22. New York, International Universities Press.)

——1933. "Problems of Femininity." *Psychoanalytic Quarterly* 2:489–518.

——1952. "Re-evaluation of the Role of the Oedipus Complex." *International Journal of Psychoanalysis* 33:335–42.

Lasch, Christopher. 1977. *Haven in a Heartless World: The Family Besieged.* New York: Basic Books.

——1979. *The Culture of Narcissism.* New York: Norton.

Layard, J. W. 1942. *Stone Men of Malekula.* London: Chatto and Windus.

Leacock, Eleanor. 1974. "Review of Steven Goldberg, *The Inevitability of Patriarchy." American Anthropologist* 76:363–65.

——1975. "Reply to Goldberg's Response to Leacock's Review." *American Anthropologist* 77:73–75.

Lemert, Edwin W. 1951. *Social Pathology.* New York: McGraw-Hill.

——1967. *Human Deviance, Social Problems and Social Control.* Englewood Cliffs, N.J.: Prentice-Hall.

LeVine, Robert. 1961. "Africa." In F. L. K. Hsu, ed., *Psychological Anthropology,* pp. 48–92. Homewood, Ill.: Dorsey.

——1973. *Culture, Behavior, and Personality.* Chicago: Aldine.

Lévi-Strauss, Claude. 1962. *The Savage Mind.* Chicago: University of Chicago Press.

Leznoff, Maurice and William Wesley. 1956. "The Homosexual Community." *Social Problems* 3:257–63.

Lichtenberg, Philip. 1969. *Psychoanalysis: Radical and Conservative.* New York: Springer.

Lieberman, Philip and Edmund Crelin. 1971. "On the Speech of Neanderthal Man." *Linguistic Inquiry* 11:203–22.

Liebert, Robert. 1971. *Radical and Militant Youth: A Psychoanalytic Inquiry.* New York: Praeger.

Linden, Eugene. 1974. *Apes, Men and Language.* New York: Saturday Review Press/Dutton.

Lipset, Seymour Martin. 1972. *Rebellion in the University.* Boston: Little, Brown.

Loewenberg, Peter. 1971. "The Psychohistorical Origins of the Nazi Youth Cohort." *American Historical Review* 76:1,457–1,502.

Lowie, Robert H. 1924. *Primitive Religion.* New York: Liveright.

Maccoby, Eleanor and C. N. Jacklin. 1975. *The Psychology of Sex Differences.* Stanford: Stanford University Press.

Maccoby, Michael. 1967. "On Mexican National Character." In *Annals of the American Academy of Political and Social Science* 370:63–73.

——1975. *The Gamesman.* New York: Simon and Schuster.

MacGregor, Gordon. 1946. *Warriors without Weapons.* Chicago: University of Chicago Press.

McIntosh, Mary. 1968. "The Homosexual Role." *Social Problems* 16:182–92.

Mahler, Margaret. 1968. *On Human Symbiosis and the Vicissitudes of Individuation.* In collaboration with Manuel Furer. New York: International Universities Press.

Mahler, Margaret, Fred Pine, and Anni Bergman. 1975. *The Psychological Birth of the Human Infant.* New York: Basic Books.

Malinowski, Bronislaw. 1927. *Sex and Repression in Savage Society.* London: Routledge and Kegan Pual.

——1930. Parenthood, the Basis of Social Structure. In C. F. Calverton and S. D. Schmalhausen, eds., *The New Generation,* pp. 113–68. New York: Macauley.

——1944. *The Scientific Theory of Culture and Other Essays.* Chapel Hill: University of North Carolina Press.

Manis, Jerome and Bernard Meltzer, eds. 1972. *Symbolic Interaction: A Reader in Social Psychology.* Boston: Allyn and Bacon.

Marciano, Teresa Donati. 1974. "Middle Class Incomes, Working Class Hearts." *Family Process* 4:489–502.

Marcuse, Herbert. 1955. *Eros and Civilization.* Boston: Beacon.

Marmor, Judd. 1968. "Changing Patterns of Femininity: Psychoanalytic Implications." In S. Rosenbaum et al., eds., *The Marriage Relationship: Psychoanalytic Perspectives,* pp. 31–44. New York: Basic Books.

Marmor, Judd, ed. 1965. *Sexual Inversion.* New York: Basic Books.

Marshall, Donald S. 1971. "Sexual Behavior on Mangaia (Polynesia)." In Marshall and Suggs 1971:103–62.

Marshall, Donald S. and Robert C. Suggs, eds. 1971. *Human Sexual Behavior: Variations in the Ethnographic Spectrum.* New York: Basic Books.

Marx, Karl. 1844. *The Economic and Philosophical Manuscripts of 1844.* Dirk Struik, ed. New York: International Publishers, 1964.

Matza, David. 1961. "Subterranean Traditions of Youth." *Annals of the American Academy of Political and Social Science* 338:102–18.

Mazlish, Bruce. 1963. *Psychoanalysis and History.* Englewood Cliffs, N.J.: Prentice-Hall.

——1972. *In Search of Nixon: A Psychohistorical Inquiry.* New York: Basic Books.

Mead, George Herbert. 1934. *Mind, Self and Society.* Chicago: University of Chicago Press.

Mead, Margaret. 1930. *Growing Up in New Guinea.* New York: Morrow.

——1935. *Sex and Temperament in Three Primitive Societies*. New York: Morrow.

——1949. *Male and Female*. New York: Morrow.

——1963. "*Totem and Taboo* Reconsidered with Respect." *Bulletin of the Menninger Clinic* 27:185–99.

——1974. "On Freud's View of Female Psychology." In Jean Strouse, ed., *Women and Analysis*. New York: Grossman.

Merriam, Alan P. 1971. "Aspects of Sexual Behavior among the Bala (Basongye) of the Democratic Republic of the Congo." In Marshall and Suggs 1971:71–102.

Merton, Robert K. 1936. "The Unanticipated Consequences of Purposive Social Action." *American Sociological Review* 1:894–904.

——1949. "Manifest and Latent Functions." In Merton, *Social Theory and Social Structure*, pp. 21–82. New York: Free Press.

Millett, Kate. 1970. *Sexual Politics*. New York: Doubleday.

Mitchell, Juliet. 1974. *Psychoanalysis and Feminism*. New York: Random House.

Mitchell, Stephen A. 1978. "Psychodynamics. Homosexuality and the Question of Pathology." *Psychiatry* 41:254–63.

Mitscherlich, Alexander. 1963. *Society Without the Father*. New York: Harcourt, Brace and World.

Mitscherlich, Alexander and Margarete Mitscherlich. 1975. *The Inability to Mourn*. New York: Grove Press.

Mitzman, Arthur. 1970. *The Iron Cage* (biography of Max Weber). New York: Knopf.

Modell, Arnold A. 1975. "The Ego and the Id Fifty Years Later." *International Journal of Psychoanalysis*, 56:57–68.

Money, John and Anke Ehrhardt. 1972. *Man and Woman, Boy and Girl*. Baltimore: Johns Hopkins University Press.

Moore, Burness. 1968. "Psychic Representation and Female Orgasm." *Journal of the American Psychoanalytic* Association 16:569–87; revised version on Blum, 1977:305–30.

Morgan, Elaine. 1972. *The Descent of Woman*. New York: Stein and Day.

Morgan, Robin, ed. 1970. *Sisterhood Is Powerful*. New York: Random House.

Morris, Desmond. 1968. *The Naked Ape*. New Haven: Yale University Press.

Moulton, Ruth. 1973. "Sexual Conflicts in Contemporary Women." In Earl Witenberg, ed., *Interpersonal Explorations in Psychoanalysis*. New York: Basic Books.

Mourant, A. E. 1973. "The Evolution of Brain Size, Speech and Psychosexual Development." *Current Anthropology* 14:30–31.

Muensterberger, Warner, ed. 1970. *Man and His Culture: Psychoanalytic Anthropology after Totem and Taboo.* New York: Taplinger.

Muensterberger, Warner et al., eds. 1960, 1962, 1964, 1967, 1972, 1975, 1976 (Series). *The Psychoanalytic Study of Society.* Vol. 1–7. (For vols. 1–6) New York: International Universities Press; (for vol. 7) New Haven and London: Yale University Press.

Myrdal, Gunnar et al. 1944. *An American Dilemma.* New York: Harper.

Nelson, Benjamin. 1954. "The Future of Illusions." *Psychoanalysis* (journal later called *Psychoanalytic Review* 2:16–37.

——1962. "Sociology and Psychoanalysis on Trial: An Epilogue." *Psychoanalytic Review* 49:144–60.

Nelson, Cynthia and Virginia Olesen. 1977. "Veil of Illusion: A Critique of the Concept of Equality in Western Feminist Thought." *Catalyst* 10–11:8–36.

Norbeck, Edward, Douglass Price-Williams, and William McCord, eds. 1968. *The Study of Personality: An Interdisciplinary Appraisal.* New York: Holt, Rinehart and Winston.

Opler, Marvin. 1965. "Anthropological and Cross-Cultural Aspects of Homosexuality." In Marmor 1965:108–23.

Ovesey, Lionel. 1969. *Homosexuality and Pseudohomosexuality.* New York: Science House.

Parin, Paul. 1972. "Der Ausgang des oedipalen Konflikts in drei verschiedenen Kulturen" (Resolution of the Oedipal Conflict in Three Different Cultures). *Kursbuch.* Berlin: Wagenbuch, 29.

Parin, Paul and Fritz Morgenthaler. 1963. *Die Weissen Denken zuviel: Psychoanalytische Untersuchungen bei den Dogon in Westafrika* (The Whites Think Too Much: Psychoanalytic Research among the Dogon of West Africa). Zürich: Atlantis; Munich: Kindler Taschenbucher, No. 2,079.

——1964. "Ego and Orality in the Analysis of West Africans." In W. Muensterberger et al., eds., *The Psychoanalytic Study of Society* 3:197–202. New York: International Universities Press.

Parin, Paul, Fritz Morgenthaler, and Goldy Parin-Matthey. 1971. *Fürchte Deinen Nächsten wie dich Selbst: Psychoanalyse und Gesellschaft am Modell der Agni in Westafrika* (Fear Thy Neighbor as Thyself: Psychoanalysis and Society in the Agni in West Africa). Frankfurt am Main: Suhrkamp.

Parsons, Anne. 1964. "Is the Oedipus Complex Universal? The Jones-

Malinowski Debate Revisited, and a South Italian Nuclear Complex." In Muensterberger et al., eds., *The Psychoanalytic Study of Society* 3:278–328. New York: International Universities Press. (Also rpt. in A. Parsons 1969 and in Muensterberger 1970.)

——1969. *Belief, Magic and Anomie: Essays in Psychosocial Anthropology.* Rose Coser et al., eds. New York: Free Press.

Parsons, Talcott. 1951. *The Social System.* New York: Free Press.

——1952. "The Superego and the Theory of Social Systems." *Psychiatry* 15:15–25. Rpt. in Parsons, 1964.

——1954. "The Incest Taboo in Relation to Social Structure and the Socialization of the Child." *British Journal of Sociology* 5: Rpt. in Parsons, 1964.

——1958. "Social Structure and the Development of Personality: Freud's Contribution to the Integration of Psychology and Sociology." *Psychiatry* 21:321–40. Rpt. in Parsons, 1964.

——1964. *Social Structure and Personality.* New York: Free Press.

——1967. *Sociological Theory and Modern Society.* New York: Free Press.

Phillips, Sheridan, Suzanne King, and Louise DuBois. 1978. "Spontaneous Activities of Female vs. Male Newborns." *Child Development* 49:590–97.

Rabow, Jerome. 1977. "Szasz, Psychoanalysis and Sociology." Paper presented at American Sociological Association meetings, Chicago.

——1979. "Psychoanalysis and Sociology: What Needs to be Done." Paper presented at Pacific Sociological Association meetings, Anaheim, Calif.

Radcliffe-Brown, A. R. 1935. "On the Concept of Function in Social Science." *American Anthropologist* 37:394–402.

——1952. *Structure and Function in Primitive Societies.* London: Cohen and West.

Reich, Charles. 1970. *The Greening of America.* New York: Random House.

Reich, Wilhelm. 1933a. *Character Analysis.* New York: Orgone Press, 1949.

——1933b. *The Mass Psychology of Fascism.* New York: Orgone Press, 1946.

——1942. *The Discovery of the Orgone.* New York: Orgone Press.

Ricoeur, Paul. 1970. *Freud and Philosophy: An Essay on Interpretation.* Denis Savage, trans. New Haven and London: Yale University Press.

Rieff, Philip. 1959. *Freud: The Mind of the Moralist.* New York: Viking.

——1966. *The Triumph of the Therapeutic*. New York: Harper and Row.

Riesman, David, Nathan Glazer, and Reuel Denny. 1950. *The Lonely Crowd*. New Haven: Yale University Press.

Ritzer, George. 1975. *Sociology: A Multiple-Paradigm Science*. Boston: Allyn and Bacon.

Robinson, Paul A. 1969. *The Freudian Left: Reich, Marcuse and Róheim*. New York: Harper and Row.

Róheim, Géza. 1925. *Australian Totemism: A Psychoanalytic Study in Anthropology*. London: Allen and Unwin.

——1930. *Animism, Magic and the Divine King*. New York: International Universities Press.

——1932. "Psychoanalysis of Primitive Cultural Types." *International Journal of Psychoanalysis* 13:150–74.

——1941. "Play Analysis with Normanby Island Children." *American Journal of Orthopsychiatry* 11:524–30.

—— 1943. *The Origin and Function of Culture*. New York: Nervous and Mental Disease Monographs.

—— 1945. *The Eternal Ones of the Dream: A Psychoanalytic Interpretation of Australian Myth and Ritual*. New York: International Universities Press.

——1947. "Dream Analysis and Field Work in Anthropology." In Róheim, ed., *Psychoanalysis and the Social Sciences*, 1:87–130. New York: International Universities Press.

——1950. *Psychoanalysis and Anthropology*. New York: International Universities Press.

——1951. "Hungarian Shamanism." In Róheim, ed., *Psychoanalysis and the Social Sciences*, 3:131–69. New York: International Universities Press.

——1952. "Culture Hero and Trickster in North American Mythology." In S. Tax, ed., *Indian Tribes of Aboriginal America*, 3:190–94. Chicago: University of Chicago Press.

——1953. *The Gates of the Dream*. New York: International Universities Press.

——1954. *Magic and Schizophrenia*. New York: International Universities Press.

——1972. *The Panic of the Gods*. Warner Muensterberger, ed. New York: Harper Torchbooks.

——1974. *Children of the Desert: The Western Tribes of Central Australia*. Warner Muensterberger, ed. New York: Basic Books.

Roiphe, Herman and Eleanor Galenson. 1973. "Object Loss and Early Sexual Development." *Psychoanalytic Quarterly* 42:73–80.

Rosenberg, Bernard and Norris Fliegel. 1965. *The Vanguard Artist*. Chicago: Quadrangle.

Ross, Ralph and Ernest Van den Haag. 1957. *The Fabric of Society*. New York: Harcourt, Brace and World.

Rowse, A. L. 1963. *William Shakespeare: A Biography*. New York: Harper and Row.

Rubin, Lillian. 1976. *Worlds of Pain: Life in the Working Class Family*. New York: Basic Books.

Ruitenbeek, Hendrik, ed. 1962. *Psychoanalysis and Social Science*. New York: Dutton.

——1963a. *The Problem of Homosexuality in Modern Society*. New York: Dutton.

——1963b. *Varieties of Classic Social Theory*. New York: Dutton.

——1963c. *Varieites of Modern Social Theory*. New York: Dutton.

Sagarin, Edward. 1969. *Odd Man In: Societies of Deviants in America*. Chicago: Quadrangle.

——1973. "The Good Guys, the Bad Guys and the Gay Guys." (Survey review essay on recent books on homosexuality.) *Contemporary Sociology* 2:3–13.

——1971. *The Other Minorities: Non-Ethnic Collectivities Conceptualized as Minority Groups*. Waltham, Mass.: Ginn.

Saghir, Marcel and Eli Robins. 1973. *Male and Female Homosexuality: A Comprehensive Investigation*. Baltimore: Williams and Wilkins.

Sahlins, Marshall. 1960. "The Origin of Society." *Scientific American* 203:76–87.

Sahlins, Marshall and E. R. Service, eds. 1960. *Evolution and Culture*. Ann Arbor: University of Michigan Press.

Schafer, Roy. 1968. *Aspects of Internalization*. New York: International Universities Press.

——1974. "Problems in Freud's Psychology of Women." *Journal of the American Psychoanalytic Association* 22:459–85. (Rpt. in Blum 1977:331–60.)

——1976. *A New Language for Psychoanalysis*. New Haven: Yale University Press.

Schaller, George B. 1963. *The Mountain Gorilla: Ecology and Behavior*. Chicago: University of Chicago Press.

Schneider, Michael. 1973. *Neurosis and Civilization*. Michael Roloff, trans. New York: Seabury Press, 1975.

Schofield, M. 1965. *Sociological Aspects of Homosexuality: A Comparative Study of Three Types of Homosexuals*. Boston: Little, Brown.

Schur, Edwin M. 1971. *Labeling Deviant Behavior*. New York: Harper & Row.

Schütz, Alfred. 1964, 1970, 1971. *Collected Papers*. vols. 1, 2, 3. The Hague: Martinus Mijhoff.

Sennett, Richard. 1970. *Families in the City*. Cambridge, Mass.: Harvard University Press.

——1977. *The Fall of Public Man*. New York: Knopf.

Shainess, Natalie. 1969. "Images of Woman: Past and Present, Overt and Obscured." *American Journal of Psychotherapy* 23:77–97.

Shibutani, Tamotsu. 1961. *Society and Personality: An Interactionist Approach to Social Psychology*. Englewood Cliffs, N.J.: Prentice-Hall.

Simmel, George. 1908ff. *The Sociology of Georg Simmel*. New York: Free Press, 1950.

Simmons, J. L. 1965. "Public Stereotypes of Deviants." *Social Problems* 13:223–32.

Simon, William and John Gagnon. 1967. "Homosexuality: The Formulation of a Sociological Perspective." *Journal of Health and Social Behavior* 8:177–85.

Skolnick, Arlene and Jerome Skolnick, eds. 1971 and later editions. *Family in Transition*. Boston: Little, Brown.

Skolnick, Jerome and Elliott Currie, eds. 1970. *Crisis in American Institutions*. Boston: Little, Brown.

Slater, Philip. 1963. "On Social Regression." *American Sociological Review* 28:339–64.

——1966. *Microcosm: Structural, Psychological and Religious Evolution in Groups*. New York: Wiley.

——1969. "The Social Basis of Personality." In Neil Smelser and James Davis, eds., *Sociology: Behavioral and Social Science Survey*. Englewood Cliffs, N.J.: Prentice-Hall.

Smelser, Neil. 1962. *The Theory of Collective Behavior*. New York: Free Press.

Smelser, Neil and William Smelser, eds., 1963, 1970. *Personality and Social Systems*. New York: Wiley.

Snodgrass, Jon. 1979. "Patriarchal Social Structure and Unconscious Knowledge: A Preliminary Statement on Psychoanalytic Sociology." MS. Based on a Paper presented at meetings of the Society for the Study of Social Problems, Boston, 1979.

Socarides, Charles W. 1968. *The Overt Homosexual*. New York: Grune and Stratton.

——1978. *Homosexuality*. New York: Jason Aronson.

Spiro, Melford. 1956. *Kibbutz: Venture in Utopia*. Cambridge, Mass.: Harvard University Press.

——1958. *Children of the Kibbutz*. Cambridge, Mass.: Harvard University Press.

Stein, Howard F. 1974. "Envy and the Evil Eye among Slovak-Americans: An Essay in the Psychological Ontogeny of Belief and Ritual." *Ethos* 2:15–46.

——1978a. "Aging and Death among Slovak-Americans." *Journal of Psychological Anthropology*, 1:297–320.

——1978b. "Judaism and the Group-Fantasy of Martyrdom." *The Journal of Psychohistory* 6:151–210.

——1979. "The White Ethnic Movement. Pan-ism and the Restoration of Early Symbiosis: The Psychohistory of a Group Fantasy." *The Journal of Psychohistory* 6:319–60.

Stein, Howard and Soughik Kayzakian-Rowe. 1978. "Hypertension, Biofeedback and the Myth of the Machine: A Psychoanalytic Culture Exploration." *Psychoanalysis and Contemporary Thought* 1:119–56.

Stierlin, Helm. 1976. *Adolf Hitler: A Family Perspective*. New York: Psychohistory Press.

Stoller, Robert J. 1975. *Perversion: The Erotic Form of Hatred*. New York: Random House.

——1977. "Primary Femininity." In Blum 1977:59–78.

Stone, Elizabeth. 1978. "A Madame Curie from the Bronx." *New York Times Magazine*, April 9, 1978, pp. 29ff.

Strehlow, C. 1915. "Die Aranda- und Loritja-Stämme in Zentral-Australien. 4: Das soziale Leben der Aranda und Loritja." *Veröffentlichungen aus den städtische Völker-Museum.* 1(4):1–103; 2:1–78. Frankfurt am Main: Joseph Baer.

Strouse, Jean, ed. 1974. *Women and Analysis: Dialogues on Psychoanalytic Views of Femininity*. New York: Grossman.

Suggs, Robert C. 1966. *Marquesan Sexual Behavior*. New York: Harcourt.

——1971. "Sex and Personality in the Marquesas: A Discussion of the Linton-Kardiner Report." In Marshall and Suggs 1971:163–86.

Sullivan, Harry Stack. 1953. *The Interpersonal Theory of Psychiatry*. New York: Norton.

Szasz, Thomas. 1961. *The Myth of Mental Illness*. New York: Paul B. Hoeber.

Talmon, Yonina. 1972. *Family and Community in the Kibbutz.* Cambridge, Harvard University Press.

Thomas, W. I. 1951. "The Persistence of Primary-Group Norms in Present-Day Society." In E. H. Volkart, ed., *Social Behavior and Personality*, pp. 35–38. New York: Social Science Research Council.

Thomas, W. I. and Dorothy Thomas. 1928. *The Child in America*. New York: Knopf.

Thomas, W. I. and Florian Znaniecki. 1918ff. *The Polish Peasant in Europe and America*. (Originally, Boston: Badger.) Rpt. New York: Dover, 1958.

Thompson, Clara. 1942. "Cultural Pressures in the Psychology of Women." *Psychiatry* 5:331–39.

——1947. "Changing Concepts of Homosexuality in Psychoanalysis." *Psychiatry* 10:183–89.

——1964. *On Women*. (Collection of Thompson's papers on feminine psychology of the 1940s.) New York: New American Library.

Tiger, Lionel. 1969. *Men in Groups*. New York: Random House.

Tiger, Lionel and Robin Fox. 1971. *The Imperial Animal*. New York: Holt, Rinehart and Winston.

Tiger, Lionel and Joseph Shepher. 1975. *Women in the Kibbutz*. New York: Harcourt, Brace, Jovanovich.

Time Magazine. 1969. Article on Harris Poll. Oct. 31, 1969.

Tripp, C. A. 1975. *The Homosexual Matrix*. New York: McGraw-Hill.

Turkle, Sherry. 1978. *Psychoanalytic Politics: Freud's French Revolution*. New York: Basic Books.

Van den Berghe, Pierre. 1978a. *Man in Society: A Biosocial View*. New York: Elsevier.

——1978b. "Sociobiology: A New Paradigm for the Behavioral Sciences?" *Social Science Quarterly* 59:326–32.

Van den Haag, Ernest. 1963. "Notes on Homosexuality and its Cultural Setting." In Ruitenbeek 1963a: 291–301.

Vanggard, Thorkil. 1972. *Phallos: A Symbol and its History in the Male World*. New York: International Universities Press.

Vidich, Arthur and Joseph Bensman. 1958. *Small Town in Mass Society*. Princeton, N.J.: Princeton University Press.

Waite, Robert. 1971a. "Adolf Hitler's Guilt Feelings: A Study in History and Psychology." *Journal of Interdisciplinary History* 1:229–49.

——1971b. "Adolf Hitler's Anti-Semitism: A Study in History and Psychoanalysis." In Wolman 1971.

Wallace, Anthony. 1961. *Culture and Personality*. New York: Random House.

Wallerstein, Robert S. and Neil Smelser. 1969. "Psychoanalysis and Sociology: Articulations and Applications." *International Journal of Psychoanalysis* 50:693–710.

Ward, David A. and Gene G. Kassebaum. 1965. *Women's Prison: Sex and Social Structure.* Chicago: Aldine.

Washington *Post.* 1965. Report on Harris Poll. Sept. 27, 1966. Cited in Weinberg and Williams 1975:19–20.

Weinberg, George. 1972. *Society and the Healthy Homosexual.* New York: St. Martin's.

Weinberg, Martin S. and Colin Williams. 1974, 1975. *Male Homosexuals: Their Problems and Adaptations.* New York: Oxford.

Weinstein, Fred and Gerald Platt. 1969. *The Wish to be Free: Society, Psyche, and Value Change.* Berkeley: University of California Press.

——1973. *Psychoanalytic Sociology.* Baltimore: Johns Hopkins University Press.

Weitz, Shirley. 1977. *Sex Roles: Biological, Psychological and Social Foundations.* New York: Oxford.

Westwood, G. 1960. *A Minority.* London: Longmans Green.

Wheelis, Alan. 1958. *The Quest for Identity.* New York: Norton.

White, Leslie. 1949. *The Science of Culture.* New York: Farrar, Straus.

——1959. *The Evolution of Culture.* New York: McGraw-Hill.

Whitney, Graig R. 1979. "Women in the Soviet Face a Stark Choice: Career or Children." *New York Times,* June 26, 1979, p. 12.

Wiedeman, Geroge. 1974. "Homosexuality: A Survey." *Journal of the American Psychoanalytic Association* 22:651–96.

Winnicott, D. W. 1958. *Collected Papers: Through Paediatrics to Psychoanalysis.* London: Tavistock.

——1960. "Ego Distortion in Terms of True and False Self." In Winnicott, 1965.

——1965. *Maturational Processes and the Facilitating Environment.* London: Hogarth; New York: International Universities Press.

——1971. *Playing and Reality.* New York: Basic Books.

Wirth, Louis. 1945. "The Problem of Minority Groups." In Ralph Linton, ed., *The Science of Man in the World Crisis.* New York: Columbia University Press.

Wilson, Edward O. 1975. *Sociobiology: The New Synthesis.* Cambridge, Mass.: Belknap/Harvard.

WNET, Channel 13, New York. 1978. *Gays at Work.* TV Program, Oct. 10, 1978.

Wolf, Kathleen. 1952. "Growing Up and its Price in Three Puerto Rican Subcultures." *Psychiatry* 15:401–33.

Wolfenstein, E. Victor. 1967. *The Revolutionary Personality: Lenin, Trotsky, Ghandi.* Princeton, N.J.: Princeton University Press.

Wolman, Benjamin, ed. 1971. *The Psychoanalytic Interpretation of History*. New York: Basic Books.

Wrong, Dennis. 1976. *Skeptical Sociology*. New York: Columbia University Press.

Yablonsky, Lewis. 1965. *The Tunnel Back: Synanon*. New York: Macmillan.

Young, Michael. 1958. *The Rise of the Meritocracy*. London: Thames and Hudson, and Pelican.

Name Index

Discontents, 100; The Future of an
Illusion, 218; Jokes and Their
Relation to the Unconscious, 100; The
Psychopathology of Everyday Life,
100, 255; Three Essays on a Theory of
Sexuality, 176; Totem and Taboo, 115
ff.;
Friedan, Betty, 220
Friedberg, Ronald, 277
Fromm, Erich, 14, 25, 35–36, 39, 193,
253, 347, 412

Gagnon, John, 260, 294, 321, 328, 369;
in Bibliography, see also Simon and
Gagnon
Galenson, Eleanor, 174, 180, 188, 191;
in Bibliography, see also Roiphe and
Galenson
Gandhi, Indira, 155
Gandhi, Mohandas K., 15, 354
Gardner, Allen, 102, 414
Gardner, Beatrice, 102; 414; in
Bibliography, see Gardner and
Gardner
Garfinkel, Harold, 28
Gebhard Paul H., 306; in Bibliography,
see also Kinsey et al.
Gerth, Hans, 12
Giallombardo, Rose, 288
Giovacchini, Peter, 25, 414, 420
Gladwin, Thomas, 411
Glenn, Jules, 180, 191
Goethe, Johann Wolfgang von, 1
Goffman, Erving, 27, 369, 373–74, 375
Goldberg, Steven, 153, 155
Goldman, Irving, 297
Goodall, Jane, 80, 102, 106
Goode, William, 158, 347–48
Gorer, Geoffrey, 37
Gornick, Vivian, 220
Gough, Kathleen, 151
Gouldner, Alvin, 27
Greer, Germaine, 220
Grunberger, Bela, 184
Guntrip, Harry, 51, 181, 204

Habermas, Jurgen, 12, 36
Hacker, Helen Mayer, 156, 158, 159,
165, 200, 316, 325, 326, 328, 418

Hampden-Turner, Charles, 351, 357, 382
Hardy, Alister, 86
Harris, Marvin, 152
Harry, Joseph, 292, 294
Hartmann, Heinz, 24, 25, 31, 32, 37, 57,
122, 173, 180
Hatterer, Lawrence, 252, 272
Hendin, Herbert, 34, 35, 38, 351, 358,
359–60, 361, 367
Herskovits, Melville, 55
Hewes, Gordon, 93, 106 ff.
Hippler, Arthur, 12, 53, 56
Hite, C., 258
Hitler, Adolf, 356
Hockett, Charles, 68 ff., 91 ff., 97, 103
Hoebel, E. A., 9
Hoffman, Martin, 294, 321, 328
Hoijer, Harry, 9; in Bibliography, see
Beals and Hoijer
Homans, George, 28
Honigmann, John, 37, 411
Hooker, Evelyn, 275–77, 328, 329
Horkheimer, Max, 13
Horney, Karen, 25, 39, 174, 179, 180,
186, 187, 189, 193, 253, 413
Hsu, Francis L. K., 411

Inkeles, Alex, 12

Jacklin, C. N., 206; in Bibliography, see
Maccoby and Jacklin
Jacobson, Edith, 39
Jahoda, Marie, 36; in Bibliography, see
Christie and Jahoda
Johanesson, Alexander, 97
Jones, Ernest, 25, 60, 179, 180, 186
Jung, Carl G., 39, 54

Kagan, J., 206
Kameny, Franklin, 321, 325
Kaplan, Bert, 411
Kaplan, E., 191
Kardiner, Abram, 25, 37, 299, 413
Karlen, Arno, 307, 308, 309, 311
Kassebaum, Gene G., 288; in
Bibliography, see Ward and
Kassebaum
Kayzakian-Rowe, Soughik, 19; in
Bibliography, see Stein and Kayzakian-
Rowe

Subject Index

Index of Tribal, Ethnic, and National Groups